CRYSTAL LAKE PUBLIC LIBRARY

3 2306 00383 5322

FIRE FROM THE SOUL

305.896 SPI
Spivey, Donald.
Fire from the soul :

MAR 2003

ω7/03   ω 5/08

D0881756

PROPERTY OF CLPL

FIRE FROM THE SOUL
A History of the
African-American
Struggle

Donald Spivey

CAROLINA ACADEMIC PRESS
Durham, North Carolina

Copyright © 2003
Donald Spivey
All Rights Reserved

ISBN: 0-89089-432-9
LCCN: 2002117149

Carolina Academic Press
700 Kent Street
Durham, North Carolina 27701
Telephone (919) 489-7486
Fax (919) 493-5668
Email: cap@cap-press.com
www.cap-press.com

Printed in the United States of America

In memory of
Richard O. Curry

CONTENTS

ACKNOWLEDGMENTS

I am deeply indebted to the past and present pioneer historians in the African and African-American fields and especially to those who take their work and commitment into the communities at large. By doing so they help to keep hope alive. My sincere thanks and appreciation to the institutions and their staffs that provided assistance in the research phases of this book, especially those of the Schomburg Research Center on Black Culture in New York, Library of Congress, National Archives, Harold Washington Chicago Public Library, University of Chicago Library, New York University Library, Oklahoma Historical Society Library, Langston University Library, Williams College Library, University of North Carolina Library at Chapel Hill, the Connecticut Historical Society Museum and Library, in particular director Christopher Bickford; the Homer P. Babbidge Library of the University of Connecticut, especially Randall Jimerson; the Otto G. Richter Library of the University of Miami most notably William Brown, head of archives and special collections, and Michael Valentine; and the Miami-Dade Public Library. A special thanks is owed to my former colleagues at the Institute for African-American Studies at the University of Connecticut where the project began, especially to Ronald L. Taylor who took time away from his busy schedule to read portions of the manuscript. Research assistance has come from many to whom I am indebted: Christine Edmonds, David Shenin, Hua Liang, Rose Lovelace, Mark Murphy, Joyce Hanson, Rogaia Abu Sharaf, Quelia Quaresma, Aldo Regalado, Emma Sordo, Keisha Duncan, Mariana Conea, Jason Bryan, Robert Davis, Cecile Houry, Logan Bailey-Perkins, Chanelle Rose, Ameenah Shakir, and James Walter.

The staff of the Department of History at the University of Miami is owed much. Jesus Sanchez-Reyes, Lenny del Granado, and Kathryn Harrison made up the extremely competent and compassionate front office. I owe them profound plaudits for their good work and for shielding me more than once from the demands that came with chairing the department that I might work on the manuscript. The College of Arts and Sciences of the University of Miami provided me with a needed year of sabbatical that made final completion of the book possible. My thanks is owed to a host of colleagues at Miami from whom I and this project have benefited, especially members of the history department that I have bounced many ideas off of and who, by their very presence and collegial support, help to make the academic environment a good one, in particular the "enhancement committee," as I call them, of Whitt Johnson, Gregory W. Bush, Robin F. Bachin, Steve Diamond, Guido Ruggiero, Steve Stein, Frank C. Stuart, Hermann Beck, Hugh Thomas, and, I would add to this list, the positive force of the new members of my department, Edmund Abaka, Edward Baptist, and Martha Few. Plaudits for providing an intellectual wellspring that enriches not only me but the entire campus go to the Center for Research on Sport in Society and my colleagues over there, Jomills H. Braddock, III., Jan Sokol-Katz, Robin Bachin, and Marvin Dawkins. A special thanks to our many teacher-colleagues from Miami-Dade County who have joined me for several summers of workshops devoted to infusing African-American history into Florida schools, especially Priscilla Dames, Thirlee Smith, Anita McGruder, and John Doyle.

I am profoundly grateful for the sound advice and spirited comments, suggestions, and criticisms the manuscript received from fellow historians: Howard O. Lindsey, Chairman of the Department of History, DePaul University; Vincent Bakpetu Thompson, Professor of History, Connecticut College; Roger Norman Buckley, Professor of History and Director of Asian Studies, University of Connecticut; Amii Omara-Otunnu, UNESCO Chair in Comparative Human Rights, University of Connecticut; Whittington B. Johnson, Professor of History, University of Miami; and Mark Naison, Professor of African-American Studies and History, Fordham University. My deepest heartfelt gratitude goes to my wife and soul-mate, Diane Marie Spivey, for her readings and critiques of the manuscript at various stages, and divine support during our never-ending confrontations with racism.

I alone, of course, am responsible for the interpretations and analyses rendered and any flaws contained herein.

The author gratefully acknowledges permission to use the following:

"Black Art" from the book *The Leroi Jones/Amiri Baraka Reader* by Amiri Baraka. Copyright © 1991 by Amiri Baraka. Appears by permission of the publisher, Thunder's Mouth Press.

PROLOGUE

"We cannot escape history," President Abraham Lincoln told the nation at the coming of the Civil War. He wisely understood that the rooted dynamics of conflicting interests would eventually surface, requiring either peaceful or painful resolution. A hundred years later Martin Luther King, Jr. was still warning the nation with the adage he often recited of William Cullen Bryant, "Truth crushed to earth will rise again." The United States of America, however, is either unable or unwilling to resolve its worst endemic and systemic flaw: racism. Today's America is rushing from its responsibilities and, with increasing frequency, espousing and implementing policies that reflect a denial or ignorance of the nation's legacy of racism. Oppression and victimization are now four-letter words and affirmative action is labeled a euphemism for reverse discrimination. Meanwhile, racism remains a part of this nation's core and is virtually pathological. It is America's disgrace, its Achilles' heel, its most glaring contradiction and inconsistency, a divisive wedge negating for millions the pledge of freedom, justice, and equality for all; life, liberty, and the pursuit of happiness. To solve the cancerous race problem is essential for the salvation of the nation. How can the race problem be solved if much of the public at large and the rising tide of political leadership are ignorant of the historic experience of African Americans? It cannot. Racism is a power relationship based on misinformation and ignorance. The belief in racial superiority, and conversely in racial inferiority, flourishes in an environment of exclusivity and lack of accurate information. It is infinitely easier to hate, despise, oppose, and misjudge a people and their problems and interests when you are unaware of their struggles, sacrifices, accomplishments, and contributions.[1]

Make no mistake about it. Racism connotes something far more insidious than discrimination, prejudice, or bigotry. We all have prejudices. We all prefer some things over others. We discriminate routinely. In fact, we complement one another for having discriminating taste. The point is not that we like and dislike but what actions we take based upon our likes and dislikes. Frankly, it is of little importance to me if an individual dislikes me because of my height, weight, politics, where I am from, my ethnic background, my gender, or my color. What is important to me is when a company, an

institution, a group, an individual, or a nation has the power to im-
plement and institutionalize its preferences, and does so; the potential employer who rejects me because of those preferences, or the
group or individual who assails me because of their preferences, or
the country and its government that establish practices and laws pre-
venting me from having the same rights and opportunities as others.
When those actions are taken because of the color of your skin or
the race to which you belong that, my friends, is racism. It is not a
noun as categorized in most standard dictionaries. It is an action. A
racist nation is one that provides or denies privileges based on race.
Thus the United States of America easily qualifies as a racist society,
having from its inception, bestowed advantages to those who possess white skin.

America's black population and its allies have waged war against
this deeply rooted and vicious sickness for almost four hundred
years without eradicating it. Within that struggle, however, are critical lessons and experiences from which we as a nation can and must
learn. Today's problems did not start today nor have the efforts to
combat them. Black folk have fought on numerous fronts and from
a variety of perspectives and strategies against the *color line*. Understanding those battles, and the successes and failures, is to better
grasp the extent and depths of the problem and the course of action
or actions warranted. How can appropriate programs be implemented to combat racism if the roots of the dilemma are not understood? They cannot. A good physician explores a patient's medical
history before rendering a diagnosis and prescribing treatment. History is the starting point for the accurate understanding of cause and
effect in the relationship between individuals, groups, societies, and
races. My goal in this work is to place the past before us and to
draw lessons from the African-American historical record to help illuminate the present and future. Mine is an offering, to those interested and willing to confront America's gravest problem, of the un-
ambiguous perspective of a member of the group whose American
dream has been and continues to be a nightmarish encounter with
the demon known as racism. The underlying philosophy of this
book is that knowledge is power and that solutions flow from understanding history. The past is our source of enlightenment and
wisdom. Indeed, our past, our history is the only thing we can know
for certain. The present and the future are evolving, and the outcome is always uncertain. What we know for sure is that failure to
embrace that past will yield a problematic outcome in the present
and future.

The struggle of African Americans against racism is a story of tragedy. It is also a story of determination and hope. It is an American saga that cannot be erased. There is some confusion as to what people of African descent in America have been fighting for and against. African Americans and others have often defined the battle ground as encompassing a variety of issues such as freedom, intolerance, tolerance, segregation, desegregation, disfranchisement, franchisement, integration, inequality, equality, nationalism, political rights, civil rights, miseducation, education, economic development, access, multiculturalism, cultural awareness, ethnicity, class, sexism, diversity, and race. I contend that all of these are important factors but, I emphatically argue, for blacks the ultimate goal, whether articulated or not, has always been self-determination and empowerment, and the ultimate barrier that subsumes all others has been and is racism.

The new *Critical Race Theorists*, as some call them, are contemporary black intellectuals offering poignant assessments of America and who conclude that the race problem is the single most important ill facing the nation. Theirs are, in my opinion, familiar cries in the tradition of earlier activists whom we proudly recognized as *Race Men and Women* and who dedicated themselves to working to uplift people of African descent in the United States and throughout the world. Those early scholar-activists saw racism as the most horrendous problem facing people of color. Out of that spirit the movement for African-American history emerged in the nineteenth century. The movement met obstacles of all sorts, clandestine and otherwise, but the activist historians fought the good fight with a commitment to getting the facts out about black folk and combating the prevailing misinformation and wrong assumptions that existed in that era. The battle continued through the centuries. Today's Eurocentrics — or anti Critical Race Theorists — I find, like those of the past, avow the supremacy of the European past and white versions of American history, and vehemently reject the importance of the African contribution and the idea that racism is a major problem. They oppose the demands for academic diversity, and likewise oppose strong civil rights measures and affirmative action programs. In this book I pull no punches in my criticisms of them. I discuss how their writings contribute to misunderstanding and also fuel the fire of contemporary racism and the reactionary political agenda that grips the nation. My position is that knowledge of Africa provides more than what the detractors label as "feel good history." It is essential to the development and progress of African Americans and crucial to the fostering of self-worth which aids empowerment. It is also a bold challenge to the faulty pillars of racism and, thus, important to the intellectual liberation of whites as well as blacks.

The relationship between blacks and whites in the United Sates is built on the enslavement of African people. Therein lies the genesis of control, disrespect, and an unlikely basis for a lasting friendship or the development of a race-free and color-blind society. Brought by force to the Americas, people of African descent were the fodder and prize of a European dream of wealth. Profit was the catalyst and racism the building blocks for the inhumane wrenching of millions of blacks from their families and African homeland to a life of forced labor and degradation in the New World. Whether in Latin America, South or Central America, the Caribbean, Haiti, Brazil, Cuba, or the colonies of North America, the Africans were relegated to the bottom of society and branded as less than human beings by virtue of their color. Blacks were at odds physically, spiritually, mentally, and culturally with the United States of America and its constitutional and moral claim of being "the land of the free." From this country's inception, Africans in America were perceived and defined as a "problem" in the making of the new nation. The treatment of blacks in Connecticut, "The Constitution State" as it is called, is illustrative. In this venerable of the early New England colonies, that exemplified America's character, Africans were viewed and treated as a major element of discord. Life for blacks under the yoke of slavery, whether in Connecticut or the cotton South, was a horrific contest for survival. That slaves found ways to somehow endure the ordeal is an affirmation of human courage, ingenuity, and strength drawn from a connectedness that transcended oceans and time back to mother Africa. Today's African Americans, and the nation, are products of their heritage including the legacy of slavery and need to substantively come to terms with that fact.

The force used to maintain the institution of slavery, and the violence required to overcome it, tell us much about America's split personality. John Brown's admonishment of slavery was also a warning to the country of continuous violence unless and until equality and justice ruled supreme for all people. Brown left a legacy from which the full spectrum of future generations of civil rights activists and black leaders drew. Brown understood the role that violence played in his day, a role and relationship that continues in contemporary society. What he and some abolitionists grasped was the full weight of America's racial divide. He understood that the nation's economic interests were so deeply invested in the institution of slavery that only violence could sever the relationship. John Brown's warning came to fruition with the Civil War. He did not attempt to foretell what might occur in slavery's aftermath, but other abolitionists did. They predicted a grisly future of struggle for blacks as racial outcasts never to be accepted in America.

What happened to black folk in the years immediately following the Civil War foretold the dismal future of race relations in America. There were substantive signs before the war ended that the lot for people of African descent would remain precarious and barrier-ridden even if the North won the war. How often historians miss the crucial aspect of the question as to whether Reconstruction was a success or failure. They have focused on the politics of radicals versus moderates, and Republicans versus Democrats, rather than on the important issue of whether racism was addressed. As blacks attempted to empower themselves after "emancipation," they were thwarted and victimized. It was difficult for them to know which whites were their friends. Yankees who came South marching to the bugles and drums of liberty did not support black autonomy. The Freedmen's Bureau failed to protect blacks or help them to build and sustain their communities. The bureau in practice reflected the movement toward reconciliation between the North and South that was premised on white nationalism and black subordination.

The precious few signs of possible white-black unity on terms approaching mutual respect and cooperation around common interests could not take hold and survive in the poisonous race baiting that escalated through the late-nineteenth and early-twentieth centuries. The detractors invoked white superiority and racist pride to chastise and brow beat those who dared suggest that poor whites and blacks have economic interests in common and that the two sides should find a way to work together. The emerging New South was a very old one to African Americans where the four "D's" ruled supreme: discrimination, disfranchisement, demonization, and death. Constitutional provisions making the freed Africans citizens and granting the males among them the right to vote were completely negated in Dixieland. In law and in practice, blacks had no rights that a white person was required to respect. The media, in all of its forms, negatively stereotyped African Americans. Demonized, powerless, and unprotected by law, it was open season on blacks to every race hater. Victimization is not a figment of the African-American imagination. Lynchings and rapes were perpetrated against blacks daily, a trend that continued well into the twentieth century. In addition, the nation embraced ideas and concepts about what it meant to be an American that were used to define blacks as unworthy and responsible for their own predicament. African-American leadership that emerged in this setting varied from conciliatory and moderate to progressive and hostile. For some blacks, separation from whites seemed the only solution. The founding of the all-black town of Langston, Oklahoma was one such result. For others, they made due with the situation in the rural South as best as possible. Still others migrated to the cities of the South and more to the urban North where their voices joined in a chorus of a new consciousness for race building and self-assertion.

Their marching feet were not simply a rejection of the rural, agricultural way of life, but a refusal to accept second-class citizenship and a willingness to fight in an articulate and organized fashion against racism. Conflicts arose in the new settings where blacks and whites met. Sometimes these conflicts became violent. Nothing, however, was going to halt the black quest for person-hood. African Americans were developing their voice and making clear and ardent demands for reform. They fended for themselves and found strength, direction, and purpose in the knowledge of self that they demonstrated through their cultural creativity. Expressions came in every form from art, literature, music, theater, religion, and politics, to organized protest from every perspective, including socialist, labor, nationalist, integrationist, and separatist.

The forward momentum, stiffly challenged under the added burden of the economic crisis of the 1930s, did not stop. The desperate economic and racial times took a devastating toll on the black family. African-American women especially rose to the occasion shouldering a great many additional responsibilities including literally placing themselves in domestic servitude for the family to survive. The black population, for the first time in its voting history, began to rethink its political allegiance to the Republican Party. They began shopping around as independent-minded voters; realigning themselves during this period with the Democratic Party and the presidential administration of Franklin D. Roosevelt. The result was access to the corridors of power for black Americans for the first time. Talk today about the need for African-American voter independence and non-political alignment is to convey an old concept that proved itself sixty years ago.

World War II ushered in a new set of challenges to African Americans in their quest to transform the racial landscape. Blacks fought in all of America's wars. They put their lives on the line and they paid dearly. The motivation behind their sacrifices was quite simple. They thought it their obligation as Americans to do their part and fight for the nation's interests, believing that these contributions would earn them the rights and privileges of full citizenship. They did much to contribute to the victories abroad. Yet the recognition they hoped for, of complete citizenship and acceptance in America as equals, was denied. For African Americans the war took place on several fronts, both foreign and domestic. It was during this period that black political consciousness expanded to include a heightened international awareness and commitment to work for the liberation of the African continent and its people. Whether focusing on the domestic scene or the international arena, black folk understood that racism was the paramount problem. Organizations that did not share that assessment, such as the Communist Party and the American Labor Movement, touted class lines or labor solidarity as primary and were only marginally successful in winning the support of the African-American community. Racism, as blacks were aware, was the major problem everywhere in America, and they attacked it in all of its settings.

Sport is an institution in which the contradiction, the inconsistency, and incompatibility of racism and discrimination with American democratic principles are most glaring and flagrant since the sanctum of athletics is premised on such doctrines as equality of opportunity, sportsmanship, and fair play. Athletics are a perfect arena for exposing and examining the dual nature of American society with its paradoxical blending of democracy and inequality, but it is often overlooked or given only scant mention in the history of the black protest movement. In sports, African-American athletes fought against racism using a variety of approaches. The protests of these athletes were profound. They generated a substantial social and political impact at the domestic and international levels and affirmed the link between sport and politics and the modern Civil Rights Movement.

The hard-won legal enactments and legislative and programmatic gains of the Civil Rights Movement of the 1950s and 1960s were a hopeful start toward eradicating the racial divide in the United States. Unfortunately all were, historically speaking, short-lived. America is an impatient nation, and a fickle one, on the question of race and equality. After President Lyndon Baines Johnson left office, the succeeding administrations began the path to the systematic dismantling of the Great Society Programs and the civil rights and affirmative action agendas. The assault intensified in the 1980s and 1990s. By any measure, the new America is anti African Americans. The historic struggle of black folk tells us that the country is in peril. The racial eruptions and conflicts in the nation that we experienced most recently have deep causal roots. The question is whether the intelligence, the foresight based on hindsight, and the national will can be summoned to eradicate racism. Given the diminished moral authority of the Presidency, the reactionary majority in Congress, and the intensifying racial intolerance and hostility to any form of diversity, the prognosis, I am sorry to say, is not good for people of color and the nation as a whole. The historical barometer is a stern warning of perilous waters ahead.

This book is, in part, an exploration of the many warnings and messages from the African-American past. It is a work of original research and makes wide utilization of published sources. It is not, however, intended as a synthesis. It is a reinterpretation and reassessment of the African-American experience within the context of what I contend is the single most pernicious and ever-present challenge to black advancement and how African Americans have dealt with it. In the following treatise I offer you a perspective, hard-hitting and meant to be, on a nation that desperately needs to make a major course adjustment for advancement in the twenty-first century.

FIRE FROM THE SOUL

RACE FIRST: AN
INTRODUCTION TO
BLACK HISTORY

THE NEW CRITICAL RACE THEORY

History is a conservative discipline and one of its greatest taboos is for the scholar to personalize the story. The primary canon of the discipline is the proclamation that research, findings, and written analysis must be objective and dispassionate. There is, in short, an underlying fallacy that historical scholarship can somehow be free of individual biases, human emotions, predilections, and that these human components can be tossed aside in the pursuit of historical truth. If that were the case, the discipline of history writing would not have all the problems that plague it. No such pristine state is attainable. History as a discipline is not a member of the sciences but the humanities. Any good humanist is an artist and does not try to deny his or her passion, feelings, and emotions. Rather, the artist uses those attributes and sensitivities in combination with training and innate skills to capture the beauty or horror of the scene as accurately as is humanly possible. The historian should do no less. The historian, like everyone else, is a conglomeration of social, political, and cultural factors, of ethnic background, beliefs and values, personal experiences, individual personality, of formal and informal education, and individual tastes and prejudices. In short, you are what you eat. The historian would serve us all better by owning up to these human qualities rather than denying their existence. The historian needs to be a dedicated researcher and intellectually honest in venturing into the realm of history writing. The following examination of the African-American experience is offered to the reader from that perspective. In various intellectual parlors, professional association meetings, and literary circles, this approach is being called the *"new* Critical Race Theory." Critical Race Theory is written work by African Americans that is often admittedly subjective in approach, beginning with a personal story or anecdote, is intended in presentation style for a general audience, as well as a scholarly one, and conveys a strong political point of view. The work inevitably concludes that *race* is the number-one problem facing African Americans. I modify the critical race approach and conclude that *racism* is the number-one problem facing African Americans.

Racism is the scourge of daily existence for black folk and, as a critical rethinking of African-American history reveals, the ever-present and paramount barrier between blacks and the American dream. Let me begin in the critical race theory mode and recount for you two personal stories. The first story that I shall share occurred at the start of the new millennium and involves the largest and most prestigious professional organization of scholars of America's history, the Organization of American Historians (OAH), of which I and ten thousand others are members. A conflict arose when it was discovered that the annual meeting of the organization, slated for the end of March of 2000, would be held at the Adam's Mark Hotel in St. Louis, Missouri. Professor Jeffrey T. Sammons of New York University, a member of the session I was scheduled to chair on "African Americans and the Olympic Games," notified me and the other members of the panel that the NAACP had filed a lawsuit against the Adam's Mark for alleged racial discrimination. After reviewing the facts in the case and the deplorable race record of the Adam's Mark, the senior members of the panel informed the leadership of the OAH that we would not attend the annual meeting unless the hotel venue was changed. The executive leadership of the organization denied our request and called for the convention to proceed, with assurances that the hotel would be monitored for any acts of discrimination against black guests. We rejected what seemed to us an act of cowardice on the part of the OAH and even more a betrayal of the organization's often proclaimed edicts against racism and discrimination. Members of our panel joined with others and formed the Committee for a New Convention Site or CNCS (pronounced *cynics*), and took on the challenge of forcing the OAH to change its mind and move the convention site. If the OAH refused, we were prepared to boycott not only the convention but the historical organization as well.

We used the skills of historians to research the race record of the Adam's Mark and to present the facts to the OAH leadership. Each member of CNCS took on an assignment to get the job done: Professor Sammons worked with the media and Professor Mark Naison of Fordham University took on development. I researched the background of the Adam's Mark and conveyed my findings to the OAH leadership in a personal letter sent email and express mail on January 29, 2000. In the letter, addressed to David Montgomery, President of the OAH, and members of the Executive Council, I made the case of "More Reasons Why the Annual Meeting of the OAH Must Not Be Held at the Adam's Mark Hotel." The letter was a follow-up to the initial communiqué of January 24 from Professor Sammons, Professor Naison, Professor Allen Sack of the University of New Haven, and me, calling for a boycott of the hotel. Our ranks expanded with Professors David Levering Lewis, Robin Kelley, Glenn Hall, Tim Tyson, and soon hundreds more. I was, in the letter, also making a personal plea and explanation of why I could not and would not set foot into an Adam's Mark Hotel and hoping that, with the additional information provided, the leadership of the OAH would come to the same decision.

The Adam's Mark Hotel Chain, which is headquartered in St. Louis, has a notorious record of flagrant racism and a continuing pattern of the most vulgar discrimination against African Americans dating back to at least 1991. I spoke with several of the attorneys for the U.S. Department of Justice and the Florida Department of Justice, a number of the individual plaintiffs involved in the class action suit against the Adam's Mark in Daytona Beach, Florida, and with other individuals intimately familiar with the pending suit. In addition, I spoke to those knowledgeable of the earlier labor complaints and successful racial discrimination suits against the Adam's Mark in St. Louis, Denver, and elsewhere. I limited quotations in some instances, as requested, because of the continuing litigation against the Adam's Mark Hotel Chain, CEO Fred Kummer, and the HBE parent corporation in which he and his family hold controlling interest. What I conveyed in the letter was information that had been made available in sworn depositions, public records, and personal interviews I conducted.

In the first major racial discrimination suit against the Adam's Mark (Helms & Ey v. Adam's Mark: 1994), a jury found the hotel, its owner, and its management guilty. The hotel had fired Dewey Helms (an African American) because of his race, and fired Helm's supervisor, Bruce Ey (who is white) because he refused to carry out the racially motivated order to dismiss Helms. The plaintiffs were awarded punitive damages totaling $4,800.000. The amount was reduced in January 1998 after a lengthy appeal process. Nevertheless, the Appellate Court upheld the guilty verdict against Kummer, the St. Louis Adam's Mark, and the HBE Corporation.

The Appellate Court's rendering, in E.E.O.C. v. HBE CORP. 135 F. 3d 543 8th Cir. 1998, is telling. The Court upheld that the Adam's Mark in St. Louis maintained an environment that was "hostile" to blacks, and "that hotel managers showed bias against African Americans, sought to exclude them from management positions and all but the lowest level positions at the hotel that were visible to the public, and sought to banish music and other atmospheric traits that they associated with African Americans" [548]; that black employees at the hotel were routinely underpaid in comparison to whites; that Kummer did not want his hotel to become "too dark" [too many African Americans] especially at Chestnut's, the hotel cafe near the entrance to the hotel [550]; that Kummer used "codes" to discriminate against black employees, informing management that any position that began with "the" was for whites only, such as "the hotel manager," "the personnel director," etc.; that Kummer stated on numerous occasions that he did not like blacks and that he often used racial epithets to describe them and Jews [550–552]. The court concluded: "These actions, many years after the laws forbidding racial discrimination became widely known, support a finding of outrageous conduct and an award of punitive damages." [558].

In other litigation against the Adam's Mark, six of the chain's twenty-one hotels, were identified as special bastions of racism. The two at the top of the list were the Adam's Mark in St. Louis, Missouri and the Adam's Mark in Daytona Beach, Florida. The actions of the Florida hotel were particularly appalling to me. I am African American and also a resident of Florida. We had already passed on to President Montgomery and others a laundry list of abuses that African Americans suffered at the Daytona Beach Adam's Mark during the Black College Reunion in April of 1999. I carefully examined the complaints that African Americans made against the Adam's Mark Hotel in Daytona Beach during the reunion, and can only think of words such as reprehensible, beastly, and demonic to characterize the treatment they suffered. One of the complainants described it best when she accused the hotel of having engaged in racial terrorism. The terrorism included a requirement that blacks wear bright orange wrist bands to identify them as guests of the resort—a requirement not made of whites also staying there. Blacks were also charged higher room rates and required to pay the entire cost at the time of reservation, and in cash. Security deposits of three hundred dollars were required for use of the room mini bar and for telephone privileges. Barriers were placed to prevent the black guests from using the driveway leading to the front entrance of the hotel. The blacks were denied garage and valet privileges. Furnishing such as couches, chairs and lamps in the lobby of the resort were removed on the day Black College Reunion attendees were ex-

pected to arrive. Some room amenities, such as pictures, were removed, and room service was suspended. One would think that the
abuse could not have sunk any lower, but it did. Eye witnesses in
the kitchen area observed that many of the African-American guests
were served second-hand food.

A group of the Black College Reunion participants who stayed at
the Adam's Mark subsequently joined with the NAACP in filing a
class action lawsuit against the hotel, its management, and ownership. The evidence was so powerful, the actions of the hotel so vulgar, and the hotel owner so unrepentant, that the U.S. Department
of Justice investigated the complaint and also joined in the suit. The
Department of Justice issued the following in its *Complaint for In-
junctive Relief, The United States of America, Plaintiff, v. HBE Corporation, d/b/a Adam's Mark Hotels, Defendant* (16 December
1999): Title II Violations. "8. Defendant, acting through its officers,
employees, and agents, has engaged in policies and practices which
deny to persons, on account of race or color, the full and equal en-
joyment of goods, services, facilities, privileges, advantages, and accommodations of its hotels and the restaurants, bars, lounges, or
clubs located therein. 9. Defendant, acting through its officers, employees and agents, has carried out such policies and practices of
racial discrimination by, among other ways: a. applying different
and more onerous terms and conditions to non-white persons at its
hotels with regard to such things as prices for goods and services,
provision of services, and requirements related to security, identification and reservations, than those applied to white persons; b. offering and renting to non-white persons less desirable hotel rooms than
those offered and rented to white persons during comparable stays
or special events; c. segregating non-white persons in rooms in less
desirable locations than those offered and rented to white persons;
and d. implementing policies and procedures to exclude or limit the
number of non-white clientele in its hotels and the restaurants, bars,
lounges, or clubs located therein. 10. The conduct of Defendant described in paragraphs 8 and 9 above constitutes a pattern or practice
of resistance to the full and equal employment by non-white persons
of rights secured by 42 U.S.C. 2000a *et seg.*, and the pattern or
practice is of such a nature and is intended to deny the full exercise
of such rights."

This was the first time that the Justice Department's Civil Rights
Division has filed a suit against a hotel chain nationwide. "We are
talking about very egregious practices," said Bill Lann Lee, Assistant
Attorney General. Lee added: "The federal government will not tolerate this type of behavior." The statement that Attorney General

Janet Reno issued is compelling: "This kind of behavior is simply unacceptable. It is hard to believe that 35 years after the Civil Rights Act was passed by Congress, this type of discrimination still exists."

Even the State of Florida, which is not exactly known for its willingness to fight for civil rights compliance, took firm action against the Adam's Mark and joined in the lawsuit. The Florida Justice Department's investigation of the complaints and the hotel chain concurred with what the U.S. Department of Justice also found through its investigation: "The inferior treatment of black guests was part of a corporate-wide policy implemented by Fred S. Kummer, president of the resort's parent company, and that the policy was designed to discourage or eliminate events which attract a large number of African Americans." Florida Attorney General Bob Butterworth said in a press release after filing the motion in U.S. District Court in Orlando: "Black patrons of the Adam's Mark resort were singled out and treated like second class citizens. Not only were their civil rights violated, their rights as consumers were trampled. The disgraceful behavior of the Adam's Mark cries out for action on all fronts."

I contacted the national office of the NAACP for clarification of its position. The national office was understandably cautious in the statements issued and in press releases regarding the Adam's Mark Hotel because of its active suit against the hotel. What they were willing to say, and make perfectly clear, was that it was misleading for anyone to suggest that NAACP President Kweisi Mfume in his press release of December 16, 1999, in anyway suggested that it was acceptable to do business with the Adam's Mark. The salient point in Mfume's press release statement was this: "We are tired of giving our dollars to businesses that treat us as second-class citizens. The time has long passed when the African-American community will continue to economically support businesses that provide substandard services and a hostile environment. Provided with the facts, our membership and the African American community can make an informed and intelligent decision as to where to apply their economic support."

Mr. James Morgan, President of the St. Louis Branch of the NAACP, had no such reservations in his condemnation of the Adam's Mark and only praise for those groups and individuals who refused to do business with the hotel. He conveyed, in emphatic terms, his appreciation to those who decided not to patronize the Adam's Mark Hotel in St. Louis and elsewhere. He went on to say: "Because the Florida State Conference of the NAACP is presently engaged in litigation against the Adam's Mark Hotel, the national

[NAACP] has not called for a boycott of the Adam's Mark but I personally would not attend any function or conduct any business with that hotel chain until this matter has been resolved. I would go even further and say that anyone that continues to do business with the Adam's Mark Hotel supports the racist acts that they have been accused of." The City of Clayton, a St. Louis suburb, turned down HBE's proposal to build a new hotel complex after questioning the chain's record of racial and sexual harassment charges, according to Gregory Freeman of the St. Louis Post-Dispatch in a piece dated December 21, 1999. This was powerful evidence to support Mr. Morgan's claims of the sorry record of Adam's Mark and the level of opposition to its practices.

The statements cited above, whether taken together or separately, did not require a rocket scientist, a lawyer, or a historian to recognize which side the NAACP was on regarding the question of whether or not organizations and individuals should give their patronage to the Adam's Mark Hotel. Moreover, the Organization of American Historians should not have needed the NAACP to tell it what was right or wrong, and what course of action should or should not be taken. Nor should the professional historical organization been willing to place its African-American members in an environment where equal treatment was unlikely.

I had been a member of the OAH for nearly thirty years and heard and read its many inspiring words and messages of progress and commitment to social justice and equality over those years. This was that moment of truth when the organization had to bridge the gap between rhetoric and practice. To do otherwise would bring into serious question the commitment of the OAH to civil rights. The villain here was not the OAH but was Mr. Kummer and his Adam's Mark Hotel Chain and HBE Corporation. The protesters hoped that the historical organization would not become tainted with the brush aimed at the Adam's Mark and its ownership. This, however, was not an issue on which the OAH could be inactive or halfhearted. This issue called for our organization to be unequivocal in its opposition to racism, in its intolerance of discrimination, and in its unwillingness to compromise and do business with racists.

CNCS spread the word still further, and finally the OAH leadership, with the growing number of historians demanding action, came out forcefully against the Kummer corporation and its practices, and moved the convention out of the Adam's Mark Hotel. We worked with our fellow historians in the St. Louis area, especially Professors Leslie Brown and Jackie Dace, in setting up protest rallies against racism that were to be held at the same time of the convention. Just days before the convention and the rallies were to commence, Kummer and his HBE Corporation capitulated and settled the lawsuits, agreeing to pay the plaintiffs eight million dollars. It was, however, only a partial victory. Kummer refused to admit any wrongdoing.

The rallies to "Make Racism History" took place in the park [in view of the courthouse where the Dred Scott Decision had been rendered] across from the Adam's Mark on March 31 and April 1 as scheduled. We recognized that the issue was bigger than the Adam's Mark and Fred Kummer. Racism is still alive and well in America and must be fought against continuously and on every front. We also understood, as the events and the protest rallies against racism demonstrated, the links between politics and scholarship. Struggling against racism is everyone's business including historians. Doing the right thing made the 2000 convention of the OAH the most significant in the organization's ninety-three year history, a powerful statement to "Make Racism History," and front page news in the St. Louis Post-Dispatch on April 1, 2000.

The second personal story of battling against racism, that I want to share with you, took place not in the United States but in Africa. It was an incident that left me feeling simultaneously both insulted and pleased. Let me explain. I had the privilege of attending an international conference in Accra, Ghana. I was back home in the motherland there on the West Coast of Africa. I must confess to you that one of the reasons I decided to participate in the conference was because of the location. I wanted to share ideas and so forth, but most of all I wanted to visit Ghana. The West African nation was the first African nation to regain its independence in 1957. Ghana was the birthplace of the great Pan-African leader and the country's first president Kwame Nkrumah, and the final resting place of the incomparable scholar-activists W.E.B. Du Bois and Shirley Graham Du Bois. My colleague and I did attend sessions at the conference, but spent more time at the various cultural sites such as the Artist Market Place where local artists sold their goods: tremendous, beautiful carvings and sculptured items of splendid quality. We had a strategy there at the Market. We agreed to go through first and see everything, and then go back and focus on what we wanted to buy. We were, as one must, haggling and negotiating with one of the artists over several pieces we were interested in purchasing. My colleague took him to the side to speak with him brother-to-brother in a last ditch effort to bargain the price downward. I was left there by the booth, so I pulled up a chair and sat down. A European woman came along and picked up one of the art pieces and then said to me:

"How much is this? You speak English don't you? How much is this?" I was simultaneously insulted and pleased by the white woman's presumptuousness; I was momentarily insulted because she saw me as just another one of the many Africans yet quite pleased because she saw me as one of them. The many derivations of my visage since my forebears were taken from Africa hundreds of years ago were not recognizable to her. She saw me as just another indistinguishable black face in the land of the blacks. I loved it. I was home. At any rate, she had asked me the price of the object and seemed to be demanding an answer. I could not resist so I blurted out: "It's a thousand." She retorted: "That's way too much, you are trying to rob me blind." Virtually right on cue, the artist rushed over, momentarily halting his negotiations with my colleague, sensing a possible quick sale. The European woman snapped at him in stern voice: "How much?" He responded: "One hundred." No doubt thinking that her assertive tone had made these boys discount the price to a bargain level, she quickly purchased the item with no further negotiations and left. The artist, my colleague, and I, stared at one another for a few seconds—a pregnant pause—and then broke out in laughter. The woman had certainly over-paid for the item, the brother had made a tidy profit, and we concluded our negotiations getting the pieces we wanted and at a substantial discount.

Of course I knew what was going on the moment the white woman began speaking to me. It was a common occurrence for me in the United States to have a white person see me in a store or in some other establishment or at a formal event and assume that I worked there. If not an employee, who then was this neatly dressed black person? He could not possibly be someone of importance; certainly not a college professor, a delegate, a trustee, or one of the honorees. Yes, I have been insulted in each one of such settings. I shall not attempt to recount the hundreds, if not thousands, of major and minor abuses I have experienced as a black person. It is a story all too familiar to any black man or woman in America. Blackness in the racist world in which we live conjures up in the white mind a person of lower station, a servant, an inferior or, worst yet, a criminal, a threat, a brute.

The trial of the white police officers for the beating of Rodney King is illustrative. How could their actions be denied since they were captured on videotape? In the trial, which is very often erroneously referred to as the "Rodney King trial," the defense attorneys did not attempt to deny the act but to explain to the all-white Simi Valley jury why such force and the repeated blows were necessary. The attorneys characterized Rodney King to them as a "hulk of a man." The officers testified that he possessed "tremendous brute strength" and, with his "nostrils flaring," charged them "snorting like a bull." Hence, what the world witnessed on the videotape was an illusion and the three or four officers beating and stomping King while he was on the ground was merely appropriately-applied force to bring such a brute under control. The dehumanizing, vilifying and bestializing descriptions of King were repeatedly given throughout the trial. The defense played to the white jury's fears and stereotypes about blacks. The jury found the police officers not guilty. Following the announcement of the acquittal on April 29, 1992, South-Central Los Angeles burst into flames in what became one of the nation's costliest race riots. Where was the outrage from the white community on the issue of black dehumanization and the freeing of the police officers who had been videotaped in their criminal action? We, however, experienced a relentless barrage of white outrage when a predominantly black jury, with two white members and a Hispanic, unanimously voted O. J. Simpson not guilty of the charges of murdering his former wife, Nicole Brown Simpson, and Ronald Goldman.[1]

What happened to Rodney King cannot be explained by a class analysis. Even the loftiest of African Americans experience these same double standards of being viewed in accordance to the color of their skin. Former United Nations Ambassador Andrew Young tells the story of when he was coming out of the fashionable Waldorf Astoria Hotel in New York from a formal reception and dressed in his tuxedo. He was waiting out front of the entrance for his chauffeur to bring the limousine around when a young white man pulled up in a sports car, jumped out of it, and threw Ambassador Young the keys telling him to park it for him. The driver of the car saw Young standing there in a tux and instantly assumed that he must be the doorman. Why else would a black man be dressed formally and standing in front of the Waldorf? One of the parking attendants who witnessed the incident came over and apologized to the Ambassador. Young quipped that he thought about keeping the car since the guy gave him the keys.

Debbie Allen, actor, director, and choreographer, recounts what happened to her when shopping for jewelry in exclusive Beverly Hills. She was admiring a particular piece in the display case when a white clerk came over and said to her that the item she was looking at was very expensive and could show her something more in her price range. The clerk had no idea what Allen's price range was, only that she was black. Incensed, Allen pulled out her credit card and purchased the jewelry on the spot. I would not have taken that approach and given the store my business, but Allen's reaction is understandable.

General Colin Powell, recounts one of the experiences he had on the National Security Advisory Staff just before he became National Security Advisor. He was assigned the task of meeting and briefing at the airport a foreign dignitary who would be between flights with only a few minutes available for discussion. Powell pulled up on time in front of the airport location. He described the car he was in as one of those with antennae coming from everywhere. He was wearing a classic Washington business suit and tie. Powell went into the private waiting area where he and the dignitary were to meet, and did not see anyone who appeared to be looking for him. General Powell waited fifteen minutes, then went to the desk to speak with the person in charge of the private lounge area. He queried the attendant about the dignitary, and she pointed him out. Powell walked over to the individual and introduced himself. The man did a double take, according to Powell. Moreover, the dignitary had seen Powell arrive, but evidently figured that he could not be the person he was to meet. Why? Because all this individual saw was a black person, and he no doubt expected to see a white man in such an important position. When he saw Powell come through the door, the man just knew *he* could not be a National Security Advisor to the President of the United States.[2]

Allow me to give you one final example involving entertainer Lionel Richie. Ambassador Howard Dawson, former United States Ambassador to Nigeria, Ghana, Sierra Leone, and Liberia, recounted this story to us at a dinner party held in his honor. Ambassador Dawson and his wife have known Richie since he was a student in college, and were special guests at a concert he gave in Washington. Afterwards, they went to the hotel where he was staying and entertaining after the concert. When the couple arrived, they found Richie and his entourage in uproarious laughter about an incident that had occurred that evening on the elevator. Richie, like any celebrity these days, travels with bodyguards, and that evening he had three stout African-American men who were with him in that capacity. When he and his three bodyguards got on the hotel elevator that evening, a white couple sheepishly got on as well. As the elevator was going up, Richie realized that he had not pressed the button for his floor. One of his guys was close to the buttons and Lionel shouted to him "Hit the floor!" The two whites in the front of the elevator went spread eagle on the floor. They evidently assumed it was a stickup and that the criminals were ordering them to lie down. Richie and bodyguards were momentarily stunned, then broke out in thunderous laughter. They had been laughing ever since. Richie later acquired the identity of the white couple that had been on the elevator and sent them flowers along with a note informing them that he wanted to pay for their hotel stay in appreciation of them giving him the best laugh he had experienced in years.

The list of such stories is endless. Is there any black person in America who has not experienced these types of racial micro aggressions? Black folk experience micro aggressions on a regular basis: the clerk who checks your credit card repeatedly; walking by an automobile and hearing the doors being snapped shut and locked; approaching a white woman on the street and seeing her clutch her purse; or having a waiter or clerk pass you by to serve someone else though you have been waiting longer. Having been chair of a department, one of my favorites was having a student come into my office and ask "Where is the chairman of the department?" Obviously *I* could not have been the chairperson. These racial micro aggressions are a regular part of black life, day in and day out, the little, and often not so little, aggressions suffered because of skin color. To get a feel for what it is to be black, imagine yourself as one of the African-American Secret Service agents refused service at the Denny's Restaurant in Baltimore, or a black employee of the Texaco Company overhearing racist remarks and experiencing daily discrimination and harassment that executives of the company boasted about committing while being tape recorded. Take those incidents and multiply them by thirty million and you will have a slight idea of what it means to be black in America for a single day.

The few examples of racial indignation that I have recited here, including my two personal stories, are in keeping with the critical race theory approach and the growing body of literature from that genre. Take, for example, Derrick Bell's *And We Are Not Saved*, *Faces at the Bottom of the Well: The Permanence of Racism*, and *Confronting Authority*. Bell, the former Harvard University Law Professor who resigned when Harvard failed to hire a black woman professor at the law school, uses the fictitious character Geneva Crenshaw as a heroine and literary tool allowing him to move freely and hurl theoretical criticism of laws and legislation impacting civil rights and especially African Americans. Patricia Williams's *The Alchemy of Race and Rights* is literally based on the daily diary of this talented black law professor at the University of Wisconsin and her encounters with students, colleagues, and administrators as she reflects on her struggle to elevate the consciousness level of those around her about the racial and civil rights impact of past and present legal decisions as they are carried out in everyday life. A similar treatment is offered in Stephen L. Carter's *Reflections of an Affirmative Action Baby*. Carter, now professor of law at Yale University, talks about the personal difficulties and benefits of growing up in the era of affirmative action programs. He even recounts his days as a youngster in Ithaca, New York and attending a public school where many of the Cornell faculty sent their kids, and how he triumphantly competed against them. From there he went on to Stanford University and was accepted into law school at Yale after rejection by Harvard (Harvard later rescinded its rejection letter, he tells us, when they learned that he was black). Personal anecdotes abound. Lani Guinier, a leading civil rights attorney who was nominated by President Clinton for the position of Assistant Attorney General of the United States in charge of Civil Rights enforcement and whose nomination was rescinded when she came under attack by right-wing forces for her liberal views, begins *The Tyranny of the Majority*, by telling of an experience she had when eight years old. Lani was a Brownie, and she entered a contest with other children to see who had made the best piece of clothing. She finished second. The mother of the girl who won the contest made her daughter's entry in clear violation of the rules. Guinier writes: "To me, fair play means that the rules encourage everyone to play. They should reward those who win, but they must be acceptable to those who lose. The central theme of my academic writing is that not all rules lead to elemental fair play. Some even commonplace rules work against it." Cornel West's *Race Matters* fits the parameters of the critical race theory approach. West, who was professor of religion and director of African American Studies at Princeton and is now professor of religion at Harvard University, begins his book by retelling his experience of trying to catch a cab on his way to a photo-shoot in New York for the cover of his forthcoming book. West and his wife had driven in to New York City from Princeton, New Jersey. West writes: "I dropped my wife off for an appointment she had on 60th Street between Lexington and Park Avenues. I left my car — a rather elegant one — in a safe parking lot and stood on the corner of 60th Street and Park Avenue to catch a taxi. I felt quite relaxed since I had an hour until my next engagement. At 5:00 p.m. I had to meet a photographer who would take the picture for the cover of this book on the roof of an apartment building in East Harlem on 115th Street and 1st Avenue. I waited and waited and waited. After the ninth taxi refused me, my blood began to boil. The tenth taxi refused me and stopped for a kind, well dressed, smiling female fellow citizen of European descent. As she stepped in the cab, she said, 'This is really ridiculous, is it not?' Ugly racial memories of the past flashed through my mind. Years ago, while driving from New York to teach at Williams College, I was stopped on fake charges of trafficking in cocaine. When I told the police officer I was a professor of religion, he replied 'Yeah, and I'm the Flying Nun. Let's go, nigger!' I was stopped three times in my first ten days in Princeton for driving too slowly on a residential street with a speed limit of twenty-five miles per hour. (And my son, Clifton, already has similar memories at the tender age of fifteen.)." Similar personal anecdotes appear in Judge Constance Baker Motley's *Equal Justice Under Law*, Randall Robinson's *Defending the Spirit*, Houston Baker's *Black Studies, Rap and the Academy*; and Charles Johnson's *Being and Race*.[3]

There is little that is actually new about the new Critical Race Theoretical approach. In March of 1887 the inaugural meeting of the American Negro Academy was held in Washington, DC. William Crogman, Francis James Grimke, Alexander Crummell, Walter Hayson, Paul Lawrence Dunbar, and Kelly Miller heralded the forum as a call to arms of leading intellectuals of the race and, in their words, to challenge the lies of the "cultural despisers" and "to aid the vindication of the race from vicious assaults." Theirs was an intellectual and scholarly mission, also one that out of necessity was partially political, social, cultural, and personal. Given the nadir that black folk faced at the start of the twentieth century, how could it have been otherwise? Given the new nadir that we face at the start of the new millennium, how can it be otherwise? W.E.B. Du Bois, the great intellect of the twentieth century, the Harvard trained historian, who later called himself a sociologist, was a renaissance thinker who spoke and wrote in many voices to address the single-most important barrier facing African Americans. Du Bois used scholarship, history, politics, poetry, verse, prose, spiritualism, psychology, and music. He used all the tools at his mighty intellectual disposal to decipher what he identified as the problem of the 20th century: "The problem of the color line." It is that same persistent problem that John Hope Franklin warns a new generation of readers of in his book, *The Color Line: Legacy of the Twenty-First Century*. Franklin, beginning his book in the Critical Race Theory approach, tells a personal story of his arrival at a speaking engagement at the University of Missouri: "My friend and host, Arvarh Strickland, met me at the St. Louis airport and greeted me warmly, and soon we were on our way to Columbia. After exchanging family news, we moved on to discuss the activities of historians, ranging from profound and unique reinterpretations of the field by some of them, to marriages, divorces, deaths, and various other events in their lives. Then, I asked if the jury in the Rodney King trial had reached a verdict. The question gave Arvarh a jolt, for he had heard of the 'not guilty' verdict just before my arrival and, in the excitement of our reunion, had failed to mention it."

What the Critical Race Theory scholars have in common is that they are Race Men and Women. They write with a purpose; some are more politically charged than others and some use a wider variety of techniques to get at the problem. They see the problem for what it is: racism, an active and systemic plague upon the American nation.[4]

THE POLITICS OF THE SCHOLARSHIP
OF AFRICAN-AMERICAN HISTORY

For the African-American historian—that is, the *race man* or *race woman* who writes and teaches black history—the world is one of duality, of seemingly contradictory purposes. You are the scholar who has pledged to be objective, but as a race warrior you are waging an intellectual battle for the liberation and progress of the race. Then you are being subjective. I have already said that human beings are what they eat; and that in the real world or even in the world of ideas there is no such creature as objectivity. We all bring to our work who we are, where we are from, what are our personal values. To be intellectually honest, we should proclaim our subjectivity; put it right out front and tell all: "This will be a subjective treatment." That is the truth. If you are a race man or woman who teaches and researches African-American history you have a scholarly *and* a political agenda. Admit it. The agenda should not be a hidden one. L.D. Reddick, former professor of history at Temple University, articulated the point when he said in his 1936 address to the Association for the Study of Negro Life and History: "Negro History has a purpose which is built upon a faith. It has the generalized objective which it shares with all scholarship of seeking the advancement of knowledge plus the specific design as a lever of what might be termed 'racial progress.'"[5]

The writing of African-American history did not grow out of some weekend recreational sport or fondness for pontificating about certain dates and events. The struggle for black history, indeed what can be termed the Black History Movement, began in the early nineteenth century with the efforts of James W.C. Pennington, William Cooper Nell, and William Wells Brown. All three men were dedicated abolitionists, and Pennington and Brown were former slaves.

Nell was born a freeman in the North. Their struggle through the writing of black history was to combat oppression and racial intolerance by proving the worth and great deeds of the descendants of Africa, particularly those in the United States. The chronicling of the achievements of blacks characterized their writings. What they were simply and eloquently trying to do was to question how this nation could hold fellow human beings in bondage, human beings who had contributed to world civilization, who were taken from a continent not of savages but of people of great worth. The idea was to prove the worth of black human beings by documenting their history, and thus winning the hearts and minds of even the slave masters. These early writers of black history attempted to play upon America's morality and the often expressed sacred tenets of freedom, liberty, equality, and justice for all. Thus African-American history grew out of a political context, not some mere freewheeling nice thing to do, or what James Baldwin called "an intellectual masturbatory delusion." It had a purpose.

These early writers did their best to be objective and truthful in their history writing. But there was no separating the historical truth from the reality of the day: the enslavement in America of people of African descent. History was one weapon that Pennington, Nell, and Brown believed could be mustered against the process and institution that exploited and dehumanized black folk. From the very beginning, these early writers of black history were attempting to expose the truth and to use it in a political context. To speak today about "political correctness" subverts and undermines what has been a proud part of African-American history writing: correctness and truthfulness that comes with the telling of the full story of America including the experiences of its people of African descent. Neither Pennington, Nell, nor Brown had formal training in history, but what they lacked in academic preparation they made up for in sheer determination.

George Washington Williams, born in 1849, approached the endeavor with similar energy, dedication, and with some formal degree of historical training. He was committed to getting the record straight and making the history of black folk accessible. Williams authored several monumental books in the late nineteenth century on the African-American experience and earned a reputation of spending years researching and writing on a topic before venturing to have his work published.

It was W. E. B. Du Bois who ushered in the era of the formally trained scholar of black history. Du Bois acquired a formal education that was second to none. He earned a B.A. from Fisk University in 1888; a B.A., cum laude, from Harvard University in 1890; studied history and economics as a graduate student at the University of Berlin from 1892 to 1894; and received a Ph.D. in history from Harvard in 1896. He used that education in the struggle for black advancement as he became a virtual publishing machine. The number of Du Bois's published works in the field of African-American history is astronomical. He authored at least twenty-one books and approximately three hundred articles and pamphlets; edited fifteen books and was founder and editor of several major periodicals, among them *Crisis*—the official oracle of the NAACP—and *Phylon: A Review of Race and Culture*, published out of Atlanta University. Du Bois ranks as one of the most prolific scholars of all time. He never saw a contradiction between his scholarship and the use of history to confront America's racism. Du Bois was a fighter for social justice and initiated the Niagara Movement in 1905 to organize African-American leaders. He was also a founding member of the NAACP and served in the organization for thirty years. Through his writings, scholarship, and social activism, he challenged the color line and the Eurocentrists who defended and supported racism by dismissing the contribution of blacks. He was not alone.

Carter G. Woodson (1875–1950), founder of the *Journal of Negro History* in 1916 and the *Negro History Bulletin* in 1937, was another highly educated student of history and twentieth-century fighter for racial justice. Along with authoring twelve major books, edited volumes, many path-breaking articles, and edited works, Woodson established the Association for the Study of Negro Life and History (ASNLH). He had contemplated the idea for such an organization for many years, and at a meeting held in Chicago with Alexander Jackson, George Cleveland, W.B. Hartgrove, J.E. Stamps, Kelley Miller, Reverend Jesse Mooreland and others, this new association was born in 1915. The organization would bring together like-minded individuals who wanted to get the full story of the contributions of black folk to black folk and others, and to fight against the evil lies being perpetuated that blacks were inept and worthless. Each time we celebrate Black History Month, a time of remembrance of the contributions that people of African descent have made to human progress in America and throughout the world, we should give thanks to Carter G. Woodson. He was the force behind this national month of recognition. Woodson, after receiving his doctorate in history from Harvard University in 1912, turned his thoughts and energies almost exclusively to the black history crusade. He stood toe to toe against the forces of racism in the midst of an era that was one of the most vile and horrendous in the nation's history. Historian Rayford W. Logan aptly dubbed the period from 1877 to 1920 as the Great Nadir. During that period, black folk were intimidated, humiliated, and violated in every conceivable fashion on a daily basis: Jim Crow laws, segregation, discrimination, theories of racial and social supremacy, and violence of every sort were constant realities for blacks. The Ku Klux Klan, Knight Riders, and the White Citizen Councils were all too familiar sights, especially in the South. More than three thousand blacks were lynched in America during this period. Justice, equality, franchisement, and equal educational and job opportunities were things that blacks could only dream about and hope would eventually come to pass in a kinder and gentler nation. America at every turn was telling black folk to stay back, we do not want you included.

Woodson tried to make the dream of a multiracial society a reality. To accomplish this, he sought to help America to understand its black component. He believed in useful history whose purpose went beyond traditional approaches and limitations and helped to open the public mind. In his effort to reach the public, Woodson used an idea originated by several members of the Omega Psi Phi fraternity in 1926, and turned it into a nationwide celebration of black achievement: Negro History Week (expanded and christened Black History Month in 1976). The second week of February was chosen for this celebration because the birthdays of Abraham Lincoln and Frederick Douglass fall on that week, making it an especially appropriate time to focus on race relations. Woodson argued for activist history and the bringing into play of the formerly dismissed and hidden elements of societal wrongs. Black scholars then, as now, should be emboldened by his challenge to understand the importance of history to the liberation of black people; and thus, to research and write about, in Woodson's words, the "useful Negroes of whom editors and authors take no account." He reasoned that if the true story of the black was more widely known, America might have a change of heart toward its citizens of color. Woodson's dream was, in a sense, much like that of Pennington, Nell, Brown, Williams, Du Bois, Benjamin Brawley, Anna Cooper, J.A. Rogers, Charles H. Wesley, Leo Hansberry, Benjamin Quarles, Shirley Graham Du Bois, John Hope Franklin, and all the other race men and women, past and present. He worked to bring the black contribution center stage.[6]

Similar in mission, the first Black Studies program began shortly before 1920 at Atlanta University under the tutelage of W.E.B. Du Bois. Throughout the 1920s, black colleges initiated specific courses devoted to examining the African-American experience. Such was the case at Fisk University in the 1920s offering courses on the "problems in Negro life" the "Negro in American history" and "Aboriginal Africa." Black colleges offered a nurturing environment sustaining Black Studies, and they were the first to integrate the teaching of African-American history and the black experience into all of its degree programs.

Even at black colleges, Black Studies grew out of struggle. The real impetus that gave rise to these programs at the colleges was student action. Black folks have always had to deal with their so-called own institutions to liberate them in terms of inclusion and the teaching of non-Eurocentric history. The activism of black students at predominantly black colleges in the 1920s included protest demonstrations and disruptions on the campuses. This shares many similarities with the activism of black students at predominantly white colleges and universities in the 1960s. In 1968 the first Black Studies programs at predominantly white universities were established. The first was at San Francisco State University through the efforts of Ron Karanga. These programs evolved from earlier struggles to have blacks included and to change the face of not only the textbooks, but the anti-multiracial society itself. The goal was the death of racism. This was coupled with a longing for a scholarship of liberation. The black studies advocates on campuses in the 1920s, like those of the 1960s, worked for race consciousness and identified with the problems facing black folk. They devoted substantial portions of their time to studying African-American history and avowing its lessons to all in hope of affecting social change.

The Black History Movement is an inclusive effort, politically and scholarly. Hence, it is not surprising that from its inception the movement welcomed all disciplines and approaches. Long before the Annales School in 1929 and the work of Febvre, Bloc, and Foucault, African-American history writing was demonstrating the worth of interdisciplinary scholarship. Indicative of the interdisciplinary nature of the Black History Movement, at least seventy-two percent of the articles in the *Journal of Negro History* from 1916 to 1940 cite sources and use works by non-historians. Moreover, Carter G. Woodson was a Pan-Africanist in his scholarship, studying blacks in America as well as Africa, the West Indies, and Latin America. During the 1920s he initiated a number of projects on Africa and the Caribbean. He began collecting historical and contemporary documents on Africa, gathering folktales, and corresponding with respected anthropologist Melville Herskovits, in addition to Monroe Work, and Maurice Delafosse, who were researching the African past. The Associated Publishers brought out an English translation of Delafosse's work, as well as Woodson's *African Myths Together with Proverbs*. Woodson provided novelist Alain Locke with funds for a two-year project to prepare a monograph on African art as a manifestation of African society and culture.[7]

The Black History Movement, however, was also fraught with politics as was, and is, the entire history profession. Woodson, for example, had disputes with the white racial moderates who were on the executive council of the ASNLH, including his former Harvard mentor, Albert Bushnell Hart, who resigned from the council in 1922. Woodson had to contend with those who accused him of abandoning the scientific study of Negro history to become a propagandist. To the contrary, he did not abandon the "scientific study" of history, whatever that might be, but strove to make the discipline intellectually honest and challenged its exclusivity and Eurocentrism. That behavior earned him the reputation of being a radical whose research and projects were unworthy of financial support from white foundations. Black proposals deemed to be controversial usually failed to receive funding. The most conservative black social scientists and projects were then, as they often are today, rewarded with the largest share of research money. Scholars who were deemed black nationalists, Marxists, Pan-Africanists, and ardent social challengers had little chance of receiving grants. Research projects that promoted interracial cooperation and racial accommodation received backing, and usually the most conservative black institutions such as Fisk, Tuskegee, Hampton, Howard, the National Urban League, and the National Negro Business League, for example, were awarded the lion's share of funds. Woodson correctly concluded that the foundations wanted control of what blacks thought and wrote. Thomas Jesse Jones of the Phelps-Stokes Fund, who was white and a board member, grew personally hostile to him. Jones also worked against Du Bois, whom he considered too radical. After Du Bois published *Black Reconstruction* in 1935, he no longer received any more grant support, as many characterized his book as a radical Marxist analysis. Other black scholars who were labeled as radical received similar treatment from the foundations.

Even those who claimed to be friendly to the Black History Movement often had their own hidden political agenda. The Federal Government saw the Black History Movement as a threat because it was intended to enlighten and inspire blacks to work to transform American society. By 1940 there was a widening government plot against Woodson that had begun at least twenty years earlier. Woodson was a target of Attorney General A. Mitchell Palmer and the Department of Justice. While teaching at Howard University in 1920 he learned from the institution's president that the Department of Justice sought information from the university's administration regarding his activities and publications and inferred their suspicion that he might be a closet Communist or, at the very least, a sympathizer. He was branded a Red because he spoke out for his people and wrote history that challenged and condemned racism.

During the 1940s Woodson also attracted the interest of Defense Department agents because of his interactions with historians and writers like Herbert Aptheker and James Ford, both of whom wrote books, pamphlets, and newspaper articles for the Communist Party of America (CP). Woodson's scholarship received attention in the *Daily Worker,* the CP's official newspaper in the United States. Moreover, he spoke at schools that, allegedly, had ties to the CP such as the Samuel Adams School for Social Studies in Boston, the Jefferson School for Social Studies in New York City, and the Rackham Educational Memorial School in Detroit. The Federal Bureau of Investigation monitored the sale of Woodson's books and kept purported radical bookstores under surveillance from the 1940s to the early 1970s through the end of the Vietnam War. The FBI took particular notice of books on black history, especially those that were in demand, such as works by Woodson. The United States government clandestinely plotted against black intellectuals and consciousness raising within the African-American community.

At the same time, the Communist Party of America had its own designs on the Black History Movement. Specifically, the CP wanted control of the movement. Herbert Aptheker and Philip Foner, two Jewish American historians who wrote extensively on African-American historical topics, were members of the CP and received funding from that organization. The CP often assisted with the publication of their books. Broader circulation of their written work bolstered their leadership potential in the Black History Movement. Max Yergan, the young black Communist and founder of the Council on African Affairs, taught the first formal black history course at City College of New York in 1937. He had become a CPer and spokesperson for the party in Harlem and was the first African American to teach at CCNY. W.E.B. Du Bois's second wife, Shirley Graham, had known Du Bois since her youth. As an adult she became an activist in the CP. The party was delighted by her relationship with Du Bois and encouraged her marriage to him.

Unlike the FBI, which worked to destroy the Black History Movement and the modern Civil Rights Movement, the CP was more a friend than an enemy to both. By the 1960s the FBI had a specialized unit, called Division Five, with the primary mission of focusing on black intellectual activists. This group worked in conjunction with COINTELPRO, the FBI's counter-intelligence program to neutralize the Civil Rights Movement and other black activists groups. Division Five focused on what it termed CIRM (Communist Influenced Racial Matters). Division Five wiretapped Herbert Aptheker's phone, for example. They had an informant within the prestigious Organization of American Historians, one of the OAH's officers, who reported on CP activities within the historical organization and kept tabs on suspected radical historians. W.E.B. Du Bois left his personal papers to the trust of Communist Party member and noted historian Herbert Aptheker because he considered Aptheker a person of conviction and courage. Twelve years after Du Bois's death in 1963, Aptheker was invited to be a visiting professor for one-semester at Yale University to teach a seminar on W.E.B. Du Bois. Some members of the university's history department launched a campaign that blocked the appointment on the alleged grounds that his teaching methods and editorship of the Du Bois papers were substandard. The department's action inspired a protest at Yale resulting in more than 2,000 students petitioning in support of the appointment. The politics of the scholarship of African-American history are never ending.[8]

RACE OR GENDER

The lesson from the Black History Movement is that the African-American historian must be conscious of divisive elements from every quarter. The assaults and confrontations come from within and outside, from would-be friends and avowed enemies, from the political right, left, and center, from whites and blacks, from men and women. Intellectual and political tensions that exist between some black men and black women historians are counter productive. One needs to question whether specified approaches to history writing have helped to advance or worked to hinder the continuation of the Black History Movement. What are the roles of gender and class analyses to the movement? They are useful because they help us to further dissect and unravel the multi-layers of oppression. Both class and gender are important, but secondary issues for African Americans. On the issue of class, Marxist scholars will, of course, disagree with this claim — that is, if avowed Marxists are still to be found after the total collapse of the former Soviet Union and the absolute supremacy now of capitalism. My contention is that *racism* is the single most important barrier to African-American progress, and class and gender are secondary. Gender analysis has made some important strides since its earliest stages when the focus of women's studies, as Pat Bell Scott writes, was almost exclusively upon the lives of white women. Scott also rightly points out that the early black studies courses tended to focus exclusively on black males. The point is well taken. Black males must own up to any lingering sexist behavior they may have, and abolish it. Beverly Guy-Sheftall, director of women's studies at Spelman College, makes the point that there are positives and negatives in black women studies. She, like Bell Hooks, is brilliant and perceptive. Note that Bell Hooks in her writings, *Ain't I a Woman: Black Women and Feminism*, and in *Killing Rage: Ending Racism*, does not ignore the persistent race problem within the women's movement.

It is only in the last few years, however, that the women's movement has been challenged to become more than a white women's movement and to deal with the issue of racism. Black feminist Barbara Smith demands that "overthrowing racism" must be a priority of the feminist movement. White feminist Ellen Pence offers a searching introspective on racism in the women's movement when she writes: "Knowing that we grew up in a society permeated with the belief that white values, culture, and lifestyle are superior, we can assume that regardless of our rejection of the concept [of racism] we still act out of that socialization." The most brilliant voice in this call for redirection is that of Evelyn Higginbotham. In a critical piece that appeared in *Signs*, a journal devoted to women and culture, Higginbotham argues: "Whether race is textually omitted or textually privileged, its totalizing effect in obscuring class and gender remains. This may well explain why women's studies for so long rested upon the unstated premise of racial (i.e., white) homogeneity and with this presumption proceeded to universalize 'women's' culture and oppression, while failing to see white women's own investment and complicity in the oppression of other groups of men and women." Elizabeth Spelman also takes to task the idea of "homogeneous womanhood" in her exploration of race and gender in her work, *Inessential Woman*.

Black women, historically, were not defined as women. As Deborah White presents in her book, *Aren't I a Woman: Females Slaves in the Plantation South*, black women were defined as "property." Sojourner Truth could ask prophetically: "Ain't I a Woman?" The answer was: No, you are not. You are black. Evelyn Higginbotham and Judge A. Leon Higginbotham document for African Americans the historical primacy of race over gender as exemplified in the case of *State of Missouri vs. Celia*. Celia was fourteen years old when purchased by a successful farmer, Robert Newsome. During the five years of his ownership, Newsome habitually forced Celia into sexual intercourse. At age nineteen she had borne a child by him and was expecting another. In June 1855, while pregnant and ill, Celia defended herself against further rape by her master. Her testimony reveals that she warned him she would hurt him if he continued to abuse her while sick. When her threats failed to thwart his assaults, she hit him over the head with a stick, immediately killing him. Celia was apprehended and tried for first-degree murder. Her counsel sought to lower the charge of first degree to murder in self-defense, arguing that Celia had a right to resist her master's sexual assaults, especially because of the imminent danger to her health. A master's economic and property rights, the defense contended, did not include rape. The defense rested its case on Missouri statues that "protect women" from attempts to ravish, rape, or defile. The language of these particular Missouri statues explicitly used terms such as "any woman," while other unrelated Missouri statues explicitly used terms such as "white female" and "slave" or "negro" in their criminal codes. The question centered on her womanhood. Was Celia "a woman" or was she "a black?" The court found Celia guilty, declaring that if Newsome was in the habit of having intercourse with the defendant who was his slave, he had the right to do so. Celia, the court declared, committed first degree murder. She was sentenced to death. Her subsequent appeal was denied and Celia, the "black woman," was hanged in December 1855 after the birth of her child.[9]

There were few changes for black women in the years following emancipation. The power relationship of white male and female superiority in the South made black women an unprotected group as was the case for black men. Black women were sexually assaulted and exploited because they were vulnerable, as were all blacks, and found no relief or recourse in the legal system because of their race.

THE NEW ANTI-CRITICAL RACE THEORISTS

Efforts to eradicate racism or to curtail gender bias and class discrimination find no support among the intellectual right wing. Under the cloak of scholarship they defend the conservative status quo, anti civil rights agenda and all that comes along with it. Politics are inherently a part of scholarship; that is reality. There has always been a relationship between the political forces at play and the "scholarship" of the day. With the New Deal Era of Franklin D. Roosevelt's administration in the 1930s and 1940s, liberal writings came to the forefront.

These writings were followed by conservative attacks. The tumultuous period of the 1960s saw the largest explosion of African-American scholarship. In the late 1970s and 1980s, synonymous with the Reagan and Bush administrations, America experienced a preponderance of neo-conservative literature and arguments. This period was the catalyst for the new anti-critical race works of such conservative writers as Diane Ravitch, Allan Bloom, Nat Hentoff, Mary Lefkowitz, William Bennett, Dinesh D'Souza, Arthur Schlesinger, Jr. (New Dealer turned traitor), and their black sycophants such as Thomas Sowell, Walter Williams, Shelby Steele, and John McWorter.[10]

Schlesinger, a former Harvard professor and advisor to President John F. Kennedy, is author of one of the most heralded writings of the anti-critical race theorists, *The Disuniting of America*. What makes his lack of factual knowledge so appalling and inexcusable is that he is an award-winning historian. The premise of *The Disuniting of America* is as follows: "As the era of ideological conflict subsides humanity enters or more precisely reenters a possibly more dangerous era of ethnic and racial animosity." Only someone who has not experienced what it means to be black in America and who fails to grasp the long history of racial conflict in this nation could come to such a conclusion. For the African American every era has been dangerous in America. Let us recall that the experience for black folk in the United States began with slavery. In addition, there was no respite after emancipation and the end of the Civil War, and blacks fell victim to one of the worst periods in the history of race relations in this nation. The era which Rayford W. Logan described as the "Great Nadir," from the date of the Great Compromise of 1877 to the end of World War I, was a period of Jim Crowism, segregation, racism, poll taxes, grandfather clauses, and lynchings. More than one hundred blacks were lynched every year, according to the official record, which was a grossly incomplete count. So for a scholar or anyone else to say, as Schlesinger does, that we are now entering a possibly more dangerous era of ethnic and racial animosity is to have short memory.

Ethnic and racial animosities are the hallmarks of America's anti-multiracial society. For black folk the nadir can logically be extended from 1619 to the present day. To say as Schlesinger does that "ethnicity is the cause of the breaking of nations" does not help the African American whose problem has not been because he or she is of a different ethnic persuasion but because he or she is of a different color. A color defined by the majority group as a color of despair, degradation, violence, unworthiness, promiscuity, loath, and inferiority.[11]

Irish-Americans, Italian-Americans, Polish-Americans, Jewish-Americans and so forth, have all had their moments in history of being placed on the out-list and discriminated against by Anglo-Saxon Protestants. Each group has in turn discriminated against the next newcomers. Blacks were never the newcomers, however. Our history dates back to the very beginning of this nation, yet we are shunned not because of any ethnic peculiarity but because our skin color is darker than that of the Irish person, the Jewish person, the German person, the Russian person, and the "other ethnic immigrants" who *came* to this nation and who today constitute the white majority. If Schlesinger were right and today's ethnicity is the cause of the breaking of nations, America would have never been. Yes, ethnic cleansing and wars spew forward in the former Soviet Union, Myanmar (Burma), Cypress, Iraq, Lebanon, Yugoslavia, Liberia, Somalia, Nigeria, Ethiopia, and so forth. Yet to bring the picture home, the question of ethnicity is not the issue. The issue is the persistent, everlasting, constantly-with-us, tearing-us-asunder, blight-and-disgrace-to-this-nation: *racism*.

Schlesinger tells us, "Even nations as stable and civilized as Britain and France, Belgium and Spain and Czechoslovakia, face growing ethnic and racial troubles." When he speaks of Africa he focuses on "tribalism" and the problems of those societies. People of color are not included in his definition of the "highly and most civilized."

In *The Disuniting of America*, diversity is lauded while the current move toward multiculturalism is assailed. All the familiar bells of the ongoing debate are rung: "political correctness," "Afrocentrism," "reverse discrimination," "black separatism," and all the other provocative terms. Black separatism is lambasted for supposedly nourishing prejudice, magnifying differences, and stirring antagonisms. The author fails to understand that the real problem has not been separation. It has been and is white segregation and anti-multiculturalism which are byproducts of racism. Schlesinger has no problem, however, in defending the status quo and urging academic institutions to take the lead in protecting traditional teaching and subject matter: "The situation in our universities, I am confident will soon right itself once the great silent majority of professors 'cry enough,' and challenge what they know to be boggiest nonsense."

This is not boggiest nonsense. What is actually occurring is a power struggle for the hearts and minds of this nation, and the detractors will never admit the true parameters of the battle. They would like us to believe that the challenge is coming from some obtuse group that, misguided in their efforts to build their own self-esteem, want to rewrite history, falsify facts, and downright lie in the name of building racial pride. Frankly, that sounds much more like the Eurocentric tradition than anything else. There is a power struggle going on for inclusion, an inclusion of ideas, thoughts, contributions, and perspectives that American education has actively omitted. The boggiest nonsense comes from the detractors, the guardians of the privileged, who still think that the European contribution is the most important and superior and only see other contributions and people as peripheral to the main story of human progress and civilization. The author warns us in his book: "If [black] separatist tendencies go on unchecked the result can only be the fragmentation, resegregation and tribalization of American life." America is already fragmented, segregated and an exclusive society. That is the undeniable truth as seen though the eyes of any African American who possesses vision and consciousness. Cities are more segregated than ever, schools are more segregated than ever, the black unemployment rate in this country is higher than ever, and the future for people of color in this country is more in jeopardy and at peril than perhaps at any other point in the history of the United States of America. Yet Schlesinger, and folks like him, warn us about a resegregation fostered by blacks as if America had ever become desegregated and blacks held the option of integrating. He quotes out of context former New York Governor Mario Cuomo as having said that "we need to recognize and encourage and enrich diversity as well as the need to ensure that such a broadened multicultural perspective leads to unity and an enriched sense of what being an American is, and not to a destructive factionalism that would tear us apart." The sad reality is that America has never been together. If it had ever been, then racism would have ended. America is a nation built on exclusivity, particularly when it comes to those who are not like the majority of society. Schlesinger contends, however, that the bonds of national cohesion are "sufficiently fragile already. Public education should aim to strengthen those bonds, not to weaken them."

Africa and its people are ridiculed in *The Disuniting of America*. Schlesinger employs such dated and pejorative labels as "tribalism" to describe African society. According to him, no one "can hope to understand African history without understanding loyalties, rituals, blood feuds, tribalism." He talks of "the orgies of war and sacrifices of human beings" in West African society and claims that these negatives are never mentioned in the new liberal curriculums. The book is laden with quotes from other members of the new right like Diane Ravitch who the author says, "sensibly asks how in the world does one lose knowledge by sharing it?" The right, however, only wants certain information shared. To teach, for example, that Africans visited the Americas before Columbus and that one of the most powerful and beautiful women of Egyptian history was black are types of information that Schlesinger wants to avoid. He says: "Is Afro-centric chauvinism any different from the Irish and American myth making satirized by John Killahere. Does not the uncritical glorification carry us back to Plato's noble lie?" Is the author saying that Africans had not visited the Americas before Columbus and that Nefertari was not black or, as Egyptologists like to say, of "mixed race"? They did and she was. How can we trust an individual who claims objectivity and then gives us half-truths at best and misinformation in general and in the name of an enlightened perspective? He is so culturally arrogant that he contends "any homogeneity among slaves derived not from the African tribe but from the American plantation." Perhaps blacks should be thankful that they were brought to America where they were forced into solidarity and homogeneity as a result of the plantation system? Let African Americans be grateful then for enslavement.[12]

You can see Schlesinger's utter disrespect for African tradition when he discusses what occurred at Professor Asa Hillard's conference focusing on the infusion of African and African-American history into the school curriculum. At that conference, the distinguished African-American historian, Professor John Henrik Clarke, was honored in the traditional manner of an Ashanti Instoolment Ceremony with individuals blowing horns, beating drums, and placing Clarke symbolically upon the seat of respect. Schlesinger describes this as looking "rather silly." The Africanization of black Americans has, in his opinion, "not gotten very far." He is wrong as usual and cites Nathan Huggins, who was also wrong on this point, when Huggins wrote, "An Afro-American and the grandson of a Polish immigrant will be able to take more for granted between themselves than the former could with a Nigerian or the latter with a Warsaw worker." That hypothesis is preposterous for African Americans given the existence of racism and the formidable color line in America. In addition, the hypothesis begs a disconnectedness between African Americans and Africans as a result of the American experience. Citing the support of William Raspberry, columnist for the *Washington Post*, hardly makes Schlesinger's assertions correct. Where did Raspberry do his training in African and African-American history? Why not look to the huge contingent of race scholars, particularly those in the fields of African and African-American history? They, in the main, have a very different perspective from that proclaimed in *The Disuniting of America*, and a vast degree more knowledge of the subject.

Even the term "African American" is denigrated in the book. The author points an accusing finger at The Reverend Jesse Jackson for having criticized the use of the term *black*. Jackson was right but neither was Jackson the first to note the inconsistency and historical inaccuracy of the term black. Jackson rekindled the old need and the old argument to identify the continent, country, and ethnicity of the individual or group. In the case of African Americans it is Africa. It would be historically correct, rather than politically correct, to make that connection known. It makes no difference that Schlesinger cites a so-called survey done by the *Washington Post* reporting that sixty-six percent of blacks polled favor being called "black" over "African American." More recent polls, however, now show an overwhelming support of the term "African American" among African Americans. It is not a question of which term is favored but which term is accurate. African American is a historically precise and accurate term.[13]

The major spur for writing *The Disuniting of America* was the lost battle against the New York State Task Force on Curriculum revision of the public schools' social studies curriculum which, in its infinite wisdom, recommended replacing the Eurocentric curriculum in favor of a multicultural one. Schlesinger's book is a manifesto against African-American cohesiveness and demands for inclusion in the school curriculum. The author, furthermore, contends that identifying with Africa, or learning African American history, will not change the problems black kids face in the ghettoes of today. He asserts: "Even if history is sanitized in order to make people feel good there is no evidence that feel-good history promotes ethnic self-esteem and equips students to grapple with their lives." If his reasoning has merit, then hearing about the successes of Europeans and white Americans most certainly will not do black youngsters any good. Eurocentric oriented history promotes white superiority and blacks have been fed those stories in school since day one. If anything, those stories lower African-American self-esteem.

Professor Schlesinger is convinced that whenever ethnic and religious groups assert a right "to approve or veto anything that is taught in public schools, the fatal line is crossed between cultural pluralism and ethnocentrism. An evident causality is the old idea that whatever our ethnic base we are all Americans together." His contention is hyperbole that miserably fails confirmation in the experience of African Americans. What we are really taking about here is empowerment and others now want some of it and to have their contributions and experiences recognized and taught. Schlesinger, however, calls all of this a "betrayal of a noble profession." This is the same history profession that has for most of its organizational life lied, distorted, abused, and excluded black folk and other people of color in every general American history text written until the serious challenges to it began in the 1940s and crystallized in the 1960s, and continues to this day. To laud the history profession for its "dispassionate analysis," as the author does, is intellectually dishonest. We need to be intellectually honest about the subjectivity of any teaching. Each instructor who enters the classroom, comes with a particular background, point of reference, racial, gender, ethnic group, and class experience, a certain world view, political and ideological bent that will color that instructor's teaching no matter how objective that particular instructor believes he or she is or attempts to be. By nature of the materials they include or do not include, books they assign or do not assign, material they choose to talk about in class or do not address, one is being subjective and it would be fair, honorable and academically truthful to admit that fact up front to all who hear the words of the professed sage.

The traditional disciplinary canons, according to *The Disuniting of America*, must be protected whatever the cost. After all, the author says, "A canon means only that because you can't read everything you give some books priority over others." Therein lies the problem. The right champions a restricted intellectualism based on time limitations. The goal of multiculturalism is not the replacing of the old canons of Western classics with new ones of African-Latin, American-Indian-Third World-gender laden texts. Rather, it seeks to expand the canon to include those other voices that make up the rest of the story. To do otherwise is to say that only one perspective, the European perspective, is important enough to be considered. This is anti-intellectualism. Things European do not constitute the entire world. Europe, and for that matter the white race, is a minority when one considers the population of the so-called Third World which includes Africa, Asia, Latin America, the Caribbean, and India. People of color constitute eighty percent of the world population, and growing. The right will eventually be forced to deal with the inevitability of a changing world that demands attention to other voices. Instead, *The Disuniting of America* poses such fear-riddled questions as: "Is the Western tradition a bar to progress and a curse on humanity? Would it really do America and the world good to get rid of the European legacy?" The answer is no. The issue is offering Western tradition and the European legacy as the complete record of humankind with the contributions of others marginalized, if considered at all.

Other voices from the right, including Dinesh D'Souza in his treatise, *Illiberal Education: The Politics of Race and Sex on Campus*,
champion the same cause as demonstrated in *The Disuniting of
America* with equally flawed reasoning and abuse of history. What
D'Souza does is engage in sloganeering. What he calls "political correctness" does not exist. What we should be talking about in this
nation is the need to appreciate multiculturalism and diversity.
Racism exists on college campuses and throughout society. Is to
challenge the racism of America, and demand that the nation honor
the principles it professes, being politically correct? There is no such
thing as political correctness. It is a sloganeering and defining campaign initiated by the right wing or so-called conservatives in their
efforts to trivialize the legitimate need for openness to diversity, sensitivity, mutual respect, equal opportunity, and an end to discrimination and racism. It is the D'Souza types of the world who engage
in the old adage of Oscar Wilde's: "If you can not answer a man's
argument, do not panic. You can always call him names." The outpouring of rejection that D'Souza and people who share his position
receive when they speak on college campuses brings into question
why they are given a platform to speak from anywhere in the nation. Intelligent and informed people are highly unlikely to join an
audience to hear something from someone foreign-born in 1961,
who has only been in the United States since 1978, and without
benefit of historical training and advanced degrees, now claims to be
an expert on the historical problems of America and the "liberal establishment." D'Souza quotes three whites in making his assertion
that even some liberals agree with his arguments. What is a "liberal," particularly in D'Souza's ultra conservative way of thinking?
Does being a liberal make you free from racism? Arthur Schlesinger,
in years past, called himself a liberal. It is not surprising that D'-
Souza cites Schlesinger as one of those liberals who support his
ideas. Noticeably absent from his short list of supporters are any
African-American scholars or race men and women. D'Souza is simply a reductionist who, lacking the depth of understanding and
training in American history, and having no real experience and
first-hand grounding in American racism, reduces the historical
legacy of racism to slogans and superficial diatribes and polemics.
The issue is not political correctness on or off campus; the issue is
racism on and off campus, and beyond that, strong doses of sexism
and opposition to any people of difference. The D'Souza types have
been on the warpath in tune with the Reagan and Bush administrations of the 1980s and continue to dig in, trying their best to save
white male supremacy. William F. Buckley immediately gravitated

toward D'Souza while he was an undergraduate at Dartmouth and editor of the radical conservative and racist *Dartmouth Review*. D'Souza's reasoning is not based on scholarly expertise or serious academic historical research. His is the shallow philosophy indicative of the novice, the immature, and the misinformed.

D'Souza further demonstrates the extent of his lack of understanding when he espouses that the American universities "are nevertheless intellectual and social enclaves, by design somewhat aloof from the pressures of the real world." Only the naive or uninformed could maintain that romanticized view of a university campus. It is assuredly not the case for African Americans and anyone else with sensitivity and who is a member of a minority group. Colleges and universities are most often microcosms of the larger society and all of its problems including racism. While D'Souza may say in writing that he deplores the racist epithets that were written at the University of Michigan such as, for example, "A mind is a terrible thing to waste, particularly on a nigger," he only uses these incidents to launch attacks on those who are in favor of some degree of censorship to try to stop this kind of racist graffiti and public display of hatred. The real issue is this society where, even on its university campuses, the citadels of learning, racist acts abound. These acts reflect how endemic, systemic, and entrenched racism is in America. The question is not free speech; that may be a secondary issue either handled properly or mishandled on a campus. Neither is the issue preferential treatment for minorities, but whether a university truly wants to become diverse and make sure that equal educational opportunity is afforded to all. Those are the real issues. They are the same issues that have existed for so very long in this nation and have yet to be solved. At least many university campus administrations, faculties, and student bodies are taking on these issues. The D'Souzas sit back and snipe. This is not to suggest that predominantly white universities and colleges are friends of black folk. If we understand nothing else about the Bakke fiasco at the University of California at Davis in the 1970s, we should grasp that the University of California system was no friend of minorities and uncommitted to diversity or equal educational opportunity for blacks. When Bakke was denied admission to the UC Davis medical school, he filed suit claiming that his rejection was reverse discrimination because several blacks had been admitted to the school who had lower test scores than his. It is not surprising that it was an associate dean at the University of California at Davis who slipped the information to Bakke that enabled him to file his suit. That is why the NAACP and other civil rights organizations filed friend of the court briefs to bolster and strengthen the University of California's defense. The University had advanced a weak argument for its affirmative action programs; its heart was not in it. If left to its own devices, the University of California and most of the rest of the predominantly white colleges and universities would have never integrated. Thanks to the Civil Rights Movement and the tumultuous activism of the 1960s, state universities were pushed to open their doors to serve all the people of their respective states.[14]

D'Souza's attack on affirmative action programs at universities reflects his closed mindedness and opposition to integrating university campuses. He tells us that admission should simply be a matter of test scores. If this were the only criteria, there would be no guarantee of diversity in the student body. The most rewarding educational experience is a result of students from different backgrounds sharing information and perspectives. This holds true for faculty, administrators, and staff. They all benefit from diversity of makeup. Moreover, education does not simply take place in the class rooms. It also takes place in the corridors, outside the buildings, in the dormitories, in the streets, at the social gatherings, and everywhere else members of the university community make contact. Furthermore, black folk pay taxes just like other Americans and are entitled as state residents to the services of their state's public higher educational institutions. State universities have that special obligation of diversity as does most private universities since they too typically receive state and federal funding. American colleges and universities, like America itself, have a serious race problem. Donna Shalala, when president of the University of Wisconsin, offered a sage perspective when she said, "I would plead guilty to both racism and sexism. The University is institutionally racist. American society is racist and sexist. Covert racism is just as bad today as overt racism was thirty years ago." Shalala was correct even if one wants to call it politically correct. She was, more importantly, historically factual. D'Souza cites her in his book and says that Shalala's opinion was absurd and radical and labels her a weak-kneed liberal college administrator bowing to the leftist assault. Dr. Shalala should be applauded. Unlike D'Souza she understands that curriculum should be changed where necessary to foster such values as tolerance and diversity. Jane Elliott, a distinguished public school teacher of over thirty years makes the point: "Racism, bigotry, and prejudice are learned activities that the educational institutions perpetuate." Annette Kolodny, Dean of Humanities at the University of Arizona at Tucson, says: "I see my scholarship as an extension of my political activism." That activism included a stint as an organizer with the

United Farm Workers when headed by Caesar Chavez. Dean Kolodny goes on to say that the U.S.'s claim as an egalitarian nation is largely a myth. Moreover, she asserts, the U.S. has taken this "incredibly fertile continent and utterly destroyed it with a ravaging hatred."

D'Souza was a student editor at the *Dartmouth Review* when it launched its relentless and unethical assault against an African-American faculty member in the music department. He helped to establish the negative atmosphere of hate on that campus that continued to exist after he graduated. Nevertheless, he holds that African Americans who cry victimization are only imagining it. He bemoans what he calls a "revolution of minority victims taking place on campus." In his book, he focuses on six episodes at different universities, Berkeley, Stanford, Howard, Michigan, Duke, and Harvard, that are, in his words, "the vanguard of the revolution of minority victims." Note the term victim here. He obviously agrees with Professor Shelby Steele, a conservative African American. D'Souza asks why are we expelling Homer, Aristotle, and Shakespeare and "other white males from their required reading list?" There is, however, absolutely no proof that this has occurred. What transpired has been a push for reform of the Eurocentric curriculum to include important scholarship in the African-American field, Women's Studies, Hispanic Studies, and Asian Studies. Only anti-intellectuals and ideologues like D'Souza fear learning something new and broadening their horizons and expanding the reading list.

He further criticizes what he terms the new separatism, and asks: "Should universities promote integration or separatism? Why do minority students attack exclusivity, yet seem to prefer segregated institutions for themselves?" He is the one suggesting this idea of a new separatism rather than recognizing that the larger society keeps telling black folk, by word and deed, that they are unwanted. Blacks on the predominantly white campuses are usually made to feel like intruders. Let them attempt to create their own survival enclave, however, and they are accused of being black separatists. It is the twisted mindset of a society that rejects you but wants you to want in. D'Souza confuses African-American cohesion with black separatism due to his total unfamiliarity with the black experience in this country. He had only been in the Untied States a few years before considering himself qualified to write a book on the subject. The timing of his arrival was also unfortunate, as it was right at the beginning of the Reagan-Bush era and the conservative explosion of anti-black, anti-affirmative action attitudes of the 1980s. This was one of the most intellectually and socially regressive decades in the modern history of American higher education and civil rights. Thus, D'Souza is comfortable crying for meritocracy but not for a level playing field. The true meritocracy he champions is based, in his mind, solely on test scores not on equal opportunities from birth. To have a true meritocracy you must first have a society free of racism. Only a liberal society can provide a truly liberal arts education. Liberal means believing in allowing all to play without the deck stacked against them. From this nation's beginning there has never been a level playing field for people of African descent. The history of the experience of African people in America illustrates that the race is run unfairly with the starting gun being fired earliest for the privileged white majority. Meritocracy can only exist in substance and fact when you have a society where opportunities are equal at the beginning of the race. You certainly do not have a meritocracy in a society that, since its founding, kept black folk not only out of the ongoing race but completely under foot. The issue is not merely what is being taught on campus. The more profound question is whether we have a society that is just and fair in its treatment of all of its citizens. If you are black in America no one can tell you that you are not victimized because of your color.

Even for African American students on the campuses of Berkeley, Michigan, and Duke to sit together at meals draws D'Souza's wrath. Blacks on campus try to survive by forming their own associations. A Michigan black student, Heather Robinson, told the *Chicago Tribune*, "I know that I am not wanted here." Another student, Jason Dotson said, "You can feel the intensity in the classroom. You can see it in the teacher's eyes. You see it in the students' faces. You are always under scrutiny. People who basically hold your future in their hands don't want you here." These African-American students should not be labeled separatists because they seek out kindred spirits for the psychological and cultural support that may help them to survive in an unfamiliar and often hostile environment. In the past there were not enough blacks at these schools to be more than a curiosity to observing whites. Blacks were not allowed to stay in the dormitories or eat in the cafeterias, sitting together or individually. Thus the likelihood of them sitting in a "group" until most recently was zero to none. It was not until the late 1960s that blacks began to appear on these campuses in large enough numbers to be seriously counted or to approach a critical mass. There were not enough blacks on campus to count at the University of Illinois in the 1960s when I was a student. My first roommate was white and I was the only black in the entire dormitory. I was a lone black student. Much of the time in the cafeteria I sat alone or, should I say, white students did not desegregate themselves and come and sit with me. Does one African American sitting by him or herself constitute black separatism or must it be two or three or more of them sitting together? This has a striking resemblance to the white fear experienced during slavery whenever blacks gathered together. In some southern states it was against the law for blacks to gather. It is a sad commentary on the present state of race relations in this country that this sort of Negrophobia persists.[15]

D'Souza's main problem is that he thinks the history of race relations in the United States began in 1980. It did not. The legacy is much longer than that and much older than D'Souza. It is not reverse racism to challenge a Eurocentric curriculum that denies your existence. Indeed, in the university setting we have an intellectual obligation to do just that. Canons are exclusive. They keep some people in and keep other people out. Curriculums should reflect a diversity of ethnic cultures and values. Black student activist Amanda Kemp of Stanford University was right when she tersely commented that the implicit message of the traditional Western civilization course is: "Nigger go home." Again, why not expand the Western civilization courses and include more books and treatment of other peoples? Unfortunately, when you push for such inclusion the traditionalist response is that there is not enough time to devote attention to every group. Why not? It is true that you can never include all things. There is always selectivity in developing a reading list. Picking and choosing means the excluding of some and including of others. The practice is discriminatory. The selection depends upon who has the authority. Who has the power of selection?

One wonders if D'Souza and people of his political persuasion and racial-educational outlook truly believe that education is neutral? Do they believe that Western culture courses are neutral? Is Shakespeare's *Othello* neutral? Is Herman Melville's *Moby Dick* neutral? Are Faulkner's novels on southern life neutral? There is no such thing as a neutral book or a neutral education. Do you think Plato and Aristotle or Virgil are without politics? Did Hippocrates have bias? Was Lee Atwater's appointment to the Board of Trustees of Howard University a neutral act? This is the same Atwater who masterminded the race-baiting Willie Horton ad campaign for George Bush's 1988 presidential bid. D'Souza is outraged that there were a number of noted faculty members who were delighted to see the student activism at Howard that opposed Atwater's appointment to the board. A preeminent black university with Atwater on the board was more than a sad irony. His appointment made a clear statement as to where Howard was heading. D'Souza condemned the students' three-day protest and quipped, "Some were actually seen studying, while the cameras flashed." What D'Souza resented was that young blacks could think for themselves and that in their enlightenment choose a more African-centered curriculum, a curriculum more about them and one with a community service component. They rejected the traditional curriculum of white institutions, including Howard University. Moreover, the students were critics of America's racism. Howard University was never a leader in African-American Studies. The school had to be dragged, kicking and screaming, to do courses on the black experience. Students protested there in the 1920s and again in the 1960s, just as they were doing in the 1980s, against the internal and external political conservatism of Howard University. Noticeably, D'Souza is silent on the issue of racism in the 1980s and in the Reagan and Bush administrations. He eagerly embraced those administrations and was a young brigade member of the reinvigorated right wing marching to the drum of anti everything and anybody who suggested compassion for one's fellow human beings, especially if their skin was black and their politics progressive. The reasonable conclusion is that D'-Souza is fearful of blacks having a voice on campus or in anything else, unless it conforms to his political agenda. The dominant voices on university and college campuses, white or black, are typically in tune with the establishment, i.e., not venturing far in most cases from the traditional Western Eurocentric traditions. Universities are not bastions of liberalism, as D'Souza portrays them, particularly when you examine them from a race perspective. They typically mimic the larger society with all of its hopes, fears, traditions, promises, and shortcomings.[16]

The preposterous thrust of D'Souza's line of reasoning reaches its unimaginable extreme with the publication of his next book, *The End of Racism*. The book is so full of inaccuracies, misrepresentations, distortions, and flawed historical analyses that it and its author deserve complete condemnation and repudiation. Most reviews of the book were utterly negative. Historian George M. Fredrickson blasted D'Souza's misrepresentations of historical fact in his review of the book. Law professor Derrick Bell acidly condemned D'Souza for his right-wing agenda, falsification of history or sheer ignorance, and questioned how the book could have ever been published. Even a more restrained critic concluded that D'Souza idealized the dominant white culture and associated black culture with a "virtual demonization." "The scope of the book's ambition," historian Eric Foner writes, "is matched only by the extent of its failure. Its account of history is misleading, its discussion of world cultures sophomoric, its analysis of current race relations simplistic. Beneath a facade of reasonableness," he continues, "*The End of Racism* is a mean-spirited polemic" that contains "truly outrageous assertions, such as that blacks owe American society a debt of gratitude for slavery" which brought them into contact with white culture. What is perhaps even more regrettable is that the book sold nearly five hundred thousand copies in hardback, thus having a wide readership of the author's stilted and misinformed utterances about the history of American race relations. D'Souza's absurd thesis must be rejected. Any claim to the marginalization of racism is wrong, intellectually dishonest, and historically indefensible. Professor Foner sees something quite pernicious at work and questions why it is that conservatives will not stop playing the race card. "Is this because the ideas of states' rights and local autonomy are so closely tied in our history to the defense of slavery and segregation," Foner asks, "or because the federal government despised by free marketeers has been so powerful an instrument for challenging racial inequality? Perhaps it is simply the lure of the cheap vote. Conservatives may in the future, as in the past, ride to power by stigmatizing black America as degraded, immoral, and 'civilizationally' inferior. But at what cost to American society?" Sean Wilentz in his review of the book finds it unfathomable to argue that racism is declining in America especially in light of the continuous assaults against African Americans from every quarter including the recycling of the old claims of black inferiority indicative of Charles Murray and Richard Hernstein's *The Bell Curve*. The problem of racism is as grave as ever. As Wilentz says, "numerous reliable studies show that even while whites voice egalitarian sentiments about integrated schools and workplaces, they continue to discriminate against blacks in hiring and (especially) housing, and still show a propensity to regard blacks as lazier, less intelligent, and more violent that any other ethnic group."[17]

AFROCENTRISM AND THE CHALLENGE TO EUROCENTRISM

Afrocentrism is a new term for an old concept. Molefe Asante, in his book, *Afrocentricity*, and in other publications, says that the main aim of Afrocentrism is to develop "consciousness" and identification with Africa. It is a call for "action," a demand to give proper respect and attention to the African background. There is nothing new about this idea. Martin Delany, Sylvester Williams, Henry McNeal Turner, Marcus Garvey, and other Pan-Africanists advocated much the same thing. Historian John Henrik Clarke, in an interview just prior to his death, described Afrocentrism as an old idea.[18]

At the very least the new Afrocentrists are demanding that the African legacy and experiences of people of African descent be recognized and taught, that the promise of inclusion be honored and, finally, fully implemented. A few years ago, the New York City Task Force on Curriculum Reform and the American Federation of Teachers survey of secondary school history textbooks, came to much the same conclusion as surveys conducted in 1949 and 1963: that there is a need for more inclusion of racial and ethnic minorities and that this has not been achieved. Cities and states throughout the country, such as Hartford, Dayton, Chicago, and the State of Florida, have gone through similar curricular challenges in recent years. Inclusion, of course, is not enough. There must be analysis, diagnosis, an explanation of the impact and relationship of the various group issues and events. There are a few textbooks in use today that are trying to offer more than a mere touch-up. Most, however, are poor in what efforts they make, if any, to integrate into the larger story a meaningful inclusion and infusion of the ideas, values, and experiences of African Americans, women, Hispanics, Asians, Native Americans, and others.

The minimum goal is inclusion. The ultimate goal is social change. Unfortunately, many scholars working in Black Studies often find themselves at odds with the majority society in academe. The white-scholar majority, however, faces no such dilemma working in what is essentially White Studies, mainly because those studies are the focus of most classrooms in America. Black Studies were born because of the failure to integrate history textbooks and to reform curriculums despite long-standing demands. In Hartford, Connecticut, where the school system is predominantly black and Hispanic, a major effort began in 1991 to reform the social studies curriculum. I remember it well having served on that task force. It should have been unnecessary to explain the need to revamp a school curriculum to make it inclusive of those it was supposed to be educating, but it was and debated virtually every day until the blind were able to see. The theme of "immigration" was used in Hartford to tell the story of the various groups that had come and contributed to America and whose ancestors made the city and the state. The theme of immigration warrants considerable explanation, however, when African Americans are considered because the original blacks in this country did not *come* voluntarily. We were *brought* to America as slaves. Starting with the concept and definition and usage of words, there is a precision that historical accuracy, not political correctness, demands. From the very beginning, the experience of black folk has been profoundly different from that of any other group in this country.

Efforts at school reform demanding proper attention to the history of African Americans, and other traditionally marginalized groups, continuously meet with objection and hostility today. The purveyors of exclusionism rationalize their position with such arguments as "maintaining standards," "cultural literacy," "the closing of the American mind," "the disuniting of America," "an illiberal education," and "the false consciousness of race." That hostility is firmly ingrained within the establishment and its intellectual and political functionaries who defend the status quo. The assault in the 1970s against Third College at the University of California at San Diego is an example of this hostility. The program there was viciously assailed by two journalists, Richard Evans and Robert Novack, who came out continuously against Third College. They wrote in their nationally syndicated column, *Inside Report*: "On the peaceful, sun-washed, San Diego campus of the University of California, is evidence that there were worst though less obvious threats to higher education than a rock through the window of a building in flames. The threat there, hidden behind the characteristic languid surface of today's American campus, is the fledgling Third College—a new semi-autonomous institution designed to give Negroes, and Mexican American students a special break." Evans and Novack were then, as they are now, reflective of a right-wing, and virtually neo-fascist, anti-intellectualism that holds that anything painted with the brush of inclusiveness, gender, race consciousness, or openness is somehow giving someone a special advantage. They oppose a public higher educational system that serves, or attempts to serve, the entire community. they oppose having a history reflective of the multifaceted population that made it.

History is not the province of any one group. It is a dish best served up consisting of many ingredients. It should nourish the intellect, be faithful to the truth, be inclusive, and stimulate the student to engage in serious individual, local, national, and world retrospection. We, African Americans, have to fight for that inclusion and consciousness of self and environment. Who are we as a people? Are we Negroes? Are we coloreds? Are we blacks? Are we Afro-Americans? Are we African Americans? The question of definition is very important because it is a question of consciousness and understanding of the forces around you and how they shape you and how you impact on them. To understand is to define your own place, your own existence, your own significance, on your own terms. For

blacks, definition is no small matter. An African American is a precise term that defines what continent you are from, where you originated, and where you are today. That is precision. Negrophobes of
today, like those of the past, are uncomfortable with that level of
self-assertion on the part of people of African descent in America.
They are fearful of the precision, the defining, and indeed the consciousness that this reflects. It is impossible to oppress people who
have consciousness, who know what has and is happening to them.
Paulo Freire, the Brazilian educator, made the point that the oppressed must first of all understand that they are oppressed. You
have a hard time convincing someone they are oppressed who
makes a livable wage, has a place to live, food, owns an automobile,
or who has a welfare check coming every month. You might be hard
pressed to break that person out of the culture of that tolerated existence. The only way you can do it is by raising that individual's consciousness to help them understand what their condition is; why it
is, and the actions necessary for them to better their lives. The first
step is to understand who you are and your origins. One of the oldest games is that of definition. Think about Africa and the name
changes that occurred. Zimbabwe for the longest was Rhodesia,
named after Cecil Rhodes, its conqueror and exploiter, an individual responsible for the deaths of hundreds of thousands of southern
Africans. When we watch the nightly news or read a newspaper we
are bombarded with labels such as "guerrillas" and "freedom fighters." Those are loaded, pejorative terms meant to lead to a certain
conclusion. You are more apt to take sides with a freedom fighter
than with a guerrilla. There is a need for awareness. If, for example,
we accept the term "black Africa" then one must presuppose that
there is a "white Africa." Blacks cannot have their due even when it
comes to their own homeland. For the longest, Africa was called the
"dark continent" with all the negatives that implied. The definition
game is played with the term "World History." In the teaching of
that history, however, coverage of Africa was routinely omitted,
until most recently. Africa today is often marginalized or treated
only within the context of European imperialism rather than as a vibrant continent with its own history, its own background and culture that existed long before the coming of Europeans.

What we are still struggling for is inclusion and the taking of
one's rightful place among the contributors to the world's history.
We are not paranoid when we say that history writing and teaching
in America is largely Eurocentric; it has been and continues to be,
although some inroads are being made. Since those in power are the
vast and dominant majority of the writers of history, you cannot

achieve an inclusive history, a history that conveys the authentic voice and insider's legacy and experience of being black in America. One cannot count on noblesse oblige for justice to the have-nots. We have a long way to go in the long and ongoing struggle for inclusion. We must not settle for the popular touch-up approach to history. Vine Deloria, a Native American and director of Native American Studies at the University of Arizona, catches the essence of the touch-up type or what he terms the "cameo theory" of American historical writing of the modern era when he says, "The new history takes a basic manifest destiny, white interpretation of history and lovingly plugs a few feathers, woolly heads, and sombreros into the famous events of American history." There has not been that inclusion, analysis and forthrightness. There has been, at best, a token gesture of giving a name or two here and there. Nearly all the American history textbooks will, for example, mention Crispus Attucks. He was the first person to die in the cause of the American Revolution and an ideal touch-up addition because he was of African descent and also part Native American. The textbook writers get two for one. It is very much like today's hiring policies, where affirmative action is invoked. The employer, not believing in the goals of diversity, but rather meeting the letter of the law rather than the spirit of it, would enjoy most hiring an African-American hermaphrodite who is part Native American with a Spanish surname and hopefully confined to a wheel chair. That constitutes the ultimate affirmative action hire for the non-believers.[19]

African Americans must claim their African past and demand their place at the international table of history and begin to think as Malcolm X said as a "majority people." Africa is four times the size of the continental United States, from the Mediterranean to the Cape of Good Hope, a distance of five thousand miles. It is four thousand seven hundred miles from Cape Verde and Senegal to the Horn of East Africa. Africa is home to a population that we approximate at between five hundred to seven hundred million people. On size and numbers alone the mother continent warrants inclusion. Many times more important than size and numbers is Africa's centrality to world civilization and history. The mindset that denies Africa's earliest history, since much of it was unwritten history, must be challenged. The old ideas expressed in the *Encyclopedia Britannica*, and other purveyors of misinformation on Africa, are owed rejection along with Leopold Von Roche's proclamation that history, to be meaningful, has to be written. African history, a substantial part of that history, has been retained through oral tradition. The notion that the oral tradition is imprecise is wrong. The African

Griot is one of the most trusted and respected positions within African society. Select Africans began training in their youth to become the Griot for the village or the nation. They were taught their people's history on a daily basis, year after year. Their commitment was to learn and recount that history accurately. We should keep in mind that in West African society, for example, the failure of the Griot to recall the history accurately was punishable by death. That was a powerful incentive that ensured a very accurate recounting of history throughout the ages. We continue to struggle against the idea held by many that Africa has no history, at least none worthy of recording and teaching to whites as well as blacks. That ignorance pervades the American fabric as exemplified during the presidential administration of Ronald Reagan. He advocated "constructive engagement" with the racist white apartheid regime of South Africa. President Reagan shared the belief of his communications director, Pat Buchanan, that the African continent was better off under white rule since Africans did not even know of the wheel until the coming of Europeans. "No matter the cruelties committed by the European invaders," Buchanan proclaimed and President Reagan echoed, "the West's arrival was the best thing that ever happened to Africa. Europeans brought Africa out of the Stone Age and into the 20th Century."[20]

An inclusive history will educate the uninformed as to where the human race originated. The Neolithic revolution occurred in Africa long before it did in other parts of the world. The last stage of the stone age and the rise of the Oldowan culture, the oldest stone age civilization, has been dated earliest in Africa. Throughout history those who have dared to give credence to African primacy have found themselves targets of the most vile kinds of criticism that far exceeded any canons of professed professionalism. Evolutionary theorists, before the publication of Charles Darwin's *The Origin of Species* in 1859, looked to Asia and other parts of the world for the creation and evolution of humankind. Darwin's work had such profound impact because, and we tend to forget this, he also advocated that the earliest of humankind emerged first in Africa. In the *Descent of Man*, which Darwin wrote in 1871, he explained his thesis of African primacy. This was a bold and revolutionary idea. Here was a leading European intellectual who had conducted the most scientific research of the age on the question of evolution, and he concluded that in all likelihood Africa was the original home of the human species.

Many others were to follow Darwin's lead and point to Africa and its singular importance. Eurocentrism has led us so far away from the truth for so long that the world refuses to admit its own origins, to properly identify where humankind first emerged. Euro-centrism by its very nature has not only been racist and anti-intellectual but anti truth and anti nature. Fossil finds and the work of paleontologists and archaeologists reveal an overwhelming amount of evidence reinforcing the centrality and primacy of Africa. Beginning in 1924 with the finds in South Africa, Australopithecus, to the tremendous work of Louis and Mary Leakey in East Africa, the primacy of Africa has been identified and proven repeatedly. Race should know no color. It did not to the Leakeys in their challenge of the systematic denial of Africa's place. These two European paleontologists and archeologists made the most important finds the world has known. Working day in and day out, year after year, in the Olduvai Gorge in Tanzania, East Africa, eighty miles south of Kenya and one hundred and twenty miles east of the tip of Lake Victoria, the Leakeys went nearly thirty years before making their most major finds. Inspired by the pursuit of truth, they sought out what their intellects and hearts told them was there. Louis Leakey, who was raised in Kenya, spoke Swahili and Kikuyu before he did English, knew that the ancient arrowheads he found during his childhood were indicators of the unexplored historical richness of Africa. He fought beyond his English education and limitations and prejudices of his teachers. It was that spirit and thirst for knowledge that kept him going for his entire lifetime of work and discovery. A decade after the finds on Russinga Island in the late 1940s came the big discovery in the Olduvai Gorge, July 1959, when the Leakeys unearthed the first early human fossil and dubbed it Zinzanthropus Boise or Zin for short, which has been dated to have lived 1.75 million years ago. The authentication process was tainted by Eurocentrism. After making a find experts are called in to examine the evidence and to help draw conclusions. For Leakey it was a tortuous process. He was required to win over his European colleagues, leading figures of paleontology, archeology, and anthropology, who embraced the old thesis of Africa's insignificance that Leakey challenged. Locked into the Eurocentric world view, the "experts" initially refused to authenticate the prehistoric age of Zin, despite Leakey's supporting evidence and eloquent arguments. Later, the carbon dating process proved them wrong and Louis Leakey correct, making Zin, at that time, the recognized oldest relative of homo sapiens. Mary and Louis Leakey made a host of other discoveries that added support to their contention that Africa was the birthplace of humankind and the original cradle of civilization.

Basil Davidson, the great English scholar of African history, has written time and again, based on the work of the Leakeys and his own extensive research, that it is unquestionable that the basic human stock that gave rise to us all occurred first in the mother continent of Africa. I had the privilege to meet Basil Davidson for the first time at the African Studies Association conference in Denver, Colorado in 1987 and to actually shake the hand of this man who has authored so many wonderful books contributing to the recapture of Africa's proper place in history and challenging the Eurocentric world view. After I shook his hand, I did not wash mine for a week in order to savor that meeting for as long as possible.

Other Europeans have made important contributions. Louis and Mary Leakey's tradition of discovery continued with the work of their son, Richard Leakey, and his discovery of Kenya Boy. Donald Johanson's discovery of "Lucy" in Ethiopia in 1974 was a monumental find. The work of Berkeley scientists Allan Wilson and Vincent Sarich, in their application of DNA modeling to human evolution, provided further compelling confirmation of Africa's primacy. The midocandria of the cell's cytoplasm yielded a genetic marker allowing the scientists to trace the basic human gene pool to Lucy and origins in East Africa. Lucy, having existed some 3.5 million years ago, was in all probability the mother of the human race. James Wainscott of Oxford University and members of his scientific team conclude: "In other words, the regional small migration of people out of Africa had subsequently given rise to all the world's present day population." The superb Nova program, "Children of Eve," is a documentary devoted to Lucy that punctuates quite vividly the importance of the new research.[21] Recent finds suggest that Central Africa may also have been one of the earliest cradles of the human species.

Within the raging debate over African primacy and struggle for inclusion there is no greater prize or area of controversy than the question of Egypt, the premier ancient civilization. To see Egypt as a part of the African continent, as it always has been, constitutes another devastating blow to Eurocentrics. All world maps yield geographical evidence that Egypt is a part of Africa, connected by land, rivers and people. Discreditors and disclaimers say no. They argue that Egypt is part of the Mediterranean, the Middle East, not Africa, and deny that Africa made any contribution to Egyptian or to world civilization. Eurocentrics are, at the core, racists who not only believe but promote the superiority of the white race over the black under the subterfuge of the singular importance of Western civilization. They swear by Greek civilization, but conveniently turn a blind eye to what the ancient Greeks appropriated from Egypt. Ironically, there was no question to the ancient Greeks that Egypt was a part of Africa. From Herodotus to Socrates this was a matter without debate. Moreover, in ancient times, Ethiopia encompassed three-fourths of upper Egypt. No one debated that Ethiopians were an African people with dark skin. The word Ethiopian was synonymous with "land of the blacks." The magnanimity of African civilization, including Egypt, was not a point of contention in the ancient world. Noticeably, Renaissance artists routinely portrayed Africans as equals to whites in their paintings. It was with the coming of the slave trade that Westerners and their scholars began their sustained assault on the contribution of Africa to civilization. The virulent racism of the eighteenth and nineteenth centuries went hand in glove with the discrediting and dehumanizing of Africans. Egypt in the racism of the West was defined out of Africa. As Basil Davidson has said, "Racism is a rather recent sickness." Unfortunately, the present-day leading schools of classical studies, which includes Egyptology, were founded on the racism and misinformation of the earlier era. To move those scholars away from the blinds of Eurocentrism entails a difficult reclamation process and de-racialization. It means that they must learn to unlearn what they have been taught and have taught others and published. Hence, the struggle is a turf war that will not be easily won. Take, for example, the firestorm around Martin Bernal's book, *Black Athena*. His work supports the contention that Egypt is a part of Africa and largely a product of rulers who were African. There is nothing new about Bernal's thesis. African-American historians are well familiar with the work of Du Bois, Woodson, John Jackson, George James, Cheikh Anta Diop, Chancellor Williams, Yusef Ben Jochannan, Leo Hansberry, Joseph Harris, John Henrik Clarke, and R.A. Jairazbhoy. These historians have long recognized and documented the Egyptian connection to Africa as did some European scholars in the past. The efforts of the West to make it seem that everything of worth revolves in its image has cost the world greatly in historical truth and helped fortify racism.

To look back at ancient Egypt and its great dynasties beginning from 5500 BC and ending with dynasty number XXX from 378 to 342 BC is to travel through a history in which black folk, African people were central. There are many challenges in the quest to correct Egyptian history. Look at, for example, how Westerners have taken even the question of dates and stilted it in such a way that it no longer provides clarity. Why do we count backward in looking at Egyptian history from 5500 to 5300 BC as we count to the present? Should not the dates move forward? That tells us something about the efforts of the West to rewrite historical truth in its own image.

The whole world was not Christian. Christianity was a minority religion in ancient times. Yet the dates imposed upon the rest of the
world commence with BC, Before Christ, and continue with AD,
After Death of Christ. That is a reordering of the historical record
and chronology. The West does not become a major player in civilization until well "After Death of Christ." The history of the world
and civilization, however, commenced thousands of years before the
birth of Christ. If we were using the present-day calendar based on
the history of ancient Egypt we would now be at over 7,000 years.
In China, where there are still remnants of the ancient Chinese calendar, we are at more than 4,000 years.

Whichever calendar you go by, Eurocentric history omits black
folk as contributors to ancient civilization. The most ancient of the
Step Pyramids of Gyza were the designs and creations of black people, of African people. Why are we not generally taught in our
schools of the accomplishments of Imhotep? The great Egyptian genius was later deified for his monumental contributions to medicine
as physician to the pharaoh and for his masterful contributions to
architecture. Imhotep practiced advanced medical science centuries
before the birth of Hippocrates, whom the Greeks proclaimed the
"father of medicine." Imhotep performed brain surgery and advanced the study of medicine, architecture, and astronomy while
Europe was floundering in the dark ages. We know from ancient
historical records, and a sculptural likeness, that Imhotep was a
squat, bald-headed, dark complexioned man, with pronounced
African features. One has only to study the erection of the Great
Pyramids to know that the ancient Egyptians also understood the
highest levels of mathematics and the basis of the so-called
Pythagorean Theory long before the Greek's Pythagoris learned it
from them. The Eurocentric, of course, does not give credit to
Africa for these contributions.

There is no denying, no matter what Arthur Schlesinger and others may say, that the Greeks borrowed heavily from Egyptian philosophy and Mystery System. This holds true for Socrates, Aristotle,
Homer, Plato and Herodotus. We do not have to agree with everything that George James wrote in *Stolen Legacy*, but there is a preponderance of evidence available that makes the point. Why not just
simply recognize the African contribution and move on? No, the
preferred image of Africa for the Eurocentric is in the *Tarzan* novels,
comic books, and movies with the white man depicted as supreme
ruler of everything, including being crowned "King of the Jungle."
In the movie industry and in television that image did more than its
share in defiling the African contribution and painting an erroneous

picture of the African continent. When Egypt was portrayed in motion pictures it was with white pharaohs, often with British accents. If blacks were included at all, it was as slaves. The classic horror film *The Mummy*, staring Boris Karloff, is a perverse rendering of the African contribution. Note that the monstrous mummy, who desecrates Egyptian law, is named Imhotep. Was that by accident to invoke such an important name in Egyptian history and use it in this sad manner?

The Golden Era of Egypt and Amenhotep III and Akhenaten, and Tutankhamen and Rameses I, II and III are never portrayed in European accounts as they were—African people with the characteristic features associated with the race. Whether they were good or bad, they were great and mighty and thus cannot be allowed to be called African. The same holds true for how the myth makers rewrote the story of Moses who was, in fact, an Egyptian priest and had studied the Mystery System. The Ten Commandments that he later cited as the words of God were based upon Egyptian teachings and *Book of the Dead*. Within the one hundred rules of life the Egyptians professed, you find the ten that Moses later avowed came to him through divine revelation and intervention. The last African pharaoh to reign in Egypt, Ahmose II, is portrayed by the Eurocentrists as being "Libyan" or "Middle Eastern" rather than African. The fight over Queen Nefertari and the Goddess Isis continues. It is unfathomable in the racist mind that women of importance and beauty could be African or even depicted as such. After Egypt fell to the armies of King Cambyses of Persia, a long line of puppet dynasties ruled. Finally, Egypt fell to Rome in 30 BC, signaling the beginning of the whitening and distancing of its historical connection to the rest of the African continent.

How can one expect to get a truthful perspective on Egypt when those who have written most about its history have been Eurocentrists. Note, for example, that in the United States the leading institute for the study of Egypt is the Institute of Oriental Studies at the University of Chicago. The Institute, founded in 1896, was born from the interests of the university's first president, William Rainey Harper, who was a professor of Semitic languages. James Henry Breasted, the first American to receive a doctorate in Egyptology, was appointed by Harper to fill the first teaching position in Egyptian studies in the United States. To Breasted's credit he maintained that Egypt was a significant contributor to the advent of Western civilization. To his discredit he defined Egypt, as did many of the Egyptologists before him and since, as a part of the "Near East," and was blind to its African roots. The Institute's name proclaims its principle and promotion of Asia's primacy and importance to the origins of Egypt and civilization. The Institute seems oblivious that many Asians find the term "Oriental" offensive. One might think, given the focus on Egypt, that the name of the Institute might be changed to the Institute of Egyptian Studies or how about the Institute of African Studies? Frankly, let them leave the name as is; it makes identifying the Institute's perspective on the issues quite easy. Nothing much has changed at the Institute of Oriental Studies since the days I first visited it as a youngster, except some expansion of its museum component and administrative offices. You see today at the Institute, as in its earlier years, alleged "recreations" and "restoration" of Egyptian mummies in the most Caucasoid likeness imaginable, which is physiologically indefensible and an abomination of history.

The debate on Egypt intensifies further when the Ethiopian factor is added. An increasing number of scholars have been arguing that Ethiopia may have possessed a high civilization, predating that of Egypt. This has a certain plausibility, given the pyramid remnants and other archeological evidence presently being excavated in Ethiopia. Ancient Ethiopia covered three-fourths of present-day Egypt. Below the First Cataract were the thriving cities of Napata and Meroe. Let us recall too that Donald Johanson discovered "Lucy" in Ethiopia. In Egypt itself the most important indicator of the possible Ethiopian origins of Egyptian high civilization is the Edfu Text, the source document of the early history of the Nile Valley. The famous inscription found in the temple of Horus at Edfu is revealing as to the origins of Egyptian civilization. It paints a vivid picture that civilization came from the south where Ethiopia lies. Frantz Boas pointed to Ethiopia as a likely source of the early advancements made in iron smelting, architecture, domestication of animals, and structured and highly civilized society. Egyptian tombs offer further support. The pharaohs were buried pointed toward the south, the acknowledged source of civilization and life. Flowing from south to north, from Ethiopia to Egypt, the Nile River was credited by ancient Egyptians as a vital source of life, connectedness, and culture. The ancient Egyptians defined their own lands as either upper or lower Egypt; lower Egypt being in the north; and upper Egypt, containing the first of the highest civilizations in Egypt and the ancient city of Thebes, in the south. If Ethiopia was the first high civilization, this makes life considerably more difficult for Eurocentrics because the blackness of its inhabitants is indisputable. There can be no debate about the skin color of Ethiopians. They were not a "mixed race" as many of the defilers of Egyptian history will grudgingly concede as possibly the case for ancient Egyptians. Eurocentrists will next need to discredit the argument that Ethiopia also produced a high civilization that predates that of the West. At the least they will have to un-blacken the Ethiopians, which might be extremely difficult in light of contemporary consciousness.[22]

The new consciousness should also leave little doubt that ancient Africans traveled to America before Christopher Columbus. Louis and Mary Leakey's research and that of scholars from Leo Wiener to Ivan Van Sertima help form a body of evidence of the African pre-Columbian presence in the Americas. Leo Wiener's early multi-volume studies showcase brilliant applications of his linguistic and historical skills. A trained philologist, Wiener traced the roots of words in the New World to their African origins. He used those and other cultural clues found in Mexico, Central America, and South America, to prove that Africans traveled to the Americas and established their own colonies and settlements there long before the arrival of Columbus. Africans, like other human beings, were curious about what existed on the other side of the mountain, beyond the valley, over the next horizon. They too explored as human creatures and members of an ever-evolving high civilization. Moreover, the celebrants of Columbus, and his so-called discovery of the New World, still largely look upon that event from the point of view of the conqueror rather than that of the conquered who suffered the devastation that he spread through physical violence and germs that decimated entire native populations. Eurocentric history makes it possible for the close-minded to accept a one-dimensional portrait of exploration. From the standpoint of the natives of the Americas, and of Africans later brought as slaves to work the fields and mines of the New World, it was far more negative than positive.[23]

II

THE DESTRUCTION
OF A PEOPLE

THE BEGINNING OF THE
AFRICAN-AMERICAN JOURNEY FROM
RESPECTABILITY TO DEGRADATION

The destruction of black civilization and its people and the flourishing of racism were synonymous with the European conquest of Africa. All people need to be familiar with and to understand their origins. This was especially true for the victims of systematic exploitation and degradation premised on another group's belief in themselves as superior beings. The forebears of today's African Americans were people of great worth and high civilization long before the coming of outsiders who took possession of their bodies, their labor, their lands, and their history.

Ninety percent of all African Americans have their ancestral roots in the kingdoms of West Africa. Ghana was one of the oldest of these kingdoms, dating back to 300 BC. Its capital, Kumbi Saleh, was a center of economic activity and cultural greatness. Ghanaians were also accomplished in weaving, ceramics, and metalwork. The kingdom was a vital hub in the trans-Saharan trade, advantageously located. Those about to cross the Sahara desert from the west took on supplies in Ghana. The kingdom enjoyed a flourishing trade in fruits, sugar, textiles, rubber, ivory, gold, and in the most precious commodity of all, salt. Salt was an essential preservative for meats, and essential to the human body's retention of precious water during the long and sweltering Saharan crossing. Because of its continued growth and prosperity, Ghana became known as the Gold Coast by the eleventh century. The kingdom, however, fell from grace in 1076 under the holy war crusade of the marauding Moslem Almorivids.

In the wake of Ghana's decline, its southern neighbor, Mali, began its ascent to preeminence under the leadership of Mari Data. Data, who was crippled, did not allow his physical impairment to stop him from becoming one of the world's most powerful monarchs. He was an organizer, a builder, and a military strategist second to none. Under his leadership, Mali grew and flourished. After him came one of the greatest West African leaders of recorded history, Mansa Konga Musa, whose reign began in 1312. Mansa Musa became Mali's most heralded potentate, a figure of such importance that many of the maps of Africa would paint practically the entire west coast of the continent in his image. He led in the development of the great cities of Timbuktu and Gao, and added extensive territory to the empire. Mansa Musa was a visionary, strategist, and a devout Moslem. He embarked on a pilgrimage to the holy city of Mecca in 1324. That pilgrimage included seventy thousand people in his entourage, many carrying gold staffs. His caravan was loaded with gold and precious jewels. In the African tradition of the powerful monarch, he shared and displayed his wealth, gave lavishly along the hajj, distributing more than twenty thousand pounds of gold to well-wishers. As a consequence, the value of gold was depressed throughout the known world for decades after his trek. Musa recruited Koranic scholars and scientists for the famous mosque at Sankore. The mosque developed into one of the greatest centers of knowledge in the world, the University of Sankore, containing thousands of precious manuscripts in its library. As a result of Mansa Musa's efforts, Timbuktu and the University of Sankore became known and respected throughout Africa, the Mediterranean, the Middle East, and parts of Europe. Through trade and the appropriating of ambassadors and representatives he further connected Mali to the rest of the African continent and the world.

The point being that the forebears of today's African Americans were civilized human beings from structured and functioning societies. Africans had governments. They had ways to deliver services to members of society. They had a system of governors, *ferbas*, who reported directly to the sovereign or king. There were *mokhrifs* and *noi* who functioned as mayors, oversaw provinces, towns and cities. The *kois* functioned as representative or council heads. From the kois to mokhrifts to the ferbas to the emperor, a chain of command or system was in place to give voice to the people of the society. Ibn Battuta and Leo Africanus wrote of the greatness of Mansa Musa and the Mali Kingdom. Mansa Musa died in 1332, but what he had given to Africa was a contribution to world civilization.

His passing did not bring a halt to West African civilization or the emergence of societies. The Songhai Empire emerged after Mali. Songhai began its climb to prominence under the leadership of Sonni Ali in 1465. After him, Askia Mohammed, better known as Askia The Great, ruled from 1494 to 1538. Askia too made a holy pilgrimage to Mecca and lavishly displayed his wealth along the trek. His hajj, however, was a distant second to that of Mansa Musa. Like Mansa Musa, Askia advanced education, recruited scholars, and expanded the society and its cultural institutions. Mali's grand city of Gao became world renown. Officials were elected such as the ferbas, who ruled over large provinces, and the Noi, who oversaw cities and towns and reported to the ferbas. The ferbas, in turn, reported to the sovereign. Songhai had a uniform system of weights and measures. It had inspectors of produce and land. The empire's economy was largely agricultural and diverse. Songhai was known for cotton, rice, wheat, and millet. The people raised cattle and goats, traded in gold and other precious metals, and cultivated the fine arts. Songhai developed a body of written civic law. It had a system of taxation. Funds from these coffers were used to provide public services.

No public service or societal function was more important throughout the history of West Africa and its people than education. The mother was the first teacher of the child, its primary educator until age seven. After that age, the boy would then be under the charge of his father for his learning, while the girl stayed under the charge of the mother for her schooling. Ancient Africans did not consider the father's role superior to the mother's, or vice versa. The African world and cultural view differed from that of the European in many ways. In some West African societies the word "beautiful" was never used to describe a woman because in the Yoruba tradition, for example, every woman was beautiful. Traditions, folkways, mores, and values were the most sacred components of education in ancient Africa. The Griot, as historian and teacher, was entrusted with this important knowledge and passed on the history from generation to generation. That tradition later enabled author Alex Haley to trace his own African roots back to the Gambia. Timbuktu and Jenne continued to grow and develop and to appreciate education and knowledge. Leo Africanus described his adventures in Timbuktu, in addition to the many manuscripts he saw there, and the people he observed engaged in intense study and learning. The intellectual heart of Sankore was a knowledge system among the best in the world. African scholars and travelers from Tunis, Cairo, Morocco, Egypt, and Spain came to the West African centers of Gao and to Timbuktu to visit and study at the famous University of Sankore.

The history of West Africa was old and diverse, and includes civilizations such as the Hausa, Kanem, Benin, Oyo, Dahomey, and Akan. These were all people searching to find themselves and to continue to develop as human beings. The African way of life stressed the value of the family. West Africans also embraced the *poro*, an inducting of the individual into society, recognizing the individual's coming of age and the rights of citizenship and obligations to the community. That coming of age also entailed an examination of learning and understanding of the rules governing the society. Sylvia Boone wrote of the *poro* masterfully in *Radiance From the Waters*. It was not a system of strict obedience and subordination, but one of nurturing and enlightenment and fostering of growth and development based upon shared commitments and responsibilities amongst families and within the larger society of the whole. Denial of Africa's, particularly West Africa's, high culture and civilization were tools of cultural imperialism that Europeans employed to legitimize their conquest, pillaging, and enslavement of these "lesser" people.[1]

The treacherous white waters of racism run deep. The English in their earliest contact with Africans demonstrated a predisposition against people whose skin color was different from theirs. Winthrop Jordan in a brilliant book, *White Over Black*, discusses the roots of racism; the black image in the white mind. When European travelers visited parts of the African continent for the first time they told tall stories about the black folk. They were first and foremost struck by the differences they perceived. Africans looked different, their religion was different, they spoke, ate, dressed, and lived differently from that of the English man, from that of the European. That Europeans described Africans as "black" was indicative of their emphasis on the color difference. I have never seen a "black" or a "white" person. A person colored of either one of those hues likely does not exist. White paper is "white." Have you ever seen a person that color? The English characterized the Africans as a lustful people, libidinous, associating with their dark color everything evil and foul. From negative poems, diary entries, and Greek mythology, to the play upon blackness in William Shakespeare's *Othello*, to the King James version of the Holy Bible, Jordan documents that the most shocking aspect to the English person was the African's color. The difference was mesmerizing to them and negative and they devoted considerable time contemplating how the Africans could have become "black." The European looked time and again to the sun as an explanation for the Africans' color. Some fathomed that since Africans lived closer to the equator, perhaps the warmer climate and intense sun had made them over the centuries a darker people. Actually, scientific evidence supports that hypothesis. People of African descent do possess more melanin which darkens their skin and protects their bodies from the harmful rays of the sun. Light skin complexion was an adaptation to the climate of Europe with less intense sun light and heat. The reduced levels of melanin, or so-called white skin, made it easier for the body to readily absorb heat and vitamin D from the sun. We do not want to go so far as to start talking about "sun people" versus "ice people," as some have suggested, but we do know that over time human beings, like other animals and species, adapt to their environment.[2]

The negative image associated with the color black found historical longevity. In the book, *Black Like Me*, published in 1961, the investigator dyes his skin to experience living for a short period of time as a black person in the Jim Crow South. A white man who has somewhat befriended him then tries to view parts of his private anatomy out of racist curiosity. This sort of "curiosity" has always existed, and one was not sure that it has completely died out. Let us hope that it has. I recall my experience, and that of fellow athletes, years back who shared a similar encounter with a white teammate who expressed his astonishment in the team shower to find that blacks did not have tails as he had been told as a child. Negative images persist regarding the continent of Africa itself. Africa has never been darker than anywhere else. Indeed, it has great sun and warmth; due to being closer to the equator than Europe. Yet this idea of the sinister, foreboding, "dark continent," exists today. Bush Gardens in Florida, until most recently, promoted itself as "Africa U.S.A., the Dark Continent." Today we still have not moved far from the Tarzan notion of the romantic backward savages of Africa who have to be led by others and saved from themselves. Edgar Rice Burroughs's *Tarzan of the Apes* was reflective of the negative image of Africa encompassed in much of literature. White was the right color and Europe the seat of, from the old missionary song, "all things white and beautiful." It would later be claimed that the dreaded "black plague" of the late twentieth century, AIDS, began in Africa and spread from there to the rest of the world. In the long mindset of negatives, misconceptions, and loathing of the African continent and people of the dark-skinned race, Europe found rationalization that helped make it much easier for them to justify their enslavement of African people, who were defined as a deviant and villainous race undeserving of freedom and better off enslaved because it brought them in contact with civilized Europe. I remember a black college professor that I knew back in the sixties who said to me, on more than one occasion, that he thought Europeans had done us a favor by enslaving us and bringing us out of Africa to America. What a sad and ignorant sentiment. One can only hope that other African Americans did not share that professor's views, then and now.[3]

THEY CAME, WE WERE BROUGHT

Profit was the catalyst and racism the pillar for the inhumane wrenching of millions of blacks from their families and African homeland to a life of forced labor and degradation in the New World. One could rape them, murder them, do what one willed with them with impunity because they were not only depicted as inferior but, more importantly, seen as less than human beings. Racism made it easier in the European mind to justify the enslavement of Africans. What was done to Africans by outsiders defies humanity. Yet, we were expected to talk about the slave trade dispassionately. I contend that we should not be dispassionate about horror and gross acts of inhumanity. How many of Irish descent can talk about the situation in Ireland dispassionately? How dispassionately can Native Americans recount the coming of the white man? How many of Jewish descent can speak of Hitler or the Jewish holocaust dispassionately? Slavery was the holocaust for people of African descent. The Eurocentric attempts to downplay slavery, and likes to point to problems that existed in Africa prior to the coming of Europeans. We were told that there was slavery in Africa before Europeans arrived. It was, however, unquestionably clear that what the Eurocentrists call African enslavement was actually a system of captives. Africans were taken by other Africans typically as a result of warfare between nations, between groups. These prisoners of war were not taken to exploit their labor or to dehumanize or to strip them of all dignity, as was the intent and, too often, the success of European enslavement of Africans. We need to be quite clear and steadfast on this point and reject the Eurocentric view, since the Eurocentric was an activist in spreading a version that minimized Europe's dominant role in the systematic exploitation and destruction of Africa. Not for one moment should we relinquish from the indictment of the European slave trade and its unprecedented cruelty against humanity. No matter what the analysis or interpretation offered, the slave trade was barbaric and savage; a process so vile it defies description. Slaves did everything to escape, including jumping overboard into the ocean. The slave ship physician Falconbridge was one eyewitness to the desperate actions of the many slaves he personally saw devoured by sharks. Sharks began to routinely follow slave vessels all the way to the New World from the west coast of Africa, where blacks were taken on board. They had learned to associate the slave vessels with food because of the large numbers of desperate souls who jumped overboard or were otherwise laid to rest at sea. There was no need for us to fictionalize the *Middle Passage*. The actual historical record was far more heart wrenching.

The profit motive and racism were a lethal combination for Africa. Europe systematically raped the African continent. Whether one accepts the often cited figure of twelve million Africans killed, taken, or otherwise lost to the slave trade, or the more likely figure of forty million and more killed, taken, or otherwise lost to the slave trade, the impact was catastrophic for Africa and monumental for European coffers and the New World. Beginning with the Portuguese encroachment into Ghana at Elmina in 1415, to the abolishment of slavery in Brazil in 1888, the human cost to Africa of the Atlantic slave trade easily ranks as the gravest holocaust in all of human history.

People of African descent throughout the diaspora must understand that their history was largely a labor history. They were taken from Africa and brought to the New World to work, to labor by the sweat of their brows in day-to-day toil, to make wealth and profits for those who owned them. The African continent provided the labor that fueled the industrial revolution of the Western world. The horrendous Atlantic trade in "black gold" made for profits at each port of the three-pronged round-trip. These Portuguese, Spanish, Dutch, and English vessels sailed from Europe loaded, for example, with rifles and other goods that were traded in Africa for blacks who were then imported to the Americas and Caribbean. There the vessels took on rum and other commodities that were sold back in Europe. Thus, this *triangular trade* was lucrative at each leg of the journey. Profits were huge in the selling of blacks. The Papal Judgment of 1493, the Treaty of Tordesillas in 1494, the Asiento, and the other dastardly enactments relating to the slave business, and the work of the Dutch Royal African Company, the Spanish, the Portuguese, the British and all the rest confirm Europe's view of African people as nothing but an exploitable labor source for the harvesting of the wealth of the New World and the making of tremendous profits and individual fortunes. Eric Williams in his classic treatise, *Capitalism and Slavery*, persuasively demonstrated the value of the slave trade in fostering the industrial revolution in England in particular. The English seaport cities of Bristol, Liverpool, and Manchester became great profit centers owing largely to the slave business. The slave trade fueled the lumber industry for the making of the slave vessels; the insurance industry to insure the ships; provided jobs for the ships' crews and officers and workers on the docks and in the building of these ships; for farmers and others who provided food; for the merchants who opened stores in the areas and sold supplies; to the tavern owners who entertained the crews; to the landlords who rented out apartments and other facilities to those who lived in the seaport towns; the banking industry for financing the ships and businesses; and huge profits for the ships' owners. Great fortunes were made and had at the human sacrifice of tens of millions of African people. Walter Rodney correctly concluded in his seminal work, *How Europe Underdeveloped Africa*, that the taking of millions of Africa's most healthy and virile sons and daughters for exploitation in another world, never to see the light of Africa again, dealt a crippling blow to the entire future development and progress of the African continent. Eurocentrists disagree with the notion of captives and argue that Africans misused their own people, claiming that slavery existed in Africa before the coming of Europeans. In that same Eurocentric vain they deny to today's descendants of those Africans the right to make an intellectual connection with their African past, with their forebears, of seeing themselves as a people who began in Africa. Unlike European immigrants, Africans did not "come" to the Americas seeking freedom, opportunities and a better way of life. To the contrary, Africans possessed that better way of life in Africa. They were torn from their families and homeland and brought to the Americas in chains as slaves with all rights, opportunities, and basic human dignity denied.[4]

The arrival of Europeans in the New World meant disaster for the native populations they encountered and the millions of Africans they imported. Numerous voyagers had made contact with the Americas prior to Christopher Columbus's late arrival in 1492. This lost sailor had not reached Asia by traveling west as he thought. Neither was this the Indies. Never should the native inhabitants already present in this "newly discovered" land been classified as "Indians." Furthermore, how do you discover something that was not lost and already populated by other people? If we were to credit Columbus for discovering the New World then let us also give him the credit for what he delivered to the inhabitants of that world. He and his followers brought with them germs that decimated entire native populations. The depleted indigenous populations and labor sources were replenished by a constant and increasing stream of enslaved Africans brought to work the fields and mines.

The seeds of racism and anti-multiracialism were being planted throughout the world everywhere black people were implanted as slaves. There were bodies of laws, enactments, and every conceivable effort to control the social status of the enslaved Africans, and to dehumanize them as a people. This was clear despite the efforts of those who would have us believe that enslaved Africans were somehow protected by laws. The comparative school of historiography was one that has done a great deal of disservice. Frank Tannenbaum's *Slave and Citizen*, published in 1947, was instructive. Equal questioning of Stanley Elkins's work *Slavery*, published in 1959, was in order. These two works initiated the comparative approach. Why compare? Slavery was slavery. It made no sense to talk about good slavery or bad slavery. Comparing slave systems resulted in a weighing of the conditions of slavery in one society against another with the inevitable, explicit or implicit, conclusion that one was better or more humane than the other. The struggle of African people for their humanity demanded more than this kind of intellectual balderdash. To note details about each system was fine and important. To talk about them in contrasting differences and similarities also made good sense, but it needed to be tempered with a consciousness that would not allow one to fall into the trap of weighing one system as somehow better than another. Slavery was horrendous. It was an abomination in all of its forms, nuances and geographical locations throughout the New World. The differences between Iberian and Anglo-Saxon slave systems, feudal and capitalist cultures, institutional influences, the difference the church made, the state itself—all of these were important ideas but not to be taken out of context and discussed as factors that somehow mitigated enslavement.

The overwhelming percentage of African slaves was imported to Latin America and the Caribbean, particularly to Haiti, Brazil, and Cuba. We can debate the numbers again. Some would talk about the figure in Brazil as ranging from a low of eight million to a high of twenty million slaves imported. These massive figures should be appreciated in terms of the staggering cruelty they represent. Indigenous people, numbering in the millions, also perished under the onslaught of the invaders' desires and attempts to enslave them in their own country. The answer to maintaining the numbers in the workforce was the forced importation of Africans, many of whom died under the extreme toil and hardships of planting and harvesting sugar and cocoa and working the mines in insufferable conditions in the Americas.

Racism was a convenient cloak over the massive destruction of native and African people. Decimated indigenous people were seen as a weak and unsuitable breed while Africans were defined as a species best suited for hard labor in the hot climate of the Americas coming from Africa and an agricultural background. Moreover, they postulate that blacks were more receptive and amiable than the native peoples to enslavement. The slave masters were in a state of racist denial as they overlooked the high death rate, short life expectancy, and countless attempts at escape of their black slaves. Greed, racism, and mortality meant an ever-growing slave trade that lasted for more than three hundred years.

To say the least, slavery was not more humane in Latin America than it was in North America. The body of laws called the *siete partidas*, dating back to Alfonso the Wise, supposedly endowed slaves with certain protection and recognition in Latin America as compared to North America or what would become the United States. To claim that the rights of slaves were recognized in courts was sheer fantasy. Iberian slavery was as ruthless as any slavery throughout the Americas. Yet the myth makers talk about the protections that the Catholic church provided the slaves, and manumission in Brazil, Cuba, Venezuela, Peru, and Columbia as if huge numbers managed to obtain their freedom within the system. Pope John Paul recently apologized for the Catholic Church's involvement in the slave trade, apologized for the Asiento and the enslavement of millions of African people. His apology was duly noted. It was, at least, some form of recognition. Some form of monetary compensation would be much better, however, and it would have to be of mammoth proportions to even be considered a gesture for the brutalization of countless black souls over hundreds of years.

There was no debate on the terms of servitude for those enslaved in the Americas and throughout the New World. The nonsense about slavery as a type of indentured servitude was just that—nonsense. A slave was a slave forever. A white indentured servant served for a certain period of contractual time, five or perhaps ten years, while a slave was a slave for the rest of his or her life. And so were their children and their children's children. This was why, throughout the Americas, slaves were defined by the status of their mothers. This ensured the perpetuation of the institution. If they had been defined otherwise, given the numbers being born resulting from the slave masters' unbridled sexual plundering of enslaved African women, at least one fourth of the slave population would have had to be freed by the nineteenth century.

It was unseemly and historically reprehensible to attempt to suggest that slavery had redeeming virtues. Slavery's value to the enslavers was obvious. For the slaves the only "virtues" of the institution were the many lessons it taught them in how to suffer and survive or how to die. To suggest that some masters were kindly, and that paternalism existed, serves only to belittle the unspeakable cruelty, immorality, and injustice of slavery. The picture of the happy-go-lucky *darkies* who were well taken care of by the good and kind slave masters, and who indulged them in their simpleminded ways and protected them as chattel because they were unable to protect themselves, has finally been rejected by most professional historians. The slaves were routinely beaten and whipped, sexually assaulted, killed, but most of all they were worked until they could work no more. The horrors perpetuated against the slaves were legion. Physical torture was routine. At times the cruelty exceeded imagination such as the example of the mistress of the household who, angry about her husband's infidelity with a female slave, had the eyes of the slave in question gouged out and served to her husband for dessert in a jelly dish; or the mistress who had the slave's breasts cut off, her nails drawn, face and ears burned. The torture list was endless, including unique devices to inflict pain and assure obedience such as the tronco, the libambo, the algemas, the novenas, the trezenas, and anjinhos.

The technique of European enslavement of Africans was to strip them from the ranks of the human family. It was racist and an abomination of natural law. The contention that slaves were protected in the Latin Americas by the Catholic Church was an exaggeration and unfounded. Slaves were not taught to read and write. For the most part, there were stringent laws forbidding this because of the fear of what an education or any degree of literacy might produce. If a slave was found to have any ability to read, however that was attained, that reading was relegated to the Bible. It, of course, raised a number of very critical questions about religion and the uses thereof in the enslavement of African people.

Laws enacted dealing with slavery in the Latin Americas were not to protect the slaves' existence nor to recognize them as human beings, but to control their very existence and movement. The Spanish Code of 1789 clearly laid out the appropriate punishment for disobedient African slaves. This was enacted to ensure stability and the preservation of the institution and not to protect the slaves. The whipping, punishing, or rape of someone else's slave without that owner's permission was forbidden by law. This was done, however, not to grant rights to the slaves but to protect private property. Indeed, the rape of a slave woman by someone other than the master or his designate without his permission was punishable as a crime; a crime of trespass. This was not a recognition of the African woman as a woman, or as a human being, nor a law protecting her against rape. It was a statement of social control and owner's rights, and an attempt to provide rules for the harmonious exploitation of the

Africans by their enslavers to alleviate and settle disagreements amongst themselves over the disposition of their "property."[5]

It was worthless to weigh Spanish slavery against Portuguese slavery or against slavery in the British Caribbean and North America. Throughout the New World, people of African descent were confined to the bottom of society and branded as less than human beings by virtue of their color. Slaves in Cuba were dehumanized and abused as were those throughout the so-called West Indies, Latin America, and North America. The chains that bound them were strong and long-lasting. In the North American colonies, of what became the United States of America, the descendants of Africa were out of place, strangers in a new land, and whose sole purpose for existence was to benefit others. As such, Africans would naturally be at odds with the new nation, and in contradiction to it, as a slave population in the "land of the free."

III

DEMOCRACY
CONTRADICTED

BLACK IN "THE LAND OF THE FREE"

Racism served to rationalize and justify the brutal enslavement and exploitation of African people, European expansionism, the colonizing of the New World, and the slave trade. Although the English did not lead in the expansionist race, they came on fast. The English trailed the Portuguese, the Spanish, and the Dutch early in the scramble for possessions in the New World, but quickly surpassed them and other rivals, except the French, in the colonization of North America and what would become the United States of America.

English intellectuals provided the rationalization. Richard Hakluyt and his ideas of "divine right" were important here because, with the death of Queen Elizabeth in 1603, he and his following of English pro-expansionists prevailed. Convinced that it was the divine right of the English to take leadership of the "primitive people," Hakluyt argued in his 1584 thesis, "Discourse Concerning Western Planting," that North America was not only there for the taking but had to be taken by the most "civilized" people, namely the English. Taking such action, Hakluyt avowed, would also be an effective bulwark against the further expansionism of the Spanish and the dreaded nemesis of Catholicism or, as he termed it, "The scarlet whore, the church of Rome." Most of all Hakluyt understood the need for England to depopulate itself, and the potential value of the unwanted poor and others who could be put to service in the New World. Hakluyt was no lover of the poor and he held utter contempt for the non-European races, whom he dubbed as "ungodly savages of the New World."

The Reverend Daniel Price was another strong supporter of English colonization of the New World. Through sermons from the pulpit, writings, and teaching, he urged the harvesting of the areas' economic riches which, he envisioned, consisted of virtually an unlimited supply of gold and other precious metals, foods, spices, and pelts. Both Price and Hakluyt helped lay the philosophical and motivational foundation for the exploitation of the New World. That plundering would result in the decimation of entire native populations and the demise of African civilization, and the enslavement of millions. The lower class of Europe would also pay a price in the conquest of the New World. European immigrants, to subsidize their immigration to the New World, indentured themselves for sometimes as long as ten years. Indentured servitude, however despicable, was far from the slaughter, destruction, and usurpation that befell the indigenous people of the New World and Africans.

In the eighteenth century the ethnic homogeneity of the English had changed as a result of the influx of Germans, Swiss, and Scotch-Irish. By the time of the American Revolution more than half of the settler population of the New England colonies was non-English. What they all had in common, however, was that they were of European descent, and white. The new nation forged around a commonality of ideals that placed a premium on race. What was in store for non-whites was not an open hand; rather, it was a clinched fist. From its conception, America emerged as an anti-multiracial society, a country whose three unifying elements were Europeanism, capitalism, and racism, and not necessarily in that order.

The seeds of America's racism and anti-multiracialism were planted during the very founding of the nation and cultivated in the Constitution of these United States. At the very beginning of the American nation, slavery was sanctioned in its body of laws and guiding principles. The specific year of the arrival of the first Africans brought to America was of limited importance. Some have argued that it was 1619 but a more careful examination of Susan Kinsbury's *Records of A Virginia Company*, and John Roche's letter to Sir Edwin Sandys in 1625, indicate that enslaved Africans were present in the American colonies prior to 1619. At any rate, slavery was firmly established as that "peculiar" institution written into the statute books of Virginia, Maryland, and the other colonies before the end of the seventeenth century.

These early years of enslavement were crucial for us to look at for it was in these years that the Africans' debasement in America was institutionalized. That debasement was set in stone. From the outset, people of African descent in America were a contradiction, a counterpoint to the great tenets of democracy, equality, liberty and justice, and all the virtuous promise of the American Revolution; a glaring example of the hypocrisy upon which America was founded, a festering sore at the very core of the nation.

The incorporating of slavery into the fabric of the nation was not done by accident or mistake but by contemplation and deliberation. The early efforts of a few to steer the nation away from slavery failed. The preliminary draft of *The Articles of Confederation*, the building blocks to the *Constitution of the United States of America*, had contained passages prohibiting the growth of slavery. The Provisional Congress reaffirmed those sentiments on April 6, 1776. The anti-slavery passages, however, were no where to be found in the final draft of the *Constitution of the United States*, with the exception of the caveat that the slave trade—not slavery—would cease at the end of 1807. That compromise edict would do little to stifle slavery's advance. Slavery's contradiction was dismissed. The venerable Thomas Paine, in his famous *Common Sense* treatise, defended the institution of slavery and criticized the British for encouraging the enslaved Africans to revolt; which he saw as a British ploy to weaken the American Revolution from within. Thus the American Revolution was about "independence" and "freedom" for whites only. Benjamin Banneker, the famed black mathematician, astronomer, builder of the first clock in America, and architect of Washington, D.C., aptly labeled the *Declaration of Independence* and the American Revolution: "a fraud."

Yet Banneker and the many other descendants of Africa did their part in the name and spirit of the American Revolution. Blacks served, fought, and gave their lives for the American Revolution and the freedom that they thought it would encompass for all people. Blacks filed petitions throughout New England condemning slavery and begging for an end to it. Pomp, Prince, Luke, Caesar, Pruce, were slaves who wrote of the horrors of bondage and servitude and asked the legislatures of their states to free all slaves. Their prophetic pleas were for the sake of their children and their children's children. Prominent blacks of the era, among them Prince Hall, Paul Cuffe, and Phyllis Wheatley, sounded a harmonious chord for freedom, liberty, and equality for all human beings in the name of the American Revolution. These pleas fell on deaf ears. When Prince Hall was rejected for membership into the Boston lodge of the Masonic order because of his color, it was, ironically, the British who granted his black Masonic order recognition and the right to establish "African lodge no. 1" in Boston on July 3, 1776. America was saying, in unmistakable terms, that blacks were not to be included in its definition of human beings, nor those defined as having rights equal to whites. In the *Constitution*, the Founding Fathers were speaking primarily to white men of property. The leading African-American jurist of today, Leon Higginbotham, in his brilliant book, *A Matter of Color*, has spoken to this contradiction eloquently. Judge Higginbotham articulated how the basic foundation of American constitutional law was premised on inequality. That inequality must be addressed if this nation is to move beyond the pit-falls of its flawed foundation. It also raises another interesting question: How can anyone who truly believes in justice and equality be a strict constructionist? How can one hold dearly to that flawed parchment, the *Constitution*, that counted blacks as three-fifths of a human being? The contradiction was too much for the Quakers. Because of the strong opposition against slavery in Pennsylvania, led by the large Quaker population, that state became the first to abolish slavery in 1787. The New England states followed suit in the early nineteenth century. New Jersey was the last of the northeastern states to completely abolish slavery in 1860.

The *Constitution of the United States of America* from its conception was an ironical document. Those who opposed the *Constitution* were most responsible for liberating it, and bringing about protections in the name of freedom of religion and speech, freedom from persecution, and the need for due process. These anti-federalists questioned constantly whether the nation could be built on democratic republican principles. A large proportion of the people in 1787 were anti-federalists, sharing the beliefs of Montesquieu that republicanism and federalism could only exist among a homogeneous population and over a small territory. America was neither. The anti-federalists saw clearly the economic and the political differences and the sectional splits within this new nation. It was the anti-federalists who, in the skeptic tradition of Rousseau, questioned the precept of majority rule over the rights of the minority. Because of the prodding of the anti-federalists various checks and balances were attained and governmental authority divided among the three branches: legislative, executive, and judicial. Patrick Henry, a noted anti-federalist, along with George Mason and Richard Henry Lee, among others, advocated direct democracy. Although they pushed for it, it was not achieved. They did not, however, vigorously address the question of slavery and the profound contradiction it exemplified. In sum, those who were most critical of the foundation of America were most instrumental in protecting liberties and fostering the first ten amendments to the *Constitution*, the *Bill of Rights*; a senate and house of representatives to assure fairer representation between large and small states, and in the end a *Constitution* that was, to be sure, a compromise document ratified in 1787, but one that only protected the rights and privileges of white Americans. The *Constitution* held only a fig leaf of hope for non-whites, for whom the great words of equality, liberty, and the pursuit of happiness would remain an elusive dream for generations to come.

The *Constitution* was a compromise document, not only on sectional and economic issues and the structure of governance and individual liberties, but it was a compromise too on simple morality. The great document did not condemn slavery. The slave trade was allowed to legally continue until a set date, and in practice the trade continued beyond that date in extralegal fashion. Even more horrendous for the future of those of African descent was that the document stated very clearly how blacks were to be forever perceived. In deciding on the number of representatives for each state, the question arose as to how the slave population in southern states would be counted in proportioning representation in the House of Representatives. The South of course wanted their slaves counted; that meant more representatives for the southern states. The North said no because, after all, the slaves were not real people. It would make as much sense, it was argued, to count horses, cows, or corn in deciding representation. A further compromise was reached, one that would bode poorly for people of African descent in America for the next two hundred years. Blacks were to be counted as "three-fifths" of a person. What does this tell you? It is sad to look back to Article I, Section II, Paragraph Three, of the *Constitution of the United States of America*, and see yourself counted as three-fifths of a human being. From that "compromise" on, African Americans would be struggling not only for freedom and constitutional recognition and provision, but to gain full status as a human being.[1]

Africans in early America were trying desperately to gain their freedom and to live by their own will. But that was denied them at every turn. W.E.B. Du Bois's analysis in the *Souls of Black Folk* was correct when he stated that the problem of the twentieth century was the problem of the color line. It was also the problem of the seventeenth and eighteenth century. The experience of people of African descent in Connecticut, "The Constitution State" was telling. In this venerable of the early New England colonies, and one that can rightly claim a central role in the formulation of the American character, Africans were, from the beginning, seen as a problem, a point of contentiousness.

For Africans, Connecticut was a place that exemplified dichotomy and contradiction: Christian values and the conquest of Native Americans and their land, the common good and individualism, Puritan work ethic and the exploitation of black labor. From the outset, enslaved Africans were important to the prosperity of Connecticut as a literal source of direct and indirect income and wealth for whites. The colonists in Hartford, Connecticut, engaged in lucrative trade with the West Indies and Africa. Colonists in the southern part of Connecticut directly engaged in the "triangular trade," but the entire state benefited. Cornmeal produced in Connecticut became part of the basic staple that planters in the West Indies feed to their slaves. Molasses imported from the West Indies was a source for homemade rum in Connecticut. The profits garnered in connection with the slave trade helped to produce the basis of wealth for some of Connecticut's most influential families. A black as house slave or house servant or personal valet became a symbol of position and status in the seventeenth and eighteenth centuries in Connecticut, symbols of the new found wealth.[2]

Blacks did more than contribute to the wealth and ease of life for the elite majority. They fought, killed and died in the nation's war for independence. They believed in the lofty ideals of the American Revolution and that they must do their part in the fight for freedom. In the beginning, Connecticut did not want its black population to participate in the war for independence, fearing the long-term consequences if blacks were allowed to bear arms and taught to fight. This was a sentiment widely shared among Connecticut's leaders. A law enacted in 1660 exempted blacks from service in the military and made it illegal for them to bear arms. The need for troops and the other demands of the war for independence later made it necessary to rescind this law. Moreover, blacks were allowed to serve in lieu of their masters. This was a convenient way for a white to fight for the independence of the colonies without risking his own life, an option that men of wealth in Connecticut and elsewhere readily utilized.

African Americans in their contribution to the American Revolution hoped to win a seed of respect within America, and to become part of the uniting of the new nation. They envisioned being rewarded for their service after the revolution was won. This was the deep motivating force behind the gallantry that blacks in Connecticut displayed in the American Revolutionary War. The African, Jordan Freeman, distinguished himself at the Battle of Fort Griswald, where he fought and died. The black man called Cuff, slave to a Connecticut physician, was another who gave unselfishly of himself during the war. Cuff had learned much of the art of medicine while assisting his owner Dr. Langrel. Cuff enlisted in May of 1777 and served until 1781 under Captain Jeddah Hyde of the Connecticut Forth Regiment, first as a waiter to a hospital surgeon. His medical skills soon became apparent. He tended the wounds of many injured soldiers brought to the Army Hospital in Danbury from 1781 to 1783. Blacks, such as Timon Negro of Wethersfield, served with distinction. Cash Africa of Litchfield, served with Connecticut's First Regiment as did Caesar Stewart and Toby Pindall of Norwich, Joseph Hopkins and Cuff Capeny of Waterbury, and Pharaoh

Heart. Blacks served in New Haven and throughout the state as members of Connecticut's Meigs Regiment, which earned great distinction. More than four hundred Connecticut black Yankees distinguished themselves while serving in the American Revolutionary War.

Little changed for them after the war, however. As one researcher of Hartford's history observed: "Sad to say, those many acts of personal heroism and sacrifice did not substantially improve the status of black men in Connecticut." Jupiter Hammon, reputed to be the first black poet in America, composed a dialogue that was printed in Hartford in 1783. In the piece entitled, "The Kindly Master and the Dutiful Servant," he sympathetically described the continuing relationship between whites and blacks. Despite those kind of prophetic efforts, Africans would not be accepted as equals in Connecticut nor throughout New England or the rest of America. They were viewed as inferiors and expected to remain in their place. In Connecticut, as elsewhere in America, racial barriers were established that would pose unique difficulties for black people for centuries.

Neither were other groups particularly well received in the Nutmeg State. Thomas Hooker, and other founders of Connecticut, sought to establish a closed community. We like to think of Hooker and his band as leaving Massachusetts in search of tolerance in a new colony. The reality was something quite different. Africans and all other groups in Connecticut should reexamine the *Fundamental Orders* from a critical perspective. To do so helps to illuminate, reveal, and expose the true Connecticut and American mindset. Hooker and his group never really separated church from state. While there were those who proclaimed the *Fundamental Orders* the hallmark and harbinger of the American *Constitution* and democratic government, the reality was that the *Fundamental Orders* was a conservative document, a body of eleven rules of order to establish social control.

Africans were, like the Pequot Indians, exploitable labor at best; at worst, a menace. Hooker's Connecticut was exclusive. Until the nineteenth century to become a resident of Hartford, Connecticut, for example, you had to be voted in. "What Connecticut most of all wanted," wrote Ordell Shepard, "was to evade attention and to be let alone. Her best heraldic device would have been the figure of a rattlesnake, a really modest and retiring creature which only asks to be allowed to lie in the sunlight dust and not be trodden upon."

Conformity was a major issue that runs throughout the history of the State of Connecticut. People of African descent could do everything possible to conform and try to be like the dominant segment of the population. The Connecticut penchant for conformity was of particular relevance to people of color and what it conveyed to them. Conformity by its very nature said that you must be like the rest of us or you would be forsaken. Black folk could do only certain things to be like the rest of society. In the end they were ostracized. Many attempted to alter their mannerisms, folkways, dress, habits, speech, and even their beliefs, but they could not change their color. Shepard, in his book on the history of Connecticut, pondered how many generations it would take before a newcomer to Connecticut developed that "certain look" and a "Yankee nose."[3] For blacks it never happened.

The dominant concern of race relations in Connecticut from the beginning was to assure the amiability of the blacks and white control over them. Daniel Wadsworth, one of the Connecticut's most imminent leaders throughout the early 1700s, attempted to imbue the blacks with the kinds of attitudes and behavior he thought proper for them. He used the scriptures and religious sermons to convey his teachings. Wadsworth often preached in the evening to groups of blacks. His favorite passages from the Bible that he geared to black worshippers addressed salvation, proper behavior, obedience, and loyalty. When the more cerebral approach failed, out right force was used to control the black population of Connecticut. Incarceration of blacks was commonplace. The charges themselves were interesting. They ranged the gamut from disobedience to murder, from theft to refusing to work. Striking were the number of cases of African women incarcerated for infanticide in Connecticut in the eighteenth and nineteenth centuries. Why were these acts committed? Were they a result of viciousness or madness? No. They were acts of desperation and despair. The black mother who killed her newborn did so to spare her child from having to live a life of slavery.

The institution of slavery was an abomination. Slavery constituted a point of contention, debate and controversy, a challenge to American democracy. In Connecticut it presented a "problem" not easily resolved in the "land of steady habits." Those white Yankees who saw slavery as a blight on the revolutionary spirit were castigated by their fellow citizens. Connecticut was ambivalent, indecisive, and virtually schizophrenic on the question of abolition as was much of the rest of the nation throughout the history of slavery in America. Indecisive Connecticut had great difficulty abolishing slavery outright. The state passed two acts that would allow "gradual" emancipation. The first act was in 1784, the same year that the City of Hartford was officially incorporated. The second act came in

1797. Connecticut did not officially abolish slavery until 1848. Only New Jersey and New York of the northern states took longer to end the dreaded institution.

Africans greatly contributed to Connecticut in a variety of ways in their efforts to become Americans. Primus, slave of Dr. Walcott of Windsor, Connecticut, practiced medicine and assisted in the health care of thousands. The slave Purdy of Newtown, Connecticut, helped in the smallpox epidemic of 1760. He was familiar with African folk-medicine and treatments, including the African tradition of inoculations against smallpox. Horace Weston, the most famous black banjo player and musician in Derby, Connecticut, spread the joy of music throughout the state in the 1840s. In recent years, his "Minor Jig" has been revived and played in New York City.

What was happening to people of African descent in Connecticut was happening throughout New England. It was clear from William Piersen's study, *Black Yankees,* that people of African descent remained *untouchables* no matter what they did, what they produced, or how they pleaded their case for inclusion. They were slaves and, at best, distant second-class citizens. Hartford-born Maria Stewart became a heralded voice of abolition. This black woman, better known outside of her native Connecticut, traveled and lectured extensively on the evils of slavery, the need for abolition, and civil rights for black people. She was a daring visionary. She had to be. For a black woman to be a public speaker in the 1830s and to fervently challenge the status quo and American morality on the slave question was a remarkable demonstration of independence of mind and personal courage. Her lectures were published in 1835 and a second edition appeared in 1879, the year she died.

Connecticut was also fortunate for the presence of James W.C. Pennington, one of the most important personages in nineteenth century black America. The story of Pennington, *The Runaway Blacksmith* (1850), was instructive. He was a runaway slave from Maryland, who lived for a while in Pennsylvania and eventually settled in Connecticut. In 1834 he became minister of the Temple Street Congregational Church, one of the first black churches in the state. Six years later he moved to Hartford as pastor of the Talcott Street Congregational Church. A prolific writer, inspirational speaker, and dedicated abolitionist, Pennington became a national and international figure. As a leader of the Connecticut Anti-Slavery Society he traveled abroad and spoke on the organization's behalf. He raised funds for the repatriation of the Amistad Africans after the Supreme Court freed them in 1841; was a founding member and president of the Hartford Central Association of Congregational Ministers; helped organize the American Missionary Association; petitioned the Connecticut legislature to grant blacks full citizenship and the right to vote; authored a textbook on *The Origins and History of the Colored People*, making him one of the first writers of African-American history; and engaged in many other intellectual and civic initiatives. Friend to Frederick Douglass, David Ruggles, Henry Highland Garnet, and other crusaders for black freedom, Pennington too was intolerant. He was intolerant of racism, injustice and inequality and, indeed, wanted to be accepted as an American. He denounced bigotry, discrimination, hatred and apathy wherever he encountered it. And he experienced a great deal of it in Connecticut where, as he noted, a black could not even walk down the street without having his hat knocked off by a white. Pennington left the state after passage of the Fugitive Slave Act of 1850, accepting the ministerial leadership of a Presbyterian church in New York City, where he continued the fight for full abolition and freedom.

Augustus Washington became similarly disappointed with the rate of progress for black people in Connecticut. Born in New Jersey and educated at Dartmouth, he settled in the State of Connecticut in 1844. Washington was a skilled daguerreotypist and opened his own successful studio in the state's capital. Pennington likely played a key role in bringing him to Connecticut. Washington immediately began teaching children and adults at the African Free School, which was largely community supported and which Pennington headed. If Africans were to achieve an education, they would have to set up their own schools. The school held its classes in Talcott Street Church. There were other African Free Schools throughout colonial New England.

Like Pennington, Washington was an intellectual, a social firebrand, an abolitionist, a petitioner, an advocate for black citizenship and rights. He would not accept second-class citizenship. When the *Connecticut Constitution of 1818* legalized the disfranchisement of the state's blacks, Washington took every opportunity to denounce the document as the black man's version of "No Taxation Without Representation." His efforts helped to generate debate in the state legislature and a movement in 1847 to grant blacks the right to vote. The movement, however, failed. Washington became more and more convinced that blacks would never be treated as equals in America and that racism was so deep within the nation's fiber that there was no hope of extricating it. He concluded that black folk could find equality only in their native land. He abandoned his hope of inclusion and embraced the idea of African repatriation and took up the call of

"Back-To-Africa." Washington gave his support to the American Colonization Society and in 1854 he left Connecticut for Liberia, West Africa. Washington and Pennington were correct in their dismal assessment of the depth of anti-black sentiment in Connecticut. Efforts toward black uplift through education were met with continuous resistance. Blacks struggled valiantly to educate themselves. They established African Free Schools with good teachers like Roseanne Cook, Sarah Wilson, P.M. Williams, Rebecca Primus, Ann Plato, and Lucy Terry. Sometimes these schools were forcibly closed. Other educational efforts were killed before they began or halted in their infancy. The Manual Labor School idea in New Haven was an example. Arthur Tappan and William Lloyd Garrison, two stalwart white abolitionists, pushed for the building of a manual labor school for blacks in New Haven in 1830. The school was to provide blacks with a jobs-related education, nothing more. Intense anti-abolitionism reared its head in the form of violence against the school. The idea was abandoned.

In 1832, Charles B. Ray became the first black to attend Wesleyan College in Middletown, Connecticut. That same year he was asked to leave. A group of white students called a meeting requesting that Ray leave the school; they did not want a Negro there even as an experiment in education. They established a special fund to defray any of Ray's expenses incurred in coming to Wesleyan. They were even willing to let him keep any additional money raised in the buyout as long as he left the school. When Ray refused the offer, he was forced out.

The most infamous of the anti-black education efforts in Connecticut was the Prudence Crandall incident of 1831 through 1834. Prudence Crandall, the kindly Quaker woman who, by simply admitting one black student, Sarah Harris, started a wrath against her school for young girls in Canterbury, Connecticut. Her drinking well was filled with filth. Windows were broken. Crandall was jeered whenever she took the young ladies for a walk or was seen in public, and in the end she was taken to court. The State of Connecticut was literally saying, "We do not want Negroes here." If they were no longer slaves, then they were no longer of value to us. The fear was that by educating blacks they might see themselves as equals; see themselves as having a place in American society. Amalgamation, that apprehension of integration, the blending of blacks into the rest of society, was taboo in Connecticut as it was throughout the rest of the nation.[4]

Blacks, nevertheless, continued their struggle in the Nutmeg State. They attempted to advance themselves in America, tried to be a part of the nation, asserted themselves and articulated their needs as best they could under the most horrendous conditions. Blacks engaged in the futility of "electing" so-called Negro governors. They held freedom celebrations on the fifth of July and in August. Neither did the gallant contributions of Connecticut's 1,664 blacks who served in the Civil War do much to alter conditions for the state's 6,500 Africans. The status of the state's African population remained essentially unchanged in the antebellum and postbellum years. The ban against black suffrage, for example, was not completely lifted in Connecticut until 1876. Considering Connecticut, New England, and the rest of the North, placing emphasis on the South as the bastion of the nation's racial divide minimizes the totality and universality of anti-black sentiment and actions in America. The Mason-Dixon Line in that sense can be misleading geographically because anti-black sentiment did not stop at the border between the South and North. It was something that permeated the very fiber of America. Africans were constantly discriminated against, despised, and relegated to defacto-slave status in the North. Politicians, whether Democrats, Republicans, Wigs or others, were openly anti blacks. Segregation was present in everything: public conveyances and conveniences, theaters, churches, and cemeteries. Although blacks struggled continuously to elevate themselves in the early-nineteenth century North, they were kept in their place. Individuals like Frederick Douglass, Harriet Tubman, Sojourner Truth, were inspirational heroes, not just for the deeds they accomplished but for the moral character and consciousness upon which they called America to account. Blacks in the North were lucky only in the sense that plantation capitalism established itself in the South, not the North. But a lucrative interregional slave trade emerged as blacks in the North were sold southward into the slavery of the blackbelt and emerging cotton kingdom.

In the North laws were established that controlled every aspect of the African's life. There were rules against blacks gathering in large numbers and against blowing horns and beating drums. Blacks were untouchables, a group deemed inferior and incapable. Such a race, it was easy to argue, warranted enslavement or at least social castigation. The release in 1840 of the Sixth Census of the United States was used as proof that segregation of the Negro was correct because, according to the Census, a very large proportion of the free black population was "insane." It was found that in Maine, for example, according to census figures, every fourteenth black was either a lunatic or an idiot; in New Hampshire every twenty-ninth; in Massachusetts every forty-third; in Connecticut every one hundred and eighty-fourth; in New York every two hundred and twenty-fifth; in New Jersey every two hundred and ninety-seventh. Clearly those states that were the last to abolish slavery had, according to the census data, the lowest percentage of black idiots. The figures for the South, on the other hand, showed that only one out of two thousand blacks were crazy. Thus the North found justification to further segregate blacks while the South argued gleefully in the words of George Fitzhugh and John C. Calhoun that the blacks were too feeble mentally to handle freedom; freedom drove them insane. The way of the South was vindicated in the old paternalistic notion of *noblesse oblige* for the dark race because their weak minds simply buckled under the pressures that came with being free. [Can one wonder today why black folk distrust the census?] Some northern whites also attacked the vile misrepresented statistically data. Abolitionists spoke out against the alleged census findings. John Quincy Adams called for a thorough investigation and revision of the 1840 Census.

There were other forms of attack and restrictions upon "free" blacks. There was legislation to control when they could travel, where they could go; in short, to control their every move. Massachusetts and Rhode Island prohibited interracial marriage. Connecticut forbade blacks from entering the state to be educated. There were numerous instances of violence against free blacks and efforts to expel them from northern states. In Ohio and Pennsylvania codes were passed to prohibit blacks from entering the states, and efforts were made to remove those who had gotten through. Most of the northern states passed "black laws" to keep free blacks out and to further curtail their rights.

In the labor market of the North, blacks found a new slavery consisting of segregation, low wages, and no regress in the courts. Although slavery officially ended in the North sooner than it did in the South, it did not mean that blacks had found anything resembling equality. The nation was sending very clear signals to its African population that they would never be accepted and welcomed as equals in America. That was the view then, and one questions how much it has changed today. The American nation crippled emancipated Africans from the outset, doing all in its considerable power to make them nothing more than defacto slaves. This point should be kept in mind when discussing the "uniting of America." The historical record was clear: there was no intention from the beginning to make Africans into Americans. Blacks were brought to the New World to toil by the sweat of their brows. Freedom for blacks was an afterthought, and citizenship more foreign and remote. That there has been tension from the beginning between black folk and what America itself stood for should be understandable from the historical record. For people of African descent, America meant enslavement or at best "freedom" in a nation that did not want them. The *American Dream* was in reality a daily nightmare for people of color. Blacks hoped and sought to change that reality.[5]

People of African descent brought by force to the United States were the fodder and prize of a white American dream to become wealthy enough to own slaves and to have a Negro servant. The black population in the United States rapidly increased during the late eighteenth and early nineteenth centuries. There were less than one million slaves in America by official count at the beginning of 1800, but just thirty years later there were more than two million. The preeminence of slavery in the southern Atlantic states, including Virginia, Maryland, Delaware, and Florida was relinquished in the nineteenth century to the blackbelt South of Alabama, Mississippi, Georgia, Arkansas, and other states where cotton was king.

The institution of slavery dominated southern cultural institutions and the political milieu. Although the majority of whites were not slave owners, it was the wealthy planter and the plantation economy that dominated the South and the southern mindset. The masters of the large slave plantations were the South's wealthiest citizens and wielded an inordinate amount of power and prestige that white commoners desperately tried to emulate in deeds and spirit. Hence, the South and slavery were synonymous. Planters like John C. Calhoun and George Fitzhugh articulated a mindset that saw blacks as inferiors and nothing more than chattel property, a view that lower class whites eagerly embraced.

The extent of the shackles placed upon Africans in America was diabolically inclusive. The remnants of those shackles remain today. Slavery was an institution that rigorously controlled and debased blacks. In the day-to-day working of the peculiar institution every aspect of the enslaved Africans' lives was monitored. The primary goal, of course, was to maintain the institution, the exploitation of the blacks and the protection of the white population. The planters worked hard to make their slaves submissive. The process began even when the slave was a child. Under the white slave driver's watchful eye, every aspect of the slaves' work in the fields was monitored. Blacks too were used as drivers. They were forced, under the threat of flogging, to keep their fellow blacks in line. Slaves were forbidden to learn to read or to write. Who you could or could not marry, if marriage was permitted, was in the hands of the master or under the slave codes. To kill or rape a slave was not a crime in the South, not a crime in this nation, and certainly not considered to be a crime against the black person. If there was any violation under the slave codes it was the destruction or violation of a white's property rights, and thus the perpetrator could be liable to the slave owner.

Everything the slave possessed belonged to the master, including the slaves' sexuality. Thomas Jefferson availed himself of the sexuality of his slave, Sally Hemmings, for thirty-eight years, and she bore children by him. Until most recently many historians denied the relationship. The evidence of the relationship, however, was overwhelming and indisputable, including the physical presence of the progeny that were spawned. The Jefferson defenders attempted to mollify and explain his relationship with Hemmings as consensual or even a "negotiated relationship." The concept of a consensual sexual relationship between the slave master and his slave was absurd. A caged bird does not make its own free and unencumbered choices. An abolitionist writing at the time described Jefferson's relationship with Hemmings for what it was, one of "lust and rape." Be that as it may, the "founding father," and author of the *Declaration of Independence,* and Third President of the United States of America, was not legally guilty of a crime. Slaves had no rights.

The slaves could not leave the plantation without a pass or other explicit authorization. Whites' fear that blacks gathered in any group may be plotting to revolt made it illegal under most codes for three or more Africans to congregate without permission. This fear was intensified after the 1790s and Toussaint L'Overture's successful slave rebellion in Haiti. The Haitian example terrified slave masters of America, and throughout the slave-holding world, who feared that it could happen to them. They took extraordinary control measures to thwart potential slave rebellions. In parts of the South it was illegal for Africans to play drums, blow horns, or come together after dark without expressed permission. Whites feared that if blacks were blowing horns and playing drums they might be sending signals. Slave patrols were widespread throughout the South, guarding the borders, particularly between slave and free states to make sure that along these areas slaves were not moving about without permission. Both slave owners and those who did not own slaves were expected to serve their allotted amount of time, usually from three to six months, patrolling designated areas.

Slavery was a hell on earth. From the beginning of historical scholarship on American slavery, starting with Ulrich Phillips's book, *American Negro Slavery,* in the early part of the twentieth century, the Eurocentric has sought to minimize slavery, to talk about the "paternalism" of the institution and how the "darkies" and "pickaninies" were taken care of, and the benefits they received as a result of their contact with the superior race and its culture. This kind of portrayal was, we thought, finally corrected with the work of Kenneth Stampp at the University of California at Berkeley in the 1960s with his seminal treatise, *The Peculiar Institution*, which put on record again for this nation the horrors of slavery, the ruthless exploitation and inhumanity of the institution. The paternalistic argument, however, arose again, and has not completely died out. Those sad notions returned to the academic landscape in dramatic fashion with the publication of Fogel and Engerman, *Time on the Cross*, and the publications of Eugene Genovese who, in his books *Roll Jordan Roll* and in *The World the Slavemasters Made*, championed a new paternalism. Genovese admired the slave owner, George Fitzhugh, and he found much favor in the work of Phillips. Whatever the enslaved Africans managed to accomplish, in the minds of the paternalist historians, was largely with the assistance of "kind and gentle masters," rather than through their own abilities to circumvent the system.

Paternalism was a far cry from the day-to-day reality of black life in the slave South. For enslaved Africans their workday began at sunup and lasted until sunset. If you were late to the fields, the overseer's lash was waiting. After working in the fields, the slaves had to care for livestock, put away tools, cooked meals, and did repair work around the plantation before the horn sounded for bed. Cotton planting started in March or early April. Cotton picking lasted from August to Christmas. During the so-called slack period the slaves cleared forest land, built fences, repaired barns, milked cows, hoed wheat, chopped wood, and performed an assortment of other daily tasks. The average work day for the slave was 18 hours.

There was no escaping the institution and its control. Any discussion about the house Negro versus the lot of the field hand need not posit any great distinctions, because they were both slaves. In many respects while the field hand was doing the arduous work outdoors, the blacks in the big house, men and women, were doing drudgery in doors. Their situation, many times, was more precarious because they worked under the constant watchful eyes of the slave master and mistress. For any failure they were immediately punished, including those African women who were nurse maids and who breast fed the slave master's own white infants. You might think that in that relationship, nevertheless, was planted the seeds for the eventual demise of the institution of slavery. When a child slave was given to the child of the master, you might think that there was a bonding that evolved and a humanizing on the part of the young white master. If it had been, it was difficult to understand how the institution could last as long as it did. What the young white was learning, by being given this prize of his or her own slave at an early age, was that there were differences and that this African black was not a person, but your property to do your bidding and upon which to learn well the art of young master; that was, the directing, controlling, ordering, and making obedient your black possession. House blacks were frequently flogged for the smallest mistake as Lewis Clarke recalled in his slave narrative. Even on the question of quality of food, it varied in the big house. In general the house servants ate better than the field hands. They were all slaves, however. On the plantations the diets were basically enough to keep the Africans alive. The diet usually consisted of fats and poor quality meats, barely enough to sustain life. We know from the work of Leslie Owens, *This Species of Property*, that blacks did their best to supplement their meager diets with the bounty from little gardens, if they were fortunate enough to have permission to have a garden and to keep the produce from it for themselves. They also used discarded meats and fats, combining them with greens from the garden, and using their creative culinary skills to make dishes that did more than simply sustain life but that tasted good as well. Their cooking in the slave quarters, as well as in the big house, drew from the African tradition of using spices and available ingredients to create delectable dishes. These innovative initiatives gave rise to what became southern cuisine, which others would blatantly lay claim to without mention of its African creators. Yet, right there on those plantations, the enslaved Africans demonstrated on a daily basis their mastery of culinary techniques and food preparation that made dining at the big house the centerpiece of southern gracious living and entertaining for wealthy whites.

The slaves' housing was deplorable. Plantation after plantation housed the entire slave family in a single-room shack. One plantation, for example, had 180 slaves and 18 cabins. It does not take a mathematician to compute what that meant, given that the average size of each cabin was 12' x 19.' To have men, women and children crammed into such squalid confines was a disgrace to humanity. The slaves' pleading fell on deaf ears. After all, they were not seen as people but as beasts of burden who were entitled, at best, to only the minimal necessities to sustain life.

African folk sought first not to be Americans but to be free human beings. America to them was a graveyard, the place that kept them enslaved. There was no early goal on their part to unite with it; the dream was to, somehow, survive it and to, hopefully, return to Africa. They constantly sought their freedom. The number of slave runaways was an ever-increasing occurrence. There were at least twenty to forty cases of runaways reported in the South each day. Punishment for attempting to runaway was severe. Moses Roper, determined to gain his freedom, received lashes from his owner on a regular basis for his repeated attempts to escape. Despite the punishment, he continued his escape efforts and was finally successful.

Fogel and Engerman minimized the inhumanity of the institution of slavery in their zeal to apply the magic of econometrics and the computer. They attempted to quantify even the numbers of lashes that slaves received on a regular basis, and concluded that it was much smaller than historians originally believed. It was historian Herbert Gutman who set them right in very plain language. Gutman, who later wrote the monumental book, *The Black Family in Slavery and Freedom*, told Fogel and Engerman at a historical conference that the idea of minimizing or counting the number of lashes was foolishness and suggested to the authors that they allow him to give them each ten lashes "well laid" on their backs and twenty lightly applied, and for them to then offer their assessment of which punishment was the worst. Only the Eurocentric lack of consciousness and sensitivity could have allowed scholars to think for one moment that punishment could be quantified or made a theoretical abstract that could be imputed into a computer to spew forth numbers that would yield a true sense of slavery in America. The result of Fogel and Engerman's flawed thesis was an erroneous calculation and insensitive portrait of the institution of slavery and the people who suffered under it.

Most fascinating and remarkable was that blacks survived the peculiar institution at all. Even the church was no friend of Africans. Ministers routinely geared their sermons to support slavery. It was commonplace that where Africans were allowed to attend service, usually standing in the segregated section at the back, one could count on the minister's sermon to be punctuated with strong doses of "obey thy master." For that small number of white southern ministers who did not embrace the pro-slavery position, and the even smaller group who thought slavery wrong, among them the Reverend J. Thornwell, they were forced to leave the South or risk losing their lives.

Africans did everything possible to maintain their human dignity and to survive bondage. The slave family suffered. Daniel Patrick Moynihan argued in the *Moynihan Report* in the 1960s that slavery destroyed the black family, and that seeds of that destruction carried into the contemporary urban era. The notion that slavery planted the seeds for the continued deterioration of the black family was not a far flung idea. Many slaves did not want to marry. Moses Grandy told of the anguish of being a black male slave and having to stand by and watch his wife flogged. Imagine what it was like to have been a slave woman and know that at the slightest whim of the master you would have to prostitute yourself to his every wish. Your sexuality belonged to him. Imagine the psychological impact this must have had on her, her husband, and their children. No woman wanted to watch her husband flogged and belittled. What family could stand by without dying inside to watch their daughters taken by the slave master or relatives or friends of the master who he had decided to make more comfortable through the night by providing "a belly warmer." So it was understandable that many slaves on the plantation, when given the option, chose not to have a family. The family, at one level, provided some semblance of normalcy and life for the Africans. At another level it helped stabilize the institution of slavery, making it less likely for slaves to run away or to revolt. Kunta Kinte in Alex Haley's *Roots* was defiant and constantly sought to escape. After his marriage, he no longer attempted to flee because it meant leaving behind his wife and children. Many plantations were opposed to Africans having families while others encouraged it because of the economic stability the institution of marriage helped to enforce.

Have African Americans completely overcome that legacy? One wonders today if Moynihan may have offered a grain of truth back then, although his data was incorrect. The legacy of slavery and its impact may have been more negative than positive in the lessons of family under bondage. The legacy of negatives planted then when combined with the current struggles in the black community, and post-1980 trend in American society in general to be self absorbed, may help us to put into proper perspective why the African-American family suffers horrendously today. Why the rampant increase of teenage pregnancy, irresponsible fathers, and births out of wedlock? The legacy of slavery was long and deep. Also, we need to appreciate how it was possible to have successful black families despite the institution of slavery and its legacy. It speaks eloquently to the remarkable humanity, spirit, courage, and love of African people that there were compassionate and positive black families at all given the goals of slavery.[6]

THE CULTURE OF SURVIVAL

Africans fought to survive the institution of enslavement with all their creative ability, intelligence, and limited power. The power of the heart, the mind, the spirit, the soul, was something not easily defeated. African traditions, memory, and connectedness transcended time, space and oceans. Their rekindled culture and mores sustained them under the dreadful onslaught. Despite life under the peculiar institution, aspects and components of the African way of life and traditions were retained. Those traditions were evident in the practices of Africans in their daily routines on the plantation and within the slave quarters. Although Western religion was forced upon them, they took it, reworked it, blended it, and gave it an African twist and perspective. As Margaret Washington Creel demonstrated in her book, *A Peculiar People*, and Mbiti in his, *African Religions and Philosophy*, the enslaved Africans looked to their roots and self for sustenance. They prayed in ways faithful to their homeland tradition of "call and response," shouting, the repeated motif, sloganeering and rhyming, and Africanized the stories of the *Bible*. The question, of course, was did religion under slavery free the mind and soul or did it, by affording relief, help the slave to better accept bondage? Not debatable was that many of the Africans found solace and strength in their deeply held beliefs, traditions, and culture.

In dance, African traditions readily survived. Forced aboard slave ships, enslaved Africans beat out rhythms with their feet on deck as exercise; rhythms that became the foundation to the slave jig and later developed into the art of tap dancing. The square dance had its roots in Africa; yet one thinks of it as a country-western creation. Long before they were brought to America, Africans engaged in ring dances, call and response, a type of dosey-doe, exchanging of partners with circular movements. The Charleston, a dance that gained popularity in the 1920s, can be traced back to plantation days and to its origins in West Africa, with its two and three step forward and kick, two and three steps backward and kick.

Blacks continued to create despite an American society that exploited them for all that they produced and gave them credit for nothing. The music that would become the hallmark of America had its origins in Africa. The ring shouts and field hollers were African traditions. These music forms carried over and through slavery, and gave birth to the blues, gospel, jazz, soul, rock n' roll, and rap. De Crevecoeur wrote a long time ago that the slaves' cultural creations were truly American. That too was patently untrue. Their creations were not truly American. The music was African from the beginning and then blended with the American experience.

The holding of funerals at night was an African tradition as well. The African practice of the *wake* continued during slavery and beyond, as did the tradition of the *repast* after the burial, which included food, drink, and often music in a joyous tribute to the dearly departed. The Africanisms carried through in New Orleans, the somber musical procession to the graveyard, and then the return with upbeat music, singing, dancing, and good food in memory of the deceased. That style of celebration of life was African and reflected a connectedness that transcended distance and time.

The music was the elixir of life. Westerners were baffled by African music. They called it uncivilized. When early European travelers heard the music in Africa they described it as being unsophisticated. They talked about African drumming as possibly a primitive mode of communications. Actually, the drumming was tonal and a phonetic reproduction of words. The drums could speak far beyond the simplistic dot-dash-dot symbolic of the later Morse code. The superb quality of the African music and musicianship were denied and unappreciated by the insensitive and untutored European ear, unable or unwilling to discern the diatonic scale differences and polyphonic and polyrhythmically syncopated sounds of African music when heard on the continent or when emanating from the slave quarters of the New World. It was a lively musical response, rhythmic beats and words that could also be used to signify on the master without him knowing it. African music was educational. The singing of lyrics and riddles and folktales were pregnant with history. Through their music, enslaved Africans passed on their heritage despite the nation's and the peculiar institution's efforts to thwart it. Enslaved Africans made their instruments speak, speak intelligently with emotion. These traditions were expressed in the music of later generations of African-American musicians such as Ma Rainey, Bessie Smith, Huey Ledbetter, Louis Armstrong, Chick Webb, Bunk Green, Ornette Coleman, and Charlie Parker. They, and others like them, played and performed with such depth and sensitivity that listeners could feel their musical expressions. Bob Marley's tune, "Slave Driver" spoke an historical narrative. Saxophonist Gary Bartz for many years began performances with "'No Mo the Magic Stick," in the African tradition of first cleansing the area of evil spirits. Michael Larouie's wonderful recreation of American Negro slave songs recaptured the African musical tradition. African instruments survived: the African flutes, bulafo or xylophone, banjar (banjo), the organ (invented by ancient Egyptians), various horns and, of course, drums. The musical riff and vamp were African in origin. The African motif and holler survived in the musical artistry of Leon Thomas and the innovative soul stylings of Aretha Franklin, Al Green, Gil Scott Herron, and others who, in their performances and recordings, built upon African techniques and sounds established hundreds and thousands of years earlier. Rap is nothing new. People of African descent all through their history have told stories in music, in lyrics, in words. Rhyming (or rapping) was practiced by African Griots and survived the institution of slavery.

Others have laid claim to black folks' music. African-derived music has, over time, been commandeered, redistributed, redefined, and appropriated to suggest a non-black, non-African origin. We were told that rock n' roll was the creation of Elvis Presley, its "king." White America prefers to ignore that Elvis frequented Beale Street in Memphis to hear Fats Domino, Little Richard, Bo Diddley and the other true creators of what the music industry took and called its own, and defined the black artists-creators as only peripheral. African Americans have become less a presence even in jazz, another great music form which they originated. Black gospel was at one time just that; it has recently been appropriated and redefined into the more nebulous and open categorization of "gospel" that increased the number of non-black practitioners of it and decreased the number of black gospelers. White artists who were peddling a black sound were a growing breed in the recording and entertainment industry, as demonstrated annually at the Grammy Awards. Today is literally open season on African/black music. On television commercials we routinely hear popular Motown sounds from the Sixties being sung by whites while hardly a black artist is to be found. We can only hope that the music's original creators were receiving royalties.

Throughout slavery and on into modern times, African music was improvisational and innovative. The music called for response and creativity on the spot; a tradition exemplified in jazz and "playing the dozens." Can you up me one, can you top me, can you build on what I have just created? That on-the-edge innovating and one-up-manship were the hallmarks of the *dozens* and the African way of poking fun. How quick were you in responding to what was just said about you? Was your reply equally smart and creative such as: "You have big feet. You could use them for boats." "Yeah, that's okay. At least I can afford new shoes to cover mine. What's your excuse?" The *dozens*, the music, the religious practices were components of cultural retention and survival skills that enabled Africans to weather the miseries of enslavement. Psychological resilience and cleverness were the others.[7]

There was no denying that slavery had a deep psychological affect on the slaves. Students of the history of slavery debated the issue of the slave personality and whether the dominant personality type was that of the Sambo: that the enslaved Africans internalized their condition and became complete slaves. The majority type in terms of slave personality and their actions and reactions actually fell into a middle range. Long before historians attempted a corrective to the *Sambo thesis*, social psychologists offered categorization and a more sophisticated analysis of *reaction formation* with their descriptions of the *reaffirmative traditionalist*, the *compensatory emergentist* [the Samboes], and, the majority type, the *pluralist*. Most people in their reaction formations and personality types fall in the middle category. Human beings choose to be free rather than slave. When the opportunity presented itself, enslaved Africans chose freedom. They tried constantly to escape. Slave narratives provide insight into the views and perspectives of blacks in bondage on plantations, revealing that most had not fully accepted their status. The seemingly loyal house slaves fled over the border to freedom when the time and opportunity was right. There was a difference between being enslaved and succumbing to enslavement. There was no denying the dreadful impact and lingering legacy of hundreds of years of bondage on the African-American psychic, the bad habits that were formed and would have to be corrected, and yes, the negatives instilled regarding self pride and human worth; negatives that would have to be unlearned.

Today we still find many blacks who, in an earlier era, would have been defined as Samboes. Some of these blacks write within the field of the black experience. The Samboes prove themselves ever present on questions of multiculturalism and other heated issues; among them were the academic lackeys who could not wait to bow. Void of appreciation of the past and lacking sound grounding in their history, these individuals take the course of least resistance and greater personal reward. Thus, they were without the consciousness that could enable them to grasp the best course for African Americans. The Samboes of slavery times, like the academic toadies of the present day, do not serve the best interests of black folk. They do black America harm because they were given voice and claimed expertise on the issues. Rather than speaking frankly, honestly, and without apology, they tend to soften their remarks, tame their observations either willingly or unconsciously, and the result is a muddled picture that no longer raises the major issue of racism but settles to blame class and caste differences or faults affirmative action programs or alleged inherent deficiencies in the black race and family as responsible for the African-American condition.

The heart of black America's dilemma lies in the history of volatile race relations. Salvation would come when racism no longer exists. To reach that point the legacy of slavery must be fully grasped. For the enslaved Africans the American nation was no land of opportunity. Brought by force to the New World black folk had to use all of their creative powers to survive the American nightmare.[8]

TRYING JUST TO BE FREE, NOT AN AMERICAN

For nearly four hundred years the history of people of African descent in America has been one of a struggle for freedom. The historical legacy of slavery was the pillar of the relationship between blacks and the larger American society. Enslaved Africans were not brought to the New World to be equal partners in the *American Dream*. They were to be the fuel for others' dreams of life, liberty, and the pursuit of happiness, especially wealth. Black folk made every conceivable effort to sever themselves from the shackles of the American nightmare. Hence, slave revolts were constant occurrences. There were hundreds of revolts. In the Stono Rebellion of 1739, in South Carolina, slaves killed two guards in a warehouse. After securing arms they then attempted to liberate their fellow Africans in the area. The uprising was squashed after several days of fighting. Forty blacks and thirty whites were killed. There was Gabriel Prosser's planned insurrection of 1800; Denmark Vessey's in 1822 in South Carolina; Nat Turner's desperate revolt in 1831 in Virginia. One hundred enslaved Africans were killed in the Turner revolt.

Enslaved Africans in these rebellions, these revolts, were not trying to be Americans. They were trying to free themselves; they were attempting to regain the basic right of freedom that America had taken from them. Blacks were rebelling intellectually as well. African people were involuntary participants in the American experiment and the cultivation of the New World. It should have been no surprise when revolts emerged in every territory blacks were enslaved, including throughout Latin America and the Caribbean.

The Amistad Slave Revolt was a poignant example of Africans' passionate struggle against slavery and their all-consuming desire to return home to Africa. In 1839 a group of Africans, who had been taken into slavery and were being transported in the Spanish ship Amistad (which in Spanish, sardonically, means liberty), rebelled along the Cuban coast. They killed the slave ship's captain and most of his small crew, took command of the vessel and tried to set sail back to Africa. They were caught off the coast of New England and imprisoned in Connecticut to await trial on charges of "mutiny" and murder.

The trial of the Amistad Africans became a rallying cry for the abolitionist movement. An Amistad committee was formed with Lewis Tappan, a wealthy New York merchant, and Simon Jocelyn, a New Haven clergyman, and the Reverend Joshua Leavitt. They rightly saw this case as a moral cry, an issue of human and natural rights. Roger Sherman Baldwin, famed attorney, was appointed to defend the Amistad captives, and he did an able job providing persuasive clarification that the Africans had been taken illegally into slavery and thus were not property at the time of their revolt because transporting Africans to Cuba for sale into slavery after 1820 was in violation of the treaty between Spain and England. The charges of murder and mutiny were dropped in the lower courts; the only issue remaining was that of salvage rights for the white lieutenant, Gedney, and his crew, which had retaken the Amistad and brought it to the harbor of New London, Connecticut, in August of 1839.

This was a curiously complicated legal case in which Gedney and his group claimed salvage rights. Judge Thompson, who presided in the local court, believed that these were issues that would have to be settled in the U.S. district court. The trial began in January 1840 and ended with Judge Judson of the district court ruling in favor of the Africans. Partial salvage rights over the ship and its other cargo were awarded to Lieutenant Gedney and his crew. However, national and international issues were involved: the South, the Van Buren presidential administration and his reelection hopes, the Spanish government and diplomatic concerns, and abolition. The verdict was appealed. On February 22, 1841, the case was brought before the Supreme Court of the United States. John Quincy Adams and Roger Sherman Baldwin argued for the defense. They cited natural law and contended that the Amistad captives were not slaves. Attorney General Gilpin prosecuted. Gilpin's line of argument was fascinating, if not bizarre, in that it was instructive on how the world in some quarters could simultaneously view Africans as people but in others view them simply as property. Gilpin argued that the Amistad Africans were both pirates and property and that they should be found guilty of illegal seizure because the property that they took was "themselves," and that they should be returned to Spain, their rightful owners. In other words, the Amistad Africans, Gilpin contended, were guilty of stealing themselves. On March 9, 1841, the U.S. Supreme Court rendered its verdict, freeing the Amistad Africans. This was no recognition of inalienable rights or a condemnation of enslaving African people. This was a decision based on "property rights" and international agreements. The Amistad Africans were freed because of the treaty between Spain and England which made the slave trade at this point illegal. The Africans had been taken illegally and thus were not officially property. Had there been no treaty they, indeed, would have been seen as the lawful property of Spain and thereby returned.

The Amistad decision had a momentous impact. It was cited in at least thirty-two other decisions before the end of the nineteenth century. Most of these cases involved trade agreements between European nations and disputes over maritime law and salvage rights. The Amistad case was seen by the courts as primarily a property dispute, not unlike the reasoning that the Supreme Court later applied in the 1857 Dred Scott case. The petition for freedom of the enslaved African Dred Scott was rejected because he was deemed to be property and thus not recognized by the framers of the *Constitution* nor provided for in that salient document as a human being with individual rights. A horse, a cow, a mule, a house, had no rights; only their owners did. The Amistad case at least had worked to the benefit of the African captives who were set free. Many of them eventually were returned to Africa.

There was a uniqueness to the Amistad incident but also a wide commonalty as there were many slave revolts and slave ship insurrections. Before the Amistad, there were hundreds of rebellions on board slave vessels, as blacks were constantly and consistently fighting for their freedom. Africans revolted, for example on board the Albion, 1699; the Tyger, 1703; the Ann, 1717; the Ginea, 1730; the Dolphin, 1735; the Ann (again), 1750; the Hope, 1764; the Thames, 1776; the Nancy, 1793; the Charleston, 1793; the Thames (again), 1797; the Thomas, 1797; the Thomas (again), 1799; the Nancy (again), 1807; the L' Estrella, 1829. On the Robert in 1721 a cargo of Africans from Sierra Leone led by Tomba attempted to overpower their captors. Tomba formed a *poro* below deck. It was likely that Cinque, a Mande from Sierra Leone, and the leader of the Amistad slave revolt, did the same thing. The *poro,* a secret society with chosen leadership, was a Mande tradition in Sierra Leone. Tomba used a woman slave, who had the freedom of the ship, to alert them to when the time was right. They jumped the crew when most of them were asleep. Tomba personally killed at least two of the crew. His companions killed at least two others. The remainder of the ship's crew, however, were awakened and able to arm themselves and put down the rebellion. Captain Harding took incredibly cruel revenge on the insurrectionaries. As recorded in Donnan's *Documents of the History of the Slave Trade*: "Captain Harding weighing the stoutness and worth of the two slaves, did as in other countries they do by rogues of dignity, ship and scarify them only; while three other, abettors, but not actors, nor of strength for it, be sentenced to cruel deaths; making them first eat of heart and liver of one of them killed. The woman he hoisted up by the thumbs, whipp'd, and slashed her with knifes, before the other slaves till she died."

Slave ship revolts did not stop with the Amistad incident. In 1841 a revolt occurred aboard the Creole. One hundred and thirty-one enslaved blacks were being transported from Richmond, Virginia to New Orleans, Louisiana on the ship Creole. The slave trading journey was never completed. Led by Madison Washington and Ben Blacksmith, the blacks engineered a successful insurrection and made their way to the relative safety of the British colony in Nassau. With the assistance of their fellow Africans on that island, and despite the many American protests, the temporary black masters of the Creole completed their journey and were never returned to slavery. The slaves landed the Creole in Nassau harbor, where they were under the protection of British law. The United States demanded their return, but Great Britain refused to surrender them on the grounds that a slave was free as soon as he set foot on British soil. In this case, which had many reverberations in Congress, Great Britain cited, as precedence and support, the U.S. Supreme Court's decision in the Amistad case.

Africans in America and throughout the world were intellectually and spiritually tied to the Amistad captives and their plight. Blacks in the United States identified with them and discussed the issues continuously. The black community had its own voice. The subject was written about by some of those blacks in *The Emancipator*, a white abolitionist paper, as well as in their own newspaper, *The Colored American*. Blacks from numerous states throughout the country sent letters of congratulations and thanks to John Quincy Adams. Ohio blacks gave him great praise. In meeting halls in the Negro community in Philadelphia they discussed the issues constantly. Two black teachers, Henry Wilson and James Wilson, accompanied the thirty-five Mendians on their voyage home to Africa. Blacks formed the Mende Support Committee. Fund-raisers were held at Negro churches and black women were particularly active in Philadelphia in supporting the cause. In Hartford, Connecticut, the effort to help was supported by the Union Missionary Society, an organization founded by Africans in Hartford on August 18, 1841.

When the American Missionary Society and the Union Missionary Society called a meeting in support of the Amistad returnees, or repatriates, black delegates came from Massachusetts, Rhode Island, New York, and Pennsylvania. Energetic support came from black leaders such as James W.C. Pennington of New Haven and Hartford, Amos Beamon, Theodore Wright, Charles Ray, and James Cornish.[9]

Blacks were doing everything they could to gain their freedom. Forget being an American, they simply wanted to be free human beings. This was their primary concern. They attacked the evils of slavery with determined intellectual outpouring. Black intellectuals saw themselves as race men and women. In this sense they were perhaps more emancipationists than abolitionists, more revolutionists than revolutionaries. Individuals like Frederick Douglass, Alexander Crummel, and James W.C. Pennington, William Cooper Nell, William Wells Brown, Sojourner Truth, for example, did not bear arms to end slavery. They were intellectual architects on the evils of slavery and podium champions for the cause of freedom. Whereas individuals like Harriet Tubman, John M. Langston, Henry Highland Garnet, David Walker, were much more abolitionists and revolutionaries in the sense of their being willing to use any and all means to free their brothers and sisters enslaved in the South.

Black intellectuals objected to the *Fugitive Slave Act* of 1793, *Prigg v. Pennsylvania* in 1842, the *Compromise of 1850*, the *Dred Scott Decision* of 1857, and every act before and since which declared blacks to be less than human beings, slaves and property in the land of "liberty for all." Blacks had no rights. A master did not have to obtain a warrant to seize his slave even if that individual had escaped into a free state. By 1800, and throughout the mid-nineteenth century, judges routinely issued certificates of repossession similar to those in modern age for repossessing an automobile. A slave master was "legally" entitled to regain possession of his property. If the slave had escaped to a free state, he or she was still property and must be returned to his or her proper "owner" — an added moral indignation to blacks and whites who opposed the dreaded peculiar institution. Assisting runaways became very popular because it was a way to work for the destruction of the institution of slavery and what it stood for without bloodying one's hands with actual violence.

Blacks and sympathetic whites worked together in the quest to aid the runaways through the *Underground Railroad*. If an escapee had made the right contacts, he or she was aided in the flight to freedom by operators in the underground throughout Ohio, New York,

Pennsylvania, and the border states. The slaves trusted these daring compatriots. Some black conductors were former slaves. The most heroic of all of these was, without a doubt, Harriet Tubman, who made repeated trips into the slave quarters of Maryland and elsewhere to lead her fellow Africans to freedom. So daring and successful was she that rewards of up to ten thousand dollars were placed on Harriet Tubman, dead or alive. Leonard A. Grimes was another of these daring conductors speeding the slaves to freedom as were George Burrills of Illinois, William Luckas in Ohio, John Jones in New York, Elizabeth Barnes of Virginia, Harriet Jacobs and hundreds more like them. Blacks took any risk to obtain their freedom. It was worth it if freedom could be had. Henry "Box" Brown became a household word. This innovative enslaved African secured the right size crate and correct postage and mailed himself to freedom in a free state.

The Vigilance Committee aided the fugitives and provided them with food and shelter, purchased clothes for them, gave them enough money to sustain them for a period of time, arranged work, and, in short, helped them to survive in the free state. Blacks played major roles in these efforts. The most noted of these black vigilance committees aiding the cause of black freedom was the Boston Vigilance Committee and the New York Committee of Vigilance; the latter founded in 1835 by David Ruggles. Ruggles served as the committee's secretary and general agent. He put much of his own money back into the organization. The success of that committee was a result of Ruggles's hard work, courage, determination, and dedication. When Frederick Douglass successfully escaped to the North, it was Ruggles who befriended him and helped to provide for his needs. Ruggles also introduced Douglass to Anna Murray, who became Douglass's first wife. Fighting for the cause of African freedom, dedicated individuals such as Ruggles continued the struggle against all odds.

There were problems within the abolitionist movement and blacks faced the threat of slave catchers and those in the North who were friendly to southern slavery. They also had to contend with informants in their own midst. Benjamin Quarles wrote of the "tell-tell" Negroes whose loyalties, like those of the Sambo of the slave plantation, were with the slave masters and against their own kind. The black abolitionists had a unique way of dealing with them. Whenever tell-tell Negro informants were identified, their names were printed in the Negro press and, interestingly enough, be it in Baltimore, Cincinnati, New York City or Pittsburgh, these Samboes often mysteriously disappeared. Martin Delany, in the *Pittsburgh Mystery,* considered identifying tell-tell Negroes a righteous mission, charging them with treason to the black race. Black abolitionists put their lives on the line, disobeyed the laws, and faced prison terms and death in their struggle to help free their race.

The opposition was fierce. In the North, black abolitionists found themselves up against organized anti-abolitionist forces. It has been generally accepted that anti-abolitionists were a minority of uneducated lower-class whites who did not have the higher moral convictions of their countrymen. The work of Leonard Richards, in *Gentlemen of Property and Standing*, and the work of others, demonstrated that anti-abolitionism in the North was much more widespread, that these were not just lower-class but middle and upper-class individuals who were against abolition. They were particularly against white abolitionists. It was anti-abolitionist forces who killed Elijah Lovejoy in Alton, Illinois in 1837. It was the anti-abolitionist forces who attacked William Lloyd Garrison and dragged him through the streets of Boston.

Why such hostility in the words and deeds of the anti-abolitionists? The answer centers on racial fears. The anti-abolitionists were anti amalgamation. This question and issue divided even the abolitionists' ranks. Garrisonian abolitionists divided on the question of amalgamation. Even for those who could support an end to slavery, the question became: What would be done with the blacks once they gained their freedom? Would these free blacks live among the larger society as equals? Would they be employed as wage earners? Would they become competitors in the market place? Could they possibly live next door to whites? Would they eventually try to marry into white families? Here was the ancient bugaboo being brought to light again, that ultimate fear of race, the anti-multiracialism of American society. Perhaps the colonization movement was right in their belief that once blacks were free they would be better off repatriated back to Africa because America could never accept them as equals. In this regard, Thomas Jefferson, James Madison, Bushrod Washington, and other member advocates of the American Colonization Society may very well have been right in understanding the depths and the impenetrability of the nation's hatred and fear of blacks. Given such attitudes it should not be surprising that there existed within the black abolitionist ranks and that of their supporters the willingness to defend themselves and employ violence to hasten the end to slavery. John M. Langston, an early black nationalist and abolitionist, after the infamous *Prigg Decision* of 1842, became a much firmer supporter of black separatism and self defense. Langston named his daughter Cinque after the leader of the Amistad revolt. A constant factor in Henry Highland Garnet's life was his vivid memory of his parents fleeing slave catchers. In Garnet's 1843 address at the first National Negro Conference he talked about the eventual need for violence, if that were the only means to end slavery. He was becoming more and more convinced that it would take violence to end the dreaded institution. David Walker made a similar revelation back in 1839 and in his published *Appeal*. This North Carolinian free black, who had moved to Boston, urged his fellow race members to stand up, shirk off submissiveness, and fight for freedom.[10]

IV

OUTRIGHT VIOLENCE

PARALLELS TO MODERN BLACK PROTEST

It is in the context of the growing impatience with slavery that we need to examine and to appreciate the legacy of John Brown and the parallels and linkages between him and the modern black protest movement. John Brown is the only white who today still receives universal respect in the black community as a true race hero. Even Abraham Lincoln has fallen on hard times in the African-American community and has been severely criticized for his waffling on the issue of emancipation for the sake of Union and to placating the border states. There has been no such mixed opinion on John Brown. In an edited volume, *Blacks on John Brown*, Benjamin Quarles traced the importance of Brown as an icon and symbol to blacks from the 1850s through the modern era. Why has John Brown and the legacy and image of him remained firmly intact among black folk? The answer to that is that John Brown saw black people as members of the human family. He did not vacillate on the question that blacks belonged to the human race and had inalienable rights, and were thus, as Brown argued, entitled to be treated as such. Slavery was a moral wrong that had to be ended at any cost. He fought and died for that belief without equivocation. Thus, blacks do not equivocate in their view of him.

There was an ideological tie between John Brown and the modern Civil Rights Movement that was based upon a non convoluted dichotomy: thought and action; principle and practice. As Kwame Nkrumah, the leader of Ghana, often invoked: "Thought without action is meaningless." John Brown embodied that belief. He was a man of all times, a person of conviction and intolerant of the injustices and hypocrisies of American society. He was a social critic, an activist whose actions transcended time. In a real sense he was an embodiment of the double consciousness that W.E.B. Du Bois spoke of in *Souls of Black Folk*, in that he was absolutely intolerant of the contradictions in American society, the peculiar duality, as Martin Luther King, Jr. would call it, of the simultaneous existence in the nation of democracy and racism or democracy and slavery. An absolute adherent to equality, Brown was a frequent visitor to the home of blacks and vice versa. He treated them as equals and socialized with them in private and public.

While one never wants to condone violence, Brown understood that America itself was born of violence; a history of violence that the nation would forever deny. The Indian wars and annihilation of the native population, the enslaving of Africans, and the American Revolution, demonstrated the country's embrace of the use of force. Violence was as American as apple pie. Brown understood this and believed that there were worthwhile issues for which one must fight and die. He admired people who stood tall like Harriet Tubman who he praised for her bravery and good work with the *Underground Railroad*. He pushed the abolitionist movement. He would not settle for "moral suasion" like William Lloyd Garrison and others whom he described as full of "talk, talk, talk." The impact of John Brown on Henry Highland Garnet and other black abolitionists including Frederick Douglass was profound. He helped to radicalize them. After a couple of meetings with Brown, Frederick Douglass lost his faith in moral suasion as the only tactic to bring about an end to slavery. Douglass wrote: "Brown is in sympathy a black man, and as deeply interested in our cause as though his own soul had been pierced with the iron of slavery."[1]

Brown was also important to the twentieth-century Civil Rights Movement. W.E.B Du Bois and followers held the second meeting of the Niagara Movement in Harper's Ferry, Virginia, in 1906. They walked barefoot through the grass there and in a symbolic and intellectual sense connected with John Brown's revolt at Harper's Ferry half a century earlier. The resolution adopted by the members of the Niagara Movement at their meeting, which Du Bois wrote, was illustrative: "We do not believe in violence, neither in the despised violence of the raid nor the lauded violence of the soldier, nor the barbarous violence of the mob; but we do believe in John Brown, in that incarnate spirit of justice, that hatred of a lie, that willingness to sacrifice money, reputation, and life itself on the altar of right. And here on the scene of John Brown's martyrdom, we reconsecrate ourselves, our honor, our property to the final emancipation of the race which John Brown died to make free." Note the "final emancipation of the race." These were powerful words, meaningful words. Blacks saw in the days of slavery as they did throughout Du Bois's era and that of the Niagara Movement and founding of the NAACP in 1909 that the elevation of the race would continue to be a long and hard struggle in America. John Brown had another tie to the NAACP in that Du Bois and Oswald Garrision Villard, the great grandson of William Lloyd Garrison and one of the founding members of the NAACP along with Du Bois, were working on biographies of him at the same time. Du Bois, in characteristic arrogant fashion, questioned Villard directly as to why he was bothering to write a biography of John Brown since he too was engaged in the same task and would produce the superior monograph. Du Bois's biography of Brown was published in 1909 and Villard's in 1910. Both authors made important contributions to the understanding of Brown's legacy.

John Brown left a legacy from which the full spectrum of civil rights activists and black leaders could draw. Ida B. Wells Barnett and Monroe Trotter withdrew from the new NAACP because they believed that you could not trust an organization geared to help blacks but largely run by whites, unless the whites were reincarnations of John Brown. Black nationalists from Martin Delany to Marcus Garvey drew strength from John Brown. Garvey, the paramount black separatist leader of the 20th century, made it clear time and again that he had no desire to be involved with white people, unless they were of the temperament and fighting spirit of John Brown. When Garvey was imprisoned in 1927 as a result of the U.S. government's efforts against him, Dean Kelly Miller of Howard University, a moderate black leader, wrote in defense of Garvey: "It is a dangerous principle to impose legal punishment upon men for their belief rather than for their behavior. This trick is as old as political cunning and chicanery. Did they not treat Socrates, Jesus and John Brown so?"

Like Brown, many of the radical black leaders did not dismiss violence or the rhetoric of it as a tool in the civil rights struggle. Brown demonstrated the usefulness of violence as a vehicle for social change in the raid at Pottawatomie, Kansas, and his most famous assault at Harper's Ferry, Virginia. Malcolm X liked to say that the litmus test for white radicals was whether or not they were like John Brown. "Who have you killed," Malcolm asked a white liberal and would-be supporter? For Malcolm, John Brown had been the genuine personification of "By Any Means Necessary." As Malcolm said: "So when you want to know good white folks in history where black people are concerned, go read the history of John Brown. That was what I call a white liberal. But those other kind, they are questionable. So if we need white allies in this country, we don't need those kind who compromise. We don't need those kind who encourage us to be polite, responsible, you know. We don't need those kind who give us that kind of advice. We don't need those kind who tell us how to be patient. No, if we need some white allies, we need the kind that John Brown was or we don't need you." Brown prodded the public consciousness about the use of violence by those in power to maintain their hegemony. He talked about the brutality of slavery and how the slave master violated the slave woman and the black family. "Their brutal aggression must be resisted," said Brown. Brutality against the Civil Rights Movement—dogs, high pressure water hoses, brutal beatings of men, women and youngsters, the use of cattle prods, the killing of Medgar Evers, Emmett Till, the bombing of black churches and murder of children, the assassination of Martin Luther King, Jr., and many other atrocities—were wanton acts of naked violence aimed at halting the Civil Rights Movement and keeping blacks in their place. The rhetoric of violence by some black leaders of the modern civil rights struggle should be seen in that context. From Malcolm X to H. Rap Brown, the threat of blacks fighting back had its advantages. H. Rap Brown's advocacy of violence often drew press coverage and hence further attention to the cause. In a protest against the racial practices of the New York Athletic Club and Madison Square Garden, Rap Brown was asked by reporters what should be done if individuals crossed the picket line? His response: "The Garden should be blown up!" Malcolm's rhetoric of implied violence in retaliation against racism was helpful to Martin Luther King's more moderate activism. Malcolm knew this and used it effectively. When King was jailed in Selma in 1964, Malcolm went down to Alabama and spoke. His presence and words were quite helpful, as Coretta Scott King later recalled. She attested that Malcolm told her that he "wanted to help. He wanted to present an alternative; that it might be easier for whites to accept Martin's proposal after hearing him." Malcolm understood that his militancy helped to make the comparatively more moderate reform demands of King and the Southern Christian Leadership Conference an attractive alternative to the white power structure as opposed to an all-out race war and a nation in flames.[2]

Black militants of the 1960s often invoked the name of John Brown. Huey P. Newton, Bobby Seale, Eldridge Cleaver, and other leaders of the Black Panther Party for Self-Defense, injected the name of John Brown into their speeches and discussions with party and community members, explaining that the use of violence was valid, legitimate, and necessary to defend the black community and to advance the goals of the African-American struggle. Violence, in their minds, was also important for political leverage. Perhaps the point was proven in the riots of the 1960s. Beyond the many negatives of the riots, there were unacknowledged positive results. The report of the Kerner Commission and the McCone Commission report on the Watts Riots linked the violent outbursts to the sad state of race relations and lack of opportunities for blacks. The commissions strongly recommended positive intervention in the form of jobs, an infusion of capital to develop private businesses in the communities, enhanced educational support, and better public services for the residents. An increase in funding for public facilities and services to the communities in question occurred for several years thereafter. The riot in South-Central Los Angeles in 1992, that ensued after an all-white jury acquitted the white police officers in their trial for the beating of Rodney King, yielded some positive results. Dramatic attention was drawn to the area and the plight of the black community and South-Central residents for the first time since the 1960s; and the kind of attention that would never have been garnered without, unfortunately, the violence that had erupted. America's hypocrisy loomed large in its denial that violence worked. President George Bush reprimanded the community for its resorting to violence, stating that the riots would gain nothing. Within a few days, however, he boarded Air Force One and flew to Los Angeles to personally visit the site of the riots. Shortly thereafter a task force was established, and one hundred million dollars devoted to Phase One of the Rebuild LA Campaign. Community groups came together, and the city promised to do its share, as did the State of California, to address the problems. Violence's voice proved powerful in commanding attention and action.

John Brown, long before, predicted that violence would become a voice of necessity unless justice prevailed. He issued a poignant warning to mid-nineteenth century America: "You had better—all you people of the South—prepare yourselves for a settlement of this question. It must come up for settlement sooner than you are prepared for it, and the sooner you commence that preparation, the better for you. You may dispose of me very easily—I am nearly disposed of now; but this question is still to be settled—this Negro question, I mean. The end of that is not yet." It has not ended. It has not been resolved. While the question of slavery was eventually settled, the race question, the questions of amalgamation, integration, and true equality remain unresolved and at the heart of the continuing conflict and tearing of the American nation, and the leading barrier against American unity whether focusing on the South, North, East, or West. The cross burnings, racial epithets, slurs, graffiti of hate, the brick thrown through the window of a black family's home in a previously all-white neighborhood, police brutality, and the continued occurrence of race-hate murders such as the dragging death of a black man in Texas, disprove the thesis of a united and non-racist American nation. The mindset that makes possible these hideous crimes against African Americans finds solace from one generation of whites to the next in the racism passed on from one generation to the next in America. Jane Elliott, a former elementary school teacher in Iowa, who became a nationally known expert on race relations, concluded that in America "we are taught to be racists in school." She further contended: "The educational system also contributes to racism by not accurately portraying the contributions of blacks and other people of color in the annals of history. Now you need to realize the contributions that have been made to society, to civilization by brown-eyed people, by people of color. I'm talking about people of color here, folks, and most of us are not aware of those things because we live in a racist society and because we are educated in a racist school system that only teaches us about white contributions." Not only does the educational system fail to teach the African-American contribution, as Elliott lamented, it shied away from the lessons to be learned through examination of stellar white activists for equality such as John Brown. Understanding the legacy of Brown remains a vital prerequisite to comprehending the coming of the Civil War and to grasping the depths of the divisiveness within the nation on the race question and the history of failure to resolve the problem peacefully.[3]

CIVIL WAR LESSONS

The American Civil War provides clarity to the roots of this nation's present-day race dilemma when we view it for what it really was—a violent white power struggle between North and South with blacks as pawns. The American Civil War was not fought to free the slaves. It was not some great moral crusade, although portrayed as such. The American Civil War took place as a result of sectional differences between North and South and the need to resolve them once and for all. Westward expansion, after the discovery of gold in California in 1848, further flamed the question of which section of the nation would rule. Would the destiny of the nation be in the hands of the mercantile wage system (synonymous with the North) or in the hands of the agrarian slave labor system (synonymous with the South)? The Civil War was fought to preserve the Union between North and South, not to destroy it. The issue of slavery would be answered, but only as a secondary concern. There was at this point in time a relative balance between North and South in terms of the distribution of governing authority, with fifteen slave and fifteen free states. The concern for both southerners and northerners was whether the new cession territories to the west would become new states either pro mercantile Northeast or pro agrarian South. The Compromise of 1850 was an effort to maintain the balance of power. It provided that California be admitted as a free state and that territory disputed by Texas and New Mexico was to be surrendered to New Mexico. Abolition of the slave trade but not slavery was to occur in the District of Columbia. The concessions to the South were substantial. The South won the compromise in that the remainder of the Mexican cession territory was to be formed into the territories of Mexico and Utah without restriction on slavery, hence open to popular sovereignty. Texas was to receive compensation, in the amount of ten million dollars, from the federal government. In addition, a more stringent fugitive slave law, superceding the one in place since 1793, was enacted. This was an effort to maintain the Union and keep slavery intact.

Historians continue to point to the Kansas-Nebraska Act of 1854 as the last straw of compromise and directly leading the nation to war. The Kansas-Nebraska Act violated the Missouri Compromise of 1820 and the forbidding of slavery north of the sacred thirty-six thirty line. The problem was that westward expansion and the taking of new territories in the West pushed the question of national policy. It pushed America to think more of itself as a nation and the need for a coherent national economic system that did not compete against itself in terms of agrarian and slavery interests versus mercantile and industrial wage-based labor. It was not easily resolved to say the least. The Civil War would be primarily an economic power struggle with interests most easily categorized as slave states versus free states. Other evidence that the Civil War was not a moral crusade comes from the border states. States such as Ohio, Missouri, Indiana, and Kansas were ambivalent over the question of slavery and over the question of the eventual Civil War because many of them neither shared completely the vision of the mercantile northeast nor that of the slave South. Most of these states were neither slave nor free in terms of their economic system. Keeping them loyal to the Union was a major concern of President Abraham Lincoln and he played to their varied economic interests and to the anti and pro slavery issues as he did in the famous debates with Stephen A. Douglas. "I have no purpose directly or indirectly to interfere with the institution of slavery in the states where it exists," Lincoln said. "I believe I have no lawful right to do so, and I have no inclination to do so. I have no purpose to introduce political and social equality between the white and the black races. There is a physical difference between the two, which in my judgment will probably forever forbid their living together upon the footing of perfect equality, and inasmuch as it becomes a necessity that there must be a difference, I, as well as Judge Douglas, am in favor of the race to which I belong, having the superior position." Lincoln ended his remarks proclaiming his personal objection to unfree labor: "I agree with Judge Douglas that he [the black] is not my equal in many respects—certainly not in color, perhaps not in moral or intellectual endowment. But in the right to eat the bread, without leave of anybody else, which his own hand earns, he is my equal and the equal of Judge Douglas, and the equal of every living man."

From the moment of the passage of the Kansas-Nebraska Act compromise between North and South seemed impossible. One outgrowth of the Kansas-Nebraska Act was the Republican Party, born in Michigan and Wisconsin. The Republican Party was labeled a moral protest party. That was only one component of the Republican Party. The slogan of the party said it best: "Free soil, free labor, free men." That slogan spoke precisely to the question of national economic expansionism and pro wage labor system. With that broad agenda the Republicans became a catch all party attracting disgruntled Wigs, which included Abraham Lincoln, many northern Democrats, Know-Nothings, and others. What they had in common was a dislike of the Kansas-Nebraska Act. They were primarily coming together to secure their own commonalty of interests.

The abolitionist crusade found some support within the ranks of the Republican Party. The loudest voice decrying slavery and giving it the sympathetic appeal that was most palatable to many in the nation was not that of the oratorically gifted Thaddeus Stevens or Charles Sumner in the United States Congress; it was Harriet Beecher Stowe's *Uncle Tom's Cabin* published in 1852. This simplistic treatment of the institution of slavery with its vilified and glorified characters, the kindly Uncle Tom and the angelic Little Eva and the mean and merciless Simon Legree, provided the North with a well-defined moral outcry against the inhumanity of slavery. It was in a sense what the North needed and what became the sloganeered and value-added explanation to northern forces that theirs was a moral crusade. God was on their side. They were crusaders for a higher cause than simply that of preserving the Union or economic issues or to settle the questions of what power groups would rule America. The average soldier fought best with a definable cause that was clear cut and deemed as moral and right rather than no cause or one too complex and cloaked in power dynamics and the political quagmire. *Uncle Tom's Cabin* provided the North with the articulated moral imperative and rallying cry it needed. This would be a moral crusade. For the Union soldier the South was evil. Northerners were thus fighting a holy war.

For blacks, and for friends of abolition, the *Dred Scott Decision* of 1857 was a terrible blow to freedom. Dred Scott, who lived with his master for five years in Illinois and Wisconsin, both free states, sued for his freedom. It was not granted. The Taney-led U.S. Supreme Court concluded that Dred Scott was a slave and therefore property and had no rights before the courts. After all, a mule could not sue for its freedom. The decision made clear that under the laws of the United States of America blacks were not recognized as citizens nor as human beings with certain inalienable rights.

Important to keeping alive the moral indignation of slavery was John Brown's raid at Harper's Ferry, Virginia in 1859. It was not, however, the final catalyst that brought the nation to war. The election of Abraham Lincoln to the presidency of the United States in 1860 served that purpose. Immediately following his election, southern states began to secede from the nation with South Carolina the first to go, followed by the firing on Fort Sumter in 1861. The "Firing on Fort Sumter" was the first blow of the Civil War. All wars, it would seem, require that first blow and their rallying cries, be it the "Boston Massacre" or "No Taxation Without Representation" or "Give Me Liberty or Give Me Death" or the "Sinking of the Lusitania" or "Remember the Maine" or "A War to Make the World Safe for Democracy" or "The War to End All Wars" or "Remember Pearl Harbor" or even the "Gulf of Tonkin." America's advent into war has to be sparked by that first blow and that sloganeered outcry important to reducing the issues to the level acceptable and effective in rallying the masses. The Civil War, in fact, was in the North sloganeered to the tune and rallying cry of "Union Now and Forever" rather than 'let us end the dreaded institution of slavery,' although 'freeing the slaves' did play nicely as that special spiritual and righteous underpinning.

It was a war that took a tremendous human toll on both sides, with a final death toll that would forever be an estimate. The North loss 140,000 in battle; the South 94,000. Death due to dysentery, typhoid and other causes claimed higher numbers: northerners, 224,000; southerners, 190,000. In the end the nation expended 648,000 of its sons to settle the question of who would rule and lead America. The number of civilians—men, women, and children—who were casualties of the war remains unknown. This was America's most cataclysmic war in terms of the cost to the nation in human lives; the population of the United States was 21 million in 1860.

The African population in America contributed to the war. Blacks fought and served in the Civil War effort, from the famous Fifty-Fourth Massachusetts Regiment to lesser known units. More than 186,000 Africans served in that war and 40,000 paid the ultimate price with their lives. There was no equivocation on their part as to why the war was being fought or why they were fighting in it. They were fighting to free the enslaved African race in America. Even the most fervent of optimists, black or white, were not operating under the illusion that Union victory might mean equality for blacks in white America. The Emancipation Proclamation issued by President Lincoln in 1863 was a wartime maneuver to destabilize the southern states that were rebelling by freeing the slaves only in those states. It was, nevertheless, a statement of great hope as blacks and believers in abolition saw it. What happened to black folk in the aftermath of the war portended the dismal future of race relations in America and the tumultuous and circuitous travail before them.[4]

RECONSTRUCTION

There were signs even before the war ended that whether or not the North won the war the lot for African people would be precarious and barrier ridden. Blacks were expendable in the name of Union between white North and South. In late 1863 the *ten percent plan* was President Lincoln's first formal offer to re-admit the Confederate states into the Union. Under the plan, if ten percent of the 1860 electorate of a Confederate state swore an oath of allegiance to the United States government, that electorate could vote for a new state government and could send representatives to Congress. In short, it was a slap on the wrist to the secession states if they came home and promised to sin no more. If the southern states took such an oath they were to be granted amnesty and, most importantly, have their confiscated lands returned to them. This was a clear and early indication that "forty acres and a mule" was a lie and that the lands in the South were never to be divided up and dispensed to the former slaves as promised. In other words, blacks were to be set adrift in the treacherous waters of a post-slavery South without the basics for survival and advancement. Meanwhile, Lincoln offered to exclude high Confederate officials from any punishment for their actions during war. Congress refused to accept the plan. Lincoln was reelected in 1864 and a few months later assassinated on April 14, 1865. His vice president, Andrew Johnson, now president, was even more conciliatory toward reuniting North and South. President Johnson reasserted the offer of the *ten percent plan* and was also willing to grant executive amnesty to high Confederate officials. He would have had his way had it not been for the persistently critical voice of so-called radical Republicans, such as Thaddeus Stevens of Pennsylvania and U.S. Senator Charles Sumner of Massachusetts. The radical Republicans led Congress in overriding the presidential vetoes and forced stern Reconstruction policies on the South, at least for the moment. This radical minority pushed through the *Wade-Davis Bill*, demanding that southern states must in their constitutions abolish slavery, disfranchised Confederate leaders, and mandated that a majority, not just ten percent of the southern electorate, had to swear an oath of allegiance in order for them to be welcomed back into the Union as participating equals.

It was this same radical Republican minority that took the initial steps to making the transplanted Africans citizens of the United States. These radicals were responsible for the Thirteenth Amendment to the *Constitution of the United Sates* in 1865, which abolished slavery. They pushed through the *Civil Rights Bill* of 1866. They navigated into passage the *Freedmen's Bureau Bill* and the Fourteenth and the Fifteenth Amendments guaranteeing blacks rights as citizens and the right to vote. President Johnson denounced these efforts, particularly the Fourteenth Amendment, which granted black citizenship. Luckily for the now *African Americans*, the radicals were a major force at least for eight years. But by 1872 their voices had been quieted and within another five years they were without support in the Congress.

What then was the legacy of the so-called Reconstruction period from the end of the Civil War in 1865 to the Compromise of 1877? What did the nation mean when it said "Reconstruction?" Was this a reconstructing of the Old South or the true building of a New South? Even the term, "reconstruction," suggested that the nation was going to rebuild the Old South and not to change it to something new. There had been the passage of the Emancipation Proclamation and the Thirteenth, Fourteenth, and Fifteenth Amendments but were blacks truly free? Did they now actively take part in the law-making process? Could blacks build their own communities? In short, did the formal end of slavery guarantee the former slaves and their progeny a partnership in America or was the "reconstruction" period a failed opportunity or a deliberate step backward?

Historians missed the crucial barometer to gauge whether Reconstruction was a success or failure. They focused on politics, radicals versus moderates, Republicans versus Democrats, rather than on the all-important race issue in the nation and whether it improved. The Reconstruction years were a period of failure on the part of the

North to deliver what was promised to African Americans. Historians, in their earliest writings on the era, blamed blacks for the woes of the Reconstruction period. It was one of the most disgraceful episodes in history writing. Historian William A. Dunning of Columbia University led the onslaught in the early 20th century. These *Dunning School* "scholars" portrayed Reconstruction as a great American tragedy, a period of corrupt government. As Dunning liked to say, "Honest men had been thrown out of power and the South found itself under Negro rule." As the Dunningnites saw it, this was a period of scalawags, carpetbaggers, and Negroes in charge of the South. This was an absolute abomination of the truth put forth in the name of scholarship and history. In truth, at no time and place did blacks rule the South.

Dunning was followed by people like Claude G. Bowers who, in 1929, wrote *The Tragic Era: The Revolution After Lincoln*. Bowers depicted Reconstruction as years of turmoil and corruption: "Never have American public men in responsible positions directing the destiny of the nation been so brutal, hypocritical and corrupt. The southern people were literally put to the torture." The Dunningnites advocated this kind of completely distorted and erroneous perspective. E. Merton Coulter was another such advocate. Writing in *The South During Reconstruction*, in 1947, he claimed that plundering was the order of the day, that there was an "irresponsible officialdom," and that government was "transformed into an engine of destruction." The Dunningnites were on common ground in portraying the Reconstruction period as one in which carpetbaggers, scalawags, and "good for nothing Negroes" ruled the South. One white Carolinian professed not to have a solution how to rid the South of the alleged carpetbaggers and scalawags in government but did offer a solution to the "Negro problem." He suggested that a massive table be set in the immediate vicinity of the state governing body while it was in session and that it include those dishes that were irresistible to the Negro: hog bowls, crackling bread, candied yams, and a number of other Negro favorites. At a pre-arranged time, he suggested, a recess could be called for from the floor and this would bring the Negroes to the spot once their huge nostrils caught whiff of the fine delicacies. And once the niggers set down to sup, an armed band of good white citizens who had been waiting hidden in the brush, could then open up with guns and free South Carolina from Negro rule forever. The good citizen further reasoned that this process could be repeated throughout the South. In a sense, what this racist diabolically advocated during Reconstruction later received sympathetic support from the Dunningnite School of historians who validated his contempt, if not his proposed actions, by castigating blacks as an evil element in the Reconstruction South.

W.E.B. Du Bois challenged the direction of Reconstruction history in his paper presented at the annual meeting of the American Historical Association in 1909. Du Bois well recognized the mood toward white nationalism which meant the further vilification of the role of blacks during Reconstruction. "Reviewing the constructive achievements of the much maligned radical governments in the South," as historian Kenneth M. Stampp wrote, Du Bois argued that the "increased tax burden," for example, "had been necessary to correct the neglected social problems such as illiteracy, that the amount of corruption had been exaggerated, and that historians had virtually ignored the biracial, bipartisan, and bisectional nature of such corruption" that did exist. Du Bois's research documented that blacks were in positions of authority in very few instances and in very few places in the Reconstruction South and, where they did have any authority, did a highly respectable job.

Decades after Du Bois delivered his paper, revisionist historians began challenging the *Dunning School* and its erroneous contention of Negro rule. They pointed out that government in the South during Reconstruction was not that corrupt. They also documented that blacks held few positions in government during this era and that in those positions that they did hold they set impeccable standards of governmental honesty and integrity. Vernon L. Whorton, in his revisionist study, found that in Mississippi during Reconstruction, Negroes along with their Republican colleagues gave the state a government of greatly expanded functions at a cost that was low in comparison with that of almost any other state. He added that Mississippi was extremely fortunate in the character of her more important Negro Republican leaders. Historian Howard K. Beale confirmed Wharton's findings in his research, and further concluded that there was no Negro rule in the South.

W.E.B. Du Bois's *Black Reconstruction*, published in 1935, significantly advanced the understanding of the Reconstruction era and race relations. Some called Du Bois's study another revisionist effort. They were mistaken. Du Bois's book broke important new ground. He was more concerned with people, black people in particular, than he was with the politics of Reconstruction or whether it was a period of carpetbaggers, scalawags, and Negro rule. He knew, of course, that all of this was nonsense, particularly the notion of Negro rule. He was concerned with examining Reconstruction and determining whether the period afforded blacks the opportunity and the aid to stride forward and become truly free people in America.

Du Bois postulated that if the Civil War was fought to end slavery, then Reconstruction should have been the next permanent step in black advancement. He investigated whether blacks were provided the means that would help them to survive and to become self-supporting citizens. Were they to become equals in this nation? Was that part of the plan and the goal? Du Bois saw the Reconstruction period as a great opportunity for America to reconstruct itself into a democracy that it had not been prior to the Civil War. He concluded in his treatise that America failed to grasp this opportunity. In his chapter, *Back Towards Slavery*, he finds: "The lawlessness in the South since the Civil War has varied in its phases. First, it was the kind of disregard for law which follows all war. Then it became a labor war, an attempt on the part of impoverished capitalists and landholders to force laborers to work on the capitalist's own terms. From this, it changed to a war between laborers, white and black men fighting for the same jobs. Afterward, the white laborer joined with the white landholder and capitalist and beat the black laborer into subjection through secret organizations and the rise of the new doctrine of race hatred." Critics said of Du Bois's study that it moved the discussion of Reconstruction into a Marxist frame of analysis. This was nonsense. Shirley Graham Du Bois later confirmed that her husband was barely familiar with Marxism in 1935. While the Communist Manifesto was created in 1848, Marxism did not gain significant following in the United States until the 1950s. What was important to understand about Du Bois's work on the question of Reconstruction was that he addressed the crucial relationship between racism and economics. Black and white workers, Du Bois argued, needed to come together. Racism, however, won out. What he fully recognized was the role of people of African descent in America. This was an issue that simply would never go away: that African people were brought to America for their labor. When slavery legislatively ended, southerners and northerners with vested economic interests, worked to secure the tractability of black labor to continue to reap the profits from their labor. Full political participation and equal rights and opportunities were contradictory to the place of the Negro in America both during slavery and after the formal demise of the peculiar institution.

Thus, the idea of Negro rule in the South during Reconstruction was preposterous. Blacks were not in control, or even close to being in control, as John Hope Franklin has documented in his many works on southern history. The new Negro Americans (males only) did participate in governance for the first time in this country's history during Reconstruction and held a small number of public offices. Two blacks served in the United States Senate: Hiram Revels and Blanche K. Bruce, both from Mississippi. Only two African Americans have been elected to the Senate since Reconstruction: Edward Brooks of Massachusetts, in the 1960s, was the first; and Carol Mosley Braun of Illinois, in the 1990s, was the second. In the Reconstruction era, some twenty blacks served in the United States House of Representatives. It was in South Carolina that blacks held their greatest numerical strength with some eighty-seven serving in the state legislature for a brief period. Whites held control, at all times, of the state senate. African Americans had far less impact in other states. In South Carolina and elsewhere the black legislators that did exist were instrumental in developing programs that aided the South: rebuilding agriculture, roads, bridges, railroads, pushing for some form of health care and, particularly, universal education. They did their best to increase the efficiency of government and to modify the penal systems. They championed legislation to end discrimination in public accommodations. They fought inflation. They increased taxes for the various social programs that, in the final analysis, benefited more whites than blacks. Nowhere in the South did blacks push for legislation for interracial marriage as such. Black men were not in the least interested in securing a socio-sexual path to white women. They did, in several instances, put forward legislation aimed at protecting and providing for black concubines and mulatto offspring resulting from what white men had done to black women during slavery and, in some cases, where the relationships were ongoing. In the main, black legislators were fair and honorable, concerning themselves with issues crucial to all southerners, black and white, such as illiteracy, food and shelter, the state of agriculture, industrial development in the region, and jobs for everyone. The black officeholders could best be termed magnanimous in their dealings with the ex-Confederates. Incredibly, they did not engage in retribution despite what they and their forebears had suffered under slavery. Neither did they seek or desire social integration. They simply wanted to be recognized as equal human beings. P.B.S. Pinchback of Louisiana, the only black to serve as lieutenant governor, and who had a brief stint as acting governor, put it succinctly: "It is false. It is a wholesale falsehood to say that we wish to force ourselves upon white people."

Nevertheless, the image of the black in the Reconstruction South was negative, as depicted in D.W. Griffith's classic and racist film, *Birth of A Nation*, released in 1915. Blacks were portrayed as evil, hateful, divisive, and a power-hungry force that hurt the South. The popular Negrophobic jingle of the Reconstruction period, "O' If I

Was A Nigger," was illustrative: "Oh! If I was a nigger, I'd do just as I pleased, and when I took a pinch of snuff, all yankeedom would sneeze. Then congress too would worship me, and bow down at my feet, and swear that since the world began, there was nothing half so sweet." In the white mind, blacks were a despicable race whose existence was acceptable only under white authority; otherwise they should be annihilated. The ex-Confederates attempted every measure to thwart black political participation and progress. In Alabama, the "conservatives" set aside days for fasting and prayer. They often lamented a common racist prayer: "Almighty God, deliver our state from these negars and the horrors of their domination." As far as the white South was concerned, the Civil War was still being fought and the enemy to be vanquished was the black race. The white South committed itself, in thought and action, to rendering the South either a "white man's government or convert the land into a negro man's cemetery."[5]

SEEKING THE DREAM

Blacks attempted to live their own lives unencumbered by whites. The Port Royal Experiment, prior to the end of the Civil War, was one such attempt. It was a dress rehearsal for Reconstruction, acted out on the Sea Islands of South Carolina. Black and white leaders, Harriet Tubman, Oliver Otis Howard, Thomas Wentworth Higginson, christened the initiative. Missionaries of Gideon's Band, as they were called, from New York and Massachusetts, came to the area to provide education. Blacks of the Sea Islands accepted educational assistance but were intent on retaining their African heritage and culture. They named their children African names and preserved their African Gullah language. They Africanized European religious practices. The Sea Islanders celebrated their African folkways, mores, traditions, ritualistic practices, and struggled to maintain their sense of being and human worth. In short, they tried to maintain some degree of autonomy. They, consequently, found themselves at odds with white supporters such as Rufus Saxon and with the Freedmen's Bureau and others who sought to dictate to them.[6]

It was difficult for black folk to know which whites were their friends because even those who came to the South, marching to the bugles and drums of liberty, did not support black hegemony. Reconstruction historians, in mass, wrote of the Freedmen's Bureau as having been established to aid and protect the newly freed population. Closer examination revealed that the bureau in practice reflected a trend toward reconciliation between the white North and

South, and worked often to thwart blacks in their effort to build their own community. Such was the experience of the freed population of Hampton, Virginia. With all the talk about the Civil War as a war to liberate the slaves, blacks in Hampton and throughout America looked to the future with great expectations. Hampton's freedmen population quickly learned that their destinies would be very different from what they thought and hoped when Union forces liberated the area and its seven thousand black inhabitants in 1862. They soon began to distrust and fear Union soldiers almost as much as they had the slave master. Union troopers often stalked black women, debased black dwellings, and stole food from the recently freed slaves. There were numerous reports of the horror of the soldiers' actions as they confiscated crops and livestock of the freed population. Labor colonies were established and black folk found themselves conscripted into service as forced workers under Union overseers. Even those blacks who fought on the side of the Union forces in Hampton did not escape mistreatment. The all-important promise of fair wages was not honored. Ironically, the labor of blacks was claimed to be less valuable than that of whites even when it was northerners dictating the terms. Blacks were accustomed to the mistreatment of slavery but they had expected better of their liberators. Hampton presented a preview of what was in store for black folk once the Civil War ended. Missionaries in Hampton reported that the blacks thought seriously about exodus to Haiti long before the Civil War was over because of their negative encounters with northern soldiers.

There were a few reasons for blacks to be optimistic. An organization that they viewed most favorably was the Bureau of Negro Affairs, particularly its superintendent C. B. Wilder who was responsible for the bureau's activities throughout the entire Fortress Monroe, Hampton, Virginia region from 1863 to 1865. Wilder worked in earnest to aid the refugees and resident blacks. He actively sought an end to injustices. He believed that blacks should be given a share in America's wealth; that it meant nothing to simply free them without also providing the sustenance for long-term survival, namely land. He was one who believed that the old plantations should be divided up and dispensed among the black population that had once worked these lands, as slave laborers, for the benefit of others. Wilder believed in land redistribution, a true carrying through of "forty acres and a mule," as the only solution for the black race in America. He was a lone eagle without the support of the government, and when the Civil War finally ended many of the gains that he dispersed to blacks were curtailed and reversed.

The Bureau of Negro Affairs was soon replaced by the Bureau of Abandoned Lands and Refugees—better known as the Freedmen's Bureau, an organization established by act of Congress in 1865 and mandated, at least on paper, to assist the newly freed populations of the South, providing them with shelter, food, clothing, and education. White southerners characterized the bureau as the "Negro no work" program, the beginning of a free ride and public handouts for blacks (the same characterizations and misunderstandings surround the welfare program today). The reality was far different. Although C. B. Wilder temporarily headed the Freedmen's Bureau in the Hampton region, the idea of reconciliation between North and South had won out, and blacks were as expendable as their dreams. Blacks in Hampton were uprooted in spite of every effort they made to keep the land. Cases were brought before the civil and Freedmen's Bureau courts, but the verdict rendered always supported the former rebel and his reclaiming of the land.

Numerous conflicts occurred between blacks and the ex-Confederates. There were countless incidents of disrespect heaped upon the blacks. Ole massa was trying to reassert his authority and put the blacks back to work on his terms. Hampton's freedmen objected. They were not going to be returned to bondage. They wanted to build their own way of life and community. They understood that there was no difference between slavery, sharecropping, and tenant farming, and fought against this new form of subjugation. One embittered Hampton black complained that, in addition to being forced to give the land back and go to work for former masters, the rebels required that they show them the same manners and respect as they had during slavery. He objected to having again to call all whites master and mistress. For Wilder, who sided with the blacks, there were assassination attempts made on his life. He was forced to leave the area and to surrender the Freedmen Bureau activities into the hands of General Samuel Chapman Armstrong and other white leaders who were committed to restoring the old order and stability—i.e., black subordination in Hampton.

Order and subordination were precisely what General Armstrong had in mind for blacks. Born of missionary parents, he had served as the white commander of a black regiment during the Civil War. Assigned to head the Freedmen's Bureau in the Hampton region, he passionately followed his orders in returning the lands to the former Confederate owners and restoring stability to the labor situation. In point of fact, blacks were removed from the land; land that had been given to them was given back to the ex-Confederates. There was no doubt who was in charge. Contracts were drawn up between whites and blacks but the contracts did not protect the rights of blacks. It was simply a system to force the blacks back to work on legal terms. As Armstrong wrote, "Whites say niggers won't work; negroes say whites won't pay." He did not take it beyond that in terms of the blacks' concerns. His concern was with order and stability and he gave weak sympathy, at best, to the freed population. He understood only too well that blacks were being exploited. They were made to pay exorbitant rents. This was nothing more than a form of slavery for the blacks and their children, not much better than the peculiar institution. Armstrong admitted this fact. His orders were to maintain stability. Like other alleged friends of blacks had done before him and would do after him, Armstrong blamed the blacks for their own dilemma. In short, he held the oppressed responsible for their own oppression. He believed that blacks, as a class, were destitute of ambition and accepted poverty and filth rather than work to do something about it. He saw no connection between the poverty and filth and his role in Hampton in the re-subjugation of black workers. He thought that blacks worked best under the watchful eyes of whites. As Armstrong put it, "One third are eye-servants and worth little or nothing. Of the remainder, only another third could really be considered good workman." As far as he was concerned, the freedmen's entire life style was nothing more than an example of the shiftless propensity of blacks. Their complaints did not deserve to be taken seriously. Nevertheless, he considered himself the best friend of the Negroes. With friends like that, who needed enemies? He was a better friend of southern men of property. After all, as Armstrong saw it, the best class of southern whites, the men of property, would work to bring order and stability to Hampton and throughout the South. He believed that the correct course of action was to reestablish the proper class to positions of authority. In short, southern white authority was being reestablished and the freed population given no voice. For blacks who brought their cries to the freedmen's courts, the verdict was always against them. Blacks continued to agitate for their own representation on the courts, and finally Armstrong, hearing their plea in May of 1866, decided that it was a just request on their part. However, he did not feel that blacks were qualified to sit on the court. In his assessment, they did not have the mental capacity to judge or to make rational decisions—a stereotype about blacks that persists to this day (witness the O. J. Simpson trial and the reactions to the verdict rendered by the majority black jury). Armstrong appointed what he called a sympathetic white to represent blacks on the freedmen's courts. In other words, black representation was not to be considered. Armstrong was a believer in paternalism, *noblesse oblige*, but not to the extent that blacks should control their own community and destiny.

Hampton blacks became dejected and outraged and began to secure for themselves the type of power that the Freedmen's Bureau, the ex-Confederates, and anyone else could understand; the type of power that when hammer struck firing pen would come out of the end of a barrel. They were starting to arm themselves in defense of their community, not unlike more contemporary actions of groups such as the Black Panther Party for Self Defense. Hampton blacks were ready, as reports indicated, to fight both the former rebels and the bureau. There were several incidents involving an exchange of gunfire between armed freedmen and bureau soldiers. Armstrong mobilized his forces to disarm every black in Hampton, and did so with military precision. If the mission of the Freedmen's Bureau was to protect the blacks and to help them in their efforts toward freedom, why were the freedmen forced to take up arms against both the ex-Confederates and the bureau? The mission of the bureau was clear. It did not provide Hampton blacks with protection and assistance. If the goal of the Civil War was to free the slaves, the Hampton experience was a bitter betrayal and a poignant precursor of the troubles that lay ahead for blacks in the aftermath of slavery.[7]

V

THE NEW SLAVERY

IF YOU ARE BLACK, STAY BACK

The troubled situation for black folk and race relations in America worsened in the waning years of Reconstruction. Hana Tutson was a case in point. In riveting testimony to a joint select committee of Congress in 1871 the elderly black woman recounted how she and her family had been victimized by a group of racists who beat them and attempted to rape her. Their only crime was that they were black and the white thugs wanted them out of the area. How had race relations become so terrible after the promise of emancipation? There had been an era of Reconstruction and blacks for the first time participated in the government. There were the Thirteenth, Fourteenth, and Fifteenth Amendments to the *Constitution*. The reality, however, was that the Civil War had continued, in many respects, despite the armistice in 1865. The South never stopped retaliating. The acts of counter revolution had begun even before the war ended and blacks were the targets. The first assaults along these lines were the *Black Codes of 1865–1866* which were laws to circumvent the rights of blacks, secure them as a subordinate labor force, and control their activities.

Much more pernicious and problematic for the future of blacks was the *Compromise of 1877* that signaled the formal end of Reconstruction and the beginning reconciliation between white North and South. This meant that blacks were expendable and were forsaken in the name of restoring the Union. They were left to the tender mercies of the South. There were, of course, forces leading to this compromise; forces that were seen as much more important to the nation as a whole than the condition of blacks and their future. There was the economic depression after the Civil War, political scandal, and the desire for reconciliation between North and South. During the next few years the great depression, the panic that had begun in 1873, worsened. Along with the many scandals associated with the Grant presidential administration, the national economic hemorrhaging made the movement for change and reform a *fait accompli*.

The election of 1876 pitted Rutherford B. Hayes, the Republican from Ohio, against Samuel J. Tilden, governor of New York and head of the Democratic ticket. Both Tilden and Hayes had solid records as reformers. The nation, however, was ready for a new party leadership. For the first time since the Civil War the Democrats held a good chance of winning the presidency. The Congressional elections of 1874 sent Democrats back into the House of Representatives in large enough numbers to give them control of the house. Two years later, the Oval Office was in sight. When the popular vote was finally counted, Tilden had more popular votes and was only one electoral vote short of the 185 necessary for election. Hayes and the Republicans contested twenty of the electoral votes. With 165 he would need the full twenty, through the Electoral College, to be elected president of the United States. The contested electoral votes lay in the South in three traditionally Democratic states, South Carolina, Louisiana, and Florida. These states, however, were still under Republican government and a form of marshal law. Hayes and his people argued that the voting in those states had not been fair. The blacks, the Republicans contended, had not been allowed to vote. In the end, these challenges moved the election into arbitration in the House of Representatives. A committee was set up to settle the issue. The committee would literally decide who was president of the United States. Would Hayes or Tilden be the next president? The committee originally consisted of seven Republicans, seven Democrats, and one independent. The committee voted repeatedly in a deadlock of 7 to 7 with 1 abstention. Through political maneuvering on the part of the Republicans, the one independent member of the committee was replaced by another individual who was supposed to be an independent but who proved in the end to be a Republican. The final vote, giving the twenty contested electoral votes to Hayes, was 8 to 7. The Democrats claimed foul and chaos prevailed. The American constitutional form of government was in jeopardy. The Democrats were steadfast in their demand for the presidency and the Republicans were steadfast in their determination not to give it up. The result was a compromise that gave the presidency to Hayes and the Republicans and yielded to the Democrats and the South vast economic aid and regional autonomy. The South received millions of dollars for road improvements, the rebuilding of railroads, farms and agriculture, and universal education. Northern troops were removed from the region and the "Negro Problem" was left in the hands of southerners. African Americans were, in short, abandoned as part of the agreement of 1877 as an expendable cost of restoring the Union.

President Hayes's office honored the abandonment. The South was to deal with blacks as it saw fit. Any lofty goals of Reconstruction that may have existed had come to an end. President Hayes concluded that the destiny of Negroes was best left in the hands of those most familiar with the problem. This meant left in the hands of the white South. President Hayes proclaimed that "absolute justice and fair play to the Negro...could be got best and almost surely by trusting the honorable and influential southern whites." The once Negro-friendly radical Republicans were in a conciliatory mood, far outnumbered by those who carried high the banner of re-Union. African Americans, without any federal support, were left alone to fend for themselves in a hostile South that blamed them for the Civil War and loss of loved ones, and saw them as a constant threat to southern white hegemony.[1]

There were but a few hopeful signs that there could be a black-white unity on some terms approaching those of mutual respect; if not mutual respect at least mutual self-interest and common decency toward one another. It was, in a sense, a last chance for some degree of black-white unity—and that was the Populist Movement. By the last decade of the 1890s, populism was a grass root's movement emerging in the South that attempted in the beginning to play down racial differences for class interests. After all, white and black poor in the South were basically farmers and were often pitted against one another. Blacks were aware of this and so were a growing number of whites as well. In the South and southwest, white farmers had started southern farmers' alliances in an effort to stave off the middlemen who were reaping the vast profits from the labor of small farmers and tenant and sharecroppers. They wanted to form their own cooperatives to guarantee higher prices and lower transportation costs to get their produce to market. Blacks likewise formed colored farmers' alliances. The two groups from time to time attempted to come together in the name of populism. The Populists, or People's Party, were taking on the old Democratic establishment in the South and trying to develop a new day of hope and solidarity among the lower classes.

White Populists knew they needed black support or at least had to control or co-opt them to advance their agenda. Both groups could see common economic interests that went beyond racial differences. The Populists pushed forward *fusion politics*—blacks and whites and others united in their support of pro-farmer candidates no matter what the candidates' party affiliation. If the candidate was in harmony with the Populists on key issues, he was their choice. At times they endorsed minority Republicans. In 1892 and in 1894, Populists were making gains throughout the South and southwest through this type of political action.

Populism was an opportunity for America. The divisive element, however, that continued to raise its ugly head was racism. It was extremely difficult, if not impossible, for white farmers to overcome the teachings of years of racial hatred toward blacks and to start treating them as equals who suffered economic exploitation just like themselves. Outside forces, the Democratic establishment, and others who wanted to see the Populist effort and farmer unity and any kind of cooperation across economic lines fail, played upon the old bugaboo of race. The detractors invoked white superiority and racial pride to chastise and brow beat those who dared lower themselves to the level of the Negro. They played upon the greatest of all white fears—the sexual unison or marriage between blacks and whites—*miscegenation*. In the end racism won out.

The South had the opportunity to go one of two ways. One way was along the lines of the Populist Movement and to have blacks and whites work together for mutual self-interest. The second was that of *Jim Crowism* and racial segregation, discrimination and disfranchisement. The South chose the latter and heaped upon blacks poll taxes, literary tests, grandfather clauses, segregated facilities, inferior education, fear, intimidation, and violence. Second-class citizenship for blacks was sanctioned in law with passage of the monumental and infamous *Plessy versus Ferguson Decision* of 1896 and the doctrine of "separate but equal." The idea of "separate but equal" was ludicrous. Equality did not exist. The nation embraced racism in *Plessy versus Ferguson* and said that segregation, discrimination, and mistreatment based on race were not only permissible but desirable and that the black and the white races could not live together in America. The highest court of the United States of America decreed people of African descent *untouchables*. African Americans were, thus, deemed an unwanted element in America and not to be accorded the full rights and privileges of citizenship. Ironically, *Plessy versus Ferguson* was only one entry on a long list of actions against blacks.[2]

Racism was the deliberate action against a people because of their race. In its treatment of people of African descent in the late nineteenth and early twentieth century, America proved that it was a racist nation second to none in its demonizing and victimizing of people of color. Those claiming today that blacks unfairly complain and only imagine victimization are anti-historical and anti-factual. The pseudo-scientific racist scholarship of anthropologists, biologists, philosophers, and others worked against black folk in the most heinous way. Borrowing from the work of Charles Darwin— who theorized that Africa was probably the site of where the human species originated—his thesis of the survival of the fittest was put into a social context. This social context—*Social Darwinism*—provided for some the rationalization or at least the explanation for why there were those who did well and those who did poorly in society. The Englishman Herbert Spencer, along with his American disciples, including John Fiske, Jack London, and William Graham Sumner, took Darwin's views and applied them to society. The thesis of the survival of the fittest in the human-animal context held that those who achieved and advanced in society did so as a result of their abilities and those who failed likewise did so as a result of their lack of abilities. For those at the bottom of society, such as black Americans and the poor, they were there because, according to proponents of *Social Darwinism*, they were inferior and the least capable.

The racist, Social Darwinist construct provided the conceptual foundation for such venerated American ideals as the *pioneering spirit* and *rugged individualism* taught in school and church and championed by American presidents from Theodore Roosevelt to Ronald Reagan. The individual was responsible for his or her success or failure, not society or the barriers it imposed. Legislation, laws, social programs or the lack thereof, had nothing to do with it. Unfortunately, these barriers were real and not a figment of black folk's imagination. Poll taxes, literacy tests, and grandfather clauses were real and a part of the everyday arsenal of barriers imposed against African Americans. When these were not enough, outright violence was used to keep blacks in their place.

The nadir following the *Compromise of 1877* witnessed the flourishing of the Ku Klux Klan, the Knights of the White Camellia, white citizen councils, rifle clubs and other hate groups dedicated to the preservation of white supremacy and to keeping blacks subordinated. All-out violence was used constantly against blacks. At least three thousand African Americans were lynched in the years after the compromise to the end of World War I. These were only the recorded lynchings. Common sense suggests that a far higher number perished. No figures exist as to how many black women were raped in the American South of this era. The number was, no doubt, huge because blacks were not respected in racist America and African-American women could be taken by white men on the slightest whim, and without fear of punishment. It was virtually unknown in the South for a white man who raped a black woman to be charged with the crime and brought to trial. The nation, by its actions, told its black citizens that they were not real citizens nor recognized members of the human family with rights that whites had to respect.

Take, for example, the Sam Hose lynching of 1899. Two thousand white men, women and children gathered in Palmetto, Georgia and partook in the murder festivities. Hose, a black man, was burned alive for the "alleged" rape and killing of a white woman. The mob celebrated as it took his life. Children played and food was served. Before Hose's body was cool the crowd descended and cut it into pieces. His bones were crushed into small bits and his heart and liver divided up and sold as souvenirs to the crowd. That Hose was, in fact, innocent of the alleged crime meant nothing. Moreover, the Hose murder, and the festivities surrounding it, was horrendous but not uncommon. Racist and barbaric violence and defiance of the laws of humanity were perpetrated against African Americans in the South on a regular basis.

Blacks were routinely killed or otherwise brutalized in the South for what was considered "uppity" behavior or not showing proper respect and adulation or obedience to whites. The increasing numbers of blacks drawn to southern cities at the turn of the century were a source of white discontent. We often recount the riots in the urban North and forget that race riots occurred in southern and western cities as well. In 1898, angry whites in Wilmington, North Carolina, opened fire on a gathering of blacks killing seven of them as a result of an article written by a local black contending that sexual affairs between black men and white women were consensual and that the claims of rape by white women were attempts to protect their reputations after being caught with their black lovers. In 1900, parts of New Orleans were set ablaze after black nationalist Robert Charles fought back against white police officers' harassment and attempt to beat him. One of the policemen drew his gun and fired at Charles. Proving that he was, as some called him, a "bad nigger," Charles, who also carried a pistol, drew his weapon and shot one of the police officers. Escaping, he became the target of a massive manhunt through the black quarter of the city. More than twenty thousand whites, coming from as far away as Georgia and including national guardsmen, were eventually involved in the hunt. Finally surrounded, while hiding alone in the home of a friend, Charles shot it out with his pursuers rather than surrender. He killed a total of seven of them before he was killed. During the manhunt and rioting, marauding whites beat and shot a score of black citizens, killing at least twelve. In 1906, Atlanta also experienced a race riot. Becoming self-sufficient and gaining a degree of affluence were no guarantees against the capricious violence of whites. In 1921, black progress in Tulsa, Oklahoma, came to a violent halt when crazed white mobs attacked the black community, burned it to the grown, and killed an estimated three hundred of its members. The black town of Rosewood, Florida, with a population of two hundred, was completely wiped out in the winter of 1923. Long angered by the "uppityness" and success of the relatively prosperous black folk, whites from surrounding areas laid siege on the town, beating, raping, shooting, and lynching as many of the inhabitants as they could find. What precipitated the massacre was a rumor that one of the black men from the town had raped a white woman. The rumor was unfounded. The white woman had fabricated the story after a dispute with her white boyfriend. Estimates of the number killed vary. Former residents of the town claimed that as many as forty blacks were murdered. Those who survived never returned to Rosewood.

Jazz vocalist Billie Holiday, in her unique way, gave voice to the horror of violence against blacks in the hauntingly poignant lyrics of song describing the scene of a lynching, "Strange Fruit:"

> Southern trees bear a strange fruit,
> Blood on the leaves and blood at the root,
> Black body swinging in the Southern breeze,
> Strange fruit hanging in the poplar trees.
> Pastoral scene of the gallant South,
> The bulging eyes and the twisted mouth,
> Scent of magnolia sweet and fresh,
> And the sudden smell of burning flesh.
> Here is a fruit for the crows to pluck,
> For the rain to gather, for the wind to suck,
> For the sun to rot, for a tree to drop,
> Here is a strange and bitter crop.

Richard Wright in his epic poem "Between the World and Me" captured and conveyed the details and trauma of the barbarous atrocities African Americans experienced:

> And one morning while in the woods I stumbled suddenly
>   upon the thing.
> Stumbled upon it in a grassy clearing guarded by scaly oaks
>   and elms.
> And the sooty details of the scene rose, thrusting themselves
>   between the world and me...
> There was a design of white bones slumbering forgottenly
>   upon a cushion of ashes.
> There was a charred stump of a sapling pointing a blunt fin-
>   ger accusingly at the sky.

There were torn tree limbs, tiny veins of burnt leaves, and a scorched coil of greasy hemp;

A vacant shoe, an empty tie, a ripped shirt, a lonely hat, and a pair of trousers stiff with black blood.

And upon the trampled grass were buttons, dead matches, butt-ends of cigars and cigarettes, peanut shells, a drained gin-flask, and a whore's lipstick;

Scattered traces of tar, restless arrays of feathers, and the lingering smell of gasoline.

And through the morning air the sun poured yellow surprise into the eye sockets of a stony skull....

And while I stood my mind was frozen with a cold pity for the life that was gone.

The ground gripped my feet and my heart was circled by icy walls of fear—

The sun died in the sky; a night wind muttered in the grass and fumbled the leaves in the trees; the woods poured forth the hungry yelping of hounds; the darkness screamed with thirsty voices; and the witnesses rose and lived:

The dry bones stirred, rattled, lifted, melting themselves into my bones.

The gray ashes formed flesh firm and black, entering into my flesh.

The gin-flask passed from mouth to mouth; cigars and cigarettes glowed, the whore smeared the lipstick red upon her lips,

And a thousand faces swirled around me, clamoring that my life be burned....

And then they had me, stripped me, battering my teeth into my throat till I swallowed my own blood.

My voice was drowned in the roar of their voices, and my black wet body slipped and rolled in their hands as they bound me to the sapling.

And my skin clung to the bubbling hot tar, falling from me in limp patches.

And the down and quills of the white feathers sank into my raw flesh, and I moaned in my agony.

Then my blood was cooled mercifully, cooled by a baptism of gasoline.

And in a blaze of red I leaped to the sky as pain rose like water, boiling my limbs.

Panting, begging I clutched childlike, clutched to the hot sides of death.

Now I am dry bones and my face a stony skull staring in
yellow surprise at the sun....

African Americans were lynched and brutalized well into the
1950s and 1960s in the South. In the 1980s there were yet instances
of lynching in the South, and in 1998 James Byrd, Jr. was chained
to a pickup truck and dragged to death by three white supremacists
in the eastern Texas town of Jasper. These atrocious acts of violence
were rooted in the long tradition of demonizing and vilifying African
Americans, especially black men. The words of Senator Ben Tillman, affectionately known as "Pitchfork," of South Carolina, an
outspoken Negrophobe and opponent of black rights, epitomized
the tradition. Senator Tillman thought of blacks as nothing more
than beasts of burden. He spoke openly of his belief that blacks resembled human beings but had none of the qualities. To him the
African Americans were incapable of exercising the higher functions
of civilization. They were, he contended, closer to baboons than humans. Tillman liked to say, "It takes something else besides having
the shape of a man to make a man and Negroes are so near akin to
the monkey that scientists are yet looking for the missing link. The
record of this ignorant and debased and debauched race in its
African environment was one of barbarism, savagery, cannibalism
and everything which is low and degrading." To have blacks living
amongst the majority society was, according to him, at the white
race's great peril. Nor should Senator Tillman's views have been
seen in isolation. He was a popular legislator. In his most famous
moment in the U.S. Senate in 1907, Tillman rose and spoke passionately, and with considerable applause, against anti-lynching legislation that had been introduced by a Republican senator from Wisconsin. Tillman brazenly defended the lynching of blacks as a
necessary corrective to defend white womanhood and to keep in
check what he characterized as the debauched and savage Negro
race. No anti-lynching legislation passed thanks to his racist oratory
eloquence. It was well into the post World War II era before anti-
lynching legislation was enacted in an effort to help curtail lynchings.

Senator Tillman was not alone in his assault against the black
race. The media did its part, particularly the D.W. Griffith film,
"Birth of a Nation," based on Thomas Dixon's books, *The Klans-
man* and *The Leopard Spots*. The books and the film glorified the
Ku Klux Klan as a positive, compassionate, and heroic organization, and blamed blacks for the disunion and turmoil between
North and South. Throughout the 1915 film, blacks were depicted

as evil, ignorant, dishonest, the villains of North-South unity and, along with their mulatto cohorts, desperate to be in positions of power and authority. "Birth of a Nation" was the film that made the American movie industry. The film was heralded as a cinematic masterpiece with its chase scenes and crowd shots of epic proportions, all used to glorify a racist script. The stereotypical images presented in the film would become the staple of the film industry, the movie industry, and Hollywood and television: the negative and demeaning images of shiftless and lazy blacks, the black criminals, the fat mammas, the loyal Uncle Toms and Aunt Jemimas. Woodrow Wilson, President of the United States of America, former president of Princeton University, former governor of New Jersey, and a historian, praised "Birth of a Nation," endorsed the film, and complimented the Ku Klux Klan for its work as a "great American organization."

We continue to struggle against the veil of black demonization and vilification. W.E.B. Du Bois, in his monumental book, *The Souls of Black Folk*, published in 1903, asked the United States of America to lift up the veil of its ignorance and brutality and to see beyond the veil and to appreciate other fellow human beings for their intellect, culture, human worth and dignity. The entire nation needed then as now to read Du Bois's compassionate and reasoned plea because he put in context America's number one problem: racism. As Du Bois said, "the problem of the twentieth century is the problem of the color line." For African Americans that has not changed. America has not answered the race question. The place of African Americans is defined continuously by this nation's crass economic needs, as Du Bois brilliantly articulated in his chapter "The Wings of *Atalanta*." The late nineteenth and early twentieth century witnessed the birth of what became known as the New South but for black Americans it was, in a real sense, an Old South. The emerging industrial South, laced with northern capital, wanted and needed blacks in their traditional role as cheap labor. The white population of the South in general wanted them completely controlled, subservient, subdued. "For the American Negro, the last decade of the nineteenth and the first decade of the twentieth centuries were more critical than the Reconstruction years of 1868 to 1876," Du Bois wrote in his autobiography. "This was the age of triumph for big business, for industry consolidated and organized on a world wide scale and run by white capital with colored labor. The southern United States was one of the most promising fields for this development, with a mass of cheap and potentially efficient labor..." Du Bois understood perfectly what this nation thought of its African-

American population and what it would continue to think and define as the "Negro's place" in America.[3]

AT THE BACK DOOR

In this hostile, brutal, savage South, a South barbaric in its treatment of African Americans and in its exploitation of them, a South which sought to maintain the status quo, arose the race leadership of the individual who became the most prominent and influential black person in America at the beginning of the 20th century: Booker T. Washington. He prescribed how African Americans should be willing to live and what they should think, the course they needed to pursue to survive and to prosper and to uplift themselves and the race in the South, as he saw it. The course he prescribed was one where blacks and whites could live together, supporting both their interests. The problem was that the interests of whites in charge and the interests of a subordinated black group were not the same.

Washington believed that for blacks to survive and move forward in the South they had to make themselves indispensable. They had to be loyalists to the South. It was as if Paulo Freire, in his classic study on education, *Pedagogy of the Oppressed*, had Booker T. Washington in mind when he warned that the oppressed must fight against being reduced to mere things. In order to regain their humanity, Freire said, "they must cease to be things and fight as men. They cannot enter the struggle as objects in order later to become men." Washington believed that the correct course for blacks was to fashion themselves in a coalition with whites in power by making themselves indispensable objects to the prosperity of the nation. In a very real sense, Washington's thinking was that here lie the salvation of the race by showing itself loyal and faithful rights and privileges would be granted, not by blacks actually exercising the franchise, not by actually standing up and demanding the end of the *Jim Crow* existence in the South, not by blacks voicing absolute disgust and demanding that lynchings be halted, no, but by showing themselves so loyal, so faithful, that the moral heart strings of whites would be touched.

Booker T. Washington worked along these philosophical lines all of his adult life. His education at Hampton Institute in Hampton, Virginia, under Samuel Chapman Armstrong, imbued him with the ideas of "head, hand, and heart," a philosophy of accommodationism which he learned from Armstrong and made into the cornerstone of his personal philosophy of Negro life and that of Tuskegee Institute, which he helped to found in 1881 in Tuskegee, Alabama. Washington's was a philosophy of uplift through submission, as he presented in his 1895 Atlanta Exposition Address with his analogy of the hand and how blacks and whites could work together on all questions of mutual economic interest, except when it came to social matters, Washington said, blacks and whites would be like the fingers on the hand, separate. His remarks were a harbinger of what the Supreme Court would declare just one year later in the infamous *Plessy v. Ferguson Decision.* The idea of "separate but equal" became the norm and the law of the land. The remarks of the majority opinion of the justices of the Supreme Court were in complete harmony with the Booker Washington philosophy, separate as the fingers on the hand.

Washington urged his fellow blacks to see their cheap labor as their source of strength. He believed that black folks' value to the society was as cheap and loyal labor and that those in power saw them only in those terms. Washington advocated that blacks play upon that relationship. Take any job, he would say. It was, in his philosophy, better to have a job than to have no job at all, regardless of whether the job paid the black worker less than it did the white worker. It was in this context that Washington saw civil rights as a secondary issue. Rights, he remarked, would follow later as blacks raised themselves to greater economic importance. Consequently, in speaking to both whites and blacks, Booker Washington advocated economic fellowship and downplayed social and civil rights. "We may sometimes complain about our not being privileged to be housed in certain hotels or about being refused the same consideration in restaurants as others," Washington professed. "But my friends, the average man of my race, perhaps the average man of any race, spends a very little part of his time in hotels or restaurants." Do not worry about rights, Washington said, they will come as you show yourself to be loyal and indispensable labor. He was convinced that capitalist materialism and the profit motive held a higher priority in America than humanity or love for fellow human beings. Washington understood that blacks were not viewed as humans by many in the South, certainly not by the lower elements of whites in the South, he noted. He thought that the way for blacks to survive was through non-antagonistic means, to use that commodity that whites in power most cherished: the labor of the black person. He professed that "the only thing that the white man wants or respects in general is either money or social position or political influence." Since blacks did not have these things, Washington advocated that they use the bargaining agent that they did possess. The one thing that blacks held in abundance was cheap labor. "The Negro constitutes in this country one of the most compact, reliable and peaceful elements of labor," Washington declared, "one which is almost the sole dependent for production in certain directions; and I believe that, if for no higher reason than the economic one, the people will see that it is worthwhile to keep so large an element of labor happy, contented, and prosperous, by surrounding and guarding it with every protection and encouragement of the laws."

Washington promoted this as the best strategy for the elevation of the black race: by thrift, saving, and working hard at whatever job given, they would, in that way, achieve "Negro power" or "black power." It could only be accomplished through economic means, he contended. Washington may have at least been correct in his understanding of blacks being worth less to the larger society, except what they could do by the sweat of their brow. He urged blacks to stay away from labor unions and other groups that agitated for equality of rights and higher pay. Washington thought that equal pay would spell no jobs for blacks. He believed that if equality of wages occurred, blacks would find themselves permanently out of work because the wealthy elements of whites would have no reason to hire them. Washington professed that the real friends of blacks were not the labor unions but those who owned the industries. Why employ blacks if their hiring meant no special advantage to the owners of industry? "Who Needs the Negro?" was a fair question in a racist society. Would gains in civil rights, then, put black folk out of work because they were no longer useful as exploitable and more profitable workers to their employers? What of the future for all American workers in the years to come as cheaper labor supplies became readily available in a changing world market? Washington hit upon a theme that was undeniable in the reality of the black experience after slavery.

Washington's severest failing was his belief that economics alone could bring protection and rights for blacks. The obstacles to African Americans were virtually insurmountable without meaningful reform and that meant being outspoken and assertive. A long list of black leaders, such as Du Bois, Kelly Miller, Monroe Trotter, and Ida B. Wells, disagreed with Washington's philosophy and leadership. In her work, *A Red Record*, published in 1892, Wells decried against lynchings as a moral outrage, hideous crime, and political intimidation against black people that was the utter disgrace of America. She was critical of anyone who did not stand tall and speak out forcefully in opposition to lynchings. Washington's severest critic was Du Bois, who lambasted the accommodationist leader for his prescription of race uplift only through exploitability and service to an emerging industrial South. Du Bois and the other Washington critics asserted that blacks could not survive without equality as human beings. They advocated a new sense of community and vision; one laced with equal opportunity and civil rights. As Du Bois often expressed, "One can not expect to be an equal while he voluntarily throws away his rights and any claim to equality."

The owners of the Virginia Railway sponsored Washington's travel to spread his message throughout the region. He stopped in large and small towns and spoke to black workers urging them to be loyal, faithful, and, at all times, hardworking. Booker Washington was an important tool in the effort to stabilize the black labor force of the South. After the *Compromise of 1877* there was a continuous and increasing exodus of blacks out of the South. Washington tried to get them to stay and invoked what became his most famous slogan: "Cast down your bucket where you are." He lectured to blacks that "the soil will yield crops to the blackest hand as quickly as it will to the whitest hand." He pleaded for an egalitarianism that would come out of the soil, out of agriculture. Large numbers of African Americans did not share his vision and hope for the South as his plea to stay put fell on deaf ears. Tired of the exploitation, mistreatment and brutality, blacks wanted to break loose from the circle of exploitation that ran from sharecropping and tenant farming to debt peonage and convict lease. They wanted to find their own salvation on their own terms. By the time of Booker T. Washington's death in 1915 several million blacks had left the South—a trend that continued through the first half of the twentieth century—seeking the African-American version of the *American Dream*.[4]

SEEKING THE LAND OF THE FREE AND TRYING TO MAKE YOUR OWN HOME OF THE BRAVE

Given the treatment that African Americans received on a daily basis in the United States, why would they not look elsewhere for possible salvation and a better way of life? Why would they not look to Haiti where Toussaint L' Overture had made it the hope for liberation? Why would they not look back to Africa? Indeed, most Africans brought to America would have gladly returned if they could have. America was a living hell for them, the rapes, the lynchings, the convict lease, the sharecropping, the daily abuse. Back-to-

Africa had been the hope of blacks since the beginning of their forced immigration to America. Ironically, it was a group of white American leaders, some who were slave holders, who orchestrated an early effort for the deportation or *repatriation* of unwanted blacks back to Africa with the formation of the American Colonization Society in 1816. In 1822, the ACS founded the colony of Liberia in West Africa especially for the repatriation. The American Colonization Society included some of America's most prominent citizens, John Caldwell, Henry Clay, William Crawford, Robert Findley, Andrew Jackson, Thomas Jefferson, Francis Scott Key, James Monroe, John Randolph, John Taylor, Bushrod Washington, and many others. Their main concern was what to do with free blacks whose ranks numbered nearly two hundred thousand in 1815 and continued to rise with the demise of slavery in the North, *manumissions*, and the number of freedmen in the South as a result of many slaves being set free when they became too old or feeble to work. Slave owners feared free blacks as a threat to the peculiar institution. The alternative, amalgamation of blacks into American society, was bitterly denounced throughout the nation. The ACS proclaimed that separation of the races was the only realistic solution and that free blacks should either be relegated to some territory in the West, shipped to Haiti, or sent back to Africa. They agreed on the latter.

Blacks were suspicious of the motives behind the American Colonization Society and rightly so. They believed that the repatriation scheme concealed American designs to enslave and colonize portions of Africa. Even blacks who advocated African repatriation such as Paul Cuffe, the well known ship captain and ship builder in Connecticut and Massachusetts; James Forten, Peter Williams, Daniel Coker, and John Russwurm were critical and suspicious of the ACS from the beginning. Eventually, however, Forten, Coker, Russwurm, and thousands of other blacks disgruntled over their treatment in the United States, embraced the Liberian exodus.

Liberia was a small strip of land in West Africa purchased from local native chiefs by the ACS for three hundred dollars and some beads, tobacco, gunpowder, clothing, mirrors, and rum. The name Liberia, which in Latin means free, was the choice of the first black repatriates. They named the capital of their tiny country Monrovia in honor of the President of the United States, James Monroe. From its founding to the end of the nineteenth century, twelve thousand blacks immigrated from the United States to Liberia; three thousand of whom were Africans seized from slavers in the Atlantic waters by the United States navy between 1822 and 1862. Three hundred blacks from the West Indies also repatriated back to West Africa, to

Liberia. The ACS helped the colony to survive, providing the repatriates with food, shelter, clothing, and medicine. It acquired several grants from the United States Congress that enabled the colony to expand, purchase additional land, construct homes and forts, secure tools, and develop agriculture. The goal was to send surplus black folk out of America and back to Africa. From the beginning Liberia was under the authority of white governors. Neither did the ACS envision blacks' own hegemony over themselves in Liberia. Eli Ayers, Liberia's first governor, was a white physician from Baltimore. Jahudi Ashmun was a white Methodist minister. Thomas Buchanan, who was the last of the white governors, was the brother of the future president of the Untied States. After Buchanan's death in office in Liberia in 1841, Joseph Jenkins Roberts became the first Americo-Liberian (as the repatriates were called) to govern the colony. His appointment was a result of the ACS's willingness to experiment with black self autonomy, at least at this point, and the Americos' persistent agitation for self rule as the black repatriates wanted their freedom and to lead themselves. The repatriates had come to Liberia to escape white domination and did not take favorably to the dictates of others. White governor Jahudi Ashmun was forced to seek the security of the Cape Verde Islands for several months until the rebellion against his administration, orchestrated by the Americo Lott Carey, quieted. Neither did the repatriates follow the ACS philosophy which, in the Jeffersonian tradition, avowed the superiority of the rural and agricultural way of life over that of the city, commerce, and industry. The Americos saw agriculture as beneath them, associating it with slavery and a previous life in America that they wished to forget. Their own assertiveness, coupled with the declining power of the ACS, brought about by the mounting successes of the abolitionist crusade in the United States, won them the right to form their own government. In 1847, Liberia declared itself an independent republic and elected Joseph Jenkins Roberts as its first president.

Liberia's future was trouble-filled and earmarked with difficulty between the black repatriates and the indigenous native population (commonly referred to as indigenees). Liberia, nevertheless, stood to many American blacks as a goal, as a success story of black people having gone back to mother Africa to reconnect and be free, at least in some sense of the word, of white domination.

The idea of African repatriation was an engaging concept and dream for black Americans throughout the nineteenth and early twentieth centuries. Martin R. Delany easily stands as the most prominent advocate of back-to-Africa migration prior to the Civil

War. The Civil War halted Delany's repatriation dream as blacks expected that slavery would be eradicated in America; very much the same kind of thinking and hope that had prevailed at the end of the American Revolution. The revolutionary war had been fought, they believed, for liberty, equality and justice. How could slavery have continued, they questioned? Much the same was contemplated during the Civil War as black folk looked to that war as being fought to liberate them, to end slavery. In short, there were expectations and hope among blacks that with the end of the Civil War, they would be free and equal. They had not gone so far as to question whether or not they might be welcomed as true citizens in the United States, but they were confident that a better life was coming with the demise of bondage. One thinks, in the American tradition, that with freedom at hand you were thus free to be your own person, to achieve on your own merits, your own worth. If you worked hard and tried and struggled, you would benefit from your own efforts. You could elevate yourself. No longer would your labor be taken for the benefit of others, or so you thought. Regardless of how simplistically blacks may have viewed the end of the Civil War and the coming of emancipation, they envisioned it positively. Freedom meant just that, they hoped. The coming of the Civil War diverted the energies of the colonization society and it made blacks reluctant to attempt to repatriate back to Africa, at least temporarily. The mistreatment the freedmen suffered told them in unmistakable terms that they hoped for too much from the Civil War. After Reconstruction, and with the Compromise of 1877, America's African population looked again to repatriation. America had made it clear that their place was as slaves or as second-class citizens, not as equals.

It has never been a question of simply black separatism. To separate indicated that blacks had some choice in the matter. America has been a closed society to people of African descent because of their color. It was just that simple and just that tragic. The mistreatment of blacks after the Civil War and the failure to deliver on the quest for black freedom helped to push forward again a new surge of black nationalism and African repatriation and resettlement in Africa. The hardship that blacks experienced under the heel of Union forces in Hampton, Virginia, was but one example among many and should help to explain why blacks looked to Haiti, to Canada, or to Africa, or somewhere other than the United States. In 1878, Martin Delany of South Carolina united with other blacks of the state, especially in Charleston, and launched the Liberian Exodus Joint Stock Steamship Company, to provide for immigration to

Africa, particularly to Liberia and Sierra Leone. With the goal of African repatriation they set sail in the spring of 1878 in their ship the Azor, which made that its first and only voyage that year. The inexperience, lack of planning, dishonesty of the ship's white captain, doomed to failure this effort at repatriation and the Azor ended up in auction to pay off the debts incurred. This repatriation effort of Martin Delany and his followers was one of many back-to-Africa initiatives after the Civil War. Delany himself, the great African-American leader, physician, officer during the Civil War, congressman in the Reconstruction government, and black visionary, concluded that America did not want black people and would remain a hostile environment. Delany maintained his dream of African repatriation for the race until his death in 1885.

New forces were beginning to be heard and they spoke along much the same lines as Martin Delany. They were talking too of nationalism, of repatriation, of Pan-Africanism, that connectedness that black folk needed to survive in both a real sense and a philosophical and psychological one; to see themselves as a strong and meaningful people with dignity and pride in their history and contributions as a people that predated their lowly status in America. Henry McNeal Turner was the forefather of this new intellectual and political consciousness movement. Turner became a bishop in the African Methodist Episcopal Church. He lived from 1834 to 1915 and throughout his life was a counter point against the philosophy and ideas of Booker T. Washington's race leadership of accommodationism. There were other critical voices being heard during the Washington era but Henry McNeal Turner stood far and above the most outspoken of the nationalists. He talked about blacks going home to Africa on a consistent basis in his public speeches. Until Turner's death during the era of World War I, his was a persistent voice for black nationalism and African repatriation, constantly agitating and questioning African Americans and prodding them to develop a world view that enabled them to see themselves as more than former slaves, as people of African descent whose beginnings were rooted in the rich heritage and civilizations of the world's oldest continent. Bishop Turner recognized only too well the disabilities plaguing African folk in the United States. He turned his considerable intellect, whit, vocabulary and powers of persuasion to developing race pride, to making African Americans understand that they were part of a history that began before European enslavement. This, he concluded, was essential for race uplift. Turner was a strong advocate for black history taught by blacks. In Georgia's Reconstruction politics, he was a force to be reckoned with, and he continued speaking out on the race question from the platform of bishop in the AME church. America's treatment of black folk disgusted him. He pessimistically concluded that blacks would never be treated as equals in America and able to stand tall in the world community of human families. African repatriation was the only solution. "Every man that has the sense of an animal," Turner exhorted, "must see there is no future in this country for the Negro."

Bishop Turner's religious views were also fiery and unique. He had no sympathy for those who thought of Christianity as the home of a "blue-eyed, straight-haired, projecting nosed, compressed lipped and finely robed *white* gentleman, sitting upon a throne somewhere in the heavens." Turner believed and often said that any people who failed to see God in their own image were weak and "demented." The bishop professed from his pulpit that there was no question in his mind that God was black and that the greatest of the Madonnas had to be black. He challenged people of color every where to put up pictures of black Christ figures for he held that there was nothing wrong with it: "Every race of people since time began who have attempted to describe their God by words, or by paintings, or by carvings, or by any other form or figure, have conveyed the idea that the God who made them and shaped their destinies was symbolized in themselves, and why should not the Negro believe that he resembles God as much so as other people? We do not believe that there is any hope for a race of people who do not believe they look like God." Hence, blacks would have to liken God to themselves. They had to stand up and throw off the yoke of backward thinking, Turner demanded. He saw no contradiction between religion, politics, ethnic pride and nationalism. The Bishop said: "I do not believe any race will ever be respected or ought to be respected who do not show themselves capable of founding and manning a government of their own creation. Till we have black men in the seat of power, respected, feared, hated, and revered, our young men will never rise for the reason they will never look up." Bishop Turner was an organization person who advocated that blacks come together and form their own associations to do for themselves. Edward Wilmot Blyden and Alexander Crummell were also in sympathy with black repatriation and connectedness with the African motherland.

Blacks have always had points of agreement and disagreement with actual repatriation. From the very beginning, black leadership in America identified with Africa. They considered themselves to be African people and large segments of the African-American population maintained that identification well into the twentieth century. It was true that back-to-Africa as a movement never grew to momentous proportions with blacks packing up in the tens of thousands and physically returning to Africa. That was not to be. African repatriation, however, never died out and peaked at various times in the nation's history. It seemed more feasible for later generations of African Americans to attempt to make due in the United States. Most black folk understood only too well that they were not true Americans. American racism made that unmistakable. African Americans made continuous efforts to build their community, to build a black nation within America, holding on to that black nationalist belief of "a nation within but without white America." It made perfect sense for them to move in the nationalist direction, given that the larger society rejected them. The idea of black separatism was misleading and a long misunderstood concept and goal. It was not a new separatism, for example, that black students were attempting to establish on some college campuses in the 1960s and, to a lesser extent, in the 1990s. They were simply trying to build community, to find strength within a group connectedness. The predominantly white academic community has not welcomed most black students with open arms or treated them as equals. If blacks were absorbed into American society, academic or social, that society would not be racist. Building one's own community was, thus, seen as a necessity for African-American survival in the nineteenth and twentieth centuries. Whether the goal was back to Africa or the search for community and self-autonomy within the geographical boundaries of the United States, African Americans were doing their best to flee racism and the stultifying affects of white domination. The black migration west was, in large part, born of simple human dignity and the desire to escape an inferior status and to construct a positive environment for the race. The black nationalist towns established in the West were revealing and informative examples of the African-American struggle to create their own communities free of white authority.[5]

A DREAM DEFERRED

African Americans set out to find their dream, belatedly following Horace Greely's advice to go west. Had they been more aware of those who had gone before them they might not have been as optimistic about their chances of building a new life and a nation in the West, but without white America. The experience of Asians in the West was a story, in some ways, similar to that of the black experience in the South; one replete with examples of declarations of race superiority, inferiority, labor exploitation, and hatred of a people for their differences.

Prior to the end of the Civil War, the Union Pacific and Central Pacific Railroads made great headway to the West, owing largely to the railroad labor of the Irish and the Chinese. The Chinese were indispensable to the building of railroads in the West and the development of California. They worked under all conditions: on the railroad lines, in the mines, as domestics, and in agriculture. Despite their value as workers and their proven profitability, there were those who insisted on painting the Chinese in negative stereotypes. The rise of the *penny press* as part of the newspaper mass media revolution of the mid-nineteenth century, brought a vastly increased circulation and, ironically, more room and almost desperate need for the exotic. The Chinese fit the bill perfectly for that kind of market in the American mind. Throughout the press there was an emphasis on racial differences and articles attempted to link the Chinese and other non-white races with dreaded diseases. Timing was a factor that worked against the Chinese. Brought to America during the middle of the slavery period, they faced the pseudo-scientific racial theories of the era and found themselves at the brunt of the works by Holmes, Lister, Semmelweis, and their *germ theories*. These theories had direct influence on the 1882 decision to exclude the Chinese from American society as germ-ridden and undesirable. Through the press and pseudo-science, every aspect of Chinese life was criticized. Articles appeared that alleged connections between the Chinese and dirt and filth and characterized the Asian race as "little beggars." There was even a discussion of the undergarments of the Chinese, asserting that they wore their underwear for such long periods of time that the garments disintegrated on their bodies. There was great fascination with the question of infanticide in China. In a barrage of American newspaper articles in the West, stories were told of Chinese mothers who reportedly killed their infant daughters. When those stories ran short, there were accounts of alleged atrocities of women having their breasts and buttocks cut off and their legs ripped from their bodies, and finally being decapitated. The association of cruelty with the Chinese seemed to be great fun in the American press of the West. They told of stories of canals and rivers in China that gave off terrible stench as a result of the number of bodies and rotting corpses of infants that floated along like barges. Misuse and abuse were favorite topics of the press. Stories abounded about the Chinese as polygamists and opium smokers; addicts filling opium dens, not only in China, but bringing the dreaded and degenerated practices to the United States.

The advent of the Opium War of 1839 through 1842, stimulated further rumors about the association of the Chinese with drugs and degeneracy and intensified the fear in America that they would bring these practices with them. The Chinese were depicted as a degenerate race, imbecilic and incapable of progress. There was discussion within American magazines of the homes of the Chinese in the West, describing them as extremely dirty with disagreeable odors that no civilized human being could tolerate. Of course nothing could have been further from the truth. No people were more meticulous about cleanliness than the Chinese. That bit of reality, in the face of the press's need for stories to feed American vanity and the race agenda, was expendable. There was no mention of the great inventions of the Chinese, including gunpowder, the compass, and major contributions to nautical navigation. Rather, negative stories abounded relating to opium, death, destruction, infanticide, dirt, filth, and disease.

The Chinese were part of a new servitude trade, the *coolie trade*, brought to the United States, South America and the Caribbean islands in smaller numbers than that of Africans. They too were the concern of abolitionists who condemned the *coolie trade* for what it was—another slave trade, an exploitation of a people's labor, the kidnapping of a people and trading them for their labor. Similarities can be made about the coolie trade and their Pacific crossing to the Atlantic crossing of Africans brought to the New World. Although the coolie migration was marked by cramped quarters with little room to move, stacked bunks to bring as many as possible, it in no way matched the magnitude of the enslavement and trade in Africans and the numbers that died. Nevertheless, it was horrific and inhumane.

The plight of Chinese women was despicable. Exploitation of them did not stop with work as laborers or house servants and domestics. Many of these women were brought to America to become prostitutes. So bad was the situation that in 1874 President Grant made reference to the *coolie trade* and that most Chinese who were being brought to America did not come voluntarily. Particularly abhorrent to Grant was the exploitation of Chinese women. What was happening to the women was against all professed notions of American male chivalry and honor, he said.

The literature and writings in the press, however, blamed the Chinese for their own exploitation. In China those who sold fellow Chinese into servitude espoused that the coolies were better off in America, no matter what the conditions. In the United States the racial doctrine helped rationalize and justify the *coolie trade*. The

Chinese, after all, were shown by pseudo scientists as having smaller skulls and were thus supposedly inferior and unable to progress at a normal rate. They were, therefore, deemed as "fortunate" in being brought to the high civilization of the Western world. Racist literature declared that the Chinese were unable to make moral and intellectual judgments and, like Africans and Indians, were lucky to have been placed in contact with Europeans either abroad or in America. Thus the Chinese too were defined as inferior to whites. Fortunately for them they did not, like the blacks, suffer the ultimate debilitation of being conscripted into the *Constitution of the United States* as property and inferiors void of basic human rights.

State houses and senates, particularly in California, debated whether it was advisable to bring more Chinese into the country. It was also debated at the national level. Professional associations also added their point of view, most notably the American Medical Association which launched a vicious attack against the Chinese in the 1850s that continued for nearly fifty years. The AMA associated dangerous and deadly diseases with the Chinese and blamed them for leprosy in San Francisco. According to the AMA, Chinese lepers could be found standing on many street corners. In addition, the medical association and the public faulted Chinese prostitutes for the spread of syphilis and gonorrhea among America's youth in the West. The fears and negative attitudes against the Chinese flourished. If something went wrong out West, the Chinese were the cause.

Organized labor joined in against the Asians. The most prominent labor spokesmen of the time, George McNeal, John Swinton, John P. Irish, Terrance V. Powderly, Samuel Gompers, William J. Mclauflin, and socialist Eugene Debs, were outspoken *sinophobes*. Why? Organized labor in America was fearful of the Chinese as competitors who might undermine unionization. Given the negative image of the Chinese, legislation was eventually passed to halt their further importation and immigration into the United States. This was accomplished with the *Chinese Exclusion Law* of 1882 and ten years later its indefinite extension. The Chinese, like the Africans before them, were exploitable labor and convenient scapegoats and points of attack by the promoters of Anglo-Saxon superiority. Racism and spoiled race relations were at the heart of American westward expansion.[6]

It would have been most helpful to African Americans in the late nineteenth and early twentieth century, who looked to the West as a promised land, to have known of the experiences of those who had gone before them. Given too that the Chinese were in general close to white in skin color, it portended more of a potential warning to blacks of the problematic encounters they were likely to face in the West. Blacks were the easiest targets of racism no matter where they went in the United States of America. Nevertheless, at least thirty thousand African Americans ventured west in the late nineteenth century hoping to find the *promised land* and build their own communities free from racism. Their eyes were full of star dust and hope and dreams that they could forge a life of dignity for themselves and their children. They were willing to do anything to keep that hope alive. Sadly, a portion of the price they paid came at the expense of other struggling minorities.

There would be no sorrier chapter in African-American history than the tumultuous encounter with native peoples in the West. Indeed, when African Americans were put in conflict against other minorities, they showed themselves to be true Americans; meaning, they fought, died, and participated in all the horrors and evils of inflicting America's will on those who resisted or were obstacles in its path. Unlike the stories of the black cowboys, particularly regrettable in the black experience in the West were the escapades of the buffalo soldiers. These black soldiers, called buffalo soldiers by the Native Americans because of their wool-like hair and dark color, were a part of the military forces used to conqueror the West and to defeat the Native American peoples of that region. These former slaves and sons of former slaves helped crush the indigenous population and served the expansionist interests of the same dominant majority society that held them and their forebears in contempt and bondage. Sad to say, blacks carried out their orders with heroism, zeal, and effectiveness as they played an important role in that conquest. When the Chairman of the Joint Chiefs of Staff, General Colin Powell, urged that a monument be erected in the West to the buffalo soldiers, he insulted the historical legacy of Native Americans. Why not build monuments in tribute to black-red coexistence where that happened? Blacks joined hands with the Seminoles, the Black Feet, the Piquot and other Native American groups in the South, Midwest, and Northeast. There were wrongs, to be sure, committed on both sides. Some of the so-called civilized tribes, the Cherokees and the Chippewas, actually owned slaves. Even that, however, could hardly justify blacks going west and killing Navaho, Cheyenne, Sioux, and others. The era of the buffalo soldiers was a tragic chapter in race relations between reds and blacks.[7]

The African-American migration was tertiary, spreading from the rural South to the cities of the South and from there outward. The majority would go to the North, but there were those who went to the West. Those that went west personified black nationalist ideology and the dream of black autonomy. Blacks started west in the late 1870s, looking first to Kansas and migrating there in large enough numbers that by 1879 the movement became known as the *Kansas Fever Exodus.* Benjamin "Pap" Singleton was the movement's leader. He and other black spokespersons urged their fellow race members to go to the West and to settle in Kansas with the hope of making of it an all-black state, a black man's land, a paradise here on earth. Singleton and his followers were nationalists who believed that the only way for African Americans to build for themselves was to do precisely that and be free of white domination, to move to the new territories like Kansas, develop a black enclave and later to bring the territory into the nation as a black state. His followers founded Nicademus, in Kansas, and other all-black towns throughout the West, including the towns of Boley and Langston in Oklahoma.

Langston became a unique experiment in black autonomy that demonstrated the hopes, strategies, successes, and shortcomings of the *African-American Dream.* Langston was the brainchild of Edwin P. McCabe, a black man deeply imbued with the idea of uplifting his race. McCabe was born in Troy, New York, in 1850. In his twenties he was inspired by the separatist ideas of Benjamin "Pap" Singleton and others who advocated that blacks go west and settle in Kansas and make it an all black state, a "black man's land," a paradise here on earth. McCabe worked for several years in Chicago, and then struck out for Kansas and settled in what became Nicademus, one of the all-black towns. He arrived there a full year before the heralded *Kansas Fever Exodus* of 1879.[8]

While this was a glorious dream there would be inherent inconsistencies in the actions of McCabe and his followers that served as poignant lessons for those interested in striking a black separatist cord. Separation did not, in and of itself, mean self-autonomy. Autonomy meant being self-sustaining. It was contradictory, at the least, for separatists to simultaneously hold the hope of some level of integration. The Langstonites, however, were willing to engage in cooperative ventures with whites. It was a unique experiment that has been given precious little attention in African-American history. The Langston experiment came closest to any sort of true black nationalism that black folk ever achieved in America. The idea that blacks physically leave and go back to Africa in the late nineteenth and twentieth century was unrealistic. The notion of a black nation state within white America seemed much more attainable to E. P. McCabe.

McCabe could not see the contradiction in his professing black autonomy, development and hegemony, and his own participation in the integrated world of politics as he became a key black Republican in Kansas. In 1882 he was elected to the office of auditor, the first black to hold a statewide position in Kansas. Political office, prestige and influence were not E. P. McCabe's motivating force. He was genuine in his desire and his concern for a better way of life for black people on their own terms. Despite doing well for himself in the state, he remained dissatisfied with the progress of the race as a whole. Numerous racial barriers in Kansas ended his dream of making it into an all-black nation state.

He turned his attention to the Oklahoma territory in 1889. What he and his followers envisioned was a sufficient number of blacks settling in Oklahoma and then controlling the state's political destiny and thus making it into the black promised land. The key here, he thought, was timing and selling the idea; getting blacks to migrate to the chosen area in Oklahoma in sufficient enough numbers. McCabe and followers believed that if large numbers of blacks settled in Oklahoma, whites would find the territory unattractive and leave it to the Negroes. With the numeric strength, he reasoned, came expanded black autonomy and the foundation to carry forward the failed *Kansas Fever Exodus* dream and nurture it into reality in Oklahoma.

In 1890, McCabe and his followers formed the Oklahoma Colored Immigration Bureau with the idea of developing pamphlets and leaflets to be distributed throughout the South to entice blacks to come and settle in Langston. They promised that this would be a black man's land and that black folk would indeed sustain it, run it, and develop it on their own terms. In their attempt to sell the Langston idea, the Oklahoma Colored Immigration Bureau published thousands of leaflets periodically and distributed them through a network of bureau agents. The bureau gave glowing accounts of what Langston was becoming, pushing the idea of separatism and racial autonomy. McCabe and associates reiterated constantly that the titles to the lots were to be sold only to blacks and that no white man could reside or conduct a business in Langston. They declared a strict abhorrence of *miscegenation*. They were not interested in being friends with whites. They most certainly were not interested in intermarrying with them. McCabe proclaimed: "Langston will develop along an all-Negro ideology." The dream was an interesting one in that financial, political, religious, legal, educational, and every other aspect of the community would be under black authority, or so it was promised. McCabe's philosophy was quite simple: whites do not want us and we do not want them.

The dream was interesting but advancing it beyond a stated philosophical premise to a practical existence immediately showed problems and inconsistencies. Some of these inconsistencies were self inflicted; others were a result of the reality of a dream difficult, and perhaps impossible to achieve within the United States of America. The choice of the name of Langston for the town was both a positive statement and a hint of early inconsistency in the thought and action of E. P. McCabe and followers. John M. Langston was a great African-American leader. Born a slave in Virginia he rose to become a lawyer, general inspector of education for the Freedmen's Bureau, member of the U.S. House of Representatives, and minister to Haiti. He was an outspoken advocate of higher education for blacks and a proponent of black migration out of the South. When all of that was said and done it remained that John M. Langston was no separatist in practice. He believed in black autonomy but he did not go beyond the rhetorical and philosophical in advocating that blacks could actually achieve complete autonomy on their own terms in the United States. Nevertheless, John M. Langston's namesake town became the hope for black nationalism. Langston, Oklahoma, according to McCabe, was to be a separatist town, the central city of that land where the race could prosper unencumbered by whites. McCabe and his associates advised blacks to "get away from the associations that cluster about them and to leave whites to themselves and to begin building a black man's country."

Key to the development of the Langston idea was an all-black education. McCabe had always held schooling in reverence. He was cognizant of the importance of education for the elevation of the race in the long term and in the short term. He understood very well the desire of blacks for quality schooling. McCabe insisted that the way to attain a good education, however, was not to have blacks attend white schools. He was not a proponent of integrated education and believed that it would never occur. His belief was that if blacks wanted quality education they would have to build black schools and have black teachers. One of the first things that he and his followers sought to achieve was a separatist public school system. This, he thought, offered the best hope to advance the community in terms of skills, in terms of philosophy, in terms of insightfulness and consciousness. The bureau boasted in its literature that Langston City "is a Negro city and we are proud of the fact that her city officers are all colored, her teachers are colored, her public schools furnish thorough educational advantages to nearly two hundred colored students."[9]

The blacks who settled in Langston were also eager for higher education. In only four years after the town's inception its residents were demanding college-level education for their children. The Langston community, which numbered five hundred in 1894, wanted to establish a university. Moreover, Langstonites insisted that the university had to be under their control and provide a "Negro education" to their liking. If "black education" was possible anywhere in the United States, its best hope was in Langston. The town did not choose, however, to be pure separatists or black nationalists and build the institution themselves, which would have been the appropriate course given their views. They had neither the money nor the expertise. Instead, the Langstonites deduced that since the territorial government provided a college for whites, it should also be made to provide a college for blacks. Needless to say, they believed that this institution of higher learning should be located in the most prominent all-black town — Langston. What they did not see was that any level of compromise constituted a cooperative effort that betrayed their separatist ideas and would endanger their hegemony.

The town drifted even further from the black nationalist philosophy. Similar to the story of colleges and universities everywhere, black and white, E. P. McCabe and his town looked to outside sources to assist them in their educational goals. Langston sought aid from the very forces from which it said it wanted to be separated. The Langston-led Oklahoma Association of Negro Teachers attempted to spur the territorial legislature into providing black Oklahomans with a university. To dramatize the issue the association took a black student, Cynthia Ware, to enroll at the white Normal University in Edmond, Oklahoma, in 1896. Ware was, as expected, denied admission because of her race. The black community, however, had made its point. They wanted college training available to their youth and they expected the territorial government to provide it. The effort was successful. The next year the legislation met and passed a bill in January of 1897 to set up the Colored Agricultural and Normal University at Langston.

Actually, it took more than the enrollment demonstration to win a university. McCabe and followers steeped themselves further into the outside world, moving away from pure separatism. McCabe did some old-fashioned integrated politicking. He was the most prominent black in the territory and the political forces eagerly sought his support. In 1896, McCabe lent his influence to the Republican cause in Oklahoma by endorsing the national ticket headed by William McKinley and supporting Cassius M. Barnes's bid for the territorial governorship of Oklahoma. McKinley won the presidency and Barnes became governor. Barnes dispensed the spoils of victory to those who had backed him. The Colored Agricultural and Normal University of Oklahoma was established at Langston. It was old-fashioned, deal-making, integrated politics that won the university for the community.

The Langstonites did not see their actions as a compromise of their separatist views or philosophically inconsistent. It was a necessary cooperative venture, in their estimation, and they avoided any thoughts that this might be a move toward accommodation or integration. It was not, of course, integration since blacks would have their own school and whites theirs. The funding, however, that sustained the "black institution" was dependent upon forces outside of the African-American community. Langstonites, nevertheless, saw their efforts as simply a way to get what they wanted quickly and on their own terms. An important aspect of the *Barnes-McCabe Agreement* was the promise to the Langston community of complete control over the selection of the school's teachers and administrators, and in formulating the educational philosophy of the institution. Langstonites wanted an institution that provided unlimited educational opportunity to black Oklahomans, a university free from the traditional limitations associated with the "Negro's place" in society, and they believed that the *Barnes-McCabe Agreement* guaranteed them that power, although the agreement was never put in writing. A critical evaluation of the gentlemen's agreement between McCabe and Barnes revealed certain danger signals. Black schools, at their point of conception, have exhibited an unfortunate naiveté in assessing their educational place and future in America. This was the seed of future difficulty that the Langstonites helped to plant with their own hands when they sought outside assistance to build their university. Like the other so-called black or Negro colleges and universities, Langston's financial well being would depend upon whites not blacks. The old adage of "He who pays the piper calls the tune" was ignored. White Oklahomans had their own idea as to what constituted the best and proper type of education for blacks. White Oklahoma opposed the premise of equal opportunity for black Oklahoma. Consequently, they saw black education in limited terms. They believed that blacks should be taught chiefly in compliance with the demands of labor, an idea championed by Booker T. Washington, exemplified at Hampton and Tuskegee Institutes, and embraced by the vast majority of Negro colleges at the turn of the century. Langstonites, however, despised the accommodationism and limited education associated with Booker Washington and the industrial schooling idea, although they liked very much Washington's thoughts on self-help and separation of the races. "I believe in

Booker T. Washington," one Langstonite said. "We can live in the same world as white folks but we can't live with them. Our lives must be as distinctive as the fingers on your hand. That's a good point ole Booker made." Self-help, in real terms, meant knowing how to build a house and irrigate a field, ideas quite in tune with the industrial education concept and the Langston community's stated beliefs. The town debated the merits of offering some degree of industrial training at their school. F. D. Moon, a former member of the community, reflected on the period and said that the town gave considerable discussion to the type of education blacks should have. Booker T. Washington, on the one hand, he noted, favored what was called industrial education and W.E.B. Du Bois and Kelly Miller, who was with Howard University, were opposed to that and advocated a liberal arts curriculum. Moon recalled that he, like the overwhelming majority of the community, was "on the side against Booker T. Washington." The town did agree on the necessity of the university providing a few courses in industrial skills.

Beyond these general points of agreement, the Langston community had no conception of the pragmatic difficulties ahead in laying the philosophical and practical foundation for a university. Black autonomy was a noble goal but impossible to obtain through cooperative ventures as the educational dilemma in Langston demonstrated. No one in the town, including McCabe, understood what was required to develop a college and particularly a "black" one—a problem universal among black schools. The Langstonites answer to the dilemma was to do as other Negro colleges and universities had done before them: appoint a chief administrator for the new school who they believed had the expertise and right educational philosophy, and who would deal with the problem. The town supported the application of Inman E. Page for president of Langston University. The regents quietly acquiesced and extended Page an offer, which he accepted.

Langstonites were most impressed with Page's reputation for his belief in having blacks to teach blacks, a cord of complete harmony with the separatist point of view. Page, like most blacks before him and after him, was a product of something other than a black nationalist or separatist educational training and philosophy. He was a graduate of an Ivy League school, Brown University in Rhode Island. He had served as a clerk under General Oliver Otis Howard in the Freedmen's Bureau and had been president of a "Negro school," Lincoln University, in Missouri for eighteen years. During Page's second year at Lincoln he began work on reversing the institute's policy of employing only whites as teachers. By the time he left Lincoln in 1897, its entire teaching staff and most of its administrators were black. This was accomplished, however, only in part due to the efforts of Page. The white governing board of Lincoln University had been anxious to try the experiment in black self-education.

Page committed himself to a difficult job when he accepted the position as president of Langston University in 1898, a post he would hold for seventeen years. The immediate task was to formulate a curriculum. Having no practical or substantive suggestions from the town as to the kind of educational program he should develop, except that it should be "Negro oriented." Page proceeded cautiously and conservatively. The curriculum he constructed at Lincoln included the study of ancient history, philosophy and the classics, and a small amount of training in agricultural and vocational skills. The emphasis was unquestionably on the liberal arts as reflected in the initial teaching staff hired at Langston, which consisted of a professor of English literature, an instructor of music, a mathematician, and a teacher of history and moral philosophy. While the initial four educators were African Americans, non had any particular training or background in subject matter focusing on the African-American experience. Neither was there a particular philosophy of nationalism lurking within their own brand of education. Theirs was a very traditional, classical educational espousal.

Langston University, however, had neither the finances nor the faculty to deliver the highest quality liberal arts nor vocational education. Nor did the institution develop a curriculum that was somehow uniquely African American or "black." Like other traditional Negro colleges and universities, Langston provided a service. Langstonites, students, and black Oklahomans in general supported Page's leadership of the university and favored the training being offered at the institution. The most praised aspect of the all-black school was its atmosphere. Students at Langston alluded that the all-black environment afforded them a sense of comfort, that they felt a racial affinity and camaraderie toward the faculty, and were proud of the school. Langston University students from the beginning praised the institution consistently for enabling them to develop a strong ego and high self-esteem.

The result was an intellectually active student body at Langston. Roscoe Dunjee, for example, became an author and publisher. This former Langston student said that while he was at the university he learned to appreciate the finer things of life and to develop his mind and confidence. "It was at Langston under Inman E. Page," Dunjee remarked, "that I got the inspiration to do big things." There was a shared sentiment among the Langston community that Inman E. Page was making excellent headway toward establishing the town as the "Athens of education for the Negroes of this territory."[10]

To develop an educational Athens or Timbuktu in Langston or any other African-American community was a near impossibility, given the scarcity of resources coupled with external and internal problems. In addition to the many worries that typically fell on the shoulders of a college president, Inman Page struggled against an eroding base of support both local and territorial. The university had been a major factor in attracting African-American settlers to Langston. By 1900, Langston University enrolled nine hundred students. The population of the town, excluding students, after reaching a peak of approximately two thousand five hundred inhabitants in 1900, had declined to three hundred and twenty by 1914. Much of the problem was due to the changing status of the territory. Oklahoma lost a great deal of its appeal to black settlers when it became a state in 1907. The once abundant supply of cheap land was now limited. Moreover, African Americans who had been attracted to the region by the dream of making it a "black man's land," were now awakened to the reality that this would never happen. E. P. McCabe, the spirit of Langston, recognized that the battle was lost. He left for Chicago in 1908. Inman E. Page put up a gallant fight as he contended with all of these negative factors. The increasing financial woes of the town and a growing anti-Langston attitude in the state government finally overwhelmed him. Page resigned his post as president of Langston University in 1915.

Statehood marked Oklahoma's breaking of the *Barnes-McCabe Agreement* and the beginning of the state government's assertion of its authority over Langston University. The political forces in the state became increasingly critical of the educational objective of the school and the stated mission of the town. They began to push their conviction that Langston University should be made to devote itself to industrial schooling and to making the educated black, along their way of thinking, of greater value to the community and to the state. These were trying times for Langston University and the town. During the twenty-five years after the resignation of Inman E. Page, the presidency of the school changed hands nine times. Throughout these years, however, the institution and town of Langston wavered only slightly from their position that emphasis at the university should be on liberal arts, an education that prepared blacks to achieve their full potential. Langstonites did not waver from their vision of the school as a great intellectual oasis. The *Black Dispatch*, published in Guthrie, Oklahoma, reported in 1923 that Oklahoma's

African-American population regarded Langston University as "a city on a hill which no intellectual can pass by. We must be steadfast in our line of duty and strive for the interest of our school." In the same article, I. W. Young, a former president of the university, lauded the school's commitment to a liberal arts education. The institution offered several courses in agriculture and vocational skills and Young considered that to be more than adequate. He was opposed to the university becoming an industrial institution, educating the hand instead of the mind. "The creative potential of the Negro race deserves better," Young asserted. "This race of ours is capable of doing anything that lies within the bounds of human effort and Langston University together with her former students is helping to build a race."

Underneath the glowing accolades of the Langston school, and the traditional black colleges throughout the United States, were numerous difficulties. In the case of Langston, an institution, a town, and a philosophy were in dire straits. The coming of the Great Depression killed any pretense of black separatism or nationalism in Langston and necessitated desperate measures just to keep the school open. Oklahoma cut back on its financial support to Langston University. The town of Langston was barely subsisting and could offer the university only moral support. Zack Hubert, president of the university in 1930, sought to obtain financial assistance for the school from wealthy whites in the East. Forgetting their philosophy of self-determinism, separatism, and anti-industrial schooling, Hubert applied to the Rockefeller-sponsored General Education Board for aid. The GEB was the major dispenser of private support to Negro schools. The organization, however, was primarily interested in industrial schools, particularly those in the South. Hubert perhaps had not considered this at the time of his grant proposal to the board in early 1930. In that request he described Langston as a western intellectual college. The grant was denied. In his second request for funding, President Hubert demonstrated that he had become more knowledgeable of what the GEB wanted to hear and that Langston was willing to submit. He emphasized the industrial side of Langston University. Hubert wrote that the school "is a mechanical college and also the colored agricultural college, the teachers' college, and the University." He ended with a plea: "In justice to its Negro population and the demands now made upon all its citizens, it is difficult to see how the state could cut a program of this nature and size. But you and I know that it very likely will. Hence I am again asking the aid of the General Education Board." The board voted no. The GEB considered the funding request of

Langston, but was obviously not interested in investing in the school's future. The board also, no doubt, saw the inconsistencies in the grant proposals of President Hubert, and doubted the institute's commitment to industrial education.

Langston, due to the deepening of the Great Depression, was now in terrible financial shape and continued its plea to the industrial schooling forces, moving rapidly away from its nationalist philosophy and stated goals. John W. Sanford, who served as president of the university from 1936 to 1939, submitted funding requests to the GEB. Upon receiving from Sanford a proposal for money to help the school to purchase more books, Leo M. Favrot of the GEB notified him that his application arrived late, and that the list of books was "voluminous and with no estimate of cost." Favrot then lashed out at Sanford for impropriety. "You thank me on behalf of the college and Negro citizens of the state for this promised donation," Favrot wrote. "My statement to you that the Board's present policy included appropriations of this kind to selected institutions and that you might apply for aid must not be interpreted by you or anyone connected with your institution as promise of a donation." After doing a brief feasibility study of Langston University, the GEB decided against Sanford's request. The study described the ideological basis of the school as being not fixed or final and that the course of training at the institution had no clear cut statement of purpose. The report ended with the recommendation that Langston University reassess itself and ask: "What kind of school would provide the best type of education for Negro citizens of Oklahoma?" The GEB long decided that industrial schooling was best for blacks and that anything other than that was basically a waste of time and funds.

Added to the school's problems were internal hassles that plagued the university throughout the 1930s. In April of 1937, for example, Pearl Howard, the school matron, filed suit against President Sanford and Langston University for slander and libel, charging that President Sanford had fired her for unjust cause. Sanford had dismissed Howard for her alleged moral misconduct one night in Guthrie, Oklahoma. She had a reputation as the bimbo of Langston. At any rate, the district court decided in favor of the plaintiff. The Oklahoma Supreme Court, however, overturned the decision. Citizens of Langston and many other supporters of the university applauded Sanford's actions. Langston University, with its special mission, tried desperately to have a spotless reputation. They fought to keep the university free of any scandals and misbehavior. The *Black Dispatch* saluted President Sanford for his belief in dismissing any teacher or employee for any misconduct or irregularity. Nevertheless, the school suffered bad publicity from the Pearl Howard incident. As a result, President Sanford resigned. Accepting personal responsibility, he decided that a new chief administrator could better serve the university.

It appeared that Langston University in its steadily weakening condition would be receptive to substantial changes. The state government considered the time right to move in and transform the university into the type of educational institution it had always deemed appropriate for blacks. The board of regents asserted itself in the selection of the new president of the university. The regents sought and found the individual they considered to be best suited to head the school. They chose Albert L. Turner, a quiet, accommodating person, an amiable individual with a reputation of working hard at whatever task given him. Most important, Turner was an advocate of the philosophy of Booker T. Washington, political accommodationism and the industrial schooling program. He received his education and training at Tuskegee Institute where he had served as registrar. Leon C. Phillips, Governor of Oklahoma, was impressed that Frederick D. Patterson, president of Tuskegee Institute, recommended Turner for the Langston job. The regents moved with undue swiftness and little consideration of what the Langston community wanted. Fred Holman, an Oklahoma banker and president of the board of regents, announced in September of 1939 that Albert L. Turner was the new president of Langston University, and was arriving on campus the first week of October.

Turner received a heated welcome from the Langston community. Although Langstonites had abandoned their commitment to nationalism, and the school was hurting financially, they did not embrace accommodationism. They resented the regents' efforts to change the educational direction of the university. It was clear to them that Turner would seek to redirect Langston University along the industrial education line. When Albert Turner arrived in Langston on Friday, October 6, 1939, he found a community and a university ready to fight for liberal arts education and autonomy. The result was one of the shortest terms in office for a college or university president in the history of American higher education — one day. Turner arrived on Friday and resigned Saturday evening. "It didn't take long for Albert L. Turner, newly appointed president of the Colored Agricultural and Normal University, Langston, to decide that the job was most certainly not to his liking," the *Oklahoma City Times* reported. Fred Holman and the other regents knew what had transpired. No one blamed Turner for resigning. "Those Negroes out there in Langston scared the new college president clear out of the state," Holman lamented. "I personally consider the presidency of the Langston Negro college one of the toughest positions in the state because of the Negroes who are fighting to control the institution." Of course they were fighting to control the institution. There was never any doubt that Langstonites were trying to control their institution as well as their community and their own lives. They preferred total autonomy and complete hegemony but were unable to achieve them by fault of their own and the realities of the world in which they lived, and the result was vulnerability to the dictates of the white power structure. Langston University, and the African-American community, had not exhausted their will to fight. Perhaps taking their queue from the famous packing attempts in American history (John Adams's appointment of numerous midnight judges or Franklin D. Roosevelt's plan to pack the Supreme Court), the Langston community acted to neutralize Turner's presidency and assure that the educational philosophy of their school remained the same by filling all open faculty and staff positions with individuals loyal to the university, its traditions, and its present program of liberal arts education. Turner, in his official letter of resignation, stated that he quit because numerous important faculty appointments were made prior to his arrival on campus.[11]

Langstonites won the battle. The regents relented to the town's choice for president of the university. The Langston University community wanted G. Lamar Harrison. An outspoken proponent of liberal education, Harrison was a graduate of Howard University, one of the oldest and most prestigious academic institutions for African Americans in the United States, and earned his doctorate at Ohio State University. He was a political activist. The Oklahoma branch of the NAACP also endorsed his candidacy. He was, to say the least, no black separatist or nationalist but he did believe in black solidarity. A renewed spirit of defiance and assertiveness—if not black nationalism—blossomed at Langston with the installing of Harrison as president of the university in 1940. Langstonites immediately pushed to have the name of the school officially changed to "Langston University." The official name of the institution was the Colored Agricultural and Normal University of Oklahoma, a fact Langstonites had ignored in the past. The change in name was symbolic but very important to the community as a demonstration of its viability. Representatives Carl Morgan and Louis Ritzhaupt of Logan County, which included Langston, urged their colleagues in the state legislature to comply with the community's request since changing the name of the university constituted a mere technicality. Oklahomans in general and black Oklahomans in particular had always referred to the school as Langston University. Of additional concern was a rumor emanating from Langston that failure of the legislature to honor the wishes of the community might result in several of the county buildings in Logan being accidentally set on fire. On May 1, 1941, house bill number 447 was hurriedly passed, officially changing the name of the Colored Agricultural and Normal University of Oklahoma to Langston University.

This was a hollow victory, however. The university remained financially dependent upon the state and, like traditional Negro colleges and schools everywhere, Langston University did not receive its fair share of funds. The university and the state board of regents clashed over the funding of the school on numerous occasions. In 1945, for example, the regents allocated six million dollars to the states eighteen institutions of higher education, of which Langston University received $186,000. President Harrison had asked the regents for three times that amount. He informed them that census figures showed that blacks comprised one-twelfth of the state's population and if allocations were made on the basis of population, Langston University should receive in excess of the amount he requested. Roscoe Dunjee, in an editorial in the *Black Dispatch*, remarked that the disparity in funding "should be sufficient notice to the Negroes of this state that the legislature, the governor and the state board for higher education have no sincere interest in the welfare of Negroes." The loyal alumnus, Dunjee, then leveled a criticism about the degree of support given to black educational institutions in America:

> Decent white people should by this time realize and Negroes have learned that it is by miseducation that lags are placed in the progress of minority groups, and just at this time when the whole world is crying for higher standards of living, black people are on the alert and know precisely what is happening to them. Basically, what is happening in Oklahoma is the foundation of world difficulty. Too long the strong have sought to steal light and knowledge from the weak. Not only in Oklahoma but in Damascus, Bombay and Hong Kong, the weak are crying out for an honest decent approach to human problems. Hypocrisy has just about reached its road's end. We may prate and talk about democracy in Oklahoma but the most democratic thing in all the world that government can do is to give to every citizen an equal break in the realm of knowledge.

Over time Langstonites distanced themselves completely from their earlier nationalist and separatist views and began pleading for equal treatment and inclusion. The answer did not lie in criticizing the government or begging it for help. Langstonites and black Oklahomans had failed to establish their university on a sound foundation. Consequently, the school was susceptible to the whims of those in power. The assertive attitude of the Langston University community served only to further enrage the foes of black higher education. President G. Lamar Harrison's administration found itself fighting the stiffest forces of racism and educational discrimination with the nemesis gaining steady momentum. Throughout the 1950s and 1960s, whenever the state legislature spoke of ways to cut the state budget and save the taxpayers money, there was inevitably some mention of Langston University. On June 3, 1960, William Foresman of the *Tulsa Tribune* offered a solution. In his opinion, Langston University was an unnecessary expense for the state, enough blacks had been educated, and the school should be closed. "Langston University has served its purpose," Foresman concluded, "and should become merely a memory in the state educational picture."

Outraged Langstonites counterattacked in defense of theirs and other black schools. "Until racial bias is totally eliminated from Oklahoma," Harrison wrote in response to the assault, "a college like Langston University has the peculiar function of maintaining, preserving and disseminating the cultural heritage of the Negro people. Since leadership potentialities are best developed in an environment that offers many unlimited opportunities for the exercise of leadership functions, Langston University is the only institution in the state that can provide unlimited opportunities for the personality development, social realization and educational leadership of these youth who have since birth been denied the feeling of belonging and sense of security that can develop only with the knowledge of total acceptance in the community." What Harrison was begging for was integration, inclusion. The reality of financial dependency had beaten them away from their separatist and nationalist line. If for reasons none other than the prejudice and discrimination of the day, Langston University was essential for the higher education of black Oklahomans. A new day, however, was dawning for African-American education. The Civil Rights Movement of the 1950s and 1960s helped to open doors traditionally barred to blacks. The result was an educational backlash to black colleges and universities as increasing numbers of African-American students, who in the past had no choice but to attend an all-black school, began opting to go to the better regarded white institutions. Such was now the problem facing Langston University.

The irony was that the accomplishments of the Civil Rights Movement sounded the death knell to institutions, whether in substance or in form, that were exclusionary or designated for one particular group, be it based on race, ethnicity, class, or gender. Desegregation signaled the elimination of the traditionally black colleges and universities. The Department of Health, Education and Welfare launched school desegregation suits against six states in 1970, one was Oklahoma. Eight years later, Oklahoma capitulated and presented its desegregation plan. The state promised to eliminate the enrollment disparity between black and white undergraduates at the four year traditionally white institutions by 1982–1983. It also pledged to eliminate the disparity between the proportions of black and white students receiving baccalaureate degrees by 1982 and in master's programs by 1983. It vowed also to establish a unique mission for its historically black public institution, Langston University. Davis S. Tatel, director of the Oklahoma office for civil rights, said that the state was considering about ten options, even one that would "relocate Langston University, which presently is in a rural area and has suffered declining enrollment, to an urban setting such as Tulsa where no public four-year colleges presently exist." Tatel neglected to mention that one of the ten options the state of Oklahoma was considering was to close Langston University. The unique mission prognosis was suspect in light of the reality that the curriculum of Langston, like that of virtually all Negro colleges and universities, was not substantially different from that of Oklahoma State University and the University of Oklahoma or other state and private schools, except that Langston and its counterparts usually offered a few more courses on the African-American experience. These types of courses, however, were being added to the curriculums of the traditionally white schools. In addition, predominantly white universities of Oklahoma and throughout the nation were able to matriculate more substantial numbers of students, possessed academic reputations that were usually more highly regarded, were economically more sound than Langston University and most other black schools, and began to admit blacks. The question became: Who needs Langston University? In the case of Langston, the government of Oklahoma and the federal government were ready to phase the university out. The signs were clear by the 1980s when a HEW spokesperson said that considering the institution's isolated location, its history of financial troubles, and its rapidly declining enrollment, "if there is one black school in this country that should be closed down, it has to be Langston." Supporters of Langston continued to fight efforts to close the university.

Langston University survived as a virtual ghost school in a ghost community. The university remained open thanks in large part to the small extension sites located in Oklahoma City and Tulsa, which accounted for one-third of the school's total enrollment of a mere three thousand students by 2000. The National Organization of Black University and College Students (NOBUCS) has given its support to Langston University. Luther Brown, president of the organization, maintained that what was happening to Langston University was happening to other black colleges and universities in America. NOBUCS was afraid that black schools would be trampled into extinction as state education officials took steps to desegregate. "Our chief concern," the group announced, "is that predominately white institutions may intensify recruitment efforts of students from the historically black colleges in order to fill their quotas." Ironically, the intensified effort against *affirmative action* that began in the Reagan-Bush era of the 1980s has perhaps prolonged the life of Negro colleges and universities. It is, however, a sad testimony to the state of African-American education that the historically Negro schools such as Langston University remain vulnerable to and dependent upon the changing moods of a nation where equality of educational opportunity still does not exist.[12]

There were many lessons to be drawn from the Langston, Oklahoma, experience and the migration west. To migrate out of the South was in itself a defiant act whether one was of the Benjamin "Pap" Singleton and E. P. McCabe school of thought or whether one went to the North rather than westward in hope of finding independence and a good life. The migration was an effort to escape the neo-slavery that gripped the South and to become a vibrant and free people whose destiny rested in their own hands. The black migration was thus a political statement, an act born of consciousness and desperation. These spirited pioneers made a valiant and dedicated effort in formation of the black towns in the West, such as Langston, but were at best only partially successful in attaining their dream. Defying the odds to make the dream a reality in racist America tested all the creative ability and survival skills of black folk. The hope of African Americans was eternal whether they ventured to the cities of the South, founded their own towns in the West, or followed their dreams to the North.

VI

URBAN BLACKS: NEW CONSCIOUSNESS AND NEW VOICE TO THE AMERICAN DILEMMA

NORTHERN HOPE

African Americans moved from the rural South to the cities of the South and then onward to the cities of the North. Many went directly from rural South to urban North. Whether they had that transition period in the cities of the South or took the Illinois Central, for example, straight to Chicago or other points northward to Cincinnati, to New York City, to Detroit, to Philadelphia and countless other cities of the North, they were making a statement. Their marching feet were a vote of rejectionism and hope. It was not simply a rejection of the rural, agricultural way of life, but a refusal to accept second-class citizenship any longer. Jobs were abundant in the North and migration peaked during the years of World War I and World War II as America geared up for a wartime economy. The industrial and related wartime jobs attracted blacks in the hundreds of thousands. By the 1950s, African Americans became predominantly a city people, virtually transforming the race. From the beginning of the migration African Americans found themselves constantly at odds with the increasing new immigrant population, coming largely from southern Europe, who competed against them for jobs. The reason for the explosion of their conflict was much more than simple economics. There were enough jobs to go around. America's economy was growing and booming. Industrialists advertised throughout the South and throughout Europe for workers to come to service the new American economic expansionism. The reason for the conflict between blacks and whites, particularly that exploded between 1908 and 1919 with a host of riots including Springfield, East St. Louis, Chicago, Detroit, Boston and in other major northern cities, was more than a question of economic com-

157

petition. The culprit was one that seemed almost automatic for the
new European immigrants and for those who had been in the nation
many years before them: that old bugaboo of racism and hatred of
black folk. How did European immigrants apparently develop an in-
stantaneous dislike and disrespect of blacks? Whites quickly learned
in America that blacks were the group to despise to prove your
Americanism. Racism was alive and well in the hearts of European
Americans, including new arrivals, and it manifested itself in violent
clashes with the African-American migrants.

Nothing was going to halt the black quest for person-hood in the
North. More than economics fueled the movement. Employment
beckoned and was crucial to sustain life and family and paid considerably better in the North as compared to the South. But much
more than that, the individual thrived also on dignity and pride in
self and in one's accomplishments. Attaining these things in the
South was a daily Herculean battle for black folk. The North held
the promise of basic human opportunity which was the key motivating factor for the migrants as the Works Progress Administration
(W.P.A.) Collection of black narratives confirmed. African Americans moved North in hope of fulfilling their destinies as human beings, to have simple human respect, a life free from the barbaric
mistreatment and daily humiliation of existence in the South. There
were many internal and external forces at work or, *push* and *pull*
factors, behind the black migration. The *pull* factors were the cities
of the North, their industries and their beckoning for labor. This
provided the opportunity for the African American to earn a better
wage, despite a higher cost of living, and to actually see some money
in hand, unlike black existence as a sharecropper or tenant farmer
in the South. The North sold this as a positive dream to blacks,
putting it in front of them constantly in the form of ads and announcements of job opportunities in Chicago, Detroit, Pittsburgh,
New York, and elsewhere. The "Negro letter" was another important *pull* factor. Successful blacks sent letters to relatives and friends
in the South relating their glorious triumphs in their new-found
home. Similar to letters written by immigrants in the United States,
it was common to display bravado and overstate success, opportunities and life style. The most important of any single *pull* force in en-
ticing blacks to the North was the *Chicago Defender*, one of the
most reliable and consistently published African-American newspapers through the first half of the 20th century. Begun by Robert Abbott and published on a regular basis since 1905, the *Defender* did
more than its share in telling blacks about the opportunities available in the North and challenging them to stand up as men and

women and to develop their consciousness and throw off the South's yoke of oppression. The *Defender's* editorials indicated that the motivating force behind the black migration was more than economic. The editorials in the *Defender* were not about jobs, they were about human dignity with such titles as: "Leave"; "Get Out of Hell"; "Lynching A National Disgrace"; "Mob of White Men Rape Black Girls"; "Leave Canaan Land"; "One Hundred Negroes Murdered Weekly in South"; "White Gentleman Rapes Colored Girl": "Land of Opportunity"; "Flight Out of Egypt"; "Let My People Go"; and "Uncle Sam Says Scram." The *push* factors were the familiar horrors of the South, the economic downturn there in the late nineteenth and early twentieth century spurred on by the boll weevil and drought. The virulent racism in the South and the inhumane existence were the most powerful factors pushing African Americans to seek a better life elsewhere.

Upon arrival in the urban North, African Americans quickly learned that their new homeland was not the heaven they expected. There were more opportunities for them in the North than in the South but in the North they were also segregated and despised, discriminated against in the labor force and employment, and provided with a second-class education. Throughout the urban North, protective associations sprung up to keep the Negroes in their place. In Chicago, for example, the infamous Hyde Park Improvement/Protective Association was one of many spread throughout the cities of the North under the rubric of maintaining their communities; however, their real aim was to keep blacks out. These associations were well known for covenants that prohibited real-estate agencies and community members from selling a home to blacks and for maintaining boundary lines that defended against Negro incursion. When a black somehow managed to buy into one of these communities, protective associations, as brilliantly portrayed in Lorraine Hannsberry's *A Raisin in the Sun*, came forward with offers to the black family to sell the house back to the protective association at a profit to the family. Whites were just that desperate to keep blacks out of the community. Violence was often used, including the firebombing of black homes, the burning of crosses on their lawns, racial epithets painted on the walls of their houses, and numerous other means to get them out. There were a host of other indignities and discrimination ranging from housing and education to the work place and segregated beaches. Many restaurants throughout the North refused to serve blacks and, like the South, cemeteries were segregated. The black migration spurred on the revival of the Ku Klux Klan. The new Klan, revitalized in 1915, was an organization with chapters throughout the South and North. Northern cities were thriving centers of Klan activity. The hooded night riders were in the West, in Oklahoma and California, throughout the Midwest, with strongholds in Indiana, Illinois, and Minnesota, and in the East, with large memberships in New Jersey, Massachusetts, Connecticut, and New York. In America, African Americans were being told everyday in every way and everywhere that America was for whites only when it came to advantages and equal opportunity.

Despite the racism and discrimination and bigotry in every conceivable mechanisms of Jim Crowism, and legal and illegal activities to bar and stifle their progress, blacks fought on desperately to advance and to make their dreams become a reality. Throughout the history of black folk in America, including the dastardly nadir, the terrible treatment in the South, and the barriers in the North, accomplishments were made. Contributions of blacks in the performing arts stood second to none. In the last decades of the nineteenth century, the great African-American composer, James A. Bland, wrote between four hundred to six hundred tunes, songs and ditties, many of them he sold for as little as five dollars a piece. Among the tunes he copyrighted at the turn of the century were several songs of great note that became American classics such as "Oh, dem Golden Slippers" and "Carry Me Back to Old Virginny," which became the Official State Song of Virginia. We may never know how many other great songs Bland composed because most of them were not copyrighted owing to the practiced restrictions against blacks holding copyrights and patents until near the end of the nineteenth century. While America celebrates Steven Foster, James A. Bland has been omitted. Nevertheless, accomplishments such as his were being made, national contributions not only in entertainment, music and dance, but contributions in the sciences. Inventions by African Americans were numerous, such as J. A. Burr's patented lawnmower; P. B. Downing's mailbox; Jan Matzeliger's shoemaking machine; Granville T. Woods's electric breaking system and many other patented inventions for the locomotive; Lewis Latimer's filament for the electric light bulb; Elijah J. McCoy's automatic lubricating devices and a host of other inventions that made his name synonymous with industrial quality. The phrase, "The Real McCoy," refers to him. The list goes on to include A. B. Blackburn, inventor of the railway signal; Daniel Hale Williams, the African American physician who performed the first successful open-heart surgery in the United States; and J. W. Smith, inventor of the lawn sprinkler. Every time a golfer tees up, he or she should give thanks to G. F. Grant, the Harvard graduate and black inventor of the golf tee. In addition,

Sarah G. Jones, was one of the first women and the first black woman licensed as a physician in America. J. A. Love invented the pencil sharpener; Garret Morgan carried the tradition into the twentieth century with his invention of the gas mask and the traffic stop light. These accomplishments and many more, took place in the North and were part of the reason why African Americans streamed northward. The black population in Detroit, from 1900 to 1930, grew from 4,000 to 120,000. In Chicago, over that same period of time, it went from 30,000 to 234,000; and in New York, from 60,000 to 328,000.[1]

BLACK VOICES

In the cities African Americans were developing their voice and clear statements of selfhood. Of all the urban black enclaves, Harlem was supreme. It was indeed the Mecca of the emerging black voice in America. During the years after WWI and throughout the 1920s onward, a new movement began to take place in America. Some called it the *Black Literary Movement*, the *Harlem Renaissance*, the *Black Renaissance*, the *New Negro Movement*. It was certainly a black literary advance, but it was not limited to literature alone. This was a period in which African Americans displayed their genius in every conceivable way, expressing their thoughts about America, their consciousness of heritage, and the dreams for themselves and for their children. This was a period of the blossoming of black self awareness and the center of it was Harlem, the black capitol of the United States and, for that matter, of the entire world. With so many African Americans coming together in New York's Harlem, critics predicted the rise of an instant ghetto. Nothing would prove to be further from the truth in the history of Harlem during its heyday. Harlem in the first three decades of the 20th century could not have been more removed from a ghetto. It was a black middle class environment. In those early years of the twentieth century it was impossible to find an African American who thought of Harlem as a slum or that it could ever become one. Harlem was a place of pride and joy of accomplishment. It was the *"Negro Mecca."* James Weldon Johnson believed that Harlem promised a future of hope and great possibilities for blacks as he wrote in *Black Manhattan* published in 1930. Harlem had a tremendous buoyancy and aura. It was the melting-pot of African-derived culture. It was as Johnson and many others said, the *"promised land."* Jobs were there. Labor beckoned. Harlem was a haven for black artists, writers, musicians, teachers, dreamers. If you wanted to become somebody and you were black, Harlem stood as the center for that possibility.

African Americans built a community in Harlem, not a separatist or black nationalist community, but an open and encompassing community. Whites came constantly to Harlem in its heyday to hear the music of the big band sounds of Count Basie, Duke Ellington, Joe Jordan, Cab Calloway and others, and to enjoy the joyous night life. African Americans, in the African tradition, were a sharing people and black Harlem was open to all. It was the majority society that rejected African Americans and erected the boundary, the *color line*, that said to black Harlemites that they were not welcome on the east side of New York or in any of the white communities. Blacks had Harlem and they were developing identity, developing as a people who, by choice and by force, dug in together and worked doubly hard to become something for themselves and their posterity. Harlem was the center of this activity. It was no "darkie" town. It was a place of gay music and bright ideas and clear voices, the intellectual and cultural center of the new Negro, the new African American. Black intellectuals, such as A. Philip Randolph and James Weldon Johnson, gravitated to Harlem. Organizations at the forefront of the struggle to advance people of color, such as the NAACP, the Urban League, the Universal Negro Improvement Association, were headquartered in Harlem or New York City proper. When Marcus Garvey, founder of the UNIA, came to America in 1916, he established the headquarters of his organization in Harlem. Harlem was the place. You could hear A. Philip Randolph and Chandler Owen, leaders of organized black labor, speaking for African-American advancement in the pages of their magazine, the *Messenger,* which soon became branded as the most radical Negro publication in America. Garvey's *Negro World* added to the intellectual stimulation of New York and Harlem. There was the success story of Madame C. J. Walker who, by 1920, had become a millionaire through her process for straightening black women's hair. The success stories abounded of others who had also made their fortune in Harlem. The black woman known as Pigfoot Mary made her dream of wealth come true selling pickled pigs' feet out of a cart on the streets of Harlem. Expertise and facilities in Harlem were the best in the black world. Harlem Hospital on 135th Street and Lenox Avenue was the leading black hospital in America and the world. It enticed the best black physicians to New York's Harlem. The best physicians, the best attorneys, many of the best educators, and aspiring African-American politicians, flocked to Harlem. In Harlem all things seemed possible. The National Urban League's magazine reflected the spirit of Harlem in its name—*Opportunity*. Langston Hughes's character, Jesse B. Simple, caught the essence of what Harlem was about, what urban life meant, as this simple character, who met in bars, usually over a glass of beer, and pontificated on the African-American urban experience. Readers of the black press followed with delight the escapades of Jesse B. Simple. Students of African-American history would be able to revisit the glory days of Harlem through their reading of Langston Hughes's *The Best of Simple*. In "A Toast to Harlem" Simple conveyed, in straight forward language, what made Harlem unique, a land of pride and reverence, and why blacks loved it and were willing to protect it and one another.

Harlem was an intellectual environment with the exchange of ideas going on from early morning to late at night. On any Wednesday, Friday, or Saturday evening, such imminent black intellectual leaders as Du Bois, James Weldon Johnson, Carter G. Woodson, Kelly Miller, Chandler Owen, or A Philip Randolph gave public lectures. The Harlem intellectuals were themselves caught up in the general protest spirit of the *Muckrakers*. Ida Tarbell had blasted Standard Oil. Upton Sinclair powerfully critiqued the growing industrialism and the exploitation of the immigrant in the meat packing industry in his work, *The Jungle*. Harlem Renaissance writers were a part of that, a part of the New York literary scene, although segregated from the mainstream of it. H.L. Mencken, the muckraker writer of the *Mercury*, when asked to reflect on civil liberties in America, commented that he thought the "Statue of Liberty should be taken three miles off shore and dumped into the ocean." As Mencken put it, "a people have to do more than pretend to be civilized." Speaking out against injustice, especially against blacks, no one was more relentless a muckraker than W.E.B. Du Bois. In the *Crisis*, Du Bois focused on lynchings as a public and national disgrace. He wrote constantly about it giving vivid accounts of mob actions. Through the pages of the *Crisis* the reader could practically smell the burning flesh of the victim. Du Bois ridiculed governmental leaders for giving nothing but lip service in the face of such brutality against blacks.

Harlem was a black intellectual oasis with heated debates raging such as the one over African-American participation in World War I. Du Bois, in the July 1918 issue of the *Crisis*, wrote what became a firestorm editorial, "Close Ranks," urging blacks and whites to close ranks and forget their differences and come together as Americans and fight for the interests of the United States abroad. Du Bois attracted spiritedly criticism from other segments of the African-

American intellectual leadership for his views. Marcus Garvey condemned him as being a misguided integrationist who should be more concerned with waging a war for black freedom at home than fighting for freedom over there. A. Philip Randolph, in the pages of the *Messenger*, assailed Du Bois's reasoning. Randolph said that he had previously thought of Du Bois as one of the most capable Negro leaders but now questioned that after reading his stand on the war and advice to colored Americans to participate in an imperialist war. "Close Ranks" was one of Du Bois's less stellar moments in reasoning and in advocacy. He dreamed of being a full-fledged American and forgot momentarily the depth and breadth of the *color line*.

Other vigorously debated issues of the period included the status of blacks and organized labor, black nationalism, Marcus Garvey and his organization, and the integration strategies of the NAACP. Harlem was alive with a great variety of ideas that touched on every aspect of African-American life. It was alive in music, song, dance, literature, and coffee-house chat that made it a vibrant and pivotal era in the development of African-American consciousness. African Americans were finding themselves. They realized only too clearly that America was a closed shop. Harlem, on the other hand, was a stimulating environment that could not be denied. African Americans looked into themselves through prose and verse and the blues. The 369th Infantry of WWI fame, returned home to a hero's welcome in a jazz step down Lenox Avenue. They were a part of this vibrancy, the Renaissance, the searching out, the becoming and defining of an African-American identity.

Alain Locke (1886–1954), the dynamic black scholar, a Rhodes Scholar and later professor of philosophy at Howard University, perceptively articulated the Harlem Renaissance. Through stories, poems and essays, and most importantly in his book, *The New Negro*, published during the heart of the Renaissance, Locke defined the Renaissance and gave it intellectual voice and definition. In a brilliant analysis, Locke explained that Harlem was more than a migration of black folk out of the South to the North, it was a cultural infusion, the birth of a consciousness that had crystallized in Harlem, and that in this urban setting a political, social and cultural consciousness emerged. He touted that in Harlem you did not find many of those Uncle Toms and Mammies and Samboes that you might find elsewhere. Locke postulated that the city made the difference. It was quick paced; it was plural; it was multicultural; it was vibrant; and most importantly it pushed African Americans to define themselves. In Harlem resided Africans, blacks from the South and North, West Indians, urban people, city people, village people, students, business men and women, artists, poets, musicians, workers, criminals, preachers, gamblers, and social outcasts. It was rich and didactic. "Each group has come with its own separate motives and for its own special ends," Locke found, "but their greatest experience has been the finding of one another." This discovery and defining of the ties that bind he called "race welding." We might call it nationalism. In a different context, Leopold Senghor, the scholar President of the West African nation of Senegal, defined the phenomenon as Negritude. Whatever definition or term given to it, it was race consciousness. It was a spirit of self definition and understanding that was absolutely essential for any people, if they were to advance. In Harlem, African Americans were recreating their race and putting back in place the positives that the American experience stole from them. As Locke wrote, "the Negro has been a race previously more in name than in fact" and what was needed to make a race was a "common consciousness." To recognize that shared experience, common heritage, legacy, and problems based upon race, was the essence of race consciousness. Locke was a *race man* in the best sense of the term. Without race consciousness there was, in his opinion, no hope for people of African descent in racist America. Locke knew this and complimented his fellow Harlemites for discovering their "life in common." He went on to say: "In Harlem, Negro life is seizing upon its first chances for group expression and self determination. It is or promises at least to be a race capital."

In the new race capital, literature played a sustaining role at both, what some term, a level of *high culture* and *low culture*. The Harlem Renaissance writers did not tend to make that distinction. They were simply bestowing voice to black folk at all of their levels of uniqueness. Claude McKay's *Home to Harlem* was insightful for what it told of African-American life and the connectedness not only with the streets but with a past rich with soul. McKay's character, Jake, was a gritty, one hundred percent black Harlemite who loved the music and night life, and interacted with the streets, the people, and everyday problems. There was no pretentiousness to Jake. He was straight forward and frank. Jake was a participant in the cultural revolution that took place and was a symbol of the feistiness that McKay also conveyed in the medium of verse. McKay's epic poem, "If We Must Die," may not have been intended as a revolutionary statement but Senator Henry Cabot Lodge perceived it as such and had it read into the *Congressional Record* as an indication of the revolutionary spirit simmering in black urban America. The words of that poem were famous through the 1920s and onward. One stanza, in particular, expressed the confidence and spirit of self exhibited in the New Negro Movement when McKay wrote: "If we must die, let it not be like hogs hunted and pinned in an inglorious spot while round us bark the mad and hungry dogs making their mock at our accused lot." He ends the poem with what can be thought of as a clarion call to fight the racists no matter what: "O kinsmen we must meet the common foe! Though far outnumbered let us show us brave, and for their thousand blows deal one death blow!" Langston Hughes's poem, "The Negro Speaks of Rivers" or commonly referred to as "I've Known Rivers," made the connection between contemporary black life and the African heritage while his short stories with the character Jesse B. Simple offered an insider's perspective on black urban life.

Despite the heavy ethnicity of the Renaissance's literature it, like Harlem, was open to whites and there were attempts at shared relationships between the two worlds. The patronage of whites was important to some of the Harlem Renaissance writers including Langston Hughes and Zora Neale Hurston. Carl Van Vechten, the white entrepreneur and patron of the black arts, came constantly into Harlem and hosted integrated social gatherings at his home in New York. Madame C. J. Walker, one of the first black millionaires, was instrumental in trying to cross the *color line* in the arts. The race-mixed parties that she hosted at her mansion on the Hudson became famous. She brought together blacks, writers and artists, with influential white patrons of the arts. This intermingling was important as one way of sustaining African-American art outside of the community. In another way, it made the black creative arts vulnerable to those who were interested in African-American culture strictly for their own gains. Be that as it may, the black literary movement continued to advance. The Great Depression of the 1930s could not destroy the Renaissance in African-American literature. Blacks continued to write. It was nonsense to talk, as some did, about a second Harlem Renaissance. There was one continuous Renaissance that even the Great Depression did not halt. Zora Neale Hurston bridged the gap through the thirties and forties with her works, *Moses Man of the Mountain* and *Their Eyes Were Watching God*. The writings of William Attaway, *Let Me Breathe Thunder*, and *Blood on the Forge*, also bridged the depression years. The contributions continued with the best known of the later Renaissance writers, Richard Wright, Ralph Ellison, and on to Gwendolyn Brooks, and James Baldwin, to Margaret Walker, Amiri Baraka, Nikki Giovanni, and others. The Harlem Renaissance lived and flourished, celebrated in the music of Gary Bartz with his historically punctuated jazz rendering in the 1960s of Langston Hughes's "I've Known Rivers." Moreover, the Renaissance was comprehensive, not just in literary writings but in music, theater, dance and every component of the people's cultural aestheticism and expressionism, including the all-important visual arts.[2]

African-American art has always been a part of the race's aestheticism and expressionism dating back to Henry O. Tanner (1859–1937), the son of a bishop of the African Methodist Episcopal church, who became the first of the internationally acclaimed African-American artists. Tanner decided at age thirteen to study art after viewing a landscape artist at work in Fairmont Park in Philadelphia. After studying at the Pennsylvania Academy of Fine Art, under Thomas Eakins, he went on to teach at Clark College in Atlanta and then held exhibitions in Cincinnati and elsewhere, finally fleeing to France in 1891 where he had a much better chance of his art being accepted as work of a talented artist rather than having it dismissed without receiving its proper due because the artist was a person of color. Like so many African-American cultural artists, Tanner found in France what he did not find in the United States. It was not that he rejected or separated from white America, he had taken charge of his own destiny in an attempt to be treated as a human being. This entailed moving to a foreign land where he might have a better chance of attaining his dream. America rejected him as it did countless other African Americans before and after him. There in France he married and continued his study and art, such as the "Young Sabot Maker," which won acclaim in Paris. His most heralded work, the "Banjo Lesson," exhibited a calm, quiet dignity and sense of connectedness between a grandfather-figure black man and his likely young grandson, whom the grandfather was instructing in how to play the banjo. The many reprints of that painting would adorn African-American homes throughout the nation. It took a century, however, before Tanner's artistic genius was generally recognized and celebrated in the country of his birth. In 1967, Tanner's works were displayed in the United States after rediscovery of some seventy missing paintings of his stored away in an attic in Paris for more than forty years. This spiritual boost to the black movement in the 1960s was a reaching back to a previous time of artistic greatness of expression that gave fuller resonance to the contemporary struggle.

Ironically, the Great Depression of the 1930s helped the advancement of African-American art. President Franklin D. Roosevelt's New Deal program for the recovery of the nation's economy contained a strong Federal Art Project, a division of the Works Progress

Administration that supported the arts until disbanded in 1943 during World War II. African-American artists considered worthy of public support received jobs painting murals at black institutions, post offices, and hospitals. Black artists Hale Woodruff, Charles Alston, and Romare Bearden were part of the grand guard in the art movement of the depression era. The creative genius of the black artist and long-standing African survival skills were demonstrated as the artists mastered a variety of mediums to survive the depression. Artists diversified, painting murals, easels, cataloging silver and furniture, mastering silk screening, weaving, architecture, photography. The work of Aaron Douglas, Archibald Motley, Richmond Barthe, and Jacob Lawrence demonstrated the diversification. Although these artists fought for the acceptance of African-American art, they did not receive the credit due their genius and skills. One of the most blatantly racist incidents of this rejectionism occurred at the public exhibition "Art Commentary on Lynching" held at the Arthur Newton Galleries in New York City in 1935. The exhibition focused on lynchings in the South and featured the works of John Curry, Isamu Noguishi, Thomas Hart Benton, and Paul Cadmus, but excluded the works of African-American artists. While the black experience provided the subject matter for the exhibition, the presence of African Americans as presenters was not allowed.

Nevertheless, African-American artists sustained the dedication to and perseverance of their craft in Harlem, in Philadelphia, in Chicago and other cities. In 1927 a week-long festival in Chicago, sponsored by the Chicago Women's Club, featured "The Negro in Art." Chicago had a good reputation early on for developing and promoting African-American artists. After maturing at their craft, however, many of the best of these artists moved on to the center of art in America: New York City. Whether painting murals or working in other mediums in Chicago, Harlem or elsewhere, black artists survived the Great Depression and remained faithful to their ethnic heritage and assisted the world in visualizing the African-American experience. The works of Richmond Barthe, for example, depicted African Americans at work and play. Many of his bronzes, such as "Birth of the Spirituals," became the most acclaimed African-American sculptures in the world. Barthe's "The Blackberry Woman," created in 1932, was a masterful statuette that celebrated the beauty and strength of women of African heritage; in addition to "The Harmonica Player," "Shoe Shine Boy," "The Boxer," and his most famous piece, "The Negro Looks Ahead," all conveyed the struggle and dignity of the black experience. Barthe, at his first one-man show in New York City in 1933, exhibited sculptures, paintings of

Harlem scenes, the Congo, Europeans and Hindus, and lynchings, as well as scenes of family life such as in his much heralded work, "Mother and Son."

Jacob Lawrence personified similar dedication with his own unique innovativeness in his work "Tombstones." His paintings were personal and explicit. Born in Atlantic City, New Jersey, Lawrence moved to Harlem with his mother when he was a child. His was a hard life filled with poverty, early homelessness, settlement houses, bread lines, and soup kitchens. These experiences imbued Lawrence with character and sensitivity that he conveyed in his paintings, which helped him climb to national prominence in the late 1930s and 1940s. The feeling of destitution, of being black and poor in America, was ably expressed in his piece, "They Were Very Poor." He continued to paint while serving in WW II. Recognition came for his "Migration of the Negro Series," created under the WPA, in which he depicted the African-American migration to the North. He captured, in his work, the struggle and human dignity of African Americans. There was always a realism in Lawrence's work and a vitality and respect for protest and plea for race reform. Like so many other of the Harlem Renaissance artists he too did a set of paintings devoted to John Brown, a series in 1945 titled "The Legend of John Brown." Lawrence's piece adorned the cover of a special issue of *Time Magazine* devoted to the story of black America. He also did likenesses of gospel great Mahalia Jackson and the Reverend Jesse Jackson and other prominent African-American figures. Jacob Lawrence received the NAACP Spingarn Medal in 1970 for his distinguished contribution to the betterment of race relations, becoming the first painter to receive the coveted award.

Charles White was another of the much heralded Harlem Renaissance painters and cultural activists. White's training began at the Art Institute of Chicago, studying there after his mother and father migrated from the South. Struggle was his middle name and throughout his life he fought to be recognized as an artist and respected as a black person in America. Early friendship with famed dancer Katherine Dunham put him in contact with artists and writers who shared a race consciousness and political awareness. He confided in and exchanged ideas with Archibald Motley, Gwendolyn Brooks, and Richard Wright. As an artist White worked in many forms, many mediums: chalk, crayons, inks, lithographs, oils, poster paper, cardboard and anything else to fashion his message of race pride and awareness. He depicted African-American heroes such as Sojourner Truth and John Brown, and the tenderness of family life in his rendering of "Mother and Son." Some of his likenesses resembled that of the Mexican peasants found in the work of David Alfaro Siqueiros and Diego Rivera, two artists whom White admired and studied with in Mexico. He was concerned with the exploitation of people of color throughout the world. His crowning artistic and race political statement came in "Birmingham Totem." In charcoal and Chinese ink he depicted an African American on a pile of dynamite surrounded by various scenes of black suffering in the United States. "Birmingham Totem" was done during the 1960s and part of White's "Wanted Poster Series" which was politically charged and inspired in the cause of the Civil Rights Movement and black protest. His artistic and political philosophies were intertwined. White was part of a Renaissance that gave voice to the black struggle to overcome racism in America. Other writers in the Renaissance adopted their own method of expression. Lois Jones, one of the few black women artists who achieved acclaim, created "Jennie," a warm and sensitive oil portrait presenting a strong, graceful black woman with pronounced color and beauty. Harlem Renaissance artists were saying in a variety of mediums what writer Countee Cullen stated in "Heritage," that African Americans should recognize and embrace their Africanism. They were also saying, in the words of Langston Hughes's, "I Too," that blacks were Americans and deserved to be treated accordingly. The Renaissance artists were expressing hope for a better day and a *color-blind* society.

Music was another favorite medium of expression. Innovations in music were limitless from such artists as Scott Joplin, the King of Ragtime and composer of the heralded "Maple Leaf Rag;" Jelly Roll Morton and his work, and on to the compositions of Joe Jordan, Eubie Blake and Noble Sissle, the country blues playing and singing of Blind Lemon Jefferson, Blind Blake, Huey Ledbetter and Robert Johnson, to the jazz stylings of W. C. Handy and the classic blues songs of Ma Rainey, Bessie Smith, Mamie Smith, and Victoria Spivey, to the musical expressions of the black experience from a Buddy Bolden, King Oliver and Louis Armstrong, to Fats Waller and Fletcher Henderson, Chick Webb, Fess Williams, Dave Patton, and Duke Ellington, to Roland Hayes, Marion Anderson, Paul Robeson, Dorothy Manor, Cab Calloway, Ethel Waters, and many others. The music of African-American artists spawned the "race records" boom that gave birth to the recording industry in America with the advent of such companies as Okeh Records, Vocalion Records, Paramount Records, and Columbia Records, all of which came into being and profitableness as a result of a music created by black folk and that was initially sold exclusively to a black audience.

Music and theater forged into an important venue for cultural expression. There may be a contemporary tendency to look down on the minstrel shows of bygone days as derogatory caricatures of black people. Blacks were the creators of minstrelsy on the slave plantations and the famous or infamous characters of Mister Interlocutor, Mister Bones, and Mister Jim Crow. That same *Jim Crow* became the nomenclature that characterized the segregated South. The crow was a despised bird, especially to farmers, a creature to be scorned, to be shunned, ostracized, segregated, and controlled. While the minstrel show was typically a black-faced comedy, just the opposite of the buffoonery was the Cake Walk, a dignified strutting in the West African tradition common place in black musical theater performances of the late nineteenth and early twentieth centuries. Bert Williams and George Walker were masters of minstrelsy and Cake Walking. They became internationally famous black entertainers for their plays, writings, depictions, and performances. The dynamic duo presented themselves as African characters in, "In Dahomey," a play dealing with the theme of back to Africa. Some saw the play as simply making fun of Africans, but the play also made a positive connection between black Americans and the African homeland. Williams and Walker played before the Queen of England in a command performance at Buckingham Palace. One black professor in the United States criticized them for spreading the negative stereotypes of blacks that whites wanted. Williams and Walker responded that as performers they were "playing to the audience." They, like many other black performers, were attempting to navigate the treacherous racial rapids.

On the road or backstage, blacks could be themselves. After-hours hangouts afforded the in-the-know public the opportunity to see the true face of their favorite black entertainers. "The real show," African-American performers liked to say, "began when the show was over." In the comfortable setting off stage, the black performer's Africanism inevitably showed itself. The African tradition of the "burnout" was retained and practiced. The "burnout" was a folk happening of a spirited yet friendly competition in the presence of the "home folks." Theater groups or individual performers challenged one another to see who could out dance, out play, or out perform the other. Bill "Bo Jingle" Robinson, for example, loved the burnout tradition. He could often be found backstage being himself with friends and co-workers as one of the greatest tap dancers in history, and always willing to take on challengers to his unofficial crown as the "Mayor of Harlem."

There were those black theatrical artists, such as the Johnson brothers, Roseman, Bob, and James Weldon, who pushed black mu-

sical theater from stereotypes to quiet dignity and political consciousness. The Johnson brothers were talented, dedicated, and
racially sensitive theatrical performers and musical composers
whose artistry often contained an imbedded political message.
James Weldon Johnson, composed "Lift Every Voice and Sing,"
which would become the African-American National Anthem. The
Johnsons and the team of Sissle and Blake were among the first of
the black theatrical artists who stopped wearing blackface and performed well dressed and sophisticated. Noble Sissle and Eubie
Blake, the black stars of the 1920s, began focusing more on the
music rather than the comedy in black theater. They wrote inspired
tunes. Nothing, however, was able to save black theater from the
downturn of the 1930s.

It was not the Great Depression that halted black musical theater
as much as it was white usurpation of the art form. While blacks
created minstrelsy and black musical theater, whites performing in
blackface, such as Billy Bud and Al Jolson, made the greatest fortunes from it. White audiences preferred to pay white performers in
blackface rather than to see and pay blacks who seemed to be getting too "uppity" and who no longer wanted to use cork. Black theater, which had grown to increasingly rely on white audiences, was
vulnerable; it faded into obscurity in the late 1930s, despite the support of the WPA which sponsored black plays such as "Green Pas-
tures" and assisted black theatrical troupes like the Gilpin Players in
Connecticut. Ethel Water's experience provided an example of the
divide-and-conquer mindset which black artists had to contend constantly. As the star of her own company, Waters was told by the
white theater owner that he was not able to pay the rest of the players, meaning she would be paid after the week's performances but
the remainder of her cast would not. Waters decided that she would
rather quit the business than be a tool of the exploiters. The dominance of white authority in black theater was epitomized with the
1935 production of George Gershwin's "Porgy and Bess," a highly
profitable usurpation of black musical comedy. The last hit black
theatrical play, "Shuffle Along," may have been an appropriate ending to black theater.

Even in the heyday of black theater, black performers were in
battle with whites for control of the industry. Most acts were
booked through the corrupt and exploitative white-owned Theater
Owners' Booking Agency (T.O.B.A.) which was notorious for short
changing black performers. T.O.B.A. was commonly known among
black performers as "Tough On Black Artists" and, like the *Chitlins
Circuit* in the South, put little money in the hands of the performing

black artists. Like so many other aspects of black art and African-American creations and labor, outside forces controlled and dominated the business at the top levels and harvested the major financial gain and claimed the artistic credit. African Americans sought to control their own destinies, struggling for self autonomy in a society that was relentless in its exploitation of them and everything they created, whether it was their day-to-day labor in a field picking cotton, drudgery in a factory, or playing music and singing and dancing on stage.[3]

PASSING ON THE WORD: URBAN BLACK ACTIVISM

Strong and articulate black voices of discontent and racial definition emanated throughout the urban North. One such voice was that of William Monroe Trotter in Boston. Trotter was born of a background and heritage of outspokenness. His father, James Trotter, was a black officer during the Civil War. James became a Democrat in the late 1870s in protest of President Hayes's withdrawal of federal troops from the South. He worked for General Ben Butler's Democratic campaign for governor, and Butler won. James Trotter vigorously opposed racism and took action when it reared its ugly head. He resigned his position from the post office in 1882 and accepted a post as officer of deeds in Washington, D. C., one of the highest black held positions in the nation. This spirit of defiance and independent mindedness was bestowed on his son William Monroe Trotter who was born in 1872. William recalled his childhood and how his father maintained certain rules of behavior, one of the most important one being that William better not be beaten up by any white boy or, as his father promised, he would give him another whipping at home. There was steel in James Trotter's words and demands on his son while at the same time praising him and pushing him to know no bounds, to fight for himself and his race. It was of little surprise that William Monroe Trotter became a staunch race man. Early on he only associated with those blacks possessing vision and pride of self and race. He was a friend of Archibald Grimke, nephew of the famed abolitionist Grimke sisters. After the family settled in Boston, Massachusetts, William showed himself to be a superb student, graduating with honors from high school and then attending Harvard University, where he also excelled. William, one of the first blacks to achieve Phi Beta Kappa at Harvard, graduated in 1895. This was the same year that Booker T. Washington gave his controversial Atlanta Exposition Address. William Monroe Trotter denounced Washington's words as a compromise of principles, a sellout of the black race. He later declared: "Washington's attitude has always been subservient to the white people of the South."

Dedicated to activism and working in a direction for his race considerably different from that of Washington, the young Trotter helped to organize the Boston Literary and Historical Association. He understood the power of literacy and history in the war for consciousness and direction. He joined the Massachusetts Radical Protective Association. The association brought together black activists who further attacked Booker T. Washington's accommodationist views. Trotter married a race woman, Geraldine Louise Pindell, in 1899, who had earlier dated W.E.B. Du Bois. Her background was one of radicalism, despite coming from a fairly well-to-do family. Indeed, her uncle led an early challenge of Boston's segregated public schools. There was a consciousness and outspokenness and defiance of second-class status in the woman who embraced Trotter, sharing his life and passion for activism. With her support Trotter established the *Boston Guardian* that became the voice of Boston's black activism and an arm of the Boston Literary and Historical Club. The club and the paper were similar in aim to the Hyde Park Club established by Robert Abbott, publisher of the *Chicago Defender,* and other socially conscious black Chicagoans, who wanted to make a difference in the battle to improve the race's condition in America. Northern associations tended to be anti Booker T. Washington and any other form of accommodationism. A. Philip Randolph, the black labor leader, also joined the Massachusetts Radical Protective Association, and delivered a speech before its members condemning Booker Washington's stand against organized labor.

Trotter spiritedly opposed anyone who he thought worked against the best interests of the race. He found himself at odds with the popular African American, William H. Lewis of Amherst, who was one of the first black All-America football players. Lewis was, in Trotter's assessment, a toady of the Booker Washington forces. Lewis, who became state senator from his district in Massachusetts, praised Booker T. Washington, especially after Washington's audience with President Theodore Roosevelt. Monroe Trotter saw Lewis's actions as kowtowing and denounced him for lack of race consciousness and being void of progressive thinking. Anyone connected to Booker Washington was an enemy of Trotter's and suffered his wrath. Trotter gleefully reported in the *Guardian* in fall of 1902 that Washington's daughter, Portia, flunked out of Wellesley College. He used the occasion to strike a personal blow at the industrial schooling idea that Washington professed. Trotter questioned why Washington advocated that blacks pursue the rudimentary education of industrial schooling while sending his daughter to a prestigious liberal arts college for women. Trotter wondered if the many years that Portia was exposed to the misguided industrial education philosophy ruined her chances for rigorous intellectual pursuit. He thought that, perhaps, she should have been taught to work with her hands rather than her mind, and may have faired better at Tuskegee or some other manual labor school. At every possible opportunity, Trotter attacked the "Tuskegee machine" that Washington headed. When Booker T. Washington was slated to speak in Boston, in 1903, it afforded Monroe Trotter an opportunity that he could not allow to pass. What occurred at the gathering became known as the Boston Riot. Trotter and supporters disrupted the meeting with a series of questions in opposition to the Tuskegee machine and black accommodationism. Shouts and invectives escalated into fist fights and a stabbing. After the police restored order, Trotter and his sister Maude, along with others, were spirited off to jail. W.E.B. Du Bois came to Trotter's intellectual defense. While the two of them had differed on several previous occasions and issues, Du Bois supported the demonstration and decried the Washington forces and others responsible for the jailing of Trotter, who had also been roughed up in the fracas.

In many respects William Monroe Trotter was a visionary and race nationalist. Although he could work with whites, he was not what one would call an integrationist. Trotter launched the National Negro Suffrage League, which was another anti Bookerite group, but which, by its very advocacy of political participation within the system, was a mainstream approach to solving the race problem. Participation and self assertion, in Trotter's mind, were essential for black advancement. He found Washington's complacency tantamount to race suicide and cowardice. Race came first for Trotter. He broke from the Niagara Movement and the NAACP because of the preponderance of whites in leadership positions. He questioned how an organization could be powerful, direct, and progressive on the Negro question if not led by Negroes. Mary White Ovington, a noted progressive and founding member of the NAACP, and who was white, angered Trotter when she had stated that blacks were not yet skilled enough to hold the position of executive secretary of the NAACP. Trotter found these and similar sentiments insulting. The diluting of black activism with the inclusion of large numbers of whites in key roles was, in his opinion, a fatal tactical error. He felt that whites could be included in supportive roles but, when it came to deciding the course of action best for the race, blacks must lead. Thus, Trotter and Du Bois parted company on the question of the

Niagara Movement, the NAACP, and other matters where African Americans were not in absolute control. Trotter held his tongue for no one. On the occasion when he met with President Woodrow Wilson, in 1916, he was quick to remind the President of the support he received from certain black organizations during the election, and chastised him for not ending segregation and discrimination in hiring within the postal service and other federal agencies. Wilson had also appointed a white man to the traditional Haitian ambassadorial position, and gave his endorsement to the racist film, *Birth of a Nation*. Trotter literally accused President Wilson, in person, of betraying those who held hope of fair treatment under his administration. Theirs was a tense meeting which President Wilson called abruptly to a halt, making it clear that Trotter and his organization would never be invited to the White House again. William Monroe Trotter was a principled *race man* who was unapologetic and uncompromising in his demand for unencumbered progress for African-Americans. He kept up his feisty activism until his death in 1934.[4]

THE MESSENGER'S MESSAGE

Harlem was the "Mecca" for black awareness and protest. From 1917 to the mid 1930s, one the most consistently piercing, provocative and radical voices emanating from Harlem was that of A. Philip Randolph. Born in Jacksonville, Florida, Randolph moved to New York and became the articulate and tireless fighter for civil rights and labor solidarity. Founder of the Brotherhood of Sleeping Car Porters, Randolph and his protégé, Chandler Owen, also founded the *Messenger* magazine in 1917. Owen's input into the magazine was minimal. The *Messenger* belonged to Randolph and he dominated its editorial page and policy throughout the life span of the magazine. The philosophy of Randolph was given in the first editorial of the *Messenger*:

> Our aim is to appeal to reason, to lift our pens above the cringing demagogy of the times and above the cheap, peanut politics of the old, reactionary Negro leaders. Patriotism has no appeal to us; justice has. Party has no weight with us; principle has. Loyalty is meaningless; it depends on what one is loyal to. Prayer is not one of our remedies; it depends on what one is praying for. We consider prayer as nothing more than a fervent wish; consequently the merit and worth of a prayer depend upon what the fervent wish is. Still we never

forget that all wishes, desires, hopes—must be realized thru the adoption of sound methods. This requires scientific education—a knowledge of the means by which the end aimed at may be attained.

The *Messenger* attempted to introduce the black community to socialism. Throughout the pages of the magazine, Randolph and Owen advocated that the working class, particularly blacks, rally behind socialism. Randolph preached social revolution. He firmly believed that America needed a new foundation. Capitalism, he hypothesized, was by nature exploitative and, in the end, self-destructive. He advocated abandoning capitalism and pledged the *Messenger* to that effort. The *Messenger* was the first voice of radical, revolutionary, economic and political action among Negroes in America. Sterling D. Spero and Abram L. Harris accurately pinpointed the philosophical underpinning of the *Messenger's* radical socialism, and at the same time revealed the racial motivation underlying Randolph's acceptance of socialism. They believed that he attributed race prejudice to capitalism. Spero and Harris surmised that Randolph held that in an individualistic economic system, competition for jobs and the profitability of race prejudice to the capitalist class were incentives to race conflict. Therefore, the removal of the motive for creating racial strife was conditioned upon the socialization of industry and the rationalization of land. In short, the elimination of racism rested upon the elimination of economic individualism and the installing of competition through social revolution. In 1918, Randolph fully endorsed the Socialist Party and urged all blacks and whites to do the same. He held that the Socialist Party was the only party of principle. That year the Socialist Party garnered twenty-five percent of the vote in New York's mayoral election thanks to the efforts of Randolph's and the *Messenger's* endorsement of the party.

Randolph did what he could to keep blacks abreast of national and international issues, which he believed held the key to consciousness and group uplift. The first editions of the magazine dealt with the Russian Revolution and World War I. Randolph approved of the Russian Revolution, calling it the greatest achievement of the twentieth century. He further suggested that every country follow the lead of Russia and throw off their exploiting rulers and administer public utilities for public welfare and disgorge the exploiters and profiteers. Taking an adamant stand against WWI and, in particular, America's involvement and interests in the war, the first edition of the *Messenger* included the article "Business and the War" by

Scott Nearing. Nearing accused American business interests of using the world crisis as an occasion for making money, making profits out of the United States government since this country entered the war, and using the war as an excuse for a great drive to strangle the American labor movement. Randolph did more than attack the war issues in the *Messenger*. He came out against the war from the speaker's platform. While speaking on the war issue at a gathering in Cleveland, he was literally yanked from the podium and thrown into jail. Due to his constant radical orations, Randolph and the *Messenger* grew in popularity. The *Messenger* soon became the most widely circulated radical publication in America.

In public addresses and in the *Messenger*, Randolph broadened his attack, taking on civil rights and the exploitation of labor. From 1918 to 1920, he published a combined total of more than two-hundred articles and editorials dealing with civil rights and the problems of workers. In covering the struggle for civil rights, the *Messenger* carried articles with titles such as: "The Negro Business Man"; "Negro Women in Politics"; "Mary White Ovington"; "Du Bois and the N.A.A.C.P."; "Mixed Juries for the Riot Trials"; "Negro Leaders Compromise as Usual"; "The Negro and High Rents"; "Republicans and the Jim-Crow Car"; "Radical Organization on the Negro Question"; "The Friends of Negro Freedom"; "Lily-Whiteism"; "The Fort San-Houston Court Martial"; and "How to Stop Lynching." Some of the topics touched upon devoted to labor were: "Organizing the Negro Actor"; "The Brotherhood of Elevator and Switchboard Operators of New York"; "The Independent Labor Party of England"; "Industrial Program Peonage"; "$300,000,000 to Labor—$800,000,000 to Capital"; "Sacco and Vanzetti"; "Labor Leaders and Negro Leaders in Council"; "Unionism among Negroes"; "Tenant Farming"; "Woman Labor"; "Child Labor"; "Break Up the A.F. of L."; "Triple Alliance of Labor in Great Britain"; "Negro Workers: The A.F. of L or I.W.W."; "The Steel Strike"; and "Reasons Why White and Black Workers Should Combine in Labor Unions." In short, Randolph was an integrationist at least to the extent that he believed that blacks and whites should come together around points of common interest, particularly when it came to labor. Ironically, he sounded like Booker T. Washington when he spoke of common interests; however, labor organization, of course, was not an issue that Washington believed in, as he was a leading anti-labor spokesman. Randolph professed just the opposite, believing that labor solidarity was the key to uplift for the black race and all workers.[5]

In light of the voracity and consistency with which Randolph attacked inequities and injustices through the pages of the *Messenger*, and considering the mainstream public and management opinion on the labor movement and civil rights during the first two decades of the twentieth century, it was not surprising that the United States government considered Randolph to be radical and dangerous. By 1920, he had been branded "The Most Dangerous Negro in America." Those who had the slightest affiliation with the *Messenger* radicals, as they were dubbed, became targets of attack. The Rand School, an organization established for the purpose of educating workers in economics and politics, voiced its support for Randolph and the *Messenger*. The United States Department of Justice labeled the school, therefore, subversive and an academy for American Bolshevism.

Nothing could dissuade Randolph, as he believed that the real question was first labor and not race, the pages of the *Messenger* consistently beseeched black and white laborers to consolidate. "We all have one common interest," Randolph commented, "the getting of more wages, shorter hours and better working conditions." His was wishful thinking that whites could see beyond race and join hands with blacks in common economic interests. It was too bad that he was mistaken. He was convinced that the history of the labor movement in America proved that the employing class recognized no race lines. Randolph believed that black and white labor should and could combine for the reason that all workers should come together: to increase their bargaining power, which would enable them to obtain their demands. Randolph constantly reminded his readers: "Every member which is a part of the industrial machinery, must be organized if labor would win its demands. Organized labor cannot afford to ignore any labor factor of production which organized capital does not ignore." Unfortunately, white labor did not practice this and organized labor as a whole was terribly segregated and exclusive.

Randolph did more than write about the needs of labor to organize. He was an activist and he took his cry to the streets and became directly involved in initiating trade union organizations. He helped organize the "Friends of Negro Freedom" in 1920. This organization conducted political and labor forums all across the United States in an attempt to make the masses aware of the benefits that could be obtained through organization. He helped Willard Townsend to organize the redcaps into the United Transport Service Employees of America. It was Randolph's grandest hope for "one big union" that would represent all labor, black and white. The established labor organizations, except for the floundering Industrial Workers of the World, were racially exclusive and craft oriented. The American Federation of Labor, Randolph noted, was essentially a craft or trades union organization, while Negroes were mostly unskilled laborers. The interests of black Americans, Randolph maintained, lie with that group which neither discriminates against workers on account of color or on account of being unskilled. Randolph suggested that, since all labor wanted better wages and better working conditions, "The only problem then, which the colored worker should consider, as a worker, is the problem of organizing with other working men in the labor organization that best expresses the interests of the whole working class against the slavery and oppression of the whole capitalist class."

The American Federation of Labor failed to serve as that very much needed positive force for the organizing of all labor, black and white, skilled and unskilled. Randolph, through the *Messenger*, never relented in his criticism of the Federation for its racial and craft exclusiveness. Randolph advocated breaking up the A.F. of L. He accused the Federation of being organized upon unsound principles. He wrote: "Break up the A.F. of L. and let's get a real constructive labor movement! The whole machinery of the American Federation of Labor needs to be destroyed. It cannot be reformed. Form a labor movement of workmen—not white men—but all men who work without regard to race, nationality or color. Retire the American Separation of Labor to the tall timbers and obscurity from which it ought never to emerge."

An organization that he thought could be the rallying point for all labor was the Industrial Workers of the World (IWW). If you are a wage-worker you are welcome in the IWW halls, no matter what your color, Randolph proclaimed. He informed his audience that blacks and whites should view the IWW not as a white man's union, nor a black or red or yellow man's union, but a working man's union. He shared the IWW's dream of the entire working class brought together in "one big union." The *Messenger* radicals fervently defended the IWW. When W.E.B. Du Bois made the mistake of equating support of the IWW with a pro-Germany position in the *Crisis*, he received a severe scolding from Randolph in a *Messenger* editorial titled "The Crisis of the Crisis." The *Messenger* stated that although they considered Du Bois more intelligent than most Negro editors, he was nevertheless, in their opinion, comparatively ignorant of the world problems of sociological and economic significance. They reasserted that "the IWW is the only national organization of labor unions that does not discriminate against Negroes. A Negro, therefore, should be the last person to try to cast aspersion upon the IWW." The Randolph critiques of Du Bois's position ended with an overall assessment of African-American leadership. "The chief problem of the American Negro today," he concluded, "is the ridding himself of misleadership of all kinds, and especially that of so-called organs of public opinion."

Randolph denounced all who stood opposed to his views. Black leaders like Kelly Miller, Robert R. Morton, and Marcus Garvey, were all denounced. Miller and Morton warned against joining hands with white laborers for, as they saw it, unity with whites meant the displacement of blacks by whites at all levels of employment. Marcus Garvey believed that blacks should move in a separatist direction, become self-autonomous, and certainly not become a part of the white-dominated labor unions. The respected black journal, *Challenge*, disfavored black and white labor unity. The *Challenge* maintained, unlike Randolph, that the problem was the *color line* not the class line. Black newspapers, except for Monroe Trotter's *Boston Guardian*, disfavored the union of black and white workers. The *Chicago Defender*, the *Chicago Whip*, the *Pittsburgh Courier*, the *Cleveland Advocate*, and the *Atlanta Independent* all opposed unionism of whites and blacks, and agreed that black and white labor solidarity was not a question of *class line* or *color line*, but a question of the bread-line. Many African Americans contended that one big union meant one big unemployment line for blacks. Randolph, through his *Messenger*, constantly struck back at the black leaders, journals, and newspapers that opposed his platform.

His assault on Marcus Garvey, however, exceeded all others in intensity, candor and ruthlessness. In 1920, Randolph began a series of articles in the *Messenger* on the Garvey Movement in order that the people, whites and blacks, might get, what he called, a clear understanding of the true impact, the political, economic and social consequences of the Garvey Movement. Randolph's interests rested in "disabusing the minds" of the people of the idea that the editors of the *Messenger* were connected in any way with the Garvey Movement. No thoughtful individual really believed that Randolph and Garvey shared a similar outlook on America and philosophy for black advancement. Randolph vowed to examine the value of the Garvey Movement to the average working man and promised that if he found upon examination that the Garvey Movement was opposed to the interests of working people, and since ninety-eight per cent of blacks were working people, he would denounce Garvey as a definite menace to blacks. As Randolph saw it, the Garvey Movement would prove unnecessary if the labor problem was addressed. Proceeding in a different direction was a waste of time. "Negroes constitute a laboring element," Randolph reminded his listeners. "Unrest is widespread among them, even in the South. Radical white labor groups are reported to be calling to them. Washington, Chicago, Arkansas and Tulsa race riots show that Negroes are discontented and are ready to strike back. The increasing demand of Negroes for the abolition of the Jim-Crow car, disfranchisement, lynching; the insistence of a small minority for every right, even social equality; the trend of Negroes into labor unions; the activities of Negroes in the Socialist movement—all indicate the birth of a new consciousness." The view of African Americans as informed workers with a pro-union position may have been wishful thinking on his part. The new consciousness, however, was real. In Randolph's view, to accept Garveyism was to "divert the Negroes' mind away from these fundamental problems." He also attacked Garvey for his back-to-Africa philosophy and apparent pro-capitalist stand. Strikes and struggles of black workers in an Africa for Africans, Randolph predicted, would be dealt with in about the same way they are dealt with in all other countries. There would be a black mastery over black wage workers. Distinctions along class lines, he contended, would be the same as in all other capitalist countries. It was a stated belief in the *Messenger* and of the *Messenger* radicals that the Garvey back-to-Africa movement was unrealistic and counter productive for the black race. The solution, Randolph advocated, was to get rid of Garvey, and he urged: "Marcus Garvey Must Go!" In January of 1923, the *Messenger* radicals intensified their attack on Marcus Garvey in a short editorial titled, "A Supreme Negro Jamaican Jackass." Garvey was called a traitor to the race, a fool and ignoramus who understood nothing about the problems of the working class and even less about the problems of the black race. The editorial bitterly denounced Garveyism as being totally illogical. "Such logic," Randolph wrote, "could emanate only from the diseased brain of this Supreme Negro Jackass from Jamaica."[6]

Despite the important and timely issues that the *Messenger* addressed and the information it provided, the magazine's readership went into a steep decline in the mid 1920s. It was during this time that Randolph turned his attention to active unionization work. By mid-1925, the *Messenger* had adopted a new rallying cry—the case of the Pullman porters. In July of that year, Randolph wrote a piece titled, "The Case of the Pullman Porters" in which he elaborated on the plight of the porters, who suffered a miserable and tragic existence with low wages, long hours, and bad conditions. The porters had no effective voice in the regulation of the conditions on the job. Few workers in America were as lacking in support and lower in the industrial world yet rendered an essential contribution to the country's transportation system. Randolph demanded that something be done and done quickly. The problem of "doubling back" was particularly horrendous. Porters were made to return on the same train, the same night or day of arrival, and to work the entire return trip without sleep or rest. The porters' health was at risk. In addition, while the porter had to survive the rigors of "doubling back" he received no pay for the return trip. Randolph thought it bad enough to be compelled to do two days and two nights work on a stretch, but worse to receive nothing for it. For the Pullman porters there were no designated and regularized work hours. They worked until their cars reached the appointed destination, however far that may have been from the place of origin. Randolph told of how porters were often on the road for weeks and months at a time, without adequate linen or food, snatching a little sleep when and whenever they could. They had no certainty with respect to time with their families. It was a vile injustice that needed rectifying. The *Messenger* radicals had no patience with company unions and warned the porters to beware of Greeks bearing gifts. Randolph elucidated: "The employer seldom shows any genuine concern about the welfare of the employee. The emancipation of the slave never originates with the master. Landlords don't institute movements to reduce rents. It is not to his interest to do so. Nor is a company union for the benefit of the employees. It is by, of and for the company. The company organized and controlled it. The officials of the company union are the tools of the company. They serve the company for the company pays them. He who pays the fiddler calls the tune."

Randolph received a great deal of favorable response for his treatise on the plight of the Pullman porters. In August of 1925, he printed an article in the *Messenger* titled, "Pullman Porters Need Own Union." He attacked the Pullman Company for job discrimination stating that the Pullman Company provides for the promotion of every other worker in the company except the porter. Randolph noted that free assemblage of porters was banned. The job of the porter was similar to the dilemma facing all blacks as workers. He concluded the article by telling porters to organize, and informed his readers that the next issue of the *Messenger* would tell how to organize. In the following issue of the *Messenger*, he diagnosed the porters' condition, and prescribed that organization was the only hope. In a mass meeting in Harlem on August 25, 1925, the Brotherhood of Sleeping Car Porters was formally launched and

Randolph elected head of the new union with the title of general organizer. In the January 1926 issue of the *Messenger* one of the Brotherhood porters was given space to express his sentiments about the Pullman Company and the plight of the porters. The porter wasted no time in getting to the crux of his feelings toward the Pullman Company. "These human buzzards," he said, "would feast upon the bodies of our wives and children in order to live in ease and luxuries, but their days are numbered and they cannot pass." Pullman, however, did everything possible in order to pass. Randolph's response in the *Messenger* was revealing. "It is unfitting though interesting," he remarked, "to note how the Pullman Company is desperately trying to make a case for the wages and treatment it now gives the porters by sentimentally appealing to the name of Abraham Lincoln." In 1928, Randolph was as the forefront of the Brotherhood's general strike vote against the Pullman Company. The strike centered on the issues of pay, conditions, and opportunities for advancement and their declaration ended with the demand that porters should receive conductor's pay for performing conductor's duties, and be considered for promotion to the position of conductor when vacancies became available.

The Pullman Company was shrewd in its ability to handle strikes. The company announced that it would look more favorably on the Brotherhood and its demands if A. Philip Randolph were removed as the organization's president. This tactic seriously undermined the strike and the confidence of the porters was sadly shaken. As membership in the Brotherhood rapidly declined, another victim became apparent—the *Messenger*. The depression years were being felt in black communities and luxuries such as newspapers and magazines were forsaken. The *Chicago Defender's* circulation fell by one-third at the beginning of 1928. The culmination of forces and events was too much for the *Messenger* radicals, and at the beginning of 1929, publication of the magazine was suspended. Although the Brotherhood's prestige and membership declined, achievements were attained. The strike demonstrated that there existed an organization of porters. The American Federation of Labor recognized the organization and granted a charter to the Brotherhood of Sleeping Car Porters. Finally, in 1935, the Pullman Company recognized the BSCP and made concessions to its black workers. It was difficult to measure Randolph and the *Messenger's* overall importance to black America. What was clear was that in the life of the magazine, and in the much longer lifetime of A. Philip Randolph, there existed a powerful and articulate voice calling for solidarity to advance black folk and the entire laboring class in America.[7]

WORKING FROM WITHOUT

The seminal advocate of black race solidarity or black nationalism, and its most prominent organizer in the twentieth century was Marcus Garvey, who embodied and articulated a vision of self-rule, independence, and empowerment that black folk in America and many throughout the world embraced. Scholars examining the impact of Garvey found his appeal, charisma, the problems associated with his movement, and the times that spawned it, fascinating. The revision in scholarship began to reflect an evolution in the thinking about black nationalism and black protest movements that rejected integration and Americanization. The early academic treatments of Garvey rarely gave him proper due. Garvey amassed one of the largest black organizations and mass movements in the history of the United States, with well over one hundred thousand dues paying members, making him the most successful black organizer. Garveyism was, to be sure, more than the sum of its parts, just as the scholarship on him was more than its sum. Writings on Garvey and the movement echoed the climate and the eras in which they were produced and the sentiments of the individuals doing the writing. The work that stood for the longest as the definitive history of Garvey was David Cronon's book, *Black Moses*, published in the 1960s. It was a period in which almost anything that had a black title could be published, and Cronon's work was symbolic in that it was a hurried expansion of a master's thesis that reflected the author's shallow research and limited knowledge of the subject. Cronon painted Garvey as nothing more than a black charlatan who used a pie-in-the-sky dream about blacks returning to Africa to defraud a gullible black public. His work, to say the least, was unkind in its treatment of Garvey's organization, the Universal Negro Improvement Association (UNIA), and his philosophy and ideas. It was an even sadder testimony that a work of this caliber could have been heralded as a major contribution on such an important topic. White-dominated academe failed for far too long to give important black topics and issues the respect warranted. One of the first positive breakthroughs in the treatment of Garvey was Theodore Vincent's *Black Power and the Garvey Movement*. Vincent saw Garvey through new eyes. Although a white writer himself, Vincent had no problem in appreciating the positive components of Garveyism. The Garvey movement, indeed, had flaws and shortcomings. Vincent, however, gave Garvey credit for being a visionary who founded a tremendous organization that dared to challenge inequalities and American racism. Garvey stood bold and rejected America, urging black folk to stand on their own. The scholarly portrait of the movement advanced, particularly with the work of John Henrik Clarke, who helped readers to understand the rightful place of Garvey and his organization. One of the first in-depth historical treatments that used a massive array of primary source materials in examination of Garveyism was Tony Martin's seminal work, *Race First: The Ideological and Organizational Struggles of Marcus and the Universal Negro Improvement Association,* published in the 1970s. The scholarship continued to evolve with other contributions. Robert Hill amassed the voluminous sources and papers world-wide related to Marcus Garvey in his edited collection published by the University of California Press. Others have raised the specter of class within the ranks of Garvey's ideology and organization. These works, while different in approach and perspective, shared an appreciation of the importance of Garvey and his movement and the times.

Garvey's background provided clues to his personal motivation and character. Born in Jamaica, in 1887, his lineage traced back to the island's Maroons, those defiant slaves who rebelled against white authority and enslavement and ran away and formed black colonies. Garvey's heritage and lineage was imbued with a fighting tradition suggesting a systemic spirit of defiance of which he was born into or, at least, raised upon. His youth was filled with books and the liberating power of knowledge. Both his father and mother constantly encouraged him to read and to absorb ideas. Steeped with the power of information early on, he thirsted for more. Growing up in the West Indies, Garvey developed sensitivity to color, race, and class distinctions. They remained forces vivid in his mind. In later years, he concluded that the major problem facing black folk was not their differences but the racism of whites who held ultimate power over the world in which they lived and who refused to recognize blacks as human beings entitled to fair treatment and equal rights. Garvey concluded that people of African descent throughout the world would have to reunite intellectually, economically, and even physically if possible. Many would later dub him a black separatist. He was actually a Pan-Africanist. Garvey held no hope of racial integration and advised blacks to "rise up you mighty race" as an independent and self-sustaining people.

Garvey's formal education was rudimental and limited. His larger education and liberation came through self initiatives. Crucial to his intellectual development were the years he spent in London, England, from 1911 to 1914. London and Paris were the centers of intellectual radicalism, free speech and pamphleteering. In London, the coffee houses became his college campus. In London, in Paris, in

Amsterdam, one could sit and talk and reflect and meet people from around the world who were thinkers and activists challenging and questioning the status quo, including that of the British empire and the European colonization of Africa. Garvey very much benefited from the London years, a crucial and vibrant time for him as he developed a vision of Pan-Africanism and an autonomous black world. He read, spoke, listened. Indeed, so many ideas were flowing around and through him that it became difficult for him to distinguish where the ideas of others stopped and his own ideas began. The concept of "Africa for Africans" was a case in point. The slogan became the rallying cry of the Garvey movement and the UNIA. Before Garvey, the concept of "Africa for Africans" was being touted about London and Paris in pamphlets that Duse Mohammed Ali authored. Many thought mistakenly that the powerful and catchy slogan was Duse Mohammed Ali's own creation. This too was incorrect. A man named Booth was the originator of the slogan. Booth was himself a fascinating figure with little know about him. He was evidently a radical missionary, perhaps a Jesuit, who spent much of his time in East and West Africa, advocating an Africa that was free from interlopers. Europeans, he preached, should pack up and leave Africa, end colonialism, and stay in their own part of the world. On one occasion when Booth was meeting with a group of African chiefs and philosophizing about the goal of "Africa for Africans," he beseeched them to expel all white folks from Africa. Booth, a white person himself, asserted to the African chiefs that white folks could not be trusted to do right and must be forced from the continent. One of the African leaders present asked a question of Booth that certainly was appropriate, given what Booth said and the fact that he was European. The African leader asked: "What should be done with Mr. Booth? Should the Africans force him to leave the continent as well?" To Booth's everlasting credit he said, "yes," that he and every other white person should be made to leave Africa, and leave "Africa for Africans."

During the London years, Garvey took freely of ideas. To his credit, he never took an idea from a second-rate mind, only first rate people, as John Henrik Clarke put it tongue in cheek. Garvey made "Africa for Africans, Those at Home and Those Abroad," a worldwide slogan of promise and hope for millions of blacks throughout the world. Garvey took these ideas back with him to Jamaica in July of 1914, and on to Harlem in the United States in 1916, one year after the death of Booker T. Washington. Garvey had read Booker Washington's *Up From Slavery* and he concluded that Washington was the greatest of the Negro leaders and espoused ideas similar to his own, particularly the advocacy of self-help and working with the hands. Garvey read into Washington's treatise a modicum of black nationalism. Self-help and working with the hands did seem to suggest autonomy and a self-sufficiency. Garvey learned over the years, however, of the shortcomings of Washington's philosophy and views. In 1923, he concluded that Booker Washington had been a misguided leader of the black race and that the ideas of industrial schooling and accommodation that Washington championed were terribly wrong and detrimental to black people.

In the United States the hope of the Garvey movement ran supreme. Possibilities seemed endless because of the wealth of the African-American community. If black America were a country it would have rated right at the top as the wealthiest black nation in the world, including all of Africa and the diaspora. These were eventful years in the United States for Garvey and the most important ones for the movement. First, Garvey raised funds for the organization. In Detroit in 1918 during his first speaking tour outside of Harlem, a heckler in the crowd hit him in the head with a rock. Garvey remained unperturbed. On a speaking tour in Chicago in 1919 he witnessed something that emboldened his faith and confidence in the spirit of black folk and their stoutness of character. In 1919, Chicago was in the midst of race riots. Whites attacked blacks and blacks fought back. Garvey noted with glee and pride that African Americans were not passively taking discrimination and mistreatment. Blacks had taken it in the South but they exchanged blow for blow in the North and retaliated against marauding white gangs that invaded their community. Garvey witnessed an incident in Chicago where blacks spread wire across an alleyway and waited for their attackers. A wagon load of white thugs tripped over the wire and were thrown to the ground. Blacks, who were waiting in ambush with baseball bats, pounced on the marauders giving them a severe beating. Garvey returned to Harlem with a new resolve and invigorated commitment to black autonomy and self rule. For him black nationalism was the only solution in the face of a hostile white America that was becoming more oppressive each day.[8]

The virulent actions of the government of the United States to halt activism during this period underscored Garvey's reasoning. The year 1919 signaled the zenith of the crack down on dissidents in the United States. The Red Raids, or so called Palmer Raids of A. Mitchell Palmer, the Attorney General of the United States, spared no expense to crush dissent in the United States. This was a time of social unrest and suppression of radicals during the years of Woodrow Wilson's presidential administration. The immigrants and the blacks were often the scapegoats, and Garvey was both black and an immigrant. The nation cracked down on any voice of discontent. Organizations such as the Industrial Workers of the World (IWW) received special focus. The IWW, headed by Big Bill Haywood, professed the idea of "one big union;" all labor organized into a single mass and dedicated to the overthrow of traditional capitalism. The United States Postal Service did its part in conspiring with other federal agencies against the IWW and against dissident organizations throughout the nation. The Post Office possessed formidable weapons. Under Section 211 of the Criminal Code, the Post Office was empowered to declare non-mailable any "indecent material." By a 1911 amendment the term indecent had been broadened to include "matter tending to incite arson, murder or assassination." Post Master General Burleson and his subordinates could also exclude anything from the mail that violated the Espionage Act of 1917 or its successor the Sedition Act of 1918.

The *Red Scare* was full blown and well underway. Attorney General Palmer's dragnet, midnight raids and quick strikes seized documents and files that were used against those individuals deemed to be enemies of the United States. A young J. Edgar Hoover, who was head of the Justice Department's Alien Radical Division, made his reputation persecuting immigrants and other "undesirables." Garvey, one of the preeminent "alien dissidents," was targeted for neutralization. The Justice Department was committed to getting the IWW, getting the Communists, and getting Marcus Garvey. They wanted immigrant dissidents deported and the Bureau of Immigration did its bidding with Hoover at the helm. Under Rule 22 of the Immigration Bureau, "detainees" were supposed to have the benefit of counsel. That "benefit" was usually ignored. Organizations like unions and individuals like Garvey were routinely denied proper legal advice and due process. Confiscated records of the suspected organizations were used against its members and others if merely mentioned in the correspondence. The government used "guilt by association" to make cases against suspected radicals. They confiscated Marcus Garvey's records of his Black Star Steamship Line and used those records against him as evidence of his alleged efforts to defraud via the mails. Hoover championed the government's efforts to get Garvey. He prodded the courts to set high bails, which they did, thus effectively keeping the undesirable dissidents in jail until deportation was possible. During the large scale round-ups in January of 1920, with many abuses to due process, Garvey was one of those successfully targeted. Secretary of Labor William B. Wilson and assistant secretary Louis F. Post agreed with the public's outrage at the Justice Department's and the Immigration Bureau's abuses and demanded that aliens be given due process and that bails be set at reasonable rates. There was fighting between the two camps as allegations of disloyalty abounded. More than six thousand dissidents were rounded up during these raids and approximately five hundred were deported.

Nothing, however, surpassed the U.S. government's efforts to neutralize Marcus Garvey. The government and its agencies devoted substantial manpower, energy and finances to bring down Garvey and the UNIA. Attorney General Palmer in his report, "Radicalism and Sedition Among the Negroes as Reflected in Their Publications," specifically listed Garvey's UNIA newspaper, Negro World, as hostile to the United States. J. Edgar Hoover stated bluntly: "Garvey is a west indian Negro and in addition to his activities in endeavoring to establish the Black Star Line Steamship Corporation he has also been particularly active among the radical elements in New York City in agitating the Negro movement. Unfortunately, however, he has not as yet violated any federal law whereby he could be preceded against on the grounds of being an undesirable alien from the point of view of deportation. It occurs to me, however, from the attached clipping that there might be some proceeding against him for fraud in connection with his Black Star Line propaganda." Reacting to the threats, Garvey responded: "Only crooks and thieves and cowards fear to go to prison. Men with principles don't care about jail." Garvey should have been a bit more worried because the U.S. government was determined to get him by any means necessary. The large financial base and membership support he garnered was seen as a threat, to people like Hoover, to the American way of life. Garvey attempted to educate the masses and motivate them to fight back for change. Hoover attempted to portray him as nothing more than a clever scoundrel and whose civil rights activities also made him a menace to America. "While he [Garvey] is clever enough to temper his propaganda with statements that he is for the Negro rather than against the white man or any government," Hoover reported, "his speeches are not lacking in many references to fighting for Negro rights and I believe that a tendency of his propaganda is to alienate the loyalty of American and British Negroes to his association."

In other words, according to Hoover, it was insurrectionary and unacceptable for blacks to fight racism and to stand up for their rights. As Garvey saw it, blacks in the United States shed their blood for the republic and for the making of America and it was time for them to finally receive the benefits of those sacrifices. Hoover and others found this unacceptable. Garvey told blacks that it was time to stop making sacrifices for America and to build for themselves. "The first dying that is to be done by the black man in the future," he declared, "will be done to make himself free." J. Edgar Hoover and the Lusk Committee found these statements incendiary and concrete examples, they believed, of the dangerous nature of the Garvey movement. Garvey's flirtations with Communism added to the volatility of the situation. He knew what he was doing. Garvey was doing this not only to agitate the American government but to strike a blow at Hoover and his paranoia with Communism. Marcus Garvey most certainly was no Communist. He believed that Communism was not the correct road for African Americans to pursue but viewed it as a positive force for the liberation of people of African descent as compared to the negatives of capitalism and colonialism. Garvey believed that the Untied States, Britain, France, Germany, Belgium and the rest of Europe were interested only in exploiting and maintaining their control over people of color throughout the United States, the Caribbean, Latin America, and Africa.

Hence, Garvey was deemed a threat to Western hegemony and qualified as a primary object of their wrath. The United States government did everything possible to get him including using the United States Secret Service, the Immigration Bureau, the U.S. Postal Service, and other agencies to plant evidence against him in order to destroy his movement. In his defense, Garvey argued that he had done nothing illegal and that the U.S. government went beyond the pale of justice in their falsification of and manufacturing of information to destroy him. James E. Amos, an ex-body guard of Garvey, was a plant of J. Edgar Hoover and provided "evidence" against Garvey. The NAACP, to its discredit, issued news releases that were harmful to Garvey receiving a fair trail, as the organization was evidently angered by his anti-white attitude and hostility to integration and the NAACP's leadership. The combination of Amos and the NAACP were all used in the government's campaign to bring down Marcus Garvey and the UNIA. After Garvey left New York in February 1921 he journeyed to Florida and from there to Havana, Cuba, where he had a triumphant visit with the island's president and other dignitaries. From there he went to Jamaica. What he did not know was that the barricades were being put in place to block his reentry into the United States. Garvey was branded as a negative force, as a radical alien who had no place in America, and he found it extremely difficult to get back into the country. The entire question of freedom of speech seemed lost when it came to voices like Marcus Garvey and his professed black nationalism. Official American harassment under Hoover and others also included efforts to thwart Garvey's annual conventions. Conventions of the UNIA were canceled. Garvey was also indicted in 1921 for income tax evasion. Evidence suggests that all of this was done to embarrass, harass, and bring down the Garvey movement. Garvey understood this as did anyone else who was in anyway connected with the movement. Records of organizations in anyway linked to Garvey were seized, and individuals identified as somehow supportive of Garveyism were targets for governmental harassment, deportation, or jail. In 1922, a meeting of the Charleston, South Carolina division of the UNIA was invaded by police. This was a common occurrence in every city where UNIA meetings were held. In Los Angeles and in New Orleans, Garvey was the target of local police and immigration officials. There had been an effort as early as 1919 to get Garvey on the Mann Act since Amy Ashwood had accompanied him on tour across state lines. Any and every effort was made to get him. The post office authorities, in conjunction with the Immigration Bureau, completely cut off the mail service to the UNIA, refusing to deliver anything including the most innocuous announcements of UNIA meetings. The UNIA organization was branded as fraudulent and Garvey himself as a criminal and an undesirable alien who should be deported to Jamaica. Garvey was arrested in 1922 on charges of mail fraud in connection with the Black Star Steamship Company, convicted, and sent to prison in February 1925. His followers established committees and did all they could to work for his release. They found themselves fighting constantly with the United States government. It was not a question of money. It was the question of a government that branded Garvey as an undesirable alien and wanted him out of the United States. The United States Supreme Court refused to review his case. It was deemed an open and shut case. Garvey was a criminal and one who would be deported from the country. Even Garvey's previous nemeses felt that the government had gone too far. Kelly Miller of Howard University wrote that it was "a dangerous principle to impose legal punishment upon men for their belief rather than for their behavior. This trick is as old as political cunning and chicanery dating back to Socrates, Jesus and John Brown," Miller complained. William Pickens of the NAACP thought that the government exceeded its authority in the Garvey case. This should have been a prime lesson to black folk throughout the United States and abroad that when you spoke in a voice of discontent, displeasure and a road to freedom not acceptable to the powers that be, you were at risk. Garvey was deported on December 2, 1927.

Hoover was still receiving reports on Garvey's activities as late as the 1930s and engaged in efforts to crush Garveyism wherever he heard that it might be gaining a foothold. After Garvey's deportation from the United States, he visited Canada on numerous occasions. He hoped that Canada might provide a basis for the continuation of his U.N.I.A. effort. There, too, the hands of the United States government were present. The movement against Garvey extended into Latin America and the rest of the world as U.N.I.A. branches were placed under surveillance and efforts to close them orchestrated by the government of the United States and other Western powers. Throughout the United States, Costa Rica, Panama, Cuba, Santo Domingo, Brazil and elsewhere, concerted attempts were made to ban Garveyism and the radicalism of black hegemony. The United Fruit Company, an organization whose history was drenched in the exploitation of black labor throughout the world, was a supporter of the surveillance and the anti-Garvey initiatives of the United States government and its allies. Leading associations of American business leaders such as the National Civic Federation supported the campaign to thwart the spread of Garveyism, believing that it stood for the agitation of people of African descent throughout the world, which meant a challenge to the capitalist relationship to black workers world-wide.[9]

Garvey nevertheless remained a voice, an idea, and a principle that circulated among black people. UNIA branches continued to function for several years after his deportation. There were chapters throughout North America, in the West Indies, in South America, and Africa. In 1931, Garvey traveled to England and made speeches in hope of revitalizing the push for black nationalism. He continued his advocacy of nationhood and empowerment for the black race abroad until his death in June of 1940. Garvey believed that black folk throughout the diaspora were destined to reunite with Africa and to assert again what they once had long before the coming of Europeans: an autonomy, a self sufficiency, a life based on principles of equality and human dignity that could not be realized under European rule or under the racism in the United Sates of America. For black America and the world, however, the Garvey dream was being rapidly pushed into the shadows under the harsh reality and daily struggle to survive the economic collapse of the 1930s.

VII
SEEKING SALVATION
DURING MORE
HARD TIMES

The Great Depression of the 1930s dealt its devastating blow to the nation as a whole and a cataclysmic one to black folk. There were some positive signals at the federal level but there, too, as throughout the nation, racism remained an ever-present force. The struggle against it and the gripping economic crisis were supreme challenges to African Americans.

Symbolic of the condition of blacks in America was the grave and diabolical and persistent occurrences of lynchings. We tend to think of lynchings happening primarily in the South. Most did occur in that region, better than eighty-five percent, but they also occurred in the West and in the urban North. In the early part of the twentieth century there were instances of blacks being lynched, hung from lampposts, in northern urban centers such as New York, New Jersey, Chicago, Cincinnati, and Boston. Lynchings, to say the least, were a national disgrace. Black folk and their allies sought the passage of anti-lynching legislation.

The NAACP also did all it could to win anti-lynching legislation. In 1919, the organization published *Thirty Years of Lynching in the United States,* which did a superb job of documenting the horror of lynchings throughout the country by race, sex, and location. Having done this, the NAACP put all of its support behind Congressman Leonidas C. Dyer of St. Louis, Missouri. The Republican congressman courageously introduced an anti-lynching bill in Congress. Dyer made no bones about it that lynching was illegal and was murder. The legislation was debated with no holds barred. The key to passage rested on whether other Republicans would rally to the cause. They did not. In the end, the Dyer Bill was defeated in 1923.

Black folk learned an important lesson regarding those they thought to be their friends in the Republican Party but who did not stand firm with Dyer and defend and vote for passage of the anti-lynching legislation. This gave added weight to the argument of black leaders that African Africans rethink their alliance to the Republican Party and become independent brokers of their own vote.

Republican presidents were of no help either. President Warren G. Harding did nothing to push for anti-lynching legislation. President Calvin Coolidge did nothing as well. The Republican Party was saying to black folk that it expected their vote but blacks should not expect anything for it. Despite the demands and efforts of African Americans to motivate the Republicans, they failed to respond. In consequence, the gap between the party and the African-American community increased during the late 1920s. The resolution passed by the NAACP at its 1926 annual convention symbolized this widening breach. The resolution read: "Our political salvation and our social survival lie in our absolute independence of party allegiance and politics and the casting of our vote for our friends and against our enemies whoever they may be and whatever party labels they carry."

In the 1928 presidential election a substantial number of black voters broke from the Republican ranks and supported the Democratic candidate Al Smith. This, in a real sense, was unprecedented and sent a clear message to the Democratic Party that blacks could be won over if the price was right, and that price was the commitment to the interests of African Americans. The presidency of Herbert Hoover was the last opportunity for the Republican Party to hold its blacks in line, to maintain their loyalty with the party. African Americans who supported Hoover may have done so out of the sense of loyalty to the Republican Party that was no longer justified. The black press reported that this was the Republicans last chance with blacks to show that it was still the party of Lincoln. The downfall of the Republican Party in 1932 was a result of the greatest economic collapse this nation has known, the Great Depression. For many, Hoover and the Republican Party gave the nation the Great Depression. The collapse of the stock market in October 1929 was a call for new leadership and the move to the Democrats to redirect the nation's future. African Americans were already wavering in their support of the Republicans and, with the collapse of the economy, they were ripe candidates for party mutiny.

It was pragmatically unfair to blame the Great Depression on Herbert Hoover. Although President of the United Sates, he was only one individual. America's economic trends were its own worst enemies. This was made clear from the causes and contributing factors to the nation's economic collapse. These factors went beyond any one party and straight to the heart and nature of American ideology. One factor was over-expansion in the fields of agriculture, industry and credit. Farmers were now producing too much and were unable to sell their produce at satisfactory prices. American industry was so over bloated and over productive that it could not sell all that it produced. In the glutted market, the over-expansion of credit and installment buying ran rampant. Add to this the decline in foreign trade as a result of high tariffs. War debts and reparations and the closing of foreign markets meant further over production of American goods that were unwanted overseas. In addition, the increased use of labor-saving devices, also known as automation, put more Americans out of work. Simply put, fewer workers were needed to produce more. In the period 1910 to 1920 output per worker in the United States increased nearly fifty percent. Labor-saving devices then as now meant in the end the replacement of more workers by machines. Another factor exacerbating the problem was the overall decline in purchasing power in the stagnant economy owing to a worsening job market, credit instability, rising prices, and low wages for those lucky enough to have a job. Finally, the grossly uneven distribution of wealth was part and parcel of America's dilemma from the very birth of the nation. Despite the generally prosperous condition of the early to mid 1920s American poverty continued to increase. The shortage of housing grew and rural and urban slums were becoming a more common phenomenon. A 1929 survey indicated that forty percent of all families in America had incomes of less than fifteen hundred dollars a year while the wealthiest twenty-five thousand families had a total income three times greater than that of the six million poorest families in the United States. The nation was in economic disarray and to blame President Hoover for the total collapse of the American economy was wrong. In all fairness to Hoover, he did take action although, as often said, he did too little too late. In 1932, President Hoover established the Reconstruction Finance Corporation, some two billion dollars allocated as loan money to financial institutions to keep them going. Hoover also initiated the Agricultural Marketing Act of 1929. This act was designed to keep farm prices from falling any lower and to loan money to farmers' cooperatives. The Federal Farm Board supervised the program. President Hoover also supported the Unemployment Relief Act that was passed in 1932. Here several billion dollars were authorized for relief on an emergency basis to the construction industry, through the erection of public buildings, thus providing jobs to that segment of the economy and to workers. It was fair to state that Hoover did act to halt the depression but it was equally fair to state that his efforts were ineffective.[1]

As far as blacks were concerned, the efforts of Hoover and the Republican Party had little or no positive effect on their condition.

African Americans received less in terms of relief moneys than did any other group, though the depression hit them and their communities the hardest. In Harlem, for example, the home of the black Renaissance, the depression was devastating. While it did not end the Harlem Renaissance, it did put a damper on it. In Harlem hand-to-mouth living became the rule of the day throughout the late 1920s and the heart of the depression era of the 1930s. By the mid 1930s most of black Harlem was destitute and barely surviving, as the average family income dropped to only eighteen dollars per week. Added to the problem was Harlem's population increase just prior to the depression. The doubling and tripling of families in what were originally one-family apartments became the norm of the day. Job discrimination against blacks was routine and continuous. Worst of the culprits were the public utilities companies of New York. The Consolidated Gas Company employed blacks only as porters. The New York Edison Company did the same. Porters and hallmen, cleaners and sweepers were all blacks could hope for in the public utilities industry. The New York Telephone Company employed blacks as messengers in addition to porters. Out of more than ten thousand employees, six hundred were blacks. Western Union Telegraph Company was a discriminator with only two blacks as clerks and a handful of them employed as messengers in the Harlem area. In its other districts, Western Union did not employ blacks in any capacity. These discriminatory practices were repeated throughout the city and state of New York. A. Philip Randolph and his organization conducted a survey of New York race discrimination in employment. In 1927 the *Messenger* sent inquires to the major public utilities companies in the city. One after another openly replied that where they did employ blacks it was as porters or other menials and that only in the fewest of instances could they cite a black as a clerk and virtually in no cases could they cite them as line workers and certainly not as middle managers or, heaven forbid, as junior executives in the company. In a written response to Randolph's inquiry, Vice President H. M. Bundage of the Consolidated Gas Company stated: "Replying to your favor of November 23, have to advice that Negroes employed by us render common labor, maid service and the like. We do not assign Negroes as stenographers, clerks or inspectors." The New York Telephone Company said the same in its response, noting that "We might say that we do employ such persons [Negroes], having some on our payroll at the present time assisting us in the conduct of our restaurant and lounge facilities." To make matters worse, there was the continuous problem of the color line within trade unions. In those areas where there might have been a glimmer of opportunity, blacks found themselves barred because they were unable to join the unions. Most craft-oriented unions maintained the color line. In New York, more than half of the major unions had restrictive racial covenants in their initiation rituals. These restrictions were rigorously adhered to until as late as the 1960s in most cases.

As the Great Depression worsened, issues of racism and of discrimination were of even lesser importance to the public. White America, especially during hard economic times, could care less about what was happening to its black citizens. People were looking inward and worrying about themselves, not their neighbors or friends next door, and least of all concerned about an outcast group such as the American Negro. Thoughts of integration and fair treatment blossomed during times of economic prosperity. During periods of economic woe and crisis the worst was demonstrated in the American population and economic sphere.

In Harlem the depression deepened. Two young black women social scientists, Ella Baker and Marvel Cooke, researching the impact of the depression on African-American women, unearthed an employment "slave mart." There were frequent complaints of exploitation of black women. Baker and Cooke began to study the problem. They published their findings in the November 1935 issue of the *Crisis* in an article they titled "The Bronx Slave Mart." What was this slave market? How did it get its name? Those were the questions that Baker and Cooke wanted answered. It was common knowledge that on any corner in the congested sections of New York City's Bronx these mushroom slave marts, as they were called, existed. The two marts where the traffic was heaviest and the bidding highest were located at 167th Street and Jerome Avenue and at Simpson and Westchester Avenues. There black women of all ages, sat on benches or leaned against the wall with the inevitable paper bundle, waiting hopefully for a white mistress to come along and buy their services for a day or a few hours. Baker and Cooke discovered that the Simpson Avenue block "exudes the stench of the slave market at its worst. Not only is human labor bartered and sold for slave wage, but human love also is a marketable commodity. But whatever it is, labor or love that is sold, economic necessity compels these women to make the sell." The women came as early as eight in the morning and stayed until the late afternoon. Rain or shine, cold or hot, young and old, black women came and waited for a Bronx housewife to buy their strength, their work, their energy, for an hour or two, or if they were lucky, for a whole day at a rate of "fifteen, twenty, twenty-five, or if luck be with them, thirty cents an hour." If not the mistress of the house, Baker and Cooke reported, their husband or their sons or brothers came and, under the subterfuge of work, "offered worldly-wise girls higher bids for their time." Who were these women? Why were they there? It was clear as Cooke and Baker documented that in the boom days before the onslaught of the depression in 1929, many of these women, who were now forced to bargain for a day's work on street corners, were employed in grand homes in the rich eighties or in the wealthier homes in Long Island and Westchester at adequate wages. Some were former industrial workers forced by slack in work to seek other means to sustain them. Unlike the vast majority of white women, most black women had always held jobs outside the home. Whatever their standing prior to the depression, these black women had not sought employment where they were now seeking it. They came to the Bronx in desperation. They needed the work. They had to support their families given the catastrophic unemployment rate for black males. This was a period that black women, more than perhaps ever before, carried the burden of economic provision for the family. Paradoxically, the crash of 1929 brought to the domestic labor market a new employer class. The lower middle class white housewife who, having dreamed of the luxury of a maid, found the opportunity readily abundant in these black women forced to the slave marts due to hardship. Ironically, blacks were forced out of many of the better paying domestic jobs when the depression hit because of the employers' declining economic means and, in other cases, because the employers felt affinity toward ethnic whites in need of work and hired them over the blacks. Pressed against the wall, black women desperately looked for any kind of employment. Hours of futile waiting in employment agencies, the fee required despite the lack of income, and the fraudulent agencies that sprung up during the depression, all "forced the day worker to fend for herself or try the dubious and circuitous road to public relief." As inadequate as emergency relief was it proved somewhat of a boom to many of the black women, for with its advent actual starvation was no longer the ever-present slave driver. In an effort to supplement the inadequate relief received, many of the black women put themselves on the line in this open market. "And what a market!," Baker and Cooke reported. "She who is fortunate (?) enough to please Mrs. Simon Legree's scrutinizing eye is led away to perform hours of multifarious household drudgeries. Under a rigid watch she is permitted to scrub floors on her bended knees, to hang precariously from window sills, cleaning window after window or to strain and sweat over steaming tubs of heavy blankets, spreads, and furniture covers. Fortunate, indeed, is she who gets the full hourly rate promised. Often, the day's slavery is rewarded with a single dollar bill or whatever her unscrupulous employer pleases to pay. More often, the clock is set back for an hour or more. Too often she is sent away without any pay at all."[2]

NEW DEAL OR OLD DEAL

The Republican Party lost the black vote and would lose the White House after the Hoover presidency. Hoover was symbolic of the dominant American ideology of rugged individualism and Social Darwinism, the belief that the individual takes care of him or herself and does not blame the government or the system for failure. He was the epitome of the rags to riches story, the Horatio Alger myth, and the rugged pioneering spirit. Hoover, who was born in Iowa and educated at Stanford, equated his success to hard work and pulling himself up by his own bootstraps. He believed in rugged individualism. The lyrics of the theme song from the hit television series of the 1970's and 1980's, "All in the Family," caught the essence of Hoover's administrative style and personal beliefs and the era as the series main characters, Archie and Edith Bunker, sung: "We could use a man like Herbert Hoover again. Didn't have no welfare states, everybody pulled his weight." The title and actual 1928 campaign song of Hoover's makes the point: "If, He's Good Enough For Lindy [Charles A. Lindbergh], He's Good Enough For Me." The success or failure of the individual was in the individual's own hands as Hoover saw it, as Lindbergh symbolized it in his heroic flight across the Atlantic, and as most Americans agreed. When the nation elected Hoover, it elected his principles, ideology, and professed philosophy. Hoover's own successful career reinforced the values of rural Protestant white America and reflected in him and in the nation the belief that achievement came through individual effort, personal merit, and that it was not a question of equality of opportunity or a helping hand.

It should have been easy for blacks to determine that Hoover would not be on their side. Though Al Smith was a northern Democrat he was still part of a party with a strong southern base. Nevertheless, some African Americans did leave the ranks of the Republican Party in 1928 and vote for the Democratic candidate. The *Chicago Defender, Baltimore Afro-American, Boston Guardian,* and the *Norfolk Journal and Guide,* all supported and endorsed Smith's candidacy. In short, the black vote was beginning to rethink its allegiance to the Republican Party. Hoover was aloof and cold to black folk. He appointed no blacks to administrative positions. He did win some favor from black for removing federal troops from Haiti. His economic policies demonstrated no interest in helping black Americans or acknowledgment of the race problem. Nevertheless, in the 1932 election most blacks stayed with the Republicans and supported Hoover. For African Americans it was a very difficult move to leave the Republican ranks and support the Democrat, Franklin D. Roosevelt. Roosevelt had no track record that engendered black confidence. African Americans recalled that Roosevelt was assistant secretary of the Navy under President Wilson during the American occupation of Haiti, and as a vice presidential candidate in 1920 he made the remark that he personally authored Haiti's constitution. FDR, now the Democratic presidential candidate, headed a ticket that included as his vice presidential running mate John Nance Garner from Texas. Blacks perceived this a negative sign, a liability for FDR in his courting of the black vote. The black Chicago vote was about the same as in 1928. In Cleveland, the Republican percentage of the black vote actually increased. FDR eventually won blacks to the Democratic ranks in forthcoming elections thanks largely to the help of his wife, Eleanor Roosevelt, whose personal appeal and charm and constant reaching out to the African-American community demonstrated to blacks that they at least had a sympathetic ear in the White House in the First Lady. FDR's own personal appeal also did much to make possible the transition of black folk from the Republican to Democratic Party possible. Although virtually none of his great fireside chats to the nation over the new media, the radio, were directed at the African-American community per se, they nevertheless played well in the black community as they did throughout the nation. Here was a president with personal appeal and a genuine sense of humanity and progressive thought that won the favor of African Americans, if not through effective legislation to counteract racism and to address their specific needs.

The first one hundred days of FDR's administration went well for the nation and the African-American community. He was a hands-on president who went against the tenets of rugged individualism and Social Darwinism to a large degree and used the power of the federal government to take on and attempt to solve the monstrous economic crisis. His style of administration was something that black citizens looked at with interest. Within his groups of liberal and conservative advisers were first-rate minds competing and offering conflicting points of view. FDR masterfully picked and chose from the exchanges, ideas, and possible courses of action. Individuals like Will Alexander of the Farm Security Administration and Harold Ickes of the Public Works Administration held high approval ratings among African Americans. Ickes, in particular, was a supporter of civil rights and member of the NAACP. The New Deal legislation, however well intended, was fraught with shortcomings. Roosevelt's first acts were to benefit the elite moneyed sector of society, as he attempted to stabilize the banking industry with passage of the Emergency Banking Act in 1933. He then put into place a deluge of recovery programs or "alphabet soup" legislation: the AAA (Agricultural Adjustment Administration), PWA (Public Works Administration), NRA (National Recovery Administration), TVA (Tennessee Valley Authority), WPA (Works Progress Administration), and hundreds more.

Two of his most important programs, however, portended ill tides for black Americans. Food and industry topped the list. The Agricultural Adjustment Administration, under Henry Wallace, focused on the nation's food, breadbasket and sustenance. The National Recovery Administration, under General Hugh Johnson concentrated on industry. The Agricultural Adjustment Administration, the AAA, was concerned with all things involving agriculture. This was important to black folks because, according to the 1930 census, a full forty percent of black wage earners were engaged in some form of agricultural work, as tenant farmers, sharecroppers, or small family farmers. The AAA did not deal with the problem of uneven distribution of income within agriculture. Had it done so, it would have better protected the rights of not only blacks but whites. One example of the failure of the AAA's implementation was the parity payments or subsidies to farmers for what they did not produce. The cotton belt received most of this money. Since there was a glutted market in agriculture, the AAA attempted to direct farmers on what not to produce and to subsidize them for their loss in production. This was better than a new deal, it was a great deal if you owned a huge farm operation to take advantage of it. Cotton was severely hurting in the late 1920s and early 1930s. The AAA approached large cotton producers with an offer to subside their not growing cotton on a percentage of their land. Since most blacks were tenant farmers or sharecroppers working the cotton industry, the impact of any cutback was especially hard on them. The AAA initiated what it called the "one-eight formula," where one-eighth of the money paid to the large cotton producer was to go for replacement wages to those workers who lost employment or were otherwise displaced as a result of the cutback in production. In actuality, none of that money reached those black tenant farmers and sharecroppers who were displaced. White tenant farmers and sharecroppers suffered a somewhat similar fate. The cotton land owners simply kept the money. Southern Democratic congressmen supported this kind of discrimination and misuse of funds, especially when the workers being displaced were black. They reasoned that blacks did not deserve the funds because black labor was "inefficient" and that to give any part of that money to them was a miscarriage of justice. This mindset dominated Congress owing to the seniority system, especially when it came to key committees. Since old-time southern Democrats were in abundance in Congress, and thus on key committees, they exerted disproportionate influence on behalf of discrimination and to the benefit of the land owners. The AAA policy actually brought greater instability to the cotton industry, although it helped the big cotton producers financially. The farm owners cut further back on cotton and other crops to receive more subsidies for not producing. The farm owner, therefore, needed less hired labor, and cut greater numbers of his workers, sharecroppers, tenant farmers, pickers, harvesters, and so forth. The 1940 census figures revealed that there were 192,000 fewer black, and 150,000 fewer white tenant farmers and sharecroppers than there had been in the 1930s. Both black and white farm laborers fell victim to well-intentioned New Deal policy in agriculture.

Under the NRA there were also problems along racial lines. Hugh Johnson, who directed the NRA, conceived of an economic stability program that, in the end, hurt as many laborers as it helped and stifled small businesses and start-up companies. Johnson's program to stabilize industry embraced big corporations, discouraging competition in industry as being counter productive to growth and stability, and attempted to gain the compliance of the labor force by promise from the corporations not to dismiss workers and to pay them a standardized wage. The policy encouraged monopolies and discrimination against blacks. White owners feared that the NRA policy codes might be misinterpreted as inclusive of all workers, including blacks. White southern businessmen traveled to Washington to attend the NRA policy hearings and to make their position clear that blacks were not entitled to wages equal to whites. Their goal was to maintain a cheap black labor force. They contended that blacks, whether sharecroppers, tenant farmers, or working in industries in the South or the North, were a less efficient form of labor, that they lived more cheaply than did whites, and therefore should not receive equal pay. J. F. Ames of Montgomery, Alabama, a business man and self proclaimed sociologist, prepared a study titled the "Subnormal Negro and the Subnormal Code," that was cited at the hearings.

Ames maintained that black labor was thirty percent less efficient than white. Southern congressmen joined in support. Roy Wilkins of the NAACP spoke out against the hearings and the misinformation, and exposed the intent behind the presentations. "The truth of the matter," Wilkins explained, "is that the Southerners want a lower wage scale because they do not wish Negroes to have wages equal to whites." Meanwhile the WPA (Works Progress Administration) helped local cotton producers get pickers at exploitative wages by closing down Negro WPA projects during the cotton picking season. The NRA let stand the various discriminatory policies. It did pass some codes for the "fair" payment of blacks and whites but manufacturers readily found loopholes in these codes. One clause in the codes provided that minimum wage scales for some classes of labor, namely blacks, should be based on wages received as of a certain date in the past. This was, as William Pickens the field secretary of the NAACP characterized it, "the grandfather clause of the NRA." Some blacks began to call the NRA the "National Run Around" and the "Negro Removal Act" since the policies of the agency resulted in large numbers of them being put out of work. Labor advocates did view as very positive the passage of Section 7A of the National Industrial Recovery Act, better known as the Wagner Act, which protected the *closed shop*. The protection of the *closed shop*, however, was decidedly anti African Americans in that the right of workers to organize was to be honored and that where it was a unionized industry only the workers who were members of the union would have the right to employment. Industries agreeing to employ only union workers was a double-edged racist barrier for black folk because most unions barred them from membership.[3]

There were some positive signs for blacks in the New Deal. Harold Ickes was a progressive and his PWA was more fair than any other New Deal agency. One reason was Ickes's second in command, Robert Weaver, the black Harvard graduate and active member of the NAACP, who constantly pushed within the administration for practices and policies beneficial to African Americans. The WPA funding of projects that aided African-American culture and the arts was extremely positive as well. Regrettably, African Americans were not organized well enough to exert more influence on New Deal agencies and policies. The rift in the NAACP in 1934 hurt any further attempt at mass organization to pressure the administration in the interest of blacks. Where positive pressure was exerted it came from within, from the wise maneuvering and coalition building of the one African American best positioned to make a difference: Mary McLeod Bethune.

WORKING FROM WITHIN

Mary McLeod Bethune, the grand matriarch of black America, was a savvy and ceaseless warrior for the advancement of her race. She worked tirelessly within the system to transform it and to make a difference. The fighting spirit was instilled within her as a child. Her mother, Patsy McLeod, born into slavery and later emancipated, was a person of exceptional understanding as was Mary's father, Sam. Both parents wanted the best for their seventeen children and their especially gifted child Mary. Patsy taught her daughter many lessons that stayed with her for her entire life. She procured an education for her daughter and pushed young Mary to always stand tall and to never run from a fight. Mary took these lessons to heart and made a personal commitment to always defend herself with reasoning. Born in South Carolina in 1875, it was in Florida that she made her permanent mark as an extraordinary educator with the founding of the Daytona School for Negro Girls in 1904, which grew to become Bethune-Cookman College. The black community gave generously of what little it had to get the school started. Serious funds to make it into a real institution and to keep it going came from northern whites. In soliciting funds for the school from wealthy northerners winter vacationing in Daytona Beach, Mary McLeod Bethune learned the art of effective maneuvering and causal solicitation, becoming adept at making the case to influential white men and women. She further honed her skills in working with whites when given introduction to the membership of the Palmetto Club for ladies. Through dint of will, glowing personality and charm, and earnestness of purpose, she won over a number of these well-to-do northern white women and the favor of their governance and financial support. Bethune never asked for money straight away. She wisely solicited the intellectual involvement of the individual first usually asking him or her to serve on the board of trustees of the school. Later on, came the plea for funds but by then the individual was already a part of the enterprise and typically gave willingly. There were always the pitfalls and slights of the hostile South and the every-present demon of racism. Bethune navigated these treacherous white waters with the aptitude and ability of an experienced ship's captain. She knocked on doors, distributed leaflets, gave Sunday musical recitals with the young students, and worked day and night to make the school a success. Through it all she always maintained the dignity of a proud and determined black woman who refused to enter through back doors or allow whites to address her by her first name, as was the customary insult to blacks in the South, rather than to call them Mrs. or Mister as blacks were required to address all whites no matter what their status or age.

Her dedication to the education of African-American youth was rooted in an all-consuming commitment to the uplift of the black race. Bethune became actively involved and helped to shape organizations that benefited African Americans, especially black women. She was an early mover and shaker in the National Association of Colored Women, founded by Mary Jane Patterson, one of the first black women in America to obtain a college degree. Mary Church Terrell shaped the NACW into national prominence and Bethune presided as its president for four years. Bethune was also a crusader for the American Red Cross and eventual director of its Florida division with headquarters in West Palm Beach; president of the Florida State Federation of Colored Women's Clubs; champion of school desegregation and improved health care for black children; a leading architect within the National Association of Colored Women to developing working relationship around common social concerns with white women, and later vice chair of the Women's Section of the Commission on Interracial Cooperation which grew out of the initiative. When Eleanor Roosevelt hosted a national luncheon at her home in New York in 1927 to bring together leaders of the women's movement, Bethune was the lone black woman in attendance. Bethune founded the National Council of Negro Women in 1935 with the mission to harness the activism of black women at the community and state levels and to integrate them into the political and federal governmental apparatus to make sure that the issues crucial to the survival of the black family such as jobs, education, health and black youth development were voiced in the national agenda.

Bethune's reputation as an educator and her network of donor contacts for her school, that she cultivated over the years, included James Gamble of the Proctor and Gamble Corporation and Thomas White of the White Steamer and Sewing Machine Company. Her community work eventually came to the attention of the White House. She served with distinction on the National Child Welfare Commission under the administrations of Presidents Calvin Coolidge and Herbert Hoover. In 1936 President Franklin D. Roosevelt approached her to head the Division of Negro Affairs within the National Youth Administration (NYA). Bethune quickly distinguished herself and became his principle adviser on matters affecting the black community, and the leading voice in the so-called "black cabinet," and the one African American in the United States with immediate access to the President. On more than one occasion she brought President Roosevelt near to tears as she described the hardships blacks were suffering during the depression. She was often personally responsible for winning program funding that went to black communities and other underrepresented minority groups, who might otherwise have been forgotten. Bethune and Robert Weaver orchestrated the inclusion of provisions for Negroes within such New Deal programs as the Public Works Administration, Works Progress Administration, and Civilian Conservation Corp. Their efforts directly benefited millions of black Americans. She also enjoyed the respect and friendship of First Lady Eleanor Roosevelt, whom she likewise offered advice and perspective on a myriad of issues ranging from expanded opportunities for African American women and men to child welfare and public health. Bethune never missed any opportunity to make contacts and to use those linkages to promote the goals of social justice and the improvement of the conditions of the race. She was eloquent and articulate in making the cases that needed to be made, and did so with optimism, missionary zeal, gentle and persistent persuasion, well reasoned and thoughtful analysis and facts, and a feisty determination. She spoke with the unquestioned moral authority of a woman of faith and humble origins whose record of accomplishments in the name of service to her race and the public were second to none. Moreover, she knew how to build coalitions and private and public trust. She brilliantly maneuvered through the corridors of power at the White House, nudging and cajoling, pleading and pressuring. Bethune led the initiative among her fellow blacks in leadership positions in federal government to band together and work in a coordinated fashion. Meeting and consulting with fellow African Americans Robert Weaver of the WPA, Federal Judge William H. Hastie, Frank Horne of the Federal Housing Authority, Assistant Attorney General Charles Houston, and confidants Venice T. Spraggs, Jeanetta Brown, and Sue Bailey Thurman of the National Council of Negro Women, a major conference was called to address the problems facing the black community and the issue of civil liberties. The Civil Liberties Conference, as it was called, convened for three days in January of 1937. The end result was the well crafted *Blue Book* that, in itself, was a reflection of Bethune's race consciousness and the aim of the conference which was, as she admonished her colleagues, predicated on their ability to "stand together as Negroes facing the problems of Negroes" and to get correct information about African Americans to those in positions of authority. In short, the idea behind the *Blue Book* was to present the case of black America from a black-American perspective. Following the conference, Bethune's colleagues charged her with the responsibility of hand delivering the document to President Roosevelt. FDR was thoroughly impressed with the results of the conference and authorized Bethune to distribute the *Blue Book* to the entire cabinet, to Congress and to key federal agencies. For the first time, the problems of African Americans, and suggested remedies, were articulated by African Americans to the highest echelons of government. Moreover, under Bethune's stewardship the tiny but influential group of blacks in federal level positions banded together on a regular basis and fought for greater access for others of the race. Superbly qualified African Americans were brought to the attention of key New Deal administrators and much time and energy given to politicking for their appointment. During her eight years as head of the Minority Affairs Division, Bethune had a hand in virtually every major black appointment in the federal government. She saw it as an obligation to her people to do all she could to get others on board and to help open as many doors for them as possible. When members of the African-American press brought to her attention that the black press was not represented at presidential press conferences because only dailies were allowed and the black papers were weeklies, she made it a personal crusade to get them in and was directly responsible for the change in rules and inclusion of minority news organizations at presidential press conferences. Her dedication to the advancement of African Americans was at the heart of her life-long commitment to the National Council of Negro Women. She was a positive role model who impacted in innumerable ways on the lives of African-American women and the entire black race.

Quintessential race woman was perhaps the best description of Mary McLeod Bethune. Her strength of character and purpose were drawn upon repeatedly as she waged a relentless crusade for the betterment of her people. Beyond the politics, the work load, the problem solving, and the many setbacks in the course to victory, there were the daily hassles and insults all too common to black folk in America. Bethune suffered a regular barrage of micro aggressions from the time she woke early in the morning until she went to bed late at night. White cab drivers refused her, restaurants denied her, train conductors insulted her, she was snubbed at teas, meetings, speaking engagements. At countless functions she was asked to identify herself, mistaken for a servant or maid or cook, she was, after all, black and certainly could not be the head of a federal agency and an adviser to the President of the United States. She never turned the other cheek or compromised her principles. She confronted her antagonists with reasoning, words to educate them, and sometimes with a brief lesson on the historical contributions of blacks to America and the world.

Bethune often credited ignorance for racial animosity. She beseeched African Americans to arm themselves with knowledge. She embraced the importance of history in the empowerment of a people and for several years served as president of the Association for the Study of Negro Life and History. She wrote weekly columns for the *Pittsburgh Courier* and the *Chicago Defender* to reach the general public. In these columns she shared with black communities her philosophy of life and practical thoughts and strategies for the advancement of the race. Knowing your background, Bethune liked to say, was the first step in deciding where you were going and the road you must travel to get there. "Knowledge is power," was undoubtedly her most often used phrase as she urged blacks to support their local educational institutions and to be determined warriors on behalf of the education of their children. Bethune received countless awards, including the Spingarn Medal, the Jefferson Award, the Medal of Honor and Merit of Haiti, and the Star of Africa, and other major recognition for public service on both a national and international level. Shortly before the end of her life in 1955, Mary McLeod Bethune placed into her diary words of wisdom that she hoped would serve as a legacy. She bequeathed, as her last will and testament, to all her love, hope, thirst for education, faith, racial dignity, desire to live harmoniously, and a call to responsibility in service to the youth and to one another. "Yesterday, our ancestors endured the degradation of slavery, yet they retained their dignity. Today, we direct our economic and political strength toward winning a more abundant and secure life. Tomorrow, a new Negro, unhindered by race taboos and shackles, will benefit from this striving and struggling," Bethune prayed. "The problem of color is world wide, on every continent. I appeal to all to recognize their common problems, and unite to solve them," she added. "I want to see my people conduct themselves in all relationships, fully conscious of their responsibilities and deeply aware of their heritage."[4]

GOD INCORPORATED

For black folk, whether in the North, or South, or West, or in rural or urban areas, or in agricultural or industrial work, the Great Depression hit them hard as it did all Americans. For African Americans in the urban North, the once glorious *promised land* turned into a living nightmare. Blacks, however, were innovative. They looked deep within themselves to be creative, to somehow survive the years of depression. Blacks have always known hard times in

America. Social activist and comedian Dick Gregory likes to quip that "black folk didn't notice the Great Depression because we have always been in a depression." Gregory was, of course, using comedic license. Yes, blacks knew tough conditions and how to make due with little. Slavery and poverty were tough taskmasters. Clifford Burke, an African-American eyewitness to the depression years of the 1930s, recalled: "The Negro was born in depression... We had one big advantage. Our wives, they could go to the store and get a bag of beans or a sack of flour and a piece of fat meat, and they could cook this. And we could eat it...Now you take the white fella, he couldn't do this. His wife would tell him: Look, if you can't do any better than this, I'm gonna leave you. I seen it happen. He couldn't stand bringing home the beans instead of steak and capon."

More than food and money, however, were needed to sustain life and African Americans, like many other Americans, sought spiritual comfort and reassurance. Some voices were more honest than others. Some had an agenda difficult to understand, while others were simply part of a growing list of panacea peddlers who offered hope to a desperate people in a desperate time. A case in point was Father Divine. He and his movement personified the trying times and psychological needs. People were most vulnerable when in a desperate situation. Historian John Henrik Clarke said of Father Divine that he "gave hope to the hopeless." That was precisely what Father Divine did. In his rhetoric, punctuated with food, he weaved together a philosophy of religion that played well in depression torn Harlem and to suffering black people in Philadelphia, New York, Connecticut's New Britain, and other urban centers.[5]

Father Divine was a real character. Black America had its share of heretics and charlatans. Divine stood alone in terms of the audacity of some of his utterances and his own persona. He often spoke a very confused rhetoric. He told those who listened that in order "to understand me you must first have to be together with me, to harmonize with me, like the oceans and seas and earth itself. There must be a balance and relationship and you must within that context, be one with me. You have to harmonize with me in opposition to your sense of feeling, in opposition to your ideas and your opinions, especially when they are not with me." There were also the practical aspects of Divine and his movement that combined with the rhetorical and spiritual attracted followers in the thousands. Divine's followers worshipped him to such a level that whenever he took a break from his office and strolled along the corridors they jumped up and down repeatedly, applauding and displaying wild adulation. He loved to be chauffeured about town in his sparkling blue Cadillac, and later a Rolls Royce, and when the car stopped crowds gathered in recognition and in awe of Divine. All of this for a man who was barely five feet tall, bald headed, portly and bowlegged. He did not fit the physical casting call for a mighty leader. He was not handsome by any definition, but he was powerful. In demonstrating that belief he later declared himself to be God. His ability to turn a phrase and to play the heart strings of African Americans was virtually without equal. Divine turned insults into positives. When asked why he, Divine (a.k.a. God), came to us in such a humble package, he retorted that appearing among the masses as one of the least of them allowed him to move freely among them and by example, not by any physical features, lead the Negro race to salvation.

Who was this Father Divine, this self-anointed miracle worker? Where did he come from? What were his origins? When asked where he was from and when was he born, Divine replied: "I was combusted one day in 1900 on the corner of Seventh Avenue and 134th Street in Harlem." In other words, like an episode from the television series *Star Trek*, if you had been standing on that corner at that time, you could have witnessed Divine's instant materialization out of nowhere. The truth was that George Baker (a.k.a. Father Divine) was born to sharecropping parents in, as best evidence indicated, about 1880 on a rice plantation in the Savannah River area of Georgia. At one time he was married and had four children, whom he abandoned. He worked in Maryland for a while cutting grass and clipping hedges for whites. Like the existence of African Americans everywhere, Baker lived in two worlds. One world was the daily drudgery to earn a living. The other was the weekend. For him, the temporal salvation of church services on Sunday was his favorite outlet. In the black church he was transformed from a humble yard man to a man of God. In church he took center stage. He was able to preach, show his intellect, and rise to prominence via his ability to sway others. Baker started off speaking on Sundays and teaching Sunday school and later becoming an assistant pastor. In the local colored Baptist church he took up with Samuel Morris, an evangelist, and traveled the circuit with him. Morris went from pulpit to pulpit as a visiting preacher but one Sunday got carried away and wound up being carried off by parishioners. That Sunday he professed to a congregation that he was not only a man of God, but that he was the Almighty Himself. Morris stepped way over the line when he claimed to be God. The church went into an uproar. Four stout black male parishioners came forward and physically removed him from the pulpit. Morris's feet only lightly touched the floor as the men escorted him down the aisle, depositing him outside the building to the enthusiastic applause of the congregation. George Baker watched in amazement and horror. If he learned anything from the experience it was to take his time to carefully cultivate the flock before crossing the line between spiritual belief and the claim of personal divinity.

Baker continued preaching at various places on Sundays and earned a living mowing lawns, driving a junk wagon, and doing other odd jobs during the rest of the week. His ability as a preacher gained him followers and a rise to prominence. By 1914 his name was being circulated throughout parts of Georgia and the Carolinas. He routinely mesmerized the local Negro church goers. Speaking to folks on street corners and from the occasional pulpit, Baker said in several of his sermons that God was reborn in him. He was successful in bringing in people from right off the streets and luring members of other churches. He was so successful in Valdosta, Georgia, that local ministers felt threatened and filed nuisance complaint charges against him contending that he was insane. The writ listed him as John Doe, alias God. There was, however, very little that could be done since he was not a raving lunatic who posed a physical threat to anyone. The complaint did not dampen his reputation nor his following. High on his list of devotees were women, primarily black women domestics who, for whatever variety of reasons, were attracted to his words and to the man. His oratory ability and growing prominence made him attractive despite his physical limitations. With his name recognition intact and an ever increasing band of followers, George Baker, also known as the Messenger, God, and increasingly as Father Divine, took his evangelism to New York State. In the Divine philosophy black folk disciplined themselves to reject attachments to members of their families and to friends, all of whom were to be left behind as family ties were secondary to their ties to Father Divine and the work of the organization. Personal possessions were permitted only at the discretion of Father Divine, to whom all material wealth and goods were entrusted. Divine's philosophy and religion took contemporary resonance in the cultism of Jim Jones and his followers whose movement ended in tragedy in Guyana, and David Korish and his cult, which came to a violent end in Texas. Father Divine professed that sex was an emotional baggage that hurt the spirit of work and oneness. Celibacy was mandated and he himself took a wife, a Miss Penny. Divine vowed, however, that he and his spouse would never engage in sexual intercourse.

As the 1930s approached, Father Divine's reputation continued to flourish. The Divine movement based itself in the town of Sayville in New York State. The "heaven," as he called the mission location, promoted scripture, Divine's own unique words of wisdom, and good food. Food proved to be a major component in the building of the Divine movement, as enormous quantities were always made available. All visitors were invited to eat until they could eat no more. A typical menu included fricasseed chicken, bacon, ham hocks, grits, spinach, cole slaw, fried chicken, beef, corn, mashed potatoes, beans, cheese, cake, cookies, pie, and an assortment of fruit drinks, tea and coffee. Following the grand meal was the inevitable sermon of Father Divine and a discussion of the movement's goal of fellowship and unity of purpose. People from all over the state began coming to hear him speak, and to eat. Each Sunday, Divine held worship at his house in Sayville. Upwards of a hundred or more people jammed into the residence. Many did whatever was necessary to get there to hear Father Divine. They came by bus, car, motorcycle, and wagon, into the predominantly white community, parking on people's lawns. The stories multiplied. It was said that Father Divine served the entire multitude from a single pot of coffee. Food, it was said, flowed like a never-ending stream from the kitchen. No one left a Divine meeting hungry for food and scripture.

Central to the Divine philosophy was his urging of African Americans to move beyond race, to stop thinking of themselves as Negroes and coloreds and begin to think of themselves as people whose color was insignificant. In a very real sense, Father Divine was one of the early advocates of a color-blind American society. He reasoned that to think in terms of color was a legacy of bondage and that one should see him or herself simply as a human being and act accordingly. Father Divine professed that black folk possessed the inner strength and ability to accomplish anything they desired. Color, he thought, was simply a tool of slavery that limited minds and potential. When he sighted his heroes whom he believed dictated the right course for African Americans, he placed at the top of that list Booker T. Washington. Father divine particularly favored Washington's professed philosophy of self-help which he likened as color-blind in terms of what it could do for any individual. Divine often quipped that the only thing holding you back from making your mark was your own denial of your abilities to accomplish. Divine's philosophy was to do for yourself, work hard, and rise up by your own bootstraps. His was, in a sense, a reaffirmation of the basic American ideology of self-help, pioneering spirit, Protestant work ethic, and rugged individualism couched in the rhetoric of the black church and assertions of ultimate divinity.

By 1931, Sayville was the center of a massive movement of African Americans associated with Father Divine. Sayville's local citizens, however, had grown tired of Divine's popularity. They wanted to rid their town of Father Divine and all the black visitors he attracted. The town leadership began a campaign of harassment directed at Divine followers and Father Divine himself. The town residents protested that Divine was a disruptive element in the community, that he illegally used his home as a business, and that he was a charlatan, cleverly duping people out of their hard-earned dollars. At the end of every one of his spiritual meetings there were efforts to collect money by passing a hat or asking individuals to contribute what they could on their way out of the door. Charges of public nuisance were filed against Father Divine and a jury trial ensued. Divine was found guilty and sentenced to one year in jail and a fine of five hundred dollars. His followers were angry and dismayed but he consoled them. He told them not to worry because he and the movement were more powerful than any jail cell. Father Divine reminded his devotees of the biblical story of the pharaoh's attempt to halt the children of Israel.

Timing was an important component of the Divine movement and Father knew how to play it for all it was worth. Divine called his trial a travesty and warned that those involved would eventually be punished. Not many people took his predilections seriously. A week after Judge Smith sentenced Father Divine, the judge fell victim to a massive heart attack and died. One of the jurors died only a few weeks after they had delivered their guilty verdict. One of Divine's followers could not wait to inform him of the judge's and the juror's demise. Divine acted absolutely stoic at the news. In fact, he informed his follower that those who passed sentence against him sealed their own fate. Playing it cool and coy, Father gave the distinct impression that he had reached out from his jail cell and struck down those who blasphemed him. The combination of timing and the notion of retribution resonated well in Divine's hands. In total he spent slightly over thirty days in jail when the Appellate Court of New York reversed Judge Smith's decision, concluding that the judge had been prejudicial. Father used this to his advantage, telling his followers that he grew tired of jail, and once he decided that the legal system and the blasphemers learned their lessons, he reached out from his cell and told the Appellate Court that it was time to release him, and they obeyed his command. Followers were now more convinced than ever that Father Divine was God and that he proved it when he freed himself from the clutches of the infidels' judicial system. Stories sprouted up everywhere about Divine's powers of retribution. Miss Lovely Heart (Father Divine enjoyed renaming his devotees such sobriquets as Lovely Heart, Beautiful Angel, Divine

Spirit, One Soul, Believable Best, etc., as he felt befitting) testified that she personally witnessed Father Divine make a nay-sayer vanish into thin air. More and more of his followers openly proclaimed that he was God, and warned that he would strike down anyone who spoke against him. One follower related how her neighbor cursed Father Divine and then, only a day later, suffered a stroke and died. Another devotee told of her friend who spoke poorly of Father Divine and was now dying painfully of a dreaded disease. Miss Beautiful Love recounted the story of a truck driver who cursed Father and only one week later drove his truck off a cliff and was killed instantly. The stories proliferated and Divine used them to perfection. He told a gathered throng of worshippers that at times he must reach out and strike down the infidels and "thus retribution rolls on, striking here and there. Things just don't happen; they happen just."[6]

By 1933, Father Divine's reputation was widespread and powerful enough to bring together audiences that numbered in the thousands. He delivered a lecture that year in New York's Rockland Palace at 155 Street and Eighth Avenue and close to eight thousand people attended the standing-room-only event. This was in the heart of the Great Depression and black folk needed to hear words that they thought might contain salvation. At the Rockland meeting, Father Divine was literally begged to come home to Harlem, the center of the Negro Mecca, to afford him the largest pulpit from which to spread his message. Later that year Divine opened his Harlem Heaven. With heavens in Philadelphia, Georgia, upstate New York, parts of Connecticut, and now Harlem, the Divine movement was big time and Harlem its center of business operations.

Harlem was in bad shape, with increasing numbers of black sharecroppers coming from the South, the worsening impact of the Great Depression, overcrowding, joblessness, and the poor health conditions of the community. Harlem was afflicted with all of the ills of the time: robbery, prostitution, and a steep rise in juvenile delinquency. In 1933, fifty percent of Harlem's black families applied for unemployment relief. Recorded cases of syphilis were seven times higher for blacks in Harlem than for whites. Medical care was severely circumscribed with only Harlem Hospital to take care of the medical needs of more than three hundred thousand African Americans. No matter how good it was, such a load asked the impossible of any single hospital. Harlemites, in these hard times, sought panaceas where they could find them, not only in real medicine but in the pseudo-medicine of psychic healers, juju spiritualists and others, and Father Divine. Harlem was full of the panacea peddlers. One of the most successful of these spiritualists during the 1930s was Madame Fu Fu Tan. She was something to behold; part African American, part Asian. Hers was an exotic look and she knew how to emphasize her exoticism, wearing flimsy and varied-colored dresses and veils, throwing bones, speaking in tongues, and making claims of receiving messages from the dead and from forces in the future. Fu Fu Tan was a competitor to Father Divine, but her major nemesis was the spiritualist down the street, Sofi Abdul Hammid, whose real name was Eugene Brown. Hammid was an interesting figure in Harlem. Jewish merchants disliked him intensely. He was a former Garveyite and advocate of black nationalism and separatism, urging that whites be thrown out of Harlem and that it become a self-sustained, all-black community, with no whites allowed to own businesses within its geographical boundaries. He was fiery and did have a substantial following of hundreds. The adversarial relationship between Fu Fu Tan and Hammid came to an end, however, when they married one another. They now combined their efforts and started their Buddhist Universal Holy Temple of Tranquility, urging African Americans to seek the healing powers they offered.

None of these spiritualists, including Father Divine, was as flashy and flamboyant as Daddy Grace, also known as Sweet Daddy. Before Father Divine arrived in Harlem, the community, in a spiritualist sense, belonged to Daddy Grace. He was a man of fine taste and an immaculate dresser who sported powder-blue suits and diamond pinkie rings. He swore to have made the blind see and the lame walk and to have driven evil out of the spirit. Women loved and flocked to Sweet Daddy, and he harvested those relationships. Every fashion of church, it seemed, from the respected Abyssinian Baptist Church of Adam Clayton Powell, Senior and Junior, to the storefront holly rollers, flourished in Harlem during the depression years. This was a period of need and desperation. Folks sought comfort within their faith.

Many in Harlem turned to Father Divine. He came full force into the black Mecca in 1933, renting a building on West 115th Street and vowing dedication to providing salvation to all Harlemites. The combination of food and sermons won him a wide following. Several days throughout the week, particularly on Wednesdays and Sundays, Harlemites formed long lines to partake of the heaven's fabulous banquets. A typical menu consisted of between fifteen and twenty items such as roast duck, fried sausage, lamb, liver, barbecued ribs, mashed potatoes, brussel sprouts, string beans, asparagus, chicken, beef, fruit salad, assorted cakes and ice creams. All of this was provided for the modest sum of ten or fifteen cents. If unable to pay, you ate for free. For thousands of black Harlemites, Father Divine was seen as an activist who helped feed the community. Critics of Father Divine questioned the source of the funds that provided the food. This was an understandable concern. One had to look no further than the followers of Father Divine to identify the source of the funds. One of the criteria for membership was to turn over all worldly possessions to the "peace mission." The "peace mission," of course, was Father Divine. Followers worked in communal fashion, pooling their resources. The funds for the banquets came from the collective and grew as the membership increased.

Among the people of Harlem, Father Divine and his organization were commonly referred to as "God Incorporated." One might question why African Americans did not follow his business example into the second half of the twentieth century. He was a black entrepreneur whose organization established stores, restaurants, boarding houses, all of which generated income. His organization leased several buildings and his followers lived there paying all the rents. Profit was made greater in that they lived military style in make-shift dormitories thus efficiently utilizing space and people. The housing was affordable. The restaurants were profitable, providing the best priced meals in Harlem. Every Divine business venture offered goods and services at the most affordable price. In total, Father Divine ran at least two dozen restaurants in Harlem where meals ran the gamut from the most simple to the more elegant. Followers worked the peace mission's restaurants, cleaners, grocery stores, vegetable and fruit wagons, fresh fish outlets, and coal business. The Divine Coal Company operated a fleet of trucks that took delivery of the coal in Pennsylvania and transported it to Harlem where it was sold at the lowest competitive rate of seventy-five cents to a dollar per ton. The coal from Father kept you just as warm, followers liked to say, and at a better price. White New Yorkers as well bought coal, fruit and vegetables from Father Divine. The Divine peace mission and heavens continued to expand, buying real-estate in Bridgeport, Connecticut; Jersey City and Newark, New Jersey; and Baltimore, Maryland. In a practical sense, Father Divine was a Communist and his communal actions were building an empire even in the worst of times. The success of his organization attracted new devotees and the growth in membership meant increase in profits. Divine estimated his organizational membership to be over one hundred thousand, with many more thousands who were disciples of his teaching. Reliable estimates put the membership figure at approximately ten thousand. His influence was far and wide but likely not in the range of three million as Father contended. The combination of the economic success and the good words and examples of his followers continued to enhance his notoriety. Add to this the occasional story of miraculous healing and divine retribution and Father was a force to be taken seriously, especially in the urban northeast.

By the mid 1930s Sofi Hammid, along with other spiritualists, declared open war on Father Divine. Hammid and his wife Fu Fu Tan were envious of Divine's success, notoriety, and swelling membership. Hammid vowed that he would drive the charlatan Divine out of New York. Hammid's followers warned that he should be careful because of Father's ability to reach out with unexplained power to destroy his enemies. Hammid branded these warnings as foolish and superstitious, which were strange comments coming from a spiritualist. As fate would have it, Hammid starting taking flying lessons and acquired an airplane. His new thrill of flying was cut short when, on one summer day in July of 1938, he crashed and was killed. In death Hammid became another important testimonial to Father Divine's powers of retribution on which he effectively capitalized. "I had nothing to do with his death," Father said to a massive banquet gathering. "I made no effort, but when he blasphemed against me, he sentenced himself."

Even the case of Daddy Grace played to Divine's advantage in the end. Daddy Grace detested Father Divine as a competitor. Grace was a powerful force in Harlem and throughout America. He was an extremely popular, articulate speaker, a charmer who, through his Houses of Prayer along the east coast and parts of the South, was overall the most popular black evangelical figure of his day. He loved to travel south to North Carolina and to Georgia where he had thousands of followers. Divine, however, was now overshadowing him as well. Daddy Grace enjoyed talking about his ability to cure the lame, make the blind see, and to expel afflictions from the human body and soul. Grace at least did not declare himself to be God. Unlike Father Divine, he made it clear on several occasions that he had no claim to be the Supreme Divinity. It was Daddy Grace, moreover, who gave Divine one of his most humiliating defeats. The building on West 115th Street that housed Divine's headquarters and followers was leased, as were most of the properties they used. Daddy Grace in a shrewd move to undercut the popularity and reputation of Divine bought the headquarters building and immediately evicted Father Divine and his followers. Daddy Grace boasted about the accomplishment to his congregation and they rolled with laughter and spread the word. As Sweet Daddy jokingly lamented, "I make no claims to being God. Only Father Divine declares himself to be God. But, I will tell you that I am the man who evicted God and threw him out into the streets. So if he is God, then who am I?" His humiliation of Divine was complete. Yet timing and circumstances gave the final laugh to Father Divine. Daddy Grace was having tax problems and the Internal Revenue Service moved in with full force charging him with income tax evasion. To avoid a jail sentence, Daddy fled the United States and sought sanctuary in Cuba where he was never heard from again.

There were problems within the ranks of the Divine believers. Miss Faithful Mary, in conjunction with Mrs. Veronica Brown, two disgruntled former Divine "Angels," and Mrs. Brown's husband, Thomas Brown, took legal action against Father Divine in 1940. Injunctions were levied against his holdings owing to ongoing charges of fraud from these and several disgruntled former followers. The Browns alleged that he had taken their personal insurance policies, cashed them in and kept the money. In the end these charges fell through. Father Divine seemed blessed in his ability to avoid ultimate prosecution. Most of his followers were loyal and toed the line. They were true believers and abided by his rules and regulations. They refrained from sex. Men and women were segregated in the heavens, and his closest group of believers, his Angels, eagerly obeyed his every wish and command. Father Divine gave another order to his followers: they were forbidden to become ill. Sickness, he declared, was an imbalance resulting from disharmony with God, Father Divine. If faith was strong, Father commanded, sickness abated. Heaven members tried to hide any illness. If you became ill, you prayed harder to mend the flaw in your faith. Physicians were not consulted. All medical problems were simply a problem of faith and could be solved by prayer. On the occasions when followers died, Father Divine had the bodies removed late at night to limit other cult members' awareness of the deaths. When the New York City Coroner's Office asked him to take possession of the bodies of followers who died in hospitals, he refused. Divine took the position that they could not be true believers of his if they became ill and died. The case of Miss Lovely Best was instructive. She came down with pneumonia and was near death in the heaven. Father Divine came to her bedside and held her hand, commanding her to recover. She did and from that point on bore witness to Father's power over illness and death. She credited Divine with giving her a second life.

Successes emboldened Father Divine beyond redemption. In 1946, he married for the second time, on this occasion to Miss Sweet Angel, a white woman follower. Divine proclaimed that this was not contradictory since color was artificial and irrelevant in his organization which went beyond race and ethnic divides. His more than twenty private secretaries were all women, and very close to him. There were men Angels as well, and a few of his followers were white. In the inner circle of women Angels were Divine's most cherished believers. He nicknamed them "The Sweets." The Sweets were consistent voices of the greatness and omnipotence of Divine. To demonstrate their loyalty to Father Divine they drew up Ten Commandments and presented these to other followers with Divine's personal approval. The Sweets' Ten Commandments were a tribute to him and his teachings and contributions. The Commandments proclaimed the followers commitment to forever obey, cherish, respect and praise Father Divine above all others; keep guile from their lips and to have but one purpose in life: to serve Father; to rejoice at the blessings he bestowed; to cherish virginity; to consecrate their hearts, minds, and souls to the cause; to love God, even if all others oppose him; to never condemn or find fault with anything Father Divine says or does; and finally they pledged to recognize at all times the power and benevolence of their Lord and Savior, Father Divine. In recognition of this outpouring, Divine mandated an Eleventh Commandment for his Sweets. For their great loyalty and devotion and praise of him, their God, Father Divine bestowed upon the Sweets ever-lasting life and announced that they were now immortal like him and were to live forever.[7]

On September 7, 1965, God died. This was an apparent contradiction to his proclamation and claim of ultimate divinity. Without Father Divine to head it, many quietly left the movement. A few of his die-hard Angels stayed together, setting a place for Father Divine at each supper and reported that he was still with them and had not died but transcended his earthly body and moved to a higher level of existence and consciousness and that those who were pure of heart could see him and continue to feel and to sense his presence. No matter what the die-hard believers professed, the demise of the Father Divine movement was inevitable. Without his charismatic leadership, the Divine mission was no more. Harlem, and black America, lost a fascinating voice. He filled a void in the depression era. Although his movement continued throughout the 1940s, the coming of World War II and the new economic prosperity accompanying it, made it possible for Harlemites, like the rest of black America, to begin a new chapter in the struggle to transform the American landscape and their situation in it.

VIII
BATTLING ON
EVERY FRONT

THE MILITARY FRONT

African Americans have fought in all of America's wars. They put their lives on the front line and they have paid dearly time and again. Their reasoning was quite simple: they wanted to prove themselves to be Americans. They thought that participating in the wars, doing their part as American citizens fighting for freedom "over there," that they would, at some point, receive freedom over here. The American Revolutionary War never gained for blacks what they had hoped. The Civil War at least brought the formal institution of slavery to an end. That spirit and hope was alive in the 1890s and was still felt when the call for volunteers came at the start of the Spanish-American War in 1898. Blacks lined up and enlisted in great numbers and were to play a distinguished role in the war in Cuba and in the Philippines. More than fifty thousand African Americans served, winning high military honors and distinctions. Notably, six blacks received the Medal of Honor for conspicuous gallantry. African Americans went into the Spanish-American War with a two-fold agenda. They wanted to win respect and acceptance in American society; and secondly, to help liberate brown people like themselves in Cuba who were victims of Spanish aggression. They identified with the Cuban, Puerto Rican, and later with their Philippine brothers and sisters of African descent, and saw these as wars of liberation for their kinsmen. A sense of Pan-Africanism existed in the African-American society of the time. When the Battleship Maine was blown up, precipitating the start of the Spanish-American War, there were blacks aboard the ship. Twenty-two of them were killed. In the African-American community the cry was just as loud to "Remember the Maine" as it was in the white community. Despite this, black volunteers and soldiers were treated miserably during the Spanish-American conflict. Blacks were thwarted when attempting to enlist and, when finally accepted into the armed forces, they were completely segregated under the charge of white officers. African Americans launched a campaign demanding that they be provided with Negro officers. As a result, nearly one hundred blacks were commissioned as officers.

African-American participation in all of America's wars was under strict scrutiny. Many white Americans believed that African Americans would not fight, had no stamina, and lacked other important attributes necessary to make them good soldiers. Blacks readily disproved this nonsense. The motto of black regiments was "no retreat, no return." They knew that they were the representatives of the race. They were, even in this context, *race men* who knew that the world was watching and that white America was eager to find fault and to condemn them if they failed to be the best among the best. In their fighting in Cuba and the rest of the Spanish-American conflict, they demonstrated the highest bravery and gallantry. The Colored Ninth and Tenth Cavalries saved Theodore Roosevelt and his Rough Riders. The charge up San Juan Hill, that Roosevelt later became famous for, would have been an utter disaster without the reinforcement and flanking assault of the black troops who kept him and his men from annihilation. In the African-American press, the blacks were saluted for their bravery. Roosevelt praised them early on as well for their heroism. He later recanted his praise for the black soldiers during his run for the presidency of the United States. He changed his rhetoric to say that the blacks tended to stay to the rear of the action and that whatever success they did have was the result of the white officers who led them.

After their defeat of the Spanish in Cuba and Puerto Rico, the Americans waged war in the Philippines. The issues here were not as clear cut to African-American troops. After all, part of their reason for fighting in these wars was to benefit their "little brown brothers." This could be justified in the war with Spain, but the Philippine conflict suggested something quite different. Filipinos were fighting for their own independence and the Untied States took the role of the colonial empire opposing the independence movement. The African-American press roundly condemned America's involvement in the Philippines and urged black troops not to participate. Throughout the African-American community there was widespread opposition to the war in the Philippines. African Americans lauded the leader of the independence movement, Emilo Alguinaldo, who earned international recognition and praise fighting the Spanish. Now he led the movement for independence from his former ally, the United States, who sent nearly one hundred thousand troops to put down the movement. From 1899 to 1902, the United States waged an all-out campaign to squash Alguinaldo's independence movement. In this effort black units were used and this heightened African-American resentment back home and the rhetoric questioning why they were fighting a kindred people. Alguinaldo's struggle for liberation, as seen in many black quarters, should have been dear to the hearts of people of color who of course wanted an end to colonialism everywhere it existed.

Alguinaldo and his group used powerful tactics to neutralize the black American troops employed against them. They distributed propaganda leaflets reminding African-American soldiers that in the United States and in the army they fought for they were routinely called "niggers" and that Filipinos were referred to likewise, and that both groups had more in common with each other than they did with whites. They pointed out that blacks were being lynched in the United States and that they, like them, were people of color who faced the same kind of hatred and violence. Alguinaldo took a step further urging blacks to put down their arms and to join his liberation struggle. These kinds of tactics were used later in the Vietnam War, as the Vietcong shrewdly attempted to propagandize America's color line. At every opportunity leaflets were distributed condemning racism and questioning why black soldiers were fighting for such a country, killing their brown brothers and sisters in Vietnam rather than helping their cause for independence and liberation. Alguinaldo's race tactic in the Philippines bore substantial success. Blacks deserted in large numbers, some actually going over to his side. They agreed that the cause of Philippine independence was just, and that America's involvement was a colonial war and morally wrong. David Fagan of the 24th Infantry of the U.S. army became the most noted black deserter. He was commissioned in Alguinaldo's army and helped orchestrate brilliant counter-offenses that gave the Americans fits as they destroyed ammunitions, supplies, and effectively counteracted American troop activity. Fagan, to be expected, never returned to the United States and adopted the Philippines as his home. The name David Fagan was well recognized and respected among the Filipinos for years after the war.[1]

African Americans in the main were loyal American citizens and fought and died for the United States of America, right or wrong. They did much to contribute to the nation's victories abroad. Yet the recognition hoped for of complete citizenship and embrace as an equal in American society was denied as illustrated in two horrendous cases of racial violence against black soldiers in the early part of the twentieth century: the cases of Brownsville in 1906 and Houston in 1917. In 1906, in Brownsville, Texas, tensions between the Colored 25th Infantry stationed at Fort Brown and the people of the small nearby Texas town grew to a head. There were allegations that black soldiers attacked a white woman, one of the most typically unfounded claims throughout the South, and one that often concluded with a black man dangling on the end of a rope. A mob of white men stormed the barracks and fired on the black soldiers. When all the shooting stopped, one white lay dead and a policeman was injured. The entire black regiment was charged with murder. The soldiers swore that they had not fired in retaliation and their white officers confirmed that position attesting that the soldiers were asleep at the time of the shooting. There was no evidence; only the accusations of whites. Many of these same black troopers were part of the forces in Cuba that came to the rescue of Theodore Roosevelt and his so-called "Rough Riders." Ironically, it was President Roosevelt who issued the executive order dishonorably discharging all one hundred and seventy of the African-American soldiers. Seventy-one years later, in 1977, the United States government reversed itself in this miscarriage of justice, and expunged the official service records of the black infantrymen, changing them to honorably discharged, although by then all of the soldiers were deceased.

In 1917, in Houston, Texas, sixty-four soldiers of the 24th Colored Infantry were accused of killing seventeen whites in a raging gun battle. In this case as well, whites started the battle by attacking the black soldiers. Armed, the soldiers fought back and in the end seventeen whites and two blacks lay dead. All sixty-four black soldiers were brought to trial. Not one white stood trial. The proceedings took only one day. In the largest murder trial in American history, the all-white military tribunal hastily convicted all sixty-four of the soldiers, sentencing thirteen of them to death and the rest to life imprisonment. This was a wake-up call to some African Americans. Outraged black newspapers poured forth heated rhetoric in condemnation of the nation's racism in the treatment of its black soldiers; African Americans who were literally putting their lives on the line in defense of the United States of America. This did little to reverse the opinion of the court, however. If a white accused a black, the black was guilty. What America was saying in the clearest of terms was that despite the willingness of African Americans to fight and die for the country, they would not be treated as equal citizens of the American nation even in the courts of law. The color line was intact, firm, and seemingly impenetrable.

Nevertheless, when the call came for Americans to step forward and defend the nation's interests during World War I, African Americans, as usual, came forth. The American military, however, no longer encouraged blacks to join. Furthermore, military directives officially sanctioned segregation of black military personnel. General Pershing, head of the American Expeditionary Forces in Europe, gave an August 1918 directive aimed at the French and how they should treat black troopers stationed in France. His directive strongly advised that there be no degree of intimacy between French officers and Negro officers, that especially there be no socializing between Negro troopers and white troopers, including eating with, shaking hands, or meeting with them in any fashion outside of military service. Despite all of these efforts at downgrading African Americans and the racism they endured, they fought in WWI for America. African Americans, like other Americans, bought into the rhetoric of making the world safe for democracy. Blacks answered the call to rally around the flag and stand tall with their white compatriots in defense of the nation's interests. In France and elsewhere they distinguished themselves. They saw their participation as a duty of citizenship; hoping yet again that through their participation the doors of democracy at home would be opened for them. W.E.B. Du Bois championed this point of view in his article, "Close Ranks," in *Crisis* magazine, which was published in 1918. Du Bois urged blacks to participate, to close ranks, to forget their differences at this time and to stand up and to defend the interests of the United States. Many other African-American leaders spoke out against his call to arms, noting quite rightly that democracy and equality were still distant dreams for African Americans in the United States and that since the nation discriminated against blacks at home, it was difficult to see why they should defend it abroad. Nevertheless, blacks stepped forward. They continued to hope that they could win recognition and respect on the battle fields "over there" and that this would translate into acceptance and full citizenship at home. After the passage of the Selective Service Act in May 1917, more than two million African Americans registered for military duty and three hundred thousand actively served. African Americans comprised one third of American forces in Europe. They fought bravely as usual. Several of the most decorated regiments of WWI were African American, and France honored them while their own nation, because of American racism and prejudice, refused to accordingly recognize African-American heroism. The 369th Colored Regiment received the Croix de Guerre, France's highest military honor. The French bestowed coveted military awards and praise on other black regiments, including the 370th, 371st, and the 372nd. African Americans repeatedly proved their bravery and French military and citizens alike recognized them for their accomplishments and contributions.[2]

Yet, not much was changing at home. Black folk were still being lynched on a daily basis in the United States of America. When the Armistice was signed in 1919, it came at the height of one of the worst racial periods in this nation's history. Black soldiers returned home to this tumultuous environment realizing they had fought for freedom abroad and were entitled to it over here. African-American leaders urged blacks to stand up for their rights at home. There was a new spirit developing and being nurtured in the African-American community because of the sacrifices made abroad in fighting for the interests of the nation. Racism, however, had not abated and doors remained firmly closed to black folk.

The bombing of Pearl Harbor hurled America into another war and again African Americans stepped forward to sign up, to do their share, to fight for the freedom of the world, with that same inevitable hope. The military remained segregated as did the home front. Ironically, the United States armed forces became the first entity, according to military proponents, to fully integrate and to allow its members to be judged on capability, to compete on a level playing field, and to rise through the ranks based on ability. When African-American forces came home after World War II, they brought with them a renewed determination to fight for freedom at home. The new spirit and demand for equality nurtured during WWII, and the positive experience of American troops abroad, particularly in France, was something that black soldiers returning to the United States demanded of their homeland. They tasted what life could be like without the color line and they wanted that same respect and freedom of opportunity in America. Underpinning the return of African-American military personnel to the United States was a maturing consciousness ready for harvesting in the struggle to move this nation forward in race relations, civil rights, and opportunities.

THE AFRICAN FRONT

The maturing black consciousness of the World War II period also complemented a heightened international awareness and spirit of Pan-African political consciousness on the part of African Americans. The identification with Africa reemerged with greater intensity and a firmer connectedness when the Italians invaded Ethiopia in 1935. Ethiopia was seen as sacred to black folk. Throughout the Caribbean it held mystic reverence. For blacks in the United States and Caribbean, Ethiopia was a land of promise and hope. They identified with it as an ancient cradle within the motherland of

Africa and honored its standing as one of the oldest civilizations of humankind. Ethiopia and, to a lesser degree, Liberia were the two nations that black folk pointed to with pride as independent African nations that survived the onslaught of European colonialism that began with the "partitioning" of the continent in 1884. Now, however, Italian forces marched headlong into Ethiopia and in a bloody scourge the one of only two remaining independent African nations fell to colonial aggression. Blacks mobilized in protest. African Americans launched a campaign to save Ethiopia. Fund drives were initiated in New York City, Boston, Chicago, Philadelphia, and other major cities. Long lines of African Americans volunteered to serve abroad, to fight for the independence and freedom of Ethiopia. A magnificent collection of photographs at the Schomburg Center for Research in African-American Culture in New York reveals the dedicated thrust of black men and women, volunteering to help Ethiopia. Africa held importance to black America as the outpouring of sentiment and support for Ethiopia demonstrated.

Italy, jealous and envious of the English, French, and Belgian conquests and colonization of Africa, asserted its "right" to additional portions of the continent. It focused on Ethiopia, wanting mineral rights and other wealth the nation possessed. The Italian attack on Ethiopia was under the pretext of violation of the Wal Wal agreement, concerning a desert strip of Ethiopia. Italy laid claims to the area as its own. Ethiopia objected but did not have the power to thwart Italy's aggression. Contrary to popular belief, France, England, and the United States were well aware of the Italian plan to invade all of Ethiopia and to occupy the country. They saw it as a small give-away to placate Italy. Why not? Ethiopia meant little to nothing to the Western powers. The one difficulty expressed by France, although a minor one for it, was how, as a member of the League of Nations, sworn to collective efforts for peace and non-aggression, could it and other League members turn a blind eye to the invasion and to Ethiopia's plea for help. The United States was not a member of the League and found it much easier to ignore Italy's move to subjugate the African nation. The United States at least tacitly approved the colonial aggression of the European powers and Italy's design on parts of Africa. No question that these powers knew of the Italian goal of conquest of Ethiopia prior to the actual invasion. Ethiopia appealed to the League of Nations and the United States prior to 1935. England quickly withdrew Addison Southard, its minister in Ethiopia; allowing them to distance themselves from the cries of Ethiopia. Italy maintained that under the terms of the Treaty of

London of 1915 it had been promised Ethiopia and now argued that just as it had taken Somali and the French had taken Morocco and the English had taken Kenya and other African territories, it was now going to take Ethiopia.

African Americans did not relent in their efforts against Italy and for Ethiopia. Some blacks fought abroad as part of the black regimental detachments connected with Ethiopia. The black press kept the issue on the front burner of black and world consciousness. African-American leaders such as W.E.B. Du Bois wrote poignantly of the injustice and inhumanity of the Italian invasion and the conquest of Africa by European nations. The Italian invasion of Ethiopia and European colonization of Africa exemplified, as Du Bois wrote, "selfishness, shortsightedness, cruelty, deception and theft." Italian subjugation of Ethiopia lasted until 1941. African-American sentiment and consciousness about Ethiopia and the rest of Africa lasted far longer. The Ethiopian crisis enlivened African-American identification with and commitment to the mother continent. Some would belatedly demonstrate their commitment abroad by joining the Abraham Lincoln Brigade and fighting to protect the democratic government of Spain against the fascist forces of Francisco Franco during the Spanish Civil War. In January 1937, sparked by an international awareness, a group of politically charged black and white Americans formed the Council on African Affairs (CAA), and dedicated the new organization to eradicating colonialism, fascism, and to liberating not only Ethiopia but the entire continent of Africa. Their premise was simple: to spread accurate information and news about the African continent and how its people were suffering; in other words, to better inform the citizenry both here and abroad about the evils of the European colonization of Africa and its people. The CAA was the brainchild of Max Yergan, a former YMCA worker. Yergan, who was a graduate of Shaw University, a traditional black liberal arts school, had spent close to twenty years in Africa, from 1916 to 1936, working with the YMCA first in parts of East Africa and then later in South Africa. His work made a difference in South Africa as he dedicated himself to the political and economic betterment of South Africans. Yergan was a force and supporter of the early labor movement and liberation movement in South Africa. He had joined with others to advance the educational mission and work of the Community Center at Fort Hare. This center later became the leading educational institution for black activists. Almost every South African activist of later years had some connection with Fort Hare, including, for example, Oliver Tambo, Walter Sisulu, Bishop Desmond Tutu, Robert Mugabe, who later became president of Zimbabwe, and Nelson Mandela, the great freedom fighter, ANC leader, and eventual President of South Africa. All of them had their roots in Fort Hare, the institution Max Yergan helped create. Yergan worked quietly and in consultation with other activists for African liberation. It was not surprising that he soon found himself at odds with the YMCA. At no time had the YMCA's mission been to liberate Africa. Yergan became concerned with his people and soon found himself at odds with the contradiction of Christian missionary work and the true liberation of the African continent. He began to embrace the South African labor movement and the new fledgling African National Congress. Faced with these contradictions, he resigned from the YMCA. That early work, however, gained him wide recognition. Yergan was one of the first to receive the Harmon Prize for Outstanding Christian Missionary Field Work. In 1933, he became the recipient of the Spingarn Medal from the NAACP for his leadership and contribution to the betterment of the Negro race, particularly for his work in Africa.[3]

He became more radicalized with his affiliation with the ANC, the South African labor movement, and political dissidents throughout the world. To put his ideas into more concrete motion he solicited the support of Paul Robeson to become both a member and supporter of his idea of a formal organization to spread correct information regarding Africa in an effort to raise the consciousness of people throughout the world about the plight of the continent and its people. Paul Robeson was easily persuaded since this struck at the very core of his own concerns for Africa. Robeson played a major role in terms of giving the CAA visibility, credibility and recognition. Dedicated to Africa's liberation Yergan and Robeson built an organization of blacks and whites in agreement on the premise of aiding the liberation of Africa. Beside Yergan and Robeson the Council attracted other important black intellectuals to its executive leadership ranks, including Ralph Bunche, who was then a professor at Howard University; Mordecai Johnson, president of Howard; Channing Tobias, a leader of the Phelps Stokes Fund; Renie Maran, a West Indian novelist in France; Herbert Delaney, a New York attorney; and Rosebery Bokwe, a South African physician and a member of the ANC. Whites who held leadership roles in the organization were noted social advocates such as Ramond Leslie Buell, who wrote substantially on African history and conditions; Mrs. John Moores, a wealthy Boston socialite; Norman McKenzie, law professor at Toronto University; Leonard Barnes, socialist author at Liverpool University; and Mary

Van Kleeck, a research director at the Russell Sage Foundation. Together blacks and whites of the CAA worked to aid the independence and advancement of the nations of Africa. The Council dropped any hint of being a pacifist organization once Germany attacked the Soviet Union in 1941 and the United States and Soviets became allies. For some this confirmed that the CAA was linked to the Communists and pro-Soviet ideology. More important to African Americans and other lovers and supporters of African liberation was the CAA's dedication to ridding Africa of colonialism.

While the Council functioned with a relatively small inner circle of twenty-five-to thirty executive members, it had a far larger following and impact outside the inner circle. CAA made a difference, its voice was being heard as it disseminated reliable information on what was happening in Africa through its publication *New Africa*. The advent of *New Africa* was an important step forward in providing accurate information about the continent, about the mother land, with the help of key individuals such as Charlette Bass, publisher of the *Los Angeles Eagle,* who had once been a follower of Marcus Garvey; Earl Dickerson, president of the National Bar Association of black lawyers; and Howard University sociology professor E. Franklin Frazier. Influential whites such as music impresario John Hammond who was long involved in political and social liberation causes aided their efforts and publication. Others included Edith Field, William Schieffelin, and William Hunton. *New Africa* had the funding behind it to make it a strong voice, and it became one of the most important oracles of its time in the United States and abroad on the question of Africa. It found its way into black churches, libraries, the offices of government officials, and among freedom fighters in Ghana, Kenya, and South Africa, London, Paris, Amsterdam, and Moscow. It was making a difference. So successful and important was *New Africa* that the Colonial Office of Great Britain officially banned it in the colonies and in England, labeling it as subversive.

By 1945 the Council's yearly operating budget had grown to approximately thirty-eight thousand dollars, most of which was used in the publication and promotion of *New Africa* and other materials including informational pamphlets and other releases. On occasion the Council was able to prompt a radio program to include information about Africa. It held a constant barrage of small to moderate size conferences to bring together intellectual leaders dedicated to Africa's liberation and to share information and knowledge on the current affairs of the continent. The CAA's most important conference, "Africa New Perspectives," was held in April of

1944 at its New York headquarters. One hundred and twenty-seven scholars, educators, labor, civic and political leaders, church representatives, and activists attended, including Kwame Nkrumah, who later became the first president of independent Ghana. The conference drew people from Africa, Europe, India, the Caribbean, and the United States. Their main focus was on how to best continue the struggle for the freedom and independence of the African continent. They exchanged ideas and information, wrote petitions and, most importantly, heightened consciousness and visibility for the cause.

The CAA was a force with which to be reckoned. Its dissemination of information and its presence in New York City had a positive impact. The headquarters itself was a place for constant meetings about Africa and other issues relating to black folk throughout the diaspora. From the outside you could see the display of books and it seemed to welcome you into the quarters. The door was often left open in the summer and visitors could walk in from the street as did many. People stopped, sat for a while, and discussed Africa. Visitors were free to browse the CAA's extensive collection of books and pamphlets and other materials on Africa. Students dropped in as did political leaders, community activists, and others thirsty for the latest information on the continent, and for lively dialogue. Thus the CAA was a major port of informational disbursement about Africa and the evils of colonization. *New Africa* was being cited throughout the world. Indeed, its circulation by 1946 was approximately three thousand issues each month; its influence was greater yet. The American State Department followed the activities of the organization as did the British Colonial Office and other offices of colonial powers. The Council was aware of the monitoring, thinking that it was just as helpful to influence and to educate the colonial powers as it was the common citizenry about the evils of colonialism. The CAA, after all, was dedicated to consciousness raising and political activism, but most of all to getting out the facts of what was occurring in Africa from the economic exploitation of its people and resources to the inhumane actions against liberation activists on the continent. When President Franklin Delano Roosevelt made his speeches for world peace and liberation in his Atlantic Charter, the CAA knew its efforts were being heard and felt.

The coming of the end of WWII also gave the organization great hope. Surely this war, fought to end German aggression and for world liberation, meant the ending of the yoke of European rule and subjugation of Africa. The Council was correct in its belief that colonialism would be on a downward slide once WWII ended, not because of the triumph of the rightness of liberation over the evils of colonialism, but because of the reconfiguration of the world order. The British empire was in total decline. The war devastated Britain. It was no longer able to amass the force necessary to assert and maintain its hegemony over colonies throughout the world, including India and, finally, Africa. France, Belgium, Germany, Italy, and the rest paid dearly during the war. The reorganization, as a result of the horrific price WWII exacted, brought about the official end of European colonization of Africa. Although colonialism was in many respects replaced with neo-colonialism, the CAA's positive contribution to African liberation was undeniable. The Council began to decline after the war ended. The external and internal struggles of the organization invariably took their toll. Moreover, the political climate in the United States made it increasingly more difficult than ever for any organization with the activist philosophy and linkages of the CAA to survive. The CAA was linked to Marxist and Communist ideology, particularly with the prominent role that Paul Robeson played. The organization, however, was not Communist. Nevertheless, the hostility against activist organizations in the postwar years, epitomized in the McCarthyism of the fifties, made it impossible for the Council on African Affairs to continue. The organization disbanded in 1955.[4]

THE COMMUNIST FRONT: BETTER RED THAN AMERICAN?

From the very beginning of the Communist movement in the United States, the Russian Revolution of 1917 and the triumph of the Bolsheviks, the American nation has had a fascination and preoccupation with branding blacks as Reds. In truth, the Communist Party movement in the United States never had strong roots in the black community because of ideological and philosophical differences that did not hit squarely on the dominate problem facing African Americans—racism. The early socialists (not to be confused with Communists), such as A. Philip Randolph and Chandler Owen, spoke of the needs of blacks to organize as laborers. They were advocates of integrated unionism and the socialist professed class over race as the major problem facing African Americans. This was not to say that Randolph and Owen were indifferent to racial issues. They believed that the economic exploitation of blacks was the main problem, not skin color. Randolph and Owen, however, never became Communists unlike Lavette Whiteman, Richard B. Moore, Otto Huiswood, and Cyril Briggs.

Socialism gained very little ground among black Americans and Communism did little better. In 1925 under the orders of the Comintern, the Communist Party (CP) initiated a campaign to become more innovative in its dealing with the Negro population of America. They believed the time was right, given the large number of blacks migrating to the North, the increasing number of urban workers and unionism, and the turmoil in the expanding cities. They saw this as an opening, as fertile ground for the CP. Their hopes proved to be overly optimistic. By 1930 there were no more than one thousand black members of the Communist Party. Part of the problem of the CP was that it failed to understand the depths of American racism. The class analysis, Marxist analysis, Leninist philosophy, all had their merits, but only a tiny minority of African Americans saw their future as dependent on joining hands with white workers in or out of unions. Most unions had color-line restrictions and were outright hostile to blacks. American labor unions traditionally did not welcome African Americans with the exception of organizations like the defunct Knights of Labor, IWW, and the CIO. The Communists' explanation to blacks that class was the reason for their problems was hardly convincing to them when they were regularly being lynched and routinely segregated, discriminated against, stereotyped, despised, shunned, and exploited. Any organization or philosophy that minimized or downplayed racism held little likelihood of success in the African-American community. Race was at the center of the American dilemma and always had been and Communist ideology minimized the importance of racism. The CP, rather, wanted to talk about the bourgeoisie versus the working class. There were socioeconomic differences, of course, even within the black community itself. Ironically, the seam uniting all African Americans, whether they wanted it to or not, was the color line. Whether upper class, middle class, or at the very bottom of any kind of class, blacks remained black and American society was actively hostile to them.

The directives from the Comintern in Russia and carried forward in the CP in America were out of touch with the black American racial plight. Progressive thinking white Communist Party members in the Untied States eventually tried to give attention to the race issue. They did not deny its existence but inevitably even those most schooled in the peculiarities of America's history of race relations spouted Communist doctrines of bourgeois exploitation and the need for class solidarity as a cure-all for blacks and whites and for the working classes of the world. African Americans knew that they were treated much differently than the white working class in the United States. That was why the CP met, at best, only limited success in bringing blacks on board in the 1930s and later, even though it tried to advance more enlightened thinking to attract larger numbers of blacks visa via its National Negro Congress and its Youth Continuation Committee, going particularly after the southern youth through its Southern Negro Youth Congress and other efforts. After the German attack on Russia in 1941, and the United States and Soviets joined together as allies against Germany, the CP in America lowered the voltage of its verbiage on the issue of laboring-class problems and black inequality. The pages of the *Daily Worker*, the official newspaper of the American Communist Party, once led the print-media criticism of American society. It now became more cautious, selective, and balanced in its critiques for the duration of the war and the Soviet-American alliance. Once the war ended, the voltage of the Communist, anti-American verbiage intensified.

By the late 1940s the CP was making its most important dint in the African-American community, especially among a few of the intellectuals such as Paul Robeson and Shirley Graham. It was a major contributor to the effort of African Americans to petition the United Nations in 1951. Robeson led the campaign to collect data and to file a formal petition in the United Nations charging the United States of America with genocide against its Negro population. The petition focused on police brutality. There was a long history in America of the phenomenon of sudden black death at the hands of law enforcement officers. The petition cited hundreds of documented cases of African Americans dying "accidentally" while being arrested or while in police custody. The 1951 Genocide Petition may have been the last gasp of the CP to place itself squarely in the African-American struggle. In the petition the CP acknowledged that racism was a major problem facing blacks; however, in keeping with party philosophy, it maintained that economic exploitation was behind the racial divide.[5]

THE LABOR FRONT

The American labor movement underwent profound changes in the 1930s and 1940s, as it fought to curtail economic exploitation, particularly with respect to mass production industries, and battled over organizing the unskilled labor segment of society. Whether blacks actually benefited from this new labor thrust was doubtful, despite the magnificent efforts of the Congress of Industrial Organizations (CIO). One of the problems with the labor movement, as the nation moved into the clutches of the Great Depression, was that the unskilled labor segment remained largely unorganized. Less than a tenth of the overall labor force of America was unionized and there was virtually no unionization in the mass production industries. Major efforts were launched to organize the growing masses of unskilled and semiskilled workers in a number of sectors. First, the American Federation of labor, an exclusionary crafts union dedicated to skilled workers, felt that the growing unskilled labor segment posed a threat to the strength of their organization and to the bargaining power of the union. The best way of neutralizing the threat, they concluded, was to bring the unskilled and semiskilled workers into the fold. There were numerous discussions on how this could be accomplished. The Committee for Industrial Organization was formed within the ranks of the AFL, with the specific mission of articulating an agenda for the unionization of the semiskilled and unskilled labor masses and integrating them into the AFL. Individuals like John L. Lewis of the United Mine Workers pushed hard within the AFL to organize common laborers. The union had difficulties reconciling the difference between industrial labor versus craft work due to the elitism of the AFL, its exclusionary traditions and its disrespect for unskilled and semi-skilled workers. John L. Lewis, chairing the Committee for Industrial Organization, had the job of articulating how this could be overcome. His committee met on this issue on numerous occasions and when the 1934 San Francisco Convention of the AFL convened, they offered a course of action. The AFL, however, rejected their recommendations. Lewis and his committee put forward a meaningful course of action again at the Atlantic City Convention of 1935 and again the leadership of the AFL rejected the plans. The result of this fateful 1935 convention was that Lewis and others of the AFL, who believed strongly in unionizing the unskilled and semiskilled workers of America, bolted from the ranks and formed their own union, the Congress of Industrial Organizations. As Lewis succinctly put it, "the mission is to organize these guys." The AFL continued to fail to take action to bring the unskilled into its ranks. Samuel Gompers, in his earlier leadership of the AFL, had also made utterances favoring the unionizing of the unskilled and semiskilled workers, but nothing ever came of it. Lewis and his group were now taking decisive action as a separate and competing union dedicated to organizing workers no matter what their status in terms of skill or craft. Lewis and his organization made great strides.

The CIO believed in integration and opened the ranks of the union to everyone. The number of African Americans brought in was unprecedented. Some would say later that the organizing of black workers was at the foundation of the mission of the CIO. Given Lewis's sensitivities and commitment, the CIO became a champion of black rights both for workers and in the area of civil liberties. In Chicago, for example, the CIO challenged the old practice of "tagging" the time cards of Negro employees in the meat packing industry. This was a common occurrence in Armour and Company, Swift, Cuddahy, and throughout the industry. The card of the African American worker would receive a black tag. This enabled the meat packing industry to more efficiently segregate and discriminate against its black workers. The black was universally paid lower wages than his or her white counterpart. The CIO took on this issue, condemning it as wrong, unconstitutional, discriminatory, and bad. The CIO organized and threatened a strike against Armour and Company, Swift, and the rest of the meat packing industry, focusing on the all-important Chicago market, the hub of meat packing. The result was an informal agreement with the Swift and Armour plants dropping the practice of tagging the time cards of Negro employees and agreeing to initiate a new policy of hiring more blacks to reach parity of representation equaling their percentage in the Chicago population. The quota hiring proved to be the only effective means to ensure fairness in hiring. Because of its successes in the Chicago meat packing industry more African-American workers turned to the ranks of the CIO. It proved itself consistently as a union that welcomed and understood the rightness of integration and the need to destroy the color line. The CIO led the charge in the change of American organized labor. The unionization of the mass production industries as a general goal was far more important to white workers than to black given that most unions, with the noted exception of the CIO, were exclusionary and did not admit blacks. This meant that the growth of the American labor movement overall was antithetical or at best marginal to the advancement of a color-blind society and African-American rights.

Labor continued to make important gains. The Railway Labor Act of 1926 and the Norris-LaGuardia Act of 1932 provided protection for workers to unionize. A major step forward, as organized labor in the main saw it, was the coming in 1935 of Section 7A of the National Industrial Recovery Act, better known as the Wagner Act. This enactment guaranteed labor's right to organize. By 1937, collective bargaining was becoming a typical occurrence in the ranks of organized labor with negotiations and advancement in the wage scale for the average worker. The average African-American worker, not including those in the CIO, witnessed only marginal advancements as a result of the Wagner Act. Ninety-eight percent of

African-American workers remained non-unionized and were unable to reap any significant advantage from the new progressive legislation. Organized labor was making progress and asserting itself, but blacks were on the periphery. Automobile workers in the sitdown strikes of 1936–1937 in Flint, Michigan, galvanized laborers in that industry and demonstrated their collective strength. The coming of World War II was advantageous to the American economy and thus to labor. Corporate profits increased dramatically and the number of the unemployed fell substantially. By December 1941, the unemployment rate had been cut in half to 3.8 million. Contracts and better working conditions were negotiated. Unions successfully negotiated for holidays and sick-time release, vacation, agreements on grievance procedures and representation. Unskilled and semi-skilled workers who unionized, obtained better deals and concessions than unorganized workers. The CIO continued at the forefront of organizing unskilled and semi-skilled workers and its reputation grew as a champion of equal rights and a color-blind society. The CIO's membership climbed from 1.5 million workers in 1940 to nearly three million just one year later, with African Americans comprising a small but growing percentage of the members. It was a start. The next five years were successful for the workers but not always successful for the union. The call to rally around the flag suggested that anyone who was doing anything that could jeopardize America's economic recovery was working against the success of the war effort. Nevertheless, with the overall prosperity brought on by war-time production, all workers, whether unionized or not, were in a better position in terms of earning a living wage. Jobs were made and people went back to work. Unions expanded their membership, although the efforts of management to paint unions as un-American and likely to jeopardize economic stability during the crucial war years steadily increased.

The anti-union trend intensified in the post-war years. The Taft-Hartley Act passed in 1947; for organized labor it was the antithesis of the Wagner Act. It was a harsh measure that reflected the trend to thwart union growth. The Taft-Hartley Act contained a long list of provisos, but four points were crippling to labor's power. Under the terms of the act, labor and management would have to give a sixty-day notice before termination of a contract which effectively meant that efforts at any type of strike, particularly wild-cat strikes, were largely thwarted. Second, the federal government could delay a strike for eighty days on the grounds of public health or safety, which meant that in the railroad industry, mining, or any other industry in which the government felt that a strike jeopardized national security or national interest, the strike could be halted for the specified period. This was to the tremendous disadvantage of the worker. Third, union leaders were made to take a non-Communist oath, a demeaning slap in the face to organized workers and their leadership and suggesting that unions were the harbingers of Communists and un-American activities. Finally, the Taft-Hartley Act prohibited the *closed shop*, meaning that efforts by unions to thoroughly unionize an industry or company was hindered. No longer could a union win ground and make it mandatory that any worker coming into a particular company be a union member. White labor saw this for what it was, a major setback. African Americans, however, did not. The policy of racial exclusion of most unions, and the *closed shop*, were a double-edged sword that worked to bar blacks from employment in many major industries. The dreaded color line too often kept black and white workers from coming together in a mutually advantageous union relationship. Racism divided white and black workers and put them both at the mercy of the employer.

Anti-union activities and the unions' own internal shortcomings were detrimental to the labor movement and union survival. Finally realizing this, the AFL embraced the CIO out of mutual self interest. They bridged their differences and in 1955 the two unions came together, forming one of the world's largest unions, the AFL-CIO. Unfortunately, they joined together in what proved to be a new conservatism. The CIO, the once great champion of black rights, moved away from the mantle of labor equality within its ranks and became mute in racial matters. With the crackdown on labor organizations and the Communist witch hunts, union membership in all groups declined in the 1950s. Quietude on race issues was apparently part of the new coalition between the CIO and the AFL. In 1959, only four years after the merger, A. Philip Randolph denounced the AFL-CIO for its new conservative attitude on discrimination against black workers, and called for major reforms. He heatedly berated the organization for embracing racist local unions that practiced exclusion against blacks. The AFL-CIO, for example, decided to admit the International Longshoremen's Association (ILA), a completely exclusionary union that constantly refused to admit African Americans despite that blacks constituted a large percentage of laborers who worked the docks. The International Longshoremen and Warehousemen's Union (ILWU), under the leadership of Harry Bridges, was the type of local that Randolph found great favor in, and said that here was the kind of organization that the AFL-CIO should embrace because Bridges had long stood for integration of his union. When the Portland, Oregon chapter of the ILWU called for a strike in 1933, Bridges challenged that local to admit blacks before it would receive the support of the national union. That was only one example of Bridges's many efforts at integrating the ILWU, and it was successfully integrated throughout the rank-in-file. The exclusionary ILA, however, was quickly admitted into the AFL-CIO while Bridges's ILWU waited a long time before being granted the same privilege. Repeatedly, A. Philip Randolph and George Meany, the head of the AFL-CIO engaged in public squabbles over the color line within the organization. Meany was furious with Randolph and doubted his union loyalty. Also in 1959, Herbert Hill, the labor secretary of the NAACP, critically assessed the Jewish Labor Council (JLC) and the International Ladies Garment Workers Union (ILGWU). The two unions represented half a million workers and no leadership positions in the organizations were held by blacks. Jews in particular, Hill noted, held a disproportionate share of important positions in the AFL-CIO. Jews branded his accusations as anti-Semitic. Hill found the charge of anti-Semitism preposterous since he was Jewish. He reiterated his charges that blacks and other minorities did not receive fair treatment in these unions, and must have more important posts, not only in the JLC and ILGWU, but in the AFL-CIO. The NAACP supported Hill's report and also criticized the AFL-CIO, challenging its racial policies. The NAACP launched formal charges against the AFL-CIO's Brotherhood of Electrical Workers (BEW), a union that from its very beginning to most recent days, was exclusionary and openly barred blacks from membership.

The challenge to the AFL-CIO's color line practices evolved through the 1960s. The most outspoken critics of union exclusionary practices were the two best known and highly respected black labor leaders in the country, Willard Townsend of the United Transport Service Employees Union and A Philip Randolph, head of the Brotherhood of Sleeping Car Porters. In 1960, unsatisfied with the token gestures of the AFL-CIO, Randolph and other black labor leaders formed the Negro American Labor Council (NALC). Within their organization they sought, among other things, an end to discrimination throughout the ranks of organized labor. To George Meany this constituted another gauntlet thrown at his feet by the trouble maker Randolph. A. Philip Randolph charged that African Americans and Puerto Ricans held no offices in the ILA and ILGWU, while they comprised at least one hundred thousand of the rank-in-file workers and thus dues-paying members of those locals. Meany essentially told Randolph to be a union man first and a NALC member second. Meany did not like adverse publicity and

most certainly did not like uppity Negroes who were challenging
and pushing the AFL-CIO to go in a direction that it was not committed.

The AFL-CIO typified and exemplified to African Americans the
paradox of being black in America. As an African American you were
brought to this nation to labor. Slavery, after all, was a forced labor
system. Blacks were brought to America to work by the sweat of
their brow. Ironically, organized labor should have been the most natural haven for African Americans and other exploited workers. It
was, instead, fraught with racial discord and failed to become the
leadership element for integration of the workplace and society. The
Civil Rights Movement and the labor movement should have been familiar bedfellows. As Martin Luther King, Jr. told the United Auto
Workers and its head, Walter Reuther, a supporter of civil rights,
"there are more ties of kinship between labor and the Negro people
than tradition." King went on to note labor's need for a wage-hour
bill and blacks need for the same, labor's need for housing legislation
and the need of blacks for the same. In short, labor's problems were
largely the same problems the African-American community faced,
King concluded to a sympathetic UAW national convention audience.[6]

The problem for African-American workers, and for American
laborers in general, was further compounded owing to international
factors. The overcoming of the color line called for a sensitivity and
consciousness that the white labor movement was unable to muster.
The International Workers of the World (IWW), also known as the
Wobblies, argued at the beginning of the twentieth century that the
labor problem was world-wide and that all workers of the world
would have to unite into "One Big Union" or suffer the consequences. The passage of time began to demonstrate that the American worker's standard of living was interrelated to the standard of
living of workers throughout the world. The success of American
industries, at one level, benefited the American standard of living
and American workers. Yet, at the same time, the exploitation of
foreign workers, particularly in the Third World, inevitably hurt all
segments of American labor as work would be shipped overseas to
to be performed by cheaper labor forces. Sadly, American organized
labor has traditionally reacted unsympathetically to the problems of
Third World workers. American organized labor sided with American big business interests rather than partnering with Third World
laboring classes. American labor, because of its nationalistic view-
point, its immediatism, and its own lingering racism, was unable to
reach out in a meaningful way to largely black, brown, and yellow
nations whom it needed desperately to form partnerships with to be

able to fend off the growing exploitation of workers both at home and abroad. There was a relationship between the big profits and the American standard of living and what labor here was paid in comparison to that paid labor in the developing world. In Bolivia, for example, the great profits that American corporations reaped in the later part of the 20th century, helped contribute to a higher American standard of living. From the days of President Hugo Benzer and his terrible exploitation of Bolivian workers, American corporations doing business in Bolivia made huge profits, and the American standard of work and living remained high. In Chile, when then President Allende sought to centralize control of his nation's copper industry, miners there knew that he was on the right track. But International Telephone and Telegraph (IT&T) and American Telephone and Telegraph (AT&T) relied on the Chilean copper and would have lost huge profits. The international community later condemned IT&T and AT&T and the United States government for their role in the assassination of Allende. The workers in Chile continued to be exploited. Rich profits were reaped by American corporations doing business there and the spoils taken from that endeavor benefited the American standard of living and thus the American worker in the short term. Gulf and Western's suppressed sugar prices in the Dominican Republic and the efforts of that nation's sugar cane workers to organize for higher wages and better working conditions. When William Bruce Konuah, minister of labor in Ghana, championed a bill to forbid trade unions in his country, it was done admittedly to keep labor costs low and profits high to attract Western corporations and investors to exploit his own nation's largest national resource—cheap labor. When Papa Doc and Baby Doc ruthlessly ruled Haiti, they increased their ties between government and the Western companies seeking cheap labor and a high profit margin. In Panama, shrimp workers were exploited yet the price and profits surrounding shrimp continued to climb while Panamanian shrimpers remained among the poorest workers in the world. Twenty percent of the chrome for American cars came from Zimbabwe, yet its miners were among the poorest paid in the world—a situation that began to change slightly only after the overthrow of colonial rule in that nation. The same held true for South African diamond and gold miners. For the pathetically small sum of five million dollars, Firestone Rubber gained exclusive rights over Liberian rubber for ninety-nine years. Liberia's work force remained among the poorest in the world. The same held true for much of Africa, Mexico, Brazil, and for Latin America, the Caribbean, Korea, China, and India.

Charles Hayes, one of the voices of reason in the black worker labor movement, head of the Organization of Black Labor Leaders (OBLL), argued that African-American workers needed to push beyond just seeing themselves as hopefully integrating with white workers and understand that a larger economic and political agenda was occurring that worked against both groups and for the continued exploitation of the Third World. Hayes tied the labor movement to the world of politics, economics and race. He contended back in 1970 that American workers, black and white, should have worked to stop the bombing of Southeast Asia, should have fought for the cause of liberation of South Africa, and should have stood opposed to the importing of chrome and anything else from Southern Africa in the era of apartheid. The OBLL supported freeing jailed activist Angela Davis and gave its support to FRLIMO, SWAPO, ANC, ZAPPO, and other liberation groups in South Africa and elsewhere. Hayes pleaded that blacks, in and out of organized labor, had to fight for world equality. As he saw it, politics and economics were one in the same, and racism and economics had blended together to exploit the world's labor force, especially its most vulnerable elements.

The division between American organized labor and the Third World was exemplified in the makeup, membership, and political positions of the WFTU and ICFTU. The World Federation of Trade Unions was an international union that had actively brought together Third World laborers and even some First World laboring groups who saw the need for having one big union of all workers of the world united in the common cause of equality and equal pay for equal work. The WFTU long advanced the argument that historian Walter Rodney and other proponents of the *underdevelopment thesis* described as a seesaw relationship of international exploitation and dependency and that as Third World workers gained strength and unionization and bargaining power and started to rise, at the one end of the economic seesaw, American workers and other First World workers who had benefited from the long exploitation of Third World workers, would experience a dramatic decline in their standard of living on the other end of the economic seesaw. Thus, the challenge was to find the middle, where all workers benefited equally. The WFTU professed such a position and universal standards. Of the affiliated unions comprising this international union, there was not one major American labor union. On the other side was the ICFTU, the International Confederation of Free Trade Unions. This organization touted capitalism and supported the interests of Western corporations in underdeveloped nations. It consistently closed its doors to Third World labor organizations. Most First World labor organizations, and all major American labor unions that had international affiliation, were with the ICFTU. American workers, white and black, failed to redefine themselves and their organizations in terms that were more sophisticated in understanding of where and how their long-term interests were best served at home and abroad.

For the African-American worker, organized labor could best be described as a missed opportunity, throughout the 20th century, to enhance and advance the cause of all workers, domestic and foreign, First World and Third World. Labor in the United States continued to rapidly lose ground. The American worker, black and white, in the context of the international sphere, has proven vulnerable to the decisions of a national and international political agenda and corporate authority that exploited cheap labor sources abroad while the standard of living of America's work force declined.[7]

THE SPORTS FRONT

Sport played a critically important role in the African-American struggle. The years immediately prior to World War II were a period of intellectual vitality in America and social and political activism as well. The Great Depression pushed Americans to examine society from a critical perspective. For blacks this was easy enough to do. These were years of continued disfranchisement, inequality in education and housing, lack of job opportunity, and the ever-present horror of lynchings. The tragedy of the Scottsboro Boys shocked, angered and motivated black and white American consciousness. The Harlem Renaissance lived. Langson Hughes, Zora Neale Hurston, Claude McKay, James Weldon Johnson, William Attaway, and Arna Bontemps challenged us with their writings. The scholarship of W.E.B. Du Bois and Carter G. Woodson enlightened and educated us. Artists Aaron Douglas and Jacob Lawrence helped black America to see itself and its heritage. Josh White wrote, sung and protested. Huey Ledbetter, Ma Rainey, Jelly Roll Morton, Bessie Smith, Blind Blake, Mammie Smith, Victoria Spivey, Billie Holiday, and Duke Ellington made black America hear itself in its music. Mary McLeod Bethune and Adam Clayton Powell, Jr. maneuvered masterfully in the halls of government and lit a fire under the political soul. Sport, like the arts, literature, and politics, was and is an important mirror of society and the search for selfhood. Two figures dominated sport in the pre-World War II years: Jesse Owens and Joe Louis. Their emergence as national symbols and sport heroes involved political and psychological dimensions as well as physical feats. Jesse Owens's four gold medals in the 1936 Olympic Games were a triumph for American democracy over nazism. They were also Owens's personal protest statement through athletic performance. Much the same can be said of Joe Louis's defeat of Max Schmeling in their second fight for the heavy-weight championship of boxing in 1938. Owens and Louis were not inert unthinking objects as they have often been portrayed. Their way of protesting against the racism that they and other blacks experienced was through proving themselves as black men and as Americans. They offered athletic victories as their statements for racial equality and the rights of full citizenship.

Owens and Louis garnered such a long list of successful athletic performances and records that it became fuel for biological racists who claimed that black athletes and the black race were physically different from whites and naturally endowed with greater speed, stamina, muscles, and jumping ability. These were long-held racist views dating back to the nineteenth century but given new life especially after Jesse Owens's record setting performance in the Olympics. William Montague Cobb, an African American who held two doctorates, a medical degree and a doctorate in physical anthropology, was so outraged by the racist declarations that he devoted careful research and writing on the subject for the rest of his career. Cobb personally examined Jesse Owens and performed scientific tests and measurements on him finding no anatomical peculiarities. He published other articles based on his life-long research and deduced that whites and blacks were physically the same. Racists refused to consider that hard work, dedication, and intelligence were the basis for the successes of Owens, Louis, and other black athletes. This same racist mindset was behind the "Tuskegee Experiment," launched in the 1930s by the U.S. Public Health Service. Over a period of forty years, four hundred uninformed black men in rural Alabama were used as human guinea pigs and deliberately withheld treatment for syphilis to study the long-term affects of the disease. Nazi Germany was not the only nation guilty of immoral and racist medical experiments.

Racism was rampant in America and in sports black athletes fought for recognition as human beings using a variety of approaches. Boxing great Henry Armstrong hammered away at discrimination on numerous occasions. Several times he refused fights in segregated arenas such as the American Legion Hall in Indianapolis, Indiana. Canada Lee, the former boxer, demonstrated his protest spirit in playing the title role of Bigger Thomas in the stage production of Richard Wright's *Native Son*. Paul Robeson, the former Rutgers All-America, continued his assertion of self-hood through acting, singing and political protest.

Sport was the institution in which the contradiction, the inconsistency and incompatibility of racism and discrimination with American democratic principles was most glaring and flagrant because the sanctum of athletics was premised on such doctrines as equality of opportunity, sportsmanship, and fair play. Athletics became a perfect arena for exposing and examining what Richard Reinhold Niebuhr, in *Moral Man and Immoral Society* and in *The Irony of American History*, characterized as the dual nature of American society, with its paradoxical blending of democracy and inequality. Understanding of this conceptual construct helped in grasping the philosophical and ideological underpinning of the coming Civil Rights Movement and its most prominent leader, Dr. Martin Luther King, Jr. King drank deeply from the wellspring of black history and political and moral philosophy. At Morehouse, Crozier Theological Seminary and at Boston University and years afterward, he wrestled with the ideas of the great social philosophers: Plato, Aristotle, Rousseau, Hobbs, Bentham, Mills; the work of Mahatma Gandhi and his principle of "Satyagraha" or truth force, non violent direct action; Hegelian Dialectics; and the writings of Walter Rauschenbush, R.H. Tawney, and Niebuhr. For King, when blacks were factored in, the overwhelming contradiction in American society and in its professed democratic ideals was painfully obvious. He despised the contradiction, the dual nature of American society, a society that could cheer for blacks as athletic heroes while denying them the rights of full citizenship.[8]

In collegiate sports, for example, the paradox was at its zenith. The collegian was seen as an amateur, a purist who played for the love of the game and not like the professional athlete for the almighty dollar. Hence, collegiate athletics, with the possible exception of the church, may best have personified American virtues and values in a working, social context of the times. The athletic field was a proving ground to verify and glorify the rightness of hard work, preparedness, self-sacrifice, team work, individual merit, stick-to-itiveness, valor and fair play. In the game the player had the opportunity to prove his or her mettle, demonstrate physical prowess, if not mental acuteness, champion a cause, defend the honor of the school, win the big one, and earn the accolades of peers. The spectators too held a similarly lauded view of the game and the role of their knights the athletes, white or black.

Black athletes at predominantly white universities found themselves cheered on Saturday during the game, but segregated and scorned during the other six days of the week at the predominantly white universities. These athletes suffered racial abuses and discrimination at the hands of opponents, teammates, coaches, spectators, sports journalists, and post season selection committees. Sometimes overlooked in examinations of the Civil Rights Movement, big-time intercollegiate sport—Ivy League, Big Ten, Big Eight, Pac Ten, Southeast, Southwest, and others of the era—was an important arena of protest movement in the pre-war years. The black athlete at the predominantly white university was both segregated and despised, yet cheered at game time ever since William H. Lewis and T.W.S. Jackson played football for Amherst in 1890–1891. This dual existence for black athletes in collegiate sports, simultaneously scorned and loved, was a microcosm of the contradictions of a racist and segregated society. Ozzie Simmons, for example, quit the University of Iowa football team because he was unable to further endure the racism on and off the playing field. Kenny Washington of UCLA, should have been everyone's All-America in 1939. On a typical Kenny Washington afternoon, this time against the University of Montana in October 1939, he ran for 163 yards in eleven carries, completed two of three passes, scored three touchdowns, all of this occurring in the span of only fifteen minutes of play. Despite being the leading ground-gainer in collegiate football that year with over one thousand yards, Washington was not selected to the All-America Team, nor invited to play in the College All-Star Game because of his color. That same year, the Cotton Bowl Committee denied Lou Montgomery, the black star running back for Boston College, the right to play in the bowl game in Dallas against Clemson. Boston College, Clemson University, and the Cotton Bowl Committee, honored the *Jim Crow* tradition in collegiate sports against having an interracial game, if one of the parties involved objected. In this case the Cotton Bowl Committee and Clemson University raised said objection. Boston College consented, leaving Montgomery at home when the team ventured to Dallas. This so-called *Gentlemen's Agreement* was a common practice in intercollegiate athletics, along with a host of other racist traditions that were tacitly accepted.

Students at New York University, however, raised a loud clamor that took the form of a mass movement against the *Gentlemen's Agreement* at their school. Their protests were profound, having substantial social, political impact, and educational, cultural, philosophical value. The student action began at NYU in October of 1940 when it was learned that Leonard Bates, who was black and the starting fullback on the Violets football team, would not be allowed to accompany his teammates to Columbia, Missouri, and play in the slated game against the University of Missouri. Missouri, like all teams in the South and most in the border states, objected to playing against Negroes. What appalled the NYU students was that their University acquiesced to Missouri's request that Bates be excluded from the game. "Bates Must Play" became the rallying cry of some 2,000 students and sympathizers as they took to the streets picketing the NYU administration building. The huge placards that the picketers bore made the demands clear: "Bates Must Play" "Don't Ban Bates" "Ban *Gentlemen's Agreement*" "End Jim Crow in Sports" "No Nazi Games" and "No Missouri Compromise." Immediately after the demonstration, the students formed the All-University Committee on "Bates Must Play." Their demands were formalized and presented to the school's administration which rejected them. The demonstrations continued. Despite this the team departed in early November to play Missouri. They were soundly defeated in Columbia by a score of 33-0. Back at NYU the defeat was celebrated as divine retribution and the protests escalated. Students held a series of meetings and debated the issues ranging from racism and the *Gentlemen's Agreement* in sports to housing, educational, and employment discrimination. They discussed, contemplated, and demonstrated. The movement intensified when it was learned that NYU held to the *Gentlemen's Agreement* in all of its sports, including their highly regarded track program. Other groups and prominent individuals picked up the cry including the NAACP, the Urban League, the Communist Party, Paul Robeson, Kenny Washington, and Adam Clayton Powell, Jr. Other colleges and universities including Notre Dame, University of Wisconsin, Boston University, began dropping the *Gentlemen's Agreement*. Student organizations and athletes of the City College of New York endorsed the NYU protesters, as did groups at Holy Cross, St. Mary's in Texas, and Rutgers University. Harvard students launched a demonstration in sympathy challenging their institution's color-line policies in sports. They then organized a nationwide conference on the Cambridge campus to discuss the issues. Four hundred delegates from 65 colleges attended. The Harvard administration reacted quickly, banning games with any team that invoked the *Gentlemen's Agreement*. Back on the NYU campus the protest was moving into a new phase, which would be a familiar protest strategy years later in the activism of the 1950s and 1960s, that of direct confrontation. A new and more broad-based student organization emerged at NYU, the Council for Student Equality. The council was formed as a permanent watchdog to fight discrimination on campus and to challenge the inaction of the University administration on the race issue. They organized rallies, public forums, workshops, distributed thousands of informational flyers, and continuously berated the administration for its position on the issue. Finally, the students initiated their boldest effort, a sit-down demonstration in the administration building on March 10, 1941. One hundred and fifty students took part. The NYU protests lasted for over a year, spawned conferences and awareness nation wide of the problem of the color line. Why, then, did not the NYU demonstrations rather than the Montgomery Bus Boycott, become the catalyst for the modern Civil Rights Movement? It might be said that it was an idea whose time had not come. Why had its time not arrived? The answer rested partially in the fragmented nature of the civil rights thrust at this time, the inability or unwillingness of NAACPers, Urban Leaguers, the Council on African Affairs, Communists, and others to seize upon the NYU demonstrations with the full force of their organizations and make of them more than the sum of their parts. Even if they had, there was yet another crucial ingredient missing. That ingredient came on December 7, 1941.

The bombing of Pearl Harbor, and America's official entrance into World War II, had a mammoth impact on American society, the blacks, the world of sports, and the protest movement. The diversion of American manpower to the war effort, left a vacuum in professional and amateur athletics. President Franklin D. Roosevelt besieged Americans to "help sports survive this era of crisis." In collegiate athletics a variety of changes were implemented to help it survive. Coach Fritz Chrysler of the University of Michigan initiated the free substitution rule to compensate for the shortage of football players. Ken Loeffler, basketball coach at Yale, advocated the adoption of the zone defense to shore-up the weak spots in the team's play resulting from the lost of most of the senior athletes to the war effort. What happened in sports confirms that the war was an important aid to black progress. The war forced athletic programs to seek talented athletes from sources they had given little or no previous attention. Black America was virtually an untapped resource of athletic talent, and it was during this era that a substantial shift took place in the athletic establishment's attitude about interracial sports. In this period, Satchel Paige and his Negro Baseball All-Star Team were given the opportunity to play the major league champions, and the Negro Collegiate All-Stars of Football played successive Games against the NFL champions. During WWII and its aftermath the number of African-American athletes in the predominantly white conferences increased substantially. Claude "Buddy" Young was given the opportunity to demonstrate his athletic prowess at the

University of Illinois and he did, dominating intercollegiate football. Jackie Robinson became the first African-American player in major league baseball, and Larry Doby the first African American to play in the American League. Professional basketball lowered the color line with the bringing in of Charles "Tarzan" Cooper and Sweetwater Clifton in 1950. That year also marked the desegregating of professional tennis when Althea Gibson won the right to compete at Forrest Hills, at the United States Tennis Championships. In short, the chaotic athletic situation of the World War II era was a vital factor in the assault on the color line in sports.[9]

At the same time the war and post war years muted the Civil Rights Movement and the organizational efforts to end Jim Crowism in sports and radicalism in general. This was a period of domestic quietude. African Americans, like all Americans, rallied around the flag. Protest was labeled as anti-Americanism. The Communist Party of America toned down its criticism of the United States. The CP had, through its sports page in the *Daily Worker*, been one of the most radical and persistent voices against discrimination in professional and collegiate athletics from the mid through late 1930s. With the German attack on Russia in 1941 and the Soviet-American alliance, the CP became less harsh about segregation in sports. From 1941 through 1945 only an occasional criticism of the American sports establishment appeared in the sports pages of the *Daily Worker*. The economic recession, the cold war mentality, and the flourishing of McCarthyism in the post war years forced the Communist Party of America to concentrate chiefly on survival. During the cold war period, Paul Robeson's name was omitted from the ranks of great All-America football players listed in Cristy Walsh's book on college sports. Branch Rickey, general manager of the Brooklyn Dodgers and the man credited for bringing Jackie Robinson into the major leagues, took part in the "red baiting" in sports. "It's time America woke up to the imminent danger of being completely infiltrated by Communists," Rickey said in 1947. "We should be made aware of the fact that Communist forces intend the overthrow of our democratic government by force." The CP lashed out at both incidents. It called the omission of Robeson's name from the great All-America players an "iron curtain blanketed around the truth" of collegiate sports. The CP was quite explicit in its criticism of Branch Rickey's remarks. It called Rickey's statement unfortunate and challenged his reputation as a liberal altruist who brought the first Negro into the majors: "Branch Rickey is a smart man, the shrewdest in baseball. His signing of qualified Negro talent wasn't done alone with an eye toward becoming a twentieth century Lincoln. Thar's gold in them there hills, and this very clever cookie knew that someday Negroes in the big leagues would be a common sight and why not cash in on it while its novelty made the cashing good?"

Intercollegiate sports was cashing in on the African-American athlete. The post war era was the coming of age of big time intercollegiate sports and the final victory in collegiate athletics of the win-at-any-cost mentality. One needed the best talent to win. The result was that recruiting abuses and scandals became the order of the day. This was not to deny that similar abuses and scandals existed in collegiate sports prior to the post war years. In 1893, for example, seven members of the University of Michigan's football team were not even students at the university, and when Yale lured James Hogan, who later became an All-America tackle, to New Haven in 1902, it was by dint of free tuition, a suite in Vanderbilt Hall, a ten day trip to Cuba, and a monopoly on the sale of score cards. In the same period, the University of Indiana and Purdue University competed for a talented high school basketball player by offering scholarships to his girl friends. In the big time intercollegiate sports programs scandals were common occurrences since the late 1940s. Four basketball stars at Long Island University were charged in 1951 with taking bribes in excess of forty thousand dollars to shave points off games. The basketball scandal at City College of New York resulted in three players being sentenced to jail. In the 1960s, for example, one of the most widely publicized scandals occurred at the University of Illinois in 1966. Eight athletes and the head coaches in football and basketball were banned forever from competing in the NCAA because of an illegal slush fund for athletes at the university. An interesting pattern emerged from the numerous scandals in big time intercollegiate sports: a disproportionately high percentage of black athletes were involved. Of the 29 substantial scandals in collegiate sports during the 1950s and 1960s, 19 occurred on teams with one or more black athletes. Of these nineteen teams, seventy-four percent of the black athletes, as compared to eleven percent of the white athletes, were allegedly involved in the rules violations. For example, three of the four athletes charged in the Long Island University basketball fixes were African American. Sherman White, the team's star center, received the harshest penalty and a likely career in the NBA never materialized. White was African-American. Of the three CCNY players sentenced to jail terms only one was actually required to serve time behind bars, Ed Warner, who was black. Of the eight athletes involved in the Illinois scandal, seven were black. In the case of the University of New

Mexico in 1979, one athlete's education and career ended because the assistant coach, Manny Goldstein, forged transcripts to make the player eligible to compete. The athlete, Craig Gilbert, was African American. This trend continued in the 1980 and 1990s. Fully, in most of the major athletic scandals of recent years at big time universities upward of ninety-five percent of the athletes involved have been African Americans. There were three contributing factors that accounted for the disproportionately high percentage of African Americans involved in the various scandals. First, the vast majority of blacks in big time intercollegiate sports were from lower class backgrounds and hence most desperately in need of financial assistance. Second, the African American athletes recruited were blue chip players and highly sought after. And third, racism.[10]

The *Brown Decision* in 1954 and the death of Joseph McCarthy appeared to remove the shackles from the Civil Rights Movement and divergent points of view. The Montgomery Bus Boycott burst onto the national scene in 1955–56. The late 1950s and the 1960s were a period of heightened social consciousness for black America and all America. The official birth of the black power movement in 1966 symbolized the intensity and the ideological differences within the protest movement. For black America its dilemma was which side to follow: the nonviolent direct action course led by Dr. Martin Luther King, Jr. or the more militant black power course articulated by Malcolm X, of which Stokely Carmichael became the leading proponent, or some other course, or no course? This new consciousness and the schisms within were reflected in the protest mood in sports in the 1960s.

From a domestic and international perspective, the 1968 Olympic boycott stands as the cornerstone in the awakening of black America, Africa, and much of the so-called Third World, to the power and utility of the international athletic contest as a political forum. The use of the Olympic boycott was not new. Egypt, Lebanon and Iraq boycotted the 1956 Melbourne Games to protest the British-French-Israeli invasion of Egypt to allegedly maintain control of the Suez Canal. In 1964, most significant to the civil rights struggle in America, Mal Whitfield, black athlete and holder of three Olympic medals, advocated that blacks boycott the 1964 Olympics to be held in Tokyo, Japan. His reasoning reflected a rising consciousness: "I advocate that every Negro athlete eligible to participate in the Olympic Games in Japan next October, boycott the Games if Negro Americans by that time have not been guaranteed full and equal rights as first class citizens." Whitfield challenged black athletes to act against racism. In his opinion, the black American struggle would have repercussions throughout the world and serve as an example, particularly for the Third World nations. His was the first clarion call for black people in America to use the international sports forum to promote the cause of human rights and the end to racism both in the United States and throughout the world. Black America, however, was not ready to meet the challenge in 1964. It was more ready and able to do so in 1968. What black America and the Third World eventually comprehended was what the powers of the West and East had long known—international sports provided a powerful platform for politics and propaganda, despite the denial of International Olympic Committee patriarch, Avery Brundage.

In the late 1960s, black athletes in the United States were showing signs of a sport-politics consciousness to combat racism. There were certainly immediate issues to stimulate them: the assassination of Dr. Martin Luther King, Jr.; the murder trial of Black Panther leader, Huey P. Newton; and the presidency of Richard M. Nixon, to name a few. The riots occurring in the cities during the period were poignant expressions of the deep-seated anger within the black communities of America. Protest sentiment was alive in every sinew of black America, including the sanctum of athletics. Black and sympathetic white athletes in the college and high school ranks boycotted the New York Athletic Club (NYAC) in 1968 because of its discriminatory policies against blacks and Jews. One of the boycott leaders was H. Rap Brown. In response to a reporter's question about what should be done if people decided not to honor the picket line and attend the track meet at Madison Square Garden, Brown answered, "the Garden should be blown up." Manhattan College, New York University, St. John's, and City College of New York refused to compete in the NYAC track meet until the club changed its racial policies. Black Students at Ohio State University protested against their institution's discriminatory policies in its academic and athletic programs. Similar protests occurred at Michigan State University, University of California at Berkeley, San Francisco State University, University of Kansas, University of Washington, Iowa State University, and others. The students demanded, among other things, that the athletic programs stop discriminating—that more black coaches and trainers be hired. Black collegiate athletes complained about a host of problems; about stacking, where a number of blacks were placed in competition for the same position; about racial stereotyping; about sports commentators biased in favor of white athletes; about the athletic associations' policing of their social activities, the most severely penalized being interracial dating; about the policy of recruiting a limited number of blacks so as not to exceed the "quota." Eight black athletes of the University of Texas at El Paso's track team refused to participate in the school's annual track meet against Brigham Young University because of the Mormon doctrine that blacks were inferior and disciples of the devil.

African-American professional athletes were speaking out louder than ever before against racism. Several black athletes within the National Football League demanded that NFL Commissioner Pete Rozelle resign because of his insensitivity to racism within the NFL. Jim Brown, upon retiring from the Cleveland Browns, denounced the racial insensitivity and intolerance of the team's owner, Art Modell, and his coaching staff. Star halfback Leroy Kelley and five other black teammates on the Cleveland Browns seconded Jim Brown's complaints. Racial turmoil on the Atlanta Falcons prompted the NAACP to threaten suit against that club unless it changed its racial attitude regarding its black players. Bobby Mitchell, black star running back with the Washington Redskins, spoke out against quotas limiting black players on NFL teams. Dallas Cowboys fullback Don Perkins of Albuquerque spoke out against the color line within and outside of the Dallas team, complaining that blacks on the team could not get decent housing in Dallas. Frank Robinson blasted major league baseball for not having a black manager and that the situation had advanced only marginally since baseball was first integrated with the signing of Jackie Robinson in 1945. Jackie Robinson, a life-long Republican, publicly criticized his party for its selection of Richard M. Nixon as the party's standard-bearer for the presidency and warned that Nixon's election would be a major step backward in the battle to abolish the color line. Tennis star Arthur Ashe summed up the feeling of many of the outspoken black professional athletes when he said: "I am not Rap Brown or Stokely Carmichael, but this country could use another three or four Browns and Carmichaels." The rhetoric and actions of the black athletes during the period were strong. Muhammad Ali, "The People's Champ," refused induction in the military because of his religious beliefs and opposition to the war in Vietnam. As a result, he was illegally stripped of his heavy weight boxing championship. Curt Flood filed suit against the Reserve Clause in professional baseball which cost him his career. Flood, too, stood on principle declaring, "A slave is a slave even if he is a one hundred thousand dollars a year slave." The actions of these athletes, particularly Ali and Flood, would make it possible for later generations of African-American athletes in professional boxing, basketball, football, and baseball to garner multi-million dollar salaries, rights, and privileges that were only dreams for the earlier black athletes.

On the international scene the proposed boycott of the 1968 Summer Games made a dramatic statement and drew attention to the plight of people of color under racism in the United States and the apartheid regime in South Africa. The boycott actually began as the idea of African nations. Two years earlier, through the Organization of African Unity and the Supreme Council for Sport in Africa, African countries started sending signals that they were seriously contemplating boycotting the 1968 Olympics if South Africa was allowed to participate. A small number of black American athletes also took up the cry of boycott. One of them was Harry Edwards, who at that time was an assistant professor at San Jose State University. He organized the "Olympic Project for Human Rights" (OPHR). It was not called the "1968 Olympic boycott" movement. Neither was the 1963 "March on Washington" simply that; it was the "March on Washington for Jobs and Freedom." The Black Panther Party was, in fact, named the "Black Panther Party for Self Defense." Full names often suggest a different perspective than presented in the media. This was significant; black folk were very sensitive about the accuracy of names, and for good historical reasons. Harry Edwards's aim was to politicize the black athlete and muster American public opinion and support the boycott and an end to racism and oppression at home and abroad. The efforts on the part of the African nations, black and white athletes in the United States, and many countries throughout the world, forced the International Olympic Committee to reverse its decision. On April 21, 1968, it rescinded the invitation to South Africa to participate in the XIX Olympiad in Mexico.

African nations, with victory in hand, participated in the XIX Olympiad. The OPHR, however, was only partially satisfied. Its mandate was twofold, and the issue of inequality in the United States remained unresolved and not addressed. Edwards proposed that black American athletes go forward with the plan to boycott the Games. The number of enthusiastic supporters of an American or black American boycott of the Olympics was drastically reduced when the issue over South Africa's participation was settled. Nevertheless, Harry Edwards, putting on virtually a one man crusade, kept the boycott threat alive.

The setting at Mexico City, and the athletes' response to it, reflected the level of political consciousness or lack thereof among the Olympians and the efforts made to keep them uninformed. Athletes as a group have been accused of political insensitivity. The very nature of organized sports, with its militaristic posture and a player-coach relationship resembling a dictatorship, discouraged political activism. If there was any level of political awareness among the Olympians, the situation in Mexico should have brought it to the surface. Political oppression in Mexico was rampant. Mexican student groups had been protesting throughout much of 1968. In part, their protest was against the forthcoming Olympics. A growing number of Mexicans were angry about their nation's expenditure of two hundred million dollars in construction of the Olympic village and other facilities while poverty, hunger, and illiteracy abounded in their country. Eight days before the Games were to begin, a clash between ten thousand demonstrators and the Mexican military left twenty-six of the protesters dead and one hundred wounded after the troops opened fire on them with automatic weapons.

Working against the proposed black American boycott of the Games were many forces, in addition to the U.S. Olympic Committee and the IOC, as one might have expected. Jesse Owens, a member of the USOC, spoke passionately against the proposed boycott and, ironic from a historical perspective, asserted that "politics and sports were incompatible." Stan Wright, an assistant track coach of the U.S. Olympic team, and himself black, lambasted the proposed black boycott of the Games and predicted its failure. The black Olympic boycott movement garnered more rhetorical than organizational support. The OPHR had only a hand full of active members, among them Tommie Smith, John Carlos, Lee Evans, and Harry Edwards. There were those who asserted that "most black athletes have been solidly against Smith and Edwards and their plan to use the Olympics as a platform to dramatize their grievances at home." Black Olympians Mel Pinder and Bob Beamon and black women Olympic athletes were staunchly anti boycott. The OPHR made practically no effort to consider the opinions and gain the support of the black women athletes. There were factors here that corresponded with what was a general pattern of treatment of women within the Civil Rights Movement. The new works on Fannie Lou Hamer, Ella Baker, Elaine Brown of the Black Panther Party, and others, demonstrated this. The gender issue has always been there as Barbara Sizemore argued. Wyomia Tyus, holder of five world records in track and a gold medal winner in 1964, remarked that the black male athletes never invited the black female athletes to attend their meetings. Jarvis Scott, a competitor in the 400-meter run, said that she supported the aims of the OPHR, but not the boycott. Scott added that she and other black women on the U.S. team were "most disappointed that our feelings were not brought out; while the men issued statements and held conferences, finding out what

we felt was only a last minute thing." Even in the case of an Evans
or a Carlos, or a Smith, it was difficult to believe that they, after
years of training and sacrifice with the goal of obtaining an Olympic
gold medal, would boycott the Games.

As the start of the Games grew nearer, the ranks of even possible
boycotters grew thinner. The black athletes assured the coaching
staff and the press that they had no intentions of boycotting. When
the press confronted Harry Edwards with this information, he made
the best out of an otherwise dismal organizational failure. Students
of rhetoric and political culture will appreciate Edwards's response.
He told the press that what the athletes were doing was in keeping
with an agreed upon strategy to create an atmosphere of confusion
for the U.S. Olympic Committee. "If I were you," Edwards said, "I
wouldn't believe everything we say. If you believe me now, that's
beautiful, and if you don't that's still beautiful. You can choose to
believe what you want to and disregard the rest. The boycott is still
alive." It was not. The Olympic events proceeded on schedule and
the black athletes competed. The proposed black boycott became, in
the final analysis, a few symbolic yet powerful gestures. Some black
Olympians wore black socks during their heats. The major incident
occurred when Tommie Smith and John Carlos, wearing black socks
and one black glove each, gave a *Black Power* salute on the victor's
stand after receiving their medals for taking first and third place in
the two-hundred meter run. Theirs was a relatively mild demonstration, and giving the black power salute was a last minute decision.
Immediately after the incident, John Carlos said to reporters that
the salute they gave on the stand—Smith with his right arm extended with black gloved clinched fist and Carlos with his left arm
extended with black gloved clinched fist—symbolized a U for black
unity. Another and more likely explanation why each wore only one
glove was that they were only able to obtain one pair of black
gloves owing to the last minute nature of their demonstration. At
any rate, their symbolic gesture was not intended as a revolutionary
action. Tommie Smith said, "As far as the black fists, it was very
quiet. We wanted black people to see, especially the young guys, to
have something to be proud of, to identify themselves with."[11]

Yet their action drew the wrath of the U.S. government and the
official reprimand of the U.S. Olympic Committee, and the International Olympic Committee. Smith and Carlos were expelled from
the Games. Neither runner would find professional athletics wel-
coming him to the fold. The reaction of other African-American athletes at the XIX Olympiad was revealing yet predictable. They took,
like the majority of humankind does, a centrists posture. The ac-

tions of human response run the gamut from radical to conservative but most fall somewhere in the middle ground. The majority of the black Olympians fell into the middle category. Black athletes at the Mexico City Games failed to take united action regarding the expulsion of Carlos and Smith. A few denounced their expulsion and a petition was circulated, but little else happened. Black Olympians sympathized with what happened to Smith and Carlos and with the problems facing black America and the Third World. But, like Bob Beamon, Ralph Boston, Wyomia Tyus, and the majority of African Americans, they adopted a centrist position. There was also the anti-protest demonstration of George Foreman at the Games who, after winning the gold medal in boxing, paraded around the ring totting a miniature American flag. The political stratification exemplified by the black athletes at the XIX Olympiad mirrored black American political consciousness: the activists, the sympathizers, the silent majority, and the anti-activists or conservative right wing. Fortunately, the 1968 Olympic boycott movement was more than the sum of its parts. The legacy of those Games was a heightened awareness and exposure of the intersection of sport and politics, the black athlete and the Civil Rights Movement.

THE CIVIL RIGHTS FRONT AND BEYOND

The Civil Rights Movement in America did not materialize overnight. The protests of the 1950s and 1960s were the results of many generations of African-American frustration. The movement was a tumultuous episode in the ongoing war against racism and all of its manifestations as African Americans and their supporters bought new vitality, determination, and strategies to the struggle. The National Association for the Advancement of Colored People played a crucial role as it challenged and won many imperative legal battles against the old nemeses, *Jim Crow* and the *color line*. In 1915, the civil rights organization won a Supreme Court decision that invalidated the Grandfather Clause. This was an important step forward for black participation in government and the electoral process. In 1927, the NAACP won a stellar Supreme Court decision against the all-white primary. The most important of the organization's victories was the *Brown Decision* of 1954, the so-called Topeka, Kansas decision. The foundation for the landmark victory had begun many years earlier with the work of NAACP lead-council, Charles H. Houston, who masterminded a string of lower court victories that whittled away at the infamous "separate but equal" doctrine that was the law of the land. Houston did not live to see the end result of his efforts. His able assistant, who became a legal giant in his own right, shepherded the work to ultimate victory in the *Brown Decision*. That singularly significant court ruling was made possible by the brilliant arguments of NAACP lead-attorney, Thurgood Marshall, and the assistance of academic experts including historian John Hope Franklin and psychologist Kenneth B. Clarke. Franklin assisted in chronicling the historical record of the racial divide. Clarke measured and demonstrated the negative psychological impact of racism on African Americans with his "Doll Test" where young black children were shown white and black dolls and asked to identify the one that was "most beautiful," "the smartest," "had the best hair," "acted the best," and finally, "which doll would you rather have." In virtually every instance the black children picked the white doll over the black doll. The solid legal, historical, and psychological arguments were not enough. Supreme Court Chief Justice Earl Warren worked long and hard behind the scenes to persuade his fellow justices of the court to render a unanimous decision reversing *Plessy v Ferguson* and finding segregated facilities inherently unequal thus declaring the illegality of segregation and the doctrine of "separate but equal." While the *Brown Decision* dealt specifically with segregated schools its implications were far broader and included educational, transportation, hospitals, public rest rooms, and other public facilities.

On the direct action protest front, A Philip Randolph and other supporters took on the issue of discrimination by threatening a march on Washington in 1941 to dramatize unfair treatment against African Americans in the public and private sectors. This march never took place because the reaction of the administration of Franklin D. Roosevelt took positive action in forming the Fair Employment Practices Commission. The commission was mandated to examine the issues and complaints and make policy changes as required. Randolph's near march on Washington was one of the early and important salvos across the bow of the nation in what would be a long and circuitous track of nonviolent direct action. Shortly after his near march and taking a cue from Randolph, the Congress of Racial Equality (CORE) was founded in 1942 in Chicago. James Farmer, a student of the tactics of nonviolent direct action, was the new organization's founding director. CORE ushered in the era of the "ins" — the sit-ins, walk-ins, lay-ins, wade-ins, the freedom rides. CORE was dedicated to desegregating public facilities and was itself a racially integrated organization.

The Civil Rights Movement had, indeed, been going on long before the heralded Montgomery Bus Boycott of 1955–56, which has been so often cited as the beginning of the modern Civil Rights Movement. The *Brown Decision* of 1954, and the brutal murder of Emmett Till in Mississippi in 1955, motivated black America to action. The Montgomery Bus Boycott was important and should not be in anyway depreciated for the dramatic change it helped to usher in. However, the boycott, specifically bus boycotts of public transportation, was nothing new. There had been at least twenty substantial bus boycott efforts prior to Montgomery: in Baton Rogue, Louisiana; Tallahassee, Florida; Vicksburgh, Mississippi; Harlem, New York; and other points in the nation. Nevertheless it was Montgomery that put the movement before the people on a scale unprecedented prior to this time. The victory came with the Supreme Court ruling November 13, 1956, that Montgomery's segregated bus service was unconstitutional. Thus too the *Brown Decision* was having an impact, stimulating activism and the nation to rethink its laws and policies and practices as related to the treatment of its black citizenry.

Viewing the Montgomery Bus Boycott as a spontaneous act of heroism on the part of Rosa Parks limits the appreciation of the boycott's and the Civil Rights Movement's intellectual depth. It was a nice story to tell of Parks, a simple black woman who one day decides that she has had enough and, when ordered to give up her seat to a white man and move to the Negro section at the rear of the bus, fights back. The bus driver stopped the bus, called the police and Parks was arrested. The defiant action on her part was courageous but was only part of the story. Rosa Parks was more than just a citizen who one day had enough. She was that but she was also a field secretary for the NAACP in Montgomery who had worked for years with Fred Shuttlesworth and E. D. Nixon. They had discussed a planned course of action to challenge the segregationist laws of Montgomery in the new light of the *Brown Decision*. With the arrest of Parks, the plan was implemented and the bus boycott began. Who would head the endeavor, however, was a concern. A charismatic leader was basic to the success of the boycott, someone who could articulate the goals and strategy, and speak to the heart of the issue and inspire the common black folk, whose participation and support of the boycott was absolutely essential for success. Nixon, Shuttlesworth, Parks were convinced that present leadership in Montgomery would not suffice. There were questions about the loyalty of that leadership and who it actually represented. Furthermore, the old guard seemed to be tied to the establishment. A fresh and spirited voice was required and a visiting assistant pastor whom many felt had the charisma, the foresight, the youthful energy, the understanding, and the education to be a good spokesperson, was approached. That young minister was Martin Luther King, Jr. He was beseeched to come and speak to a rally being held that evening to start off the boycott and to explain to the people the objective and to strengthen their resolve. King raised serious doubts to the delegation about his capability to do all that was being asked. Furthermore, he said, he had no speech prepared. He was assured that he need only speak extemporaneously and briefly. King, with many reservations, nevertheless took on this challenge to speak. The rest, as they say, is history. What was to have been a ten or fifteen minute address to the several hundred gathered in and outside of the church became a much longer and powerful oration punctuated with thunderous applause, call and response, and repeated amens. King's from-the-heart sermon was brilliant. It was a clarion call to civil rights arms to the Montgomery African-American community. They were now completely dedicated to the boycott. King had galvanized them. The Montgomery Improvement Association was formed and the young minister was chosen to be its president. King was now the voice of the Montgomery movement and, unbeknownst to him at that time, his would become the preeminent voice of the modern Civil Rights Movement.

The Montgomery Bus Boycott was a brilliant show of unity. Empty buses rolled by as black folks walked along the streets to get from place to place. Blacks formed caravans with those who owned automobiles to take others to their destinations. You could pay a nickel or, if you had no money, ride for free. Everyone gave help and support. With African Americans no longer taking the bus the impact was devastating to the bus line. It was a marvelous demonstration of black pride and organization, and an effective use of collective strength. When the boycott successfully concluded and the *Jim Crow* policies of the bus company struck down, blacks were there that glorious first day to take their seats at the front of the buses. Rosa Parks and Martin Luther King, Jr. were there riding in the front of the bus. For months following the victory, when black folk rode the buses, no one seemed willing to ride in the back of the bus, even when the front was full and plentiful seating available in the rear. Buses passed with African Americans either sitting or standing crowded in the front. They savored the victory. More importantly, a lesson was learned in Montgomery: that economics matter and nonviolent direct action works.

Taking the lessons of Montgomery and applying them on a larger scale in the South, the Southern Christian Leadership Conference was formed in 1957. Playing a key role in the founding of SCLC and later in the Student Nonviolent Coordinating Committee (SNCC), was Ella Baker, one of the most trusted and ablest civil rights organizers. Women like her, Septima Clark, and Fannie Lou Hamer of Mississippi, were pivotal in gaining grassroots support for the movement. SCLC used a particular strategy most effectively: the media, and especially television, to expose America's racism and to hopefully shame the nation into reforming. America watched on television as peaceful civil rights demonstrators were viciously beaten and jailed. They watched SCLC's efforts to desegregate Birmingham, Alabama in 1963, and witnessed the police brutalize the demonstrators with clubs, dogs, cattle prods, and high pressure water hoses. They saw pregnant women and children trampled by policemen on horseback and black citizens whipped with night sticks as they knelt in prayer. At the dinner hour, on national television, the media brought the issue home to America. President John F. Kennedy, together with Vice President Lyndon Johnson, and Attorney General Robert Kennedy, sat horrified watching the televised news report of the events in Birmingham. The virulence and barbarity of racism in this nation could not be denied as the whole world watched.

African Americans, since the founding of this country, have been a profound embarrassment to America's institutions and processes. The Civil Rights Movement laid bare the duality and duplicity that was America. Racism was and is the most glaring contradiction to the American proclamation of freedom and equality and human rights. The *Declaration of Independence* and the *Bill of Rights* lose luster in the face of slavery's legacy. Racism and the doctrine of democracy should not be compatible concepts. Martin Luther King, Jr., more than any other leader of the twentieth century, made America come face to face with its contradictions and with its racism. The Civil Rights Movement demanded that the nation live up to the great tenets it professed. As King liked to say, "Democracy is a promise of equality to be shared by all Americans." King thus was much more than a protester, a rebel rouser, a leader of a ban of disgruntled Negro citizens. He was a voice, a lightning rod, a theoretician and a student of America's history who knew his country, and its principles, well enough to chastise it: "Ever since the birth of our nation, white America has had a schizophrenic personality on the question of race. She has been torn between selves—a self in which she proudly professed the great principles of democracy and a self in which she sadly practiced the antithesis of democracy. This tragic duality has produced a strange indecisiveness and ambivalence toward the Negro, causing America to take a step backward simultaneously with every step forward on the question of racial justice, to be at önce attracted to the Negro and repelled by him. To love and to hate him. There has never been a solid, unified and determined thrust to make justice a reality for Afro-Americans." These were King's words shortly before his assassination in 1968. They symbolized the thrust of the Civil Rights Movement and its call for American consistency and an end to racism.

The strategy of nonviolent direct action that King and SCLC utilized was as old as America. King knew and articulated the antecedents in a speech to the National Jewish Committee in 1965 making the distinction between what SCLC and the movement were doing as compared to Thoreau's civil disobedience owing to his opposition to the Mexican War and refusal to pay his taxes in protest. As King said, blacks were not defying law when they opposed segregation and racism. The law, the Constitution, the *Brown Decision*, and the Civil Rights Act of 1964 were on the side of African Americans. "It is the segregationists," King explained, "who defy and break the law."

The philosophy of nonviolent direct action that King espoused had as its original architect Mahatma Gandhi of India. A strong tie, spiritually, intellectually, and strategically, existed between the American Civil Rights Movement and the movement that Gandhi orchestrated earlier in India. The American Civil Rights Movement should be embraced as part of a world wide movement to challenge colonialism, to challenge racism, discrimination, mistreatment, and any denial of basic humanity and the rights of the individual as a human being residing on the planet earth. Gandhi was the leading purveyor of the universality of the civil rights thrust. This great architect of nonviolent direct action was born October 2, 1869, in Sudamapuri, India. He experienced hardship and difficulty all his life and showed a reform spirit at an early age. As a youngster, he experimented intellectually and challenged "tradition." In his teens, Gandhi spoke out against child marriage, a Hindu and Moslem custom. He himself was forced to marry at the age of thirteen, a tradition that he would continue to oppose. Although his marriage was one of great success, he nevertheless felt that the practice of child marriage was unfair to both parties. As a youth, he once experimented with the eating of meat. Some Indians believed that the eating of meat made the British strong. Gandhi grew up and came of age in an India under British control. As a youngster, he thought the British seemed taller and stronger than the Indians. They were in charge and he wanted an explanation why. In the simple reasoning of a child he decided that it must have been because they ate meat.

Strict Hindus and Moslems were vegetarians, as was Gandhi, but he and a friend decided to experiment. They saved a few coins and bought meat and at their secret hiding place cooked it as best they could. They ate meat the entire day with the predictable end result of severe nausea, upset stomachs, and vomiting. As a result, Gandhi drew his own conclusion regarding meat and decided to refrain from eating it. He followed his vegetarian ways with strong conviction. Gandhi was a strong willed youngster and a free thinker who questioned right and wrong, a practice he continued throughout his life.

He was not particularly fond of going to school but grasped the importance of education and was an excellent student. Mahatma Gandhi graduated from high school in 1887 and enrolled in Samaldas College in his home province. He moved on successfully to pursue the study of law in England. After completing that training in 1890, he spent a short stint in Paris. His stay there was helpful in shaping his thinking because, in the late nineteenth and early part of the twentieth century, Paris was a place of great intellectual exchange, cafes, pamphleteers, soapbox speakers and street corner philosophers who shared ideas about the world around them, from questions of moral philosophy and law to colonialism and human rights. After his Paris education he traveled to South Africa in 1893 to defend a client, Abdulah Sheth, a Moslem businessman. Gandhi remained in South Africa for eighteen years. He learned much there and South Africa learned much of him and his emerging spirit of colonial defiance. Gandhi could not fathom the situation in South Africa. On his way to Durban, South Africa, he received a taste of apartheid or *Jim Crow,* South African style, when forced to give up his coach compartment and ride in a rear car because he was Indian. Gandhi argued with the conductor, but to no avail. Despite having paid for first class accommodations, they were not granted to him. He was experiencing in that incident what African Americans always experienced. No matter what your resources, you were still a second-class citizen because of your race and were thereby subjected to segregation and many other forms of mistreatment. Gandhi protested in every instance of mistreatment. He repeatedly took on the South African system during his years in that country. He orchestrated and led the massive march to protest injustices against Indians. After the 1913 march, he was jailed for several months. His march, however, was successful and after long negotiations between General Smuts and Gandhi, an agreement was reached on June 30, 1914. This agreement became the Indian Relief Act which bestowed certain rights to Indian laborers.

Gandhi left Africa in 1914 for India, where he believed that he was much needed. After all, it was home. In South Africa he had mastered the strategy of *Satyagraha* or "truth force." Gandhi believed that truth and the power of love could overcome injustice, inequity, discrimination, and racism. In *Satyagraha* one peacefully but firmly challenged the thinking, assumptions and system of inequality and institutional racism by exposing and refusing to conform to injustices that denied basic human rights and dignity. Through nonviolent, determined, dignified objection and noncompliance with the colonial system of oppression one could, Gandhi taught, attain the basic human rights entitled and be elevated to equal citizenship. With *Satyagraha* he took on the Raj, as the British were called in India, and used the tactic successfully in hundreds of protests including the Great Salt March of 1930. The British had declared it illegal for Indians to take water from the ocean and make their own salt. The colonial government declared its monopoly and control over the sea and salt. Gandhi refused to accept this proposition against what he called a "God given" human right, and led a march to the sea to take salt in defiance of British rule. The Indian demonstrators were savagely beaten but won their right in the end to the sea and its salt.

Gandhi's tactics of nonviolent resistance reached oppressed people throughout the world. In 1929, a group of African Americans led by Mordecai Johnson of Howard University and successor groups, in 1937, led by Benjamin Mays, President of Morehouse College, visited Gandhi to learn first hand of the Mahatma's philosophy and technique of *Satyagraha*. Nonviolent direct action was nothing new when striking automobile workers in Flint, Michigan used it, or when students at New York University used the technique, or when A. Philip Randolph used it in his near march on Washington. It was certainly nothing new when Martin Luther King, Jr. and others employed it in Montgomery, Alabama.[12]

King was unquestionably the leading architect and user of nonviolent direct action in America. He was a student of philosophy and reform ideas. The intellectual component behind King and the movement was a strong one. Very often African-American initiatives were branded as spontaneous and without in-depth thought and study. This premise was absolutely without merit, especially concerning King, SCLC, and the Civil Rights Movement. They were students of history and protest thought and keenly knowledgeable of the world around them and those individuals and organizations prior to them who battled for freedom and equality. In his youth, King read constantly and absorbed his mother's and his minister father's philosophy of humanity and strength of religious conviction.

Martin Luther King, Jr. built on this foundation with formal education at Morehouse College, later at Crozier Theological Seminary, and finally at Boston University, where he earned his doctorate in theology. He read, pondered, discussed, dissected, and learned. King was particularly impressed with the work and ideas of Walter Rauschenbush, and especially his book, *Christianity and the Social Crisis*. Rauschenbush was a minister and social gospeler who worked in Hell's Kitchen in New York City and professed that society must transform itself into a heaven here on earth for all of its people. Each person, in his view, was entitled to a dignified way of life, good treatment, and opportunity. The pressing survival needs of people, Rauschenbush asserted, could not wait for the goodness of the hereafter. King was moved by this philosophy and the practicality and useful power of religion which, he liked to say in the Rauschenbusch tradition, must be taken into the streets. "Jesus," Rauschenbusch and King proclaimed, "was a revolutionary."

King weighed and at times doubted nonviolent direct action, although it seemed the best course to follow. He wrote that the turning of the other cheek philosophy and loving your enemies was only valid when individuals were in conflict with other individuals. When racial groups and nations were in conflict, King reasoned, a more realistic approach was necessary. Then he heard Mordecai Johnson speak on the life and teachings of Mahatma Gandhi. This moved King to a deeper understanding of Gandhi's beliefs and the power of love. One fateful and difficult day in Montgomery, during the heat of the bus boycott, the various philosophies and teachings came together for him. He came home late one night, tired as usual but unable to sleep, to the ringing of the phone. He answered it and there on the other end was an ugly voice, filled with hate. The caller told him in substance, "Nigger, we are going to kill you and blow up your house. Kill your wife and children." King recounted putting down the phone and at that moment, shaking, although he had received many such calls and threats before and would receive many more. But the one that evening unnerved him and he went into the kitchen and made himself a cup of coffee, thinking that the coffee might give him some relief. He recalled vividly how the stress was gripping him and he finally fell to his knees and prayed for strength. Some have written about this instance as the "epiphany of the coffee cup" where King drew upon an inner strength and made an iron clad commitment with God that the movement go forward, that his own life was secondary, and that he was forever unshakably committed to the course of nonviolent direct action. King had in a sense been reborn to the movement.

King remained true to the commitment, the boycott, and the coming years of struggle. Make no mistake about it; this was a brave individual. To live under the daily threat of death and to keep the dream and the movement going was no easy task. It was an heroic output; a commitment that in the end cost King his life. He had no greater day than the 1963 March on Washington for Jobs and Freedom and his famous "I Have A Dream" speech. King's dream was a simple one, simple in the sense that it was a call for fairness, a call for equality, a call for an end to racism, and a call for America to stop *pretending* to be the land of justice for all, and to live up to its claim. Unforgettable were his words envisioning a nation where all of its citizens would be "judged by the content of their character rather than the color of their skin." That dream resonated as more of a desperate plea in a nation that, in that same year, witnessed the church bombing that took the lives of four little girls in Birmingham; and Medgar Evers, the leader of the NAACP in Jackson, shot in the back and killed.

Other more radical voices on the scene in the 1960s offered alternative strategies to nonviolent direct action for the progress of the race. The spirit of the new forces at work, the tensions, the harsher challenges to racism, the system, the society, and even calling to task those who offered the hand of friendship to African Americans, was symbolized in Amiri Baraka's genre poem, "Black Art." The poem captured with bitterness, biting sarcasm, and scathing language, the emerging revolutionary spirit and blanket demand for immediate change and empowerment of the black community. It gave a flavor of the period and the times and the gloves-off approach that many young blacks began to embrace.

"BLACK ART"

Poems are bullshit unless they are
teeth or trees or lemons piled
on a step. Or black ladies dying
of men leaving nickel hearts beating them down. Fuck poems
and they are useful, they shoot
come at you, love what you are,
breathe like wrestlers, or shudder
strangely after pissing. We want live
words of the hip world live flesh &
coursing blood. Hearts Brains
Souls splintering fire. We want poems
like fists beating niggers out of Jocks
or dagger poems in the slimy bellies

of the owner-jews. Black poems to
smear on girlemamma mulatto bitches
whose brains are red jelly stuck between 'lizabeth taylor's toes.
Stinking Whores! We want "poems that kill."
Assassin poems, Poems that shoot
guns. Poems that wrestle cops into alleys
and take their weapons leaving them dead
with tongues pulled out and sent to Ireland. Knockoff
poems for dope selling wops or slick halfwhite
politicians Airplane poems. rrrrrrrrrrrrrrrrrrrr
rrrrrrrrrrrrrrr.... tuhtuhtuhtuhtuhtuhtuhtuhtuhtuh
....rrrrrrrrrrrrrrrr....Setting fire and death to
whites ass. Look at the Liberal
Spokesman for the jews clutch his throat
& puke himself into eternity....rrrrrrrrrr
There's a negroleader pinned to
a bar stool in Sardi's eyeballs melting
in hot flame. Another negroleader
on the steps of the white house one
kneeling between the sheriff's thighs
negotiating cooly for his people.
Aggh...stumbles across the room...
Put it on him, poem. Strip him naked
to the world! Another bad poem cracking
steel knuckles in a jewlady's mouth
Poem scream poison gas on beasts in green berets
Clean out the world for virtue and love,
Let there be no love poems written
until love can exist freely and
cleanly. Let Black People understand
that they are the lovers and the sons
of lovers and warriors and sons
of warriors Are poems & poets &
all the loveliness here in the world

We want a black poem. And a
Black World.
Let the world be a Black Poem
And Let All Black People Speak This Poem
Silently

or LOUD

In "Black Art" was heard a call for abandonment of what had been a fruitful coalition between blacks and some segments of the Jewish community. Jews played a major role in the Civil Rights Movement, but that did not erase the longstanding tensions between blacks and Jews on the home front, in the apartment buildings, in the local stores, in the establishments that Jews owned and that did business with blacks. On the daily level, for the average black person, there were more negatives than positives in their relationship with Jews who were shop owners and landlords. The relationship between blacks and Jews simply was often no different from that between blacks and Anglo whites. Angry young blacks, like Baraka, viewed the relationship from a different and critical perspective as had Malcolm X, years earlier.

In the summer of 1966 a new movement burst onto the national scene that further contributed to and symbolized the widening gap in traditional alliances between blacks and liberal whites: the *Black Power* Movement. Black youth were beginning to see Martin Luther King, Jr. as too conservative. He was being challenged from fringe groups, very similar to Gandhi who also did not become more radical. As a consequence, Gandhi was killed by the far left, the Godse, discontented radical Hindus who claimed love for Gandhi but in order to radicalize the movement concluded that the nonviolent Gandhi had to be removed, and in 1948 assassinated him. King's leadership was being increasingly challenged from the growing leftist movement. RAM, the Revolutionary Action Movement, led by Robert Williams, openly urged the radicalizing of the Civil Rights Movement beyond the nonviolent direction of King, Roy Wilkins, and Whitney Young.

An increasingly angrier black America seemed receptive to the widening call for *Black Power*. The idea of black power was nothing new. *Black Power* gained a great deal of press coverage in the late 1960s. Its message was black unity, business ownership, economic and political solidarity and independence, block voting; in short, black control of the black community as Malcolm X, Marcus Garvey, Martin Delany, E. P. McCabe, and others urged blacks to do long before. In the sixties, the name Malcolm X personified the ideology of *Black Power*. The disciple of Elijah Muhammad, and national minister for the Nation of Islam, could be heard regularly on the Nation's radio station broadcast from the organization's headquarters in Chicago. There were three ingredients to *Black Power* and although Malcolm X never explicitly used the term *Black Power* he, indeed, meant it and its essence of black empowerment and black nationalism which had to be accomplished, Malcolm admonished, "By any means necessary."

It was Stokely Carmichael, an intellectually astute student of Malcolm's ideas, who became best known for *Black Power*. "Stokely" was born in Trinidad. He came of age in New York and Washington D.C., receiving a bachelor's degree from Howard University in 1964. During and after his college days, he was actively involved with civil rights organizations such as the Student Nonviolent Coordinating Committee (SNCC). In 1966, he was voted chairman of that organization. Carmichael was one of the principal organizers of the Lowdes County Freedom Organization in Alabama. That organization would help give birth to what became known as the Black Panther Party. Their full name was the Black Panther Party for Self Defense. The Panthers, founded by Huey P. Newton and Bobby Seale, were headquartered in Oakland, California. The organization advocated armed resistance against the white power structure, and would be involved in numerous bloody shoot-outs with the Oakland Police Department. In 1967, Stokely Carmichael traveled extensively throughout Africa and the Third World. He returned to the United States to organize the first Black United Front in Washington, D.C., and from 1968 to 1969 he served in a leadership role in the Black Panther Party. He and his wife, Miriam MaKeba, moved to Guinea in 1970. Stokely returned to the United States in the 1980s, but remained a citizen of the world in formulating his own All-African Peoples' Party and pushing for the adoption of a new version of socialism throughout the black world. "Ready for the revolution," was Stokely's signature admonition for the remainder of his life.

The original road to *Black Power* was for a relatively easy one for Stokely. He read Frantz Fanon, Garvey, Delany, Turner, Du Bois, and drunk most deeply of Malcolm. Stokely's advocacy of *Black Power* was on the fast track by 1966. That summer brought the perfect opportunity to thrust it onto the national scene with the attempted assassination of James Meredith.

Meredith, who had been the first black to attend the University of Mississippi, decided to lead a one man march through the back areas of Mississippi to the capitol in Jackson to promote black voter registration and civil rights. This one man march was typical of Meredith who was always something of a loner who took on issues single-handedly. On his trek to Jackson during primary election week he had hardly begun when he was shot by a would-be assassin. Black leaders hearing of this flew in from all parts of the country to be at his bedside. Floyd McKissick, national director of CORE, rushed to the hospital. Stokely Carmichael came as did other black leaders, including Dr. Martin Luther King, Jr. They beseeched Meredith to allow them to continue his march because the march was now larger than any single individual. Meredith agreed.

Within a day, ten thousand demonstrators gathered to continue the march to Jackson. It was a united campaign of blacks and whites together to dramatize the moment and the hope. Along the trek, however, there were words of division. The most telling came during the singing of "We Shall Overcome." King, way at the head of the march, heard changes to the familiar stanzas. "We Shall Overcome" became "We Shall Overrun." The stanza "blacks and whites together" was replaced with four-letter expletives ending with chants of "Ungawa, *Black Power!*" King found these elements objectionable and called a momentary respite and sent word for all leaders to meet with him at a near-by farm house there in Yazoo County. King's concern was particularly directed at Stokely, who he knew was one of the young Turks responsible for the *Black Power* advocacy. What King wanted, King got. Respecting his leadership and wishes, all agreed to refrain from any further discord, at least until completion of the march. The word was circulated and the march resumed, reaching Jackson without any other incidents. As speakers took to the steps of the capitol building to proclaim the victory in hand and what needed to be done in terms of registration, there was a widespread chant for Stokely to take center stage. "Where is Stokely? We want to hear from Stokely." King and others discretely left the scene. After repeated calls of "Stoke, Stoke, Stoke," he came to the platform and electrified the crowd with his sentiments. "The only way we goin' stop them white men from whipping us upside our heads is to take over," he exclaimed. "We've been saying freedom for six years, and we ain't got nothing. What we're going start saying now is *Black Power*. And there is nothing, nothing wrong with anything all-black, because I am black, and I am beautiful. Now don't you be afraid. And from now on when they ask you what do you want. You know what to tell them." The crowd replied in unison with repeated chants of "*Black Power, Black Power, Black Power!*"

It was a feeding frenzy for the national press. They reported that a new radical element had taken over the Civil Rights Movement. King was on the way out, they suggested, and the radical and more vociferous younger members were advocating a new black separatism. What they wanted, in fact, was neither new nor truly separatist. It was a call for African-American empowerment. The Civil Rights Movement was not, at this time, split down the middle as the media pundits reported. The movement was, as it should, giving vent to different points of view, which it always had. It was falsely reported that Martin Luther King, Jr. opposed Stokely and the ad-

vocates of *Black Power*. King believed in many of the tenets of
Black Power. He, however, found problematic the slogans of the
Black Power Movement and what he saw as a divisive element in
that movement. King argued that many of the white supporters of
the Civil Rights Movement would be excluded. He did not, for example, wish to alienate Jewish allies. He was a pragmatist and believed it politically unwise to disgorge one's friends rather than
building alliances. While he was critical of the slogan *Black Power*,
he was not critical of the ideal and stated this opinion in his book,
Where Do We Go From Here?: "It was my contention that a leader
has to be concerned about the problem of semantics. Each word, I
said, has a denotative meaning, its explicit and recognized sense and
a connotative meaning, its suggestive sense. While the concept of legitimate *Black Power* might be denotatively sound, the slogan *Black
Power* carried the wrong connotations. I mentioned the implications
of violence that the press had already attached to the phrase and I
went on to say that some of the rash statements on the part of a few
marchers only reinforced this impression." King goes on to use the
Jews as an example. He suggested that no one has ever heard the
Jews publicly chant a slogan of Jewish power, but through group
unity, determination, and creative endeavor they have gained it. The
same is true of the Irish and Italians, he said. Neither group has
used a slogan of Irish or Italian power but they have worked hard
and achieved it and Negroes, he advises, should do the same. King
concludes: "we must use every constructive means to amass economic and political power. This is the kind of legitimate power we
need. We must work to build racial pride and refute the notion that
black is evil and ugly. But this must come through a program not
merely through a slogan."

King defended the *Black Power* advocates such as Stokely. He re-
buked the critics, saying: "The Black Power slogan did not spring full
grown from the head of some philosophical Zeus. It was born from
the wounds of despair and disappointment. It is a cry of daily hurt
and persistent pain. For centuries the Negro has been caught in the
tentacles of white power. Many Negroes have given up faith in the
white majority because white power with total control has left them
empty handed. So in reality the call for black power is a reaction to
the failure of white power." As for Stokely, King lamented, "he is a
young man whose anger stems from his disappointment with the nation's failure" to do the right thing and that "he as a dedicated vet-
eran of many battles and has seen with his own eyes the most brutal
white violence against Negroes and white civil rights workers and he
has seen it go unpunished."[13]

Moreover, King was sympathetic to and in agreement with the disenchantment of *Black Power* advocates who pointed out the inconsistencies in the militaristic posture of the government and the war in Vietnam. "Over the last decade they have seen America applauding nonviolence whenever the Negroes have practiced it," King wrote. "They have watched it being praised in the sit-in movements of 1960, in the freedom rides of 1961, in the Albany movement of 1962, in the Birmingham movement of 1963, and in the Selma movement of 1965. These same black young men and women have watched as America sends black young men to burn Vietnamese with napalm, to slaughter men, women and children, and they wonder what kind of nation it is that applauds nonviolence whenever Negroes face white people in the streets of the United States but then applauds violence and burning and death when these same Negroes are sent to the fields of Vietnam." King's objection to the war in Vietnam was an issue even his closest advisors urged him to avoid in order to protect their positive relationship with the Johnson administration. King, however, felt strongly the moral imperative and that anyone who claimed to be a moral leader had to speak out against the war in Vietnam. Most respected African-American leaders opposed the war. King had much in common with many of the so-called more radical black leaders. They all wanted uplift for the African-American population, equality, justice, equal opportunities, and empowerment. The Black Muslims wanted the same thing. The Black Panthers wanted the same thing. Unlike King, however, they did not profess a commitment to nonviolent means to attain their goals.

The divergent strategies and radicalizing of the movement reflected the growing discontent within black America that erupted in the late 1960s in the nation's cities. Most texts will point to 1965 and the riots in the Watts section of Los Angeles as the beginning of a tumultuous string of violent summers that continued until 1968. In point of fact, the eruptions began a year earlier. Harlem, not surprisingly, was the first to erupt. The once affluent Mecca of black America had become the most recognizable ghetto in the country. Harlem was no stranger to race riots. The riots there in 1935 and 1943 were still vivid in the memories of the community's older residents and the precipitating factors now were much the same as they were then: unemployment and police brutality. The Harlem Riot of July 1964 ignited as a result of yet another act of police brutality and ended with one person dead and one hundred injured. Rioting followed in Rochester and Philadelphia that same summer. Two were killed and three hundred injured in the Philadelphia clash. Fair to suggest, there were substantial indicators of the depth of discontent within the black urban centers and clear warnings of the powder-keg situation before Watts exploded in August of 1965. Triggered by police action, blacks in Watts went on a rampage, smashing widows, looting, destroying stores and other properties. More than three hundred buildings were set on fire; many burned to the ground as firefighters were hindered from responding or opted not to go into the hostile environment. The National Guard was called in to reinforce the police response to the insurrection. When the riot ended, thirty-four people were dead, hundreds injured, nearly four thousand arrested, and property damage estimated at forty million dollars. Watts was the worst race riot in America's history at that point. It was not the last, however, as riots broke out in Chicago, Cleveland, Dayton, San Francisco, Atlanta, Nashville, Boston, Cincinnati, Newark, Buffalo, Milwaukee, Tampa, and the worst in Detroit. In the summer of 1967, the Detroit riot claimed forty-three lives, with more than a thousand injured, seven thousand arrested and, when the smoke finally cleared, a city in utter disarray, with property damage in excess of fifty million dollars. When Martin Luther King, Jr. was assassinated in April 1968, sections of many cities went up in flames again, including Washington, D.C., Baltimore, Hartford, and Miami. By the time of the relatively quiet, but uneasy calm of the summer of 1968, race rioting had claimed lives and property in more than one hundred of the nation's cities, North and South.

White America in general remained in a state of denial as to the causes behind the riots. Harris and Gallup polls found that the majority of whites attributed the cause of the riots to outside agitators. Ninety-five percent of African Americans polled thought just the opposite and wanted change to come at a quicker pace. For whites, the Civil Rights Movement and black struggle for freedom and equality was a contemporary event. For blacks, the struggle began during the era of slavery and was ongoing. Although he considered the violence reprehensible, Dr. Ralph Bunche, Under Secretary of the United Nations and Nobel Peace Prize recipient, nevertheless understood the causes behind the rebellions, and predicated that there would be more of them until America freed itself of discrimination and race prejudice.

But America stood firm behind the color line as white parents demonstrated in their opposition to school desegregation and especially busing. African-American children were threatened, brow beaten, and at the receiving end of the most vile epithets shouted at them as they were bused into previously all-white schools. The school desegregation experience at Central High School in Little Rock, Arkansas, in 1957, and the necessity to use National Guard troops to protect the bused children was bad enough, but the North was no different. South Boston, Massachusetts, was second to none in terms of the poisonous racial hatred, threats, and verbal abuse that white picketers there, most notably women, unleashed against the black children bused into their community on the opening day of school on September 12, 1974. The anti-busing protests continued for months. Black students were stoned and cut by shattered glass as white teenagers and parents threw rocks and smashed windows of school buses carrying the students.

African Americans struggled daily against the multiple assaults of racism, police brutality, and discrimination in employment. Since the end of Reconstruction, the black unemployment rate has averaged twice that of whites, underemployment eight times higher than that of whites, a per-family income half that of whites, individual wage income only half that of whites with the same number of years of education, and relegated to poor and segregated housing. In addition, the bombing of churches and murdering of children and killing of civil rights workers in the South and the assassination of black leaders has always been accomplished under the watchful eye of a law enforcement body that aggressively violated the constitution and sought through counter measures and planned sabotage such as COINTELPRO, initiated in the early 1960s, to neutralize or destroy black activist organizations and leaders from Malcolm X and Martin Luther King, Jr., to Angela Davis, Huey P. Newton, Bobby Seale and the Black Panther Party for Self Defense. The Federal Bureau of Investigation carried out a smear campaign to discredit those black leaders, whom bureau chief J. Edgar Hoover personally disfavored and considered particularly dangerous, such as Dr. King. The Bureau also used more lethal force. In Chicago, Illinois, for example, the local chapter of the Panthers was raided at night by a combination of FBI and local law enforcement agents, who killed Chicago Panther leaders Fred Hampton and Mark Clark as they slept.

At the time of the urban riots of the 1960s, blacks held less than 0.5 percent of managerial or executive positions in white-owned businesses. African Americans in the cities were relegated, for the most part, to the ghettos and a condition that can best be described as domestic colonization. Black communities often found themselves bound by highways and other clearly delineated physical barriers as occurred, for example, in Overtown, Liberty City, and the West Grove communities in South Florida. The National Advisory Commission on Civil Disorders, better known as the Kerner Commission, reported: "What white Americans have never fully understood—but what the Negro can never forget—is that white society is deeply implicated in the ghetto. White institutions created it, white institutions maintain it, and white society condones it." The Commission rightly found that there were two Americas, one black and one white. It aptly concluded: "Segregation and poverty converge on the young to destroy opportunity and enforce failure. Crime, drug addiction, dependency on welfare, and bitterness and resentment against society in general and white society in particular are the result." Racism was the dagger held at black America's throat and simultaneously at the entire nation's heart.

President Lyndon Baines Johnson was sensitive to America's race dilemma and took steps that suggested hope. Critics contended that the programs that Johnson initiated to tackle the domestic problems were unworkable and nothing more than an effort to pacify disgruntled blacks and to end the siege on the cities. Indeed, he did attempt to intervene and some programs were enhanced and received additional funding during the riot-torn last three years of his administration. But the historical record and sequence of programs and initiatives show that Johnson was committed to civil rights reform and social programs aimed at blacks and the rest of the nation's poor before the explosion in the cities. Upon assuming the presidency after the assassination of John F. Kennedy in November of 1963, Johnson immediately launched a nonstop support of civil rights and it was he who politically shepherded into passage the monumental Civil Rights Act of 1964 and the Voting Rights Act of 1965. His declared "War on Poverty" began during his first full day as president. The Office of Economic Opportunity (OEO) was established and the pivotal Economic Opportunities Act became law in January of 1964—all before the outbreak of riots. Johnson placed other programs on the fast track to passage, including the Elementary and Secondary Education Act of 1965, the Higher Education Act of 1965, the Medicare and Medicaid Amendments to the Social Security Act of 1965. The Community Action Program, the Job Corps, the Neighborhood Youth Corps, and Head Start were major accomplishments of his administration. The Jobs Corps and Neighbor Youth Corps gave many inner-city and rural poor youngsters their first wage paying jobs and provided them with entry-level experience vital to taking the next step to higher levels of employment and income. The Work-Study Program of 1964 gave poor teenagers and college students the opportunity to earn funds that enabled them to continue their education. The Elementary and Secondary Education Act more than quadrupled federal aid to public school systems throughout the nation. The Higher Education Act was the most progressive attempt to make college more accessible to the financially disadvantaged since the passage of the GI Bill. The flamboyant and assertive representative from Harlem, Adam Clayton Powell, Jr., chaired the powerful House Committee on Education and Labor, and with the mammoth infusion of funds to education during the Johnson years, Powell's influence reached new proportions, making him the most powerful black person in America. President Johnson was particularly dismayed that the riots occurred despite the work and accomplishments of his administration. The rioting in Watts broke out only five days after the passage of the Voting Rights Act. Moreover, the Office of Economic Opportunity provided Los Angeles with seventeen million dollars earlier in the year to fight poverty and deprivation, but the city's Mayor, Sam Yorty, and his five-member all-white advisory committee had, in violation of OEO mandates and procedures, chose not to use the funds to improve the conditions in the black community. The Johnson administration continued to provide leadership and funding targeted to help the nation's needy and to address inequities such as the Model Cities Act (1966), and the Housing Act (1968). His domestic policy and programs were overwhelmingly proactive rather than merely reactive, and he ordered cabinet members and staff not to wait but to identify and address potential problems. He proved that, besides being a shrewd politician, he was a statesman and leader.

The problem was that expectations were high in the black communities and all patience was gone. At the other end of the spectrum, white Americans in the main were not deeply committed to ending racism and discrimination and, as polling revealed, 58 percent of them favored gradualism in civil rights and felt that President Johnson was moving too fast. Johnson's support of legislation to desegregate public and private institutions, schools and facilities, alarmed most whites who, while claiming that they believed discrimination was wrong, also admitted that they did not want blacks living next to them. Johnson did not seek reelection in 1968, but remained committed to civil rights reform and to ending racism. In his last public address which was given at the Civil Rights Symposium held in Texas at the Lyndon Baines Johnson Library in December of 1972, and less than a year before his death, Johnson spoke of his own growth in understanding of the race problem in America and exhorted the scholars, activists, civic and political leaders attending the conference to move forward and continue to push for programs to address the problem. In conclusion to his speech at the symposium, and borrowing from his address to the nation seven years earlier during the signing of the Voting Rights Act, the ailing former president said in firm voice: "We have proved that great progress is possible. We know how much still remains to be done. And if our efforts continue, if our will is strong, if our hearts are right and if courage remains our constant companion, then, my fellow Americans, I am confident that *we shall overcome.*"

The black community bears some responsibility for the failure to work together and move the race forward on the basis of shared goals in a united front, as Malcolm X had urged. There were, to be sure, gains made. The Civil Rights Movement exposed to the public the hypocrisy of America and challenged the nation to live up to its great declarations. As a result of the movement, reforms were initiated. Despite President Johnson's many flaws, in particular the escalation of the war in Vietnam, his domestic programs and civil rights record position him second to none in America's history. Yet, many have spoken despairingly of the Great Society Programs, carping that they totally failed. First, the Great Society Programs had their weaknesses, but they did not all fail. The programs assisted millions of inner-city and rural poor youngsters. Unfortunately, the Great Society Programs lasted less than a decade in this nation's history. In short, they were not supported for a substantial enough period of time to yield optimum results.

America has proven itself an impatient nation, and a fickled one particularly on the question of race and equality. After President Johnson left office, the succeeding administrations began the path to the systematic dismantling of the Great Society Programs and the civil rights and affirmative action agendas. The Great Society Programs were replaced with an aggressive regression to America's old ways. The first was, most notably, with the anti-affirmative action assault of the *Bakke Decision* of 1978, followed by the *Webber Decision*, and then an all out blitzkrieg against civil rights gains under Presidents Ronald Reagan and George Bush in the 1980s. The serious bid of the Reverend Jesse Jackson in 1980 for the Democratic nomination for President of the United States was doomed from the start given the growing tide of race-reactionary conservatism, and like Congresswoman Shirley Chisholm's bid for the nomination in 1972, the act itself was an important symbolic statement of black self-assertion and quest for empowerment against racism. The flourishing tide of contemporary racism, however, or so-called conservatism, crested in the self-centered decades of the eighties and nineties with the election of Newt Gingrich as Speaker of the House of Representatives, and the other right wing Republicans of Congress, whose vision of America was exclusionary and sought to serve the privileged by diverting civil rights and opportunities from minorities. Add to the mixture a regressive ideologue U. S. Supreme Court hostile to affirmative action and the accomplishments of the Civil Rights Movement. By any measure, the America of the late 20th century was anti African Americans as reflected in the enactment of *Proposition 209* in California, and the court decision of *Hopewood v. Texas*, both striking down so-called preferential treatment based on race. The effect of these enactments has been to severely curtail the enrollment of African Americans in the colleges and universities of those states, especially in professional schools and graduate programs. President Bill Clinton, the conservative Democrat, did little to stop the war on civil rights and equal opportunities or to set a new and constructive course of action. His establishment of the President's Initiative on Race, a seven-member advisory committee headed by the venerable African-American historian John Hope Franklin, and the holding of hearings and town meetings to discuss race and racism, were positive as far as it went. The question, however, was what changed? What new legislation was enacted and programs established to help solve the nation's awful race problem? The experience of African Americans documents the collective history of a nation in peril at its core. Does the intelligence, the foresight based on hindsight, and the national determination exist to eradicate racism in the future? Given the growing conservative political mood and the flourishing racial intolerance, the answer to that question has to be "no." America seems committed, at the present moment in history, to ignoring the African-American struggle and the deeply-rooted problem of racism.[14]

RACE TO THE FUTURE

TOWARD A CONCLUSION

Where are we now and how did we get here? Hopefully, through the previous pages that question has been answered either in whole or in part. The question now is, where do we go from here? Let me borrow, for a moment, from the lessons of the South African situation. Americans do not like having their country compared to the former apartheid regime of South Africa but there is much to be learned from it. There is considerable similarity between the two situations and this is why African Americans vigorously and dedicatedly supported the long war against apartheid. As blacks struggled in the United States to make their lives better, they never became self-absorbed as a people. Black folk have always been amazing in this regard; a generous people willing to share. Even slavery could not beat that out of them or destroy their identification with Africa. African Americans are concerned about the world around them and the plight of black people throughout the diaspora. Their ties and that of other people of African descent to their African motherland remains vibrant. Africans prefer Africa over any place in the world. The dispute on Capitol Hill in the 1990s over Chinese students being allowed to stay in America, highlighted the fact that Africans have the lowest overstay record with only one thousand seven hundred African nationals in three years compared to Europeans' fifty-four thousand four hundred. It also shows the United States' dislike of people of color. The nation makes every effort to keep black people out while it opens its arms wide to whites. Note if you will the dilemma over Haitian immigration and their treatment compared to, for example, that of white Cubans. The Cubans are embraced and easily welcomed into the United States while the Haitians have obstacle after obstacle thrown in their path and are literally returned to the islands. Only the recent democratization of Haiti gives any hope that this situation will change. It is not that the United States will be more receptive to opening its borders to people of color, but perhaps Haiti can be reformed from within to make it a country that better serves the needs of all of its people.

281

No battle, however, garners more of African Americans' attention than the struggle in South Africa. There is a strong sense of a linked destiny between black Americans and the blacks of South Africa and the human suffering under racism. What the supporters of a free South Africa did was similar in strategy to the American Civil Rights Movement—to shame the oppressor, to make visible to the world the inhumanity and barbaric nature of the racist apartheid system. One of the strategies used to oppress people throughout the world has been to deny their history and to deny the onslaught against them. In a sense, the view is, out of sight out of mind. In a desperate attempt to conceal its crimes, white South Africans disallowed news coverage in the late 1980s in hopes of manipulating world opinion. Randall Robinson of TransAfrica assessed Pretoria as successful in its strategy of barring news coverage and thus lessening public and world focus on South Africa. Stephen Cohen of CBS News said that the American media had been cowardly and played into the hands of South Africa and the apartheid system. It had. The American and world media did not aggressively pursue coverage in South Africa in the face of the government's band on pictures. As with history, it can be argued that, the actual events never occurred unless somehow recorded. In the end, the news and information blackout failed. Truth crushed to the ground will rise again. History cannot be denied. When Jesse Jackson later visited South Africa as the guest of Walter Sisulu of the African National Congress and the South African Council of Churches, he was making a pilgrimage to keep the spotlight on the problems in that country.

The armed struggle of the ANC and economic direct action made the difference. U.S. government officials condemned the ANC for its use of violence, as it had the Civil Rights Movement when there were violent outbreaks. President George Bush went so far as to urge the ANC to follow the non-violent tactics of Martin Luther King. He made these utterances only a few weeks after ordering U.S. troops into Panama. The United States, a nation built on violence, seems to have no problem advocating non-violence to the people of Africa and others of the so-called Third World. Like the Montgomery Bus Boycott, economic direct action, particularly the world and American economic sanctions, helped. In October 1986, the U.S. Congress, over the objection of President Ronald Reagan, and led by representative Ronald Dellums and other members of the Congressional Black Caucus, gained passage of the sanctions bill. It was a devastating blow to apartheid. With the U.S. joining in, although reluctantly, with other nations of the world that refused to conduct business as usual with South Africa, the foreign economic sanctions cost the apartheid country thirty-two to forty billion dollars between 1985 and 1989, including four billion in lost exports. The results of South Africa's isolation during the 1980s helped turn around the thinking of its leaders who grudgingly began to recognize that the course of democratic change was irresistible and inevitable. President Frederick W. DeKlerk promised and delivered on a number of modest reforms. He freed several political prisoners, effectively legalized many formerly banned political organizations, and began desegregating South African beaches and public facilities. This was not unlike the results of the Civil Rights Movement in the United States and DeKlerk further moved the nation closer to the concept of one person one vote, released Nelson Mandela, and initiated the first phase in the dismantling of the apartheid system. Black America should recognize only too well that Dr. Motlana, a Mandela associate, was quite correct when he cautioned that white leadership of South Africa had not made the psychological leap from racist to non-racial government. In the South African context and the American context as well, the formal end of segregation or the formal end of apartheid does not mean an end to personal and institutional racism. It means, however, that there has been positive change, but change that is merely a starting point from which to develop equal opportunity and to begin empowering the formerly oppressed.

When we saw Nelson Mandela, after twenty-five years of incarceration, finally released from prison on February 11, 1990, one could not help but reflect on the historical linkages. Neither could we afford to react to Mandela's release and the promises made with a relaxation of sanctions as President Bush and other conservatives sought. Indeed, Representative Fautneroy and the Congressional Black Caucus were right in pushing for a tightening of sanctions to hasten the day of the complete collapse of apartheid. Jesse Jackson was correct in his assessment, rendered after meeting with Mandela, when he said that Nelson Mandela was not free. Mandela himself insisted that he was not free until all of his country was on an equal footing and a level playing field. When Mandela spoke in Soweto a few days after his release, he articulated a vision. For many, as reported in the world press, it seemed a cautionary vision. He was cautious and circumspect of the environment in which he was operating. He knew well the depths of the system of apartheid and the racism in the hearts and minds of the whites of his country. He also knew that racism would not end with pronouncements and denouncements but through empowerment legislation and reeducation. Mandela wanted to maintain his country by making fundamental, absolute changes for the uplift and equality of his people. He knew that rhetoric was only one aspect of this and that substance was far more important. Mandela, like Martin Luther King, understood that aggressive sounding slogans have their place, but for many others the words could be objectionable and counterproductive by alerting one's adversaries to your planned course of action. Mandela's wisdom abounded.

Nelson Mandela is a symbol not only to South Africans but to black Americans as well. He is a freedom fighter, a *race man* and warrior, an individual whose life personifies the continuing battle against the evils of racism. There is a political and spiritual tie between African Americans and Mandela and the South African struggle. The United States honored him in 1998 for his contributions to humanity and guidance of South Africa as its president, presenting him with the Medal of Freedom. Mandela symbolizes the hope of a world without racism. People analyze and contemplate his importance from a great variety of perspectives: freedom fighter, politician and statesman. We should have learned from his every move, for let us not forget that Mandela, long before becoming President of South Africa, and even before he became a brave race warrior of the African National Congress, or a trained lawyer, had been a boxer. Many people do not realize that fact or only give it minor consideration. Allow me to focus for a moment on Mandela the boxer. He had an excellent left jab which anybody familiar with the fight game knows is an essential and potent weapon. In the same year of Mandela's release from prison, heavyweight boxing champion Mike Tyson learned the hard way the effectiveness of a good jab after Buster Douglass knocked him out. Nelson Mandela also had and still has a good left jab. He is a student of the sweet science, the art of boxing. This is important for us to understand when we gage his political maneuvering between the many factions of his nation. Remember the boxer in him. A good boxer is an individual who knows that you do not just simply bull your way straight ahead all the time. You have to know when to move from side to side and when to seemingly retreat to gain effectively over your adversary. Think of Mandela in those terms and you have a sense of his motions and intellect and rhythm. A man whose love of jazz, including such greats as John Coltrane and Charlie Parker, and deep spiritualism has a connectedness that black folk share. His personality and formal and informal training made it possible for him to maintain his tough mindeness and dedication to the cause even while incarcerated. His humanity and political savvy guided his implementing of policies in the new South Africa. Remember Mandela the boxer, the individual who knows when to give and to take, who understands the necessary moves and intellectual gymnastics required for positioning. He wisely used the jab to work his way in to land solid punches against the vestiges of apartheid. Succeeding leadership must work to the body and then to the head and deliver the knock out. Mandela, who retired from office in 1999, proved himself to be a great statesman while President of South Africa. He can be counted upon to continue to maneuver sprightly and wisely in and out of the ring of recognized political office to guide in the fashioning of a new nation that is destined to become a hallmark of African freedom and the rightness of humanity and equality for all people.

Internal strife among blacks in South Africa, like that experienced by blacks in the United States, is a part of a long war to end racism and to gain empowerment. Throughout their history, African Americans have had their share of tell-tell collaborators working against the best interests of the race, or who otherwise find their greatest reward and comfort among those who hold power. There have always been those who sell their souls for a price. In South Africa, Chief Buthelezi of the Zulu comes to mind. In the United States, Ward Connerly is one among many who comes to mind. Connerly, a member of the Board of Regents of the University of California, has been placed in the forefront of the assault on affirmative action. He is neither an intellectual nor a highly successful businessman or respected community leader. He is, however, a black conservative and that is all that the forces in power need to declare his legitimacy as someone representative of a movement, that includes some blacks, against the civil rights agenda and affirmative action programs. Connerly is the product of a right-wing Republican former governor of California. He has never been an active member of any African-American community but does possess moderately dark skin pigmentation. The need for black sycophants was most vividly demonstrated with the nomination and appointment of Clarence Thomas to the Supreme Court of the United States. Clearly unqualified by standards of legal knowledge, experience, professional stature and contributions, President George Bush, nevertheless, deemed him the best choice in the entire country for appointment to the nation's highest court. Thomas's sole qualification was his politics and his race. An opponent of affirmative action and critic of civil rights laws, racial and gender equity, he was the darling of the conservative establishment and the old and new supporters of business as usual on the race question. They vigorously defended Thomas against highly creditable charges of sexual harassment during his confirmation hearings. One might only wonder if he would have been confirmed had the accuser, Anita Hill, been a white woman rather than a black one.[1]

The attack on affirmative action is a betrayal of a national promise to provide opportunities to African Americans and other groups who have been traditionally locked out. No sooner had positive movement begun in the 1960s than it was ended. The greatest beneficiaries of the Civil Rights Movement, as Martin Luther King predicted, would be whites. White women have been the largest beneficiaries of the civil rights and affirmative action programs. The access they have gained in business and professions is due in no small measure to the Civil Rights Act, Title Nine of the Higher Education Act, and affirmative action mandates for some degree of representative and diversified hiring. There is no evidence to suggest that advances made by white women, however, have aided black women or black people in general. The color line has not rescinded. White women executives now talk of having reached the "glass ceiling" while African-American women and men face a locked basement void of any windows.

In the highly competitive setting that is America, it seems more difficult to develop linkages with other races. The gap widens between Asians and African Americans as indicated by the growing number of conflicts between the two groups in the cities, particularly in New York's Harlem and south-central Los Angeles. There is blame enough on both sides. Oppression and envy also play roles. The newcomers, as a group, are progressing while black progress as a group declines or at best remains stagnant. The apparent success, for example, of Korean businesses within the boundaries of the black communities is often seen as effronteries and reminders to blacks of their failures. If the two groups communicated and developed forums for discussions of mutual problems and concerns friendly coexistence might be possible. The same holds true for relationships with Native Americans that today are almost non existent. There was a time when Native Americans and blacks shared a great deal. Runaway slaves in the deep South often found refuge with Native Americans such as the Seminoles in Florida. In the North, blacks were welcomed among the Piquot. There are many more such examples. Today outsiders are welcomed only as tourists. It is a sad commentary that when Native Americans approached African-American organizations for assistance in recent times their requests fell on deaf ears. Blacks failed to join with Native Americans in their protest against sport mascots based on caricatures of Native Americans, such as the Washington Redskins, the Cleveland

Indians, the Florida Seminoles, the Fighting Illini, and so forth. Their cry went unheeded and no support came from African Americans. The divide between African Americans and Hispanics has had only momentary reprieve, such as the limited support blacks gave Caesar Chavez and the United Farm Workers of America in the 1970s, the coalition in the 1980s in the election of Harold Washington to the office of Mayor of Chicago, and the alliance in protest against several high profile racial incidents in New York City and Los Angeles in recent years. While there have been conferences to bring together portions of the two groups, such as the Hartford symposium on "Puerto Ricans and Blacks," these are usually rare occurrences and with no long-term follow through. Given too that the Hispanic population is heterogeneous, the concerns of African Americans and Hispanic Americans are not mutual in all cases. In Miami, for example, the relationship between African Americans and the large Cuban population can best be described as tense and uncomfortable. Cuban-American city officials in Miami snubbed ANC freedom fighter and Nobel Prize Winner Nelson Mandela when he visited the area in 1990 because of his statement praising Cuban President Fidel Castro for his support of the liberation struggle in South Africa. African Americans in retaliation initiated a boycott of Miami area hotels that lasted for three years. When Cuban-American city officials also later snubbed former United Nations Ambassador Andrew Young for similar reasoning, the wedge between African Americans and Cuban Americans was driven deeper.

There has always been a wide divide in the relationship between blacks and the largest "ethnic" group—whites, one that took on a renewed expansion beginning in the late 1960s and continues on through today. One of the clearest indications of this is the realignment in white politics. The South led the way but the rest of the nation quickly followed. The white political realignment started with the successes of the Civil Rights Movement, including the legislative victories, in particular the Civil Rights Act and the Voting Rights Act. The long term cost was white flight from the Democratic Party to the Republican Party. The once solid Democratic South is today controlled by the Republican Party. Throughout the entire nation Republicanism has meant fiscal conservatism, lowering of taxes, deregulation and a free for all for industry and banking, abandonment of federal housing support, drastic cutbacks in public assistance, particularly to the bugaboo of welfare, and opposition to civil rights legislation and especially affirmative action. Under the cloak of these issues is a decidedly hidden racist agenda against African

Americans. For many whites, blacks are synonymous with all that is wrong in America. In a contested political race, he or she simply reaches into those long-rooted white fears and *nigger baits*. Opposition to welfare, in the white mind, means getting those lazy blacks and Latinos off of the public dole. Never mind the fact that the majority of people receiving welfare assistance are children and white. Crime is, without a doubt, portrayed as a problem with the blacks. To be anti crime is implicitly in the white mind putting away those troublesome and good-for-nothing blacks. The media plays into this fixation every evening with its race game. If a black did it you will be given pictures of him or her handcuffed and being lead away to the police car. Conversely, you can virtually tell when the perpetrator is white because invariably pictures will often be omitted. Note this the next time you are watching the nightly news. Any politician knows that taking a purported tough stand on crime is to send a strong race message, directly, indirectly or subliminally, that you are anti the blacks and the "liberal" agenda. In his bid for the presidency, George Bush's utilization of Lee Atwater's strategy of the Willie Horton ads was unabashed *nigger baiting* against Massachusetts Governor Michael Dukakis, as it accused him of being soft on crime by allowing a criminal type like Horton to be paroled and, without saying it in words, portrayed him as pro blacks. The strategy played on white fears of the black boogie man and, sadly, was quite effective. Some pundits have given large credit to the "Willie Horton ads" for Bush's election to the presidency in 1988. Bill Clinton, in running for the presidency in 1992, and for reelection in 1996, distanced himself as far as possible from blacks in the eyes of the white majority he courted but not so far as to lose the needed support of African-American voters. His Commission on Race, "One America," and the related forums, although important first steps, were, interestingly enough, not inaugurated until after his reelection. The Congressional elections of 1998 saw the race card being cleverly cloaked and played throughout the country. For many of the politicians the new code slogan is: "I support everyone being treated the same." Such was successfully used in the North Carolina race for the U.S. Senate. Translated the statement means: "I am opposed to affirmative action and to giving advantages to blacks over whites." White folk know what is meant and African Americans do as well. The softened rhetoric of the new so-called "compassionate conservatism" touted by Texas Republican governor and now President of the United States, George W. Bush, the son of the former president, fools no one who has lived a black life in America. Barely underneath the surface is a fierce partisanship committed to the protection of white privilege and the continuation of black disempowerment. Compassionate conservatism is nothing more than an update of his daddy's, former president George Bush's, rhetorical smoke screen of a "kinder and gentler nation," while he brutally assaulted every program remaining on the books that hinted of protecting civil rights or elevating the disenfranchised or aiding the poor. The former president's other son, Florida Republican governor Jed Bush, embarked in 2000 on what he termed a "One Florida Initiative." "One Florida" is the antithesis of President Clinton's "One America." Jed Bush's Florida initiative is to eliminate all affirmative action plans and programs in the "sunshine state" and to leave nothing in their place except a program-less promise to the state's African-American population that he will look out for their best interests. It harkens back to the days of the Old South plantation when *massa* typically proclaimed that his *negroes* did not need rights and that he knew and would do what was best for them. African Americans are well aware that they and affirmative action are under siege throughout the nation and that there is no friendly political party with which to realign. The Democratic Party, with all of its limitations, is viewed in the African-American community as the only game in town. Thus, the two-party system severely circumscribes minority interests and the efforts to vigorously combat racism.

White America is afraid of black America. One of the salient reasons that gender equity is, for black folk, far secondary to the problem of racism is because whites are in charge and the dominate power dynamics and stereotypical views cut just as deeply on either side of black gender. There is no question that African-American women are discriminated against also because they are women in a world dominated by white males. But it is likewise true that black men are discriminated against because they are men in a world dominated by white males. As several leading African-American psychologists have surmised, the white psycho-sexual pathology regarding the black male runs the gamut from a perceived "direct physical threat to penis envy." If given a choice, the white employer is more likely to hire a black woman, feeling more comfortable with her as a member of the "weaker sex" than a black man, whom he sees as a physical threat. I say this not to pit black women against black men but to reiterate that the overwhelming factor behind the mistreatment of both is racism—not gender—and never should the two groups be divided along secondary lines. Racism can be gender specific. Each gender does have disadvantages and advantages unique to it in the social setting that needs to be acknowledged and openly addressed. But the linkage of black women with white women along a feminist agenda is as logical as black men joining with white men along a male agenda. The modern Women's Movement has been severely flawed because of its failure to recognize the problem of racism. Until that issue is honestly addressed, and white women resolve their duplicity and complicity with America's racism, there is no basis for a united effort of black and white women. The notion of a gender alliance between the two makes as much sense as a wealthy mistress and her maid joining together in a movement to advance class interests.

The preferred status and images whites still feel most comfortable with for black women and black men have changed very little over the past century: the overweight, dark skin, promiscuous, childlike and jovial Black Mammy serving whites, for African-American women; and the dim-witted, clownish, chicken stealing but otherwise loyal Uncle Tom, for African-American men. These images personified the black sit-coms on televisions in the 1970s and 1980s, with such highly successful programs as "That's My Mama," "Good Times," and "The Jeffersons." When Oprah Winfrey held an open forum on her show in 1997, to discuss her new image after losing a substantial amount of weight through dieting and exercise, she was told point black by several of the white women present that they did not like her new trim and elegant appearance and that they preferred her when she was overweight. When Oprah asked one of the white women if it would have been easier for her to take if she had started off her television career trim rather than fat, the woman replied: "No. I would have never liked you at all." The black woman or man with elegance, position, fame or, heaven forbid, money, is a troubling image for whites in racist America. The treatment of African-American movie stars, professional athletes and other successful entertainers is a constant reminder of the dual nature of an American society that, as Martin Luther King would say, "simultaneously loves and hates the Negro." Without fail when a Michael Jordan, an Eddie Murphy, a Bill Cosby, or a Denzel Washington appear on a television interview or within the print media, the white host or journalist inevitably asks what Eddie Murphy calls "the Negro question." The question is: "How much money do you make?" There is a white fixation regarding any degree of black success and wealth. It is the economic envy synonymous with racism that blacks are not to do better than whites. If a black person has more money, a nicer home, a better automobile, or finer clothes, then the system has broken down. The long legacy of racism has taught whites that they are supposed to be better and to do better than blacks. Hence, African-American success is often consciously or unconsciously upsetting to whites. Larry Bird was never asked in a major interview how much money he earns. African-American celebrities are continuously berated with "the Negro question." Neither is the question relegated to athletes and entertainers. Any successful black person is subject to "the Negro question." The renown chair of the African-American studies program at Harvard University, Henry Louis Gates, when hosting a dinner party for a distinguished visitor, was asked by a reporter covering the event, "what kind of car he in fact drives" and whether or not it was true that he owned "twin Mercedes?" Gates joked for a moment, thought about it, and then pointedly responded that the question "would not have been asked if you were doing a story on a white professor." When the reporter responded saying that she routinely asks about cars, "Gates snapped back with an expletive."

Racism is built on stereotypes that reinforce loathing and disrespect for the disadvantaged and targeted group. Acts of violence in the black communities, the drive-by shootings and other black-on-black crime help perpetuate the racial divide because they lend credence to white perceptions of African Americans as an unworthy segment of society where failure is self perpetuated rather than the result of external forces. The critics give little weight to the reality that social programs and economic opportunities have drastically diminished in the black communities and inner cities of the nation over the last quarter of a century. Black-on-black crime supports racism and the negative image of inner-city youth as the undeserving poor. Who cares what happens to them? When a murder is defined as gang related or drug related, it becomes a lesser priority to the police establishment, which has proven time and again that it cannot be trusted at any rate. Being harassed by police for DWB (Driving While Black) is symptomatic of a pernicious and deep-seated disrespect. The brutal murder of Amadou Diallo in February 1999, who was shot nineteen times by police while standing unarmed in the vestibule of his home in the Bronx, is only one of many recent episodes of police violence against blacks across America. Latanya Haggerty, a twenty-six year old computer analyst, and Robert Anthony Russ, a twenty-two year old graduating senior at Northwestern University, were "accidentally" shot to death on June 4 and 5, 1999, respectively, by police in Chicago. They are only two more examples from a long national list of such "accidents" that are forever-occurring assaults against black folk with no end in sight. The 1999 conviction of one of the four policemen accused of beating and sodomizing Abner Louima, while he was in custody on August 9,

1997, does nothing to soothe the relationship between police and America's black communities. The outbreak of a race riot in Cincinnati in 2001 after yet another white police shooting of an unarmed black person necessitated a dusk-to-dawn curfew in the city for three days. Black folk are assailed from every conceivable quarter. Often the entire African-American community is unknowingly at risk. Environmental racism plagues the physical health of African Americans. U.S. Surgeon General David Satcher, in a discussion on National Public Radio on November 24, 1998, remarked that from "forty to fifty percent of those who live around hazardous dump sites and other potentially dangerous waste sites are African Americans and other minorities, including Native Americans and Hispanics."

American society has become increasingly numb to the problems of others. The outrage of the country over children killing children is vocalized but little else. Teenage pregnancy seems tolerated as a norm of the times. Panhandlers are viewed as a part of the urban landscape and homelessness is no longer shocking and intolerable to the nation. What is happening in America and what we must do to solve the problems are questions we all need to ask ourselves on a regular basis and then work collectively and individually toward solutions. As Malcolm X used to say, "You are either part of the solution or you are part of the problem." We neglect rather than help. We reject rather than accept. We hate rather than love. For the solution we must begin at the beginning and tackle the problems at their inception. Racism is a problem and product of human beings premised on ignorance. We learn to hate and pass the sickness on from generation to generation through what we teach at home, at school, in social settings, in community organizations, in individual relationships, and in our institutions of higher learning. The Kerner Commission told us nearly forty years ago that the nation's most serious problems are due to "historical amnesia that masks much of our turbulent past." To begin at the beginning is to reeducate and re-acculturate the citizenry of the present and those who come in the future. In short, I echo here what I said in testimony to the Advisory Committee of the U.S. Commission on Civil Rights and include those brief remarks for your perusal in the appendix. I urge now that we declare, similar to the War on Poverty in the 1960s, a War on Racism and its foundation, which is ignorance. My life and years as a student of history convince me that education is the key. The young and the old must start now, in and out of the formal education environment, to focus explicitly on the problem of racism and to learn to respect and appreciate the history and culture of all members of society. This will put in place the intellectual foundation that leads America to a genuine concern for one another and commitment to the common good, unity of purpose, and the end of racism. On September 18, 1998, the Advisory Committee on *One America in the 21st Century—The President's Initiative on Race* issued its report and recommendation to President Clinton. The Committee found that racism is deeply embedded within the nation. It is "essential to recall the facts of racial domination" and that "whites tend to benefit, either unknowingly or consciously, from this country's history of white privilege," the Committee reported. Stereotyping was deemed to be at the core of the nation's racial perceptions that find their way into the decision making at every level and within institutions of every form including business, government, and universities. The Committee urged that racism be dealt with in the light of day and not behind the false facade of a "colorblind" society. "The idea that we should aspire to a 'colorblind' society is an impediment to reducing racial stereotyping," committee chair John Hope Franklin wrote, and research has demonstrated that "the best way to reduce racial stereotyping is to be conscious of race" and to focus on problems openly and in every venue. The Committee recommended strong leadership and "well designed" long-term national programs to combat racism and the inequities it has spawned and to better educate the population to the diverse historical legacies that comprise America. The recent presidential election—or election debacle is a better term—gives little hope. The ascendancy of George W. Bush to the White House in 2001 tells black America, and all who would want to eradicate the cancer of racism, that there is no national will to take on this serious problem now or in the foreseeable future. As any physician will tell you, a disease let alone to fester does not improve over time. The history of African Americans is a powerful indictment of American hypocrisy and the continuing failure of a nation to do what it must to cure its internal festering.[2]

On September 11, 2001, three thousand lives were taken in the worst attack on U.S. soil, including Pearl Harbor, when four large passenger jets were hijacked and crashed. Two of the planes were flown into the World Trade Center in New York City, reducing the giant twin towers to rubble and killing most of the buildings' inhabitants. A third airliner was crashed into the Pentagon, taking more lives. A fourth flight was diverted from its intended target and crashed in a wooded area in Pennsylvania as passengers fought back for control of the aircraft. All aboard were killed. The tragedies elicited an outpouring of patriotic sentiment and cries for national unity to meet the threat to

American security. The deep schisms that historically divided the nation were, perhaps, momentarily bridged in the wake of the disaster. As the months passed and patriotic rhetoric rescinded, the nation slowly returned to normalcy with the gargantuan racial divide unaddressed and unresolved.

APPENDIX

"Racism and Intolerance on Campus UConn and Elsewhere:
Panel Presentation to the Connecticut Advisory Committee of
the United States Commission on Civil Rights"

Held at Keller Auditorium, University of
Connecticut Health Center, Farmington, CT.,
April 27, 1992

Remarks by Donald Spivey
Professor of History and Director of the
Institute for African American Studies,
University of Connecticut at Storrs

I shall be brief in hope that we will have time for discussion at the
end of our panel's presentation. Neither will I give you a string of examples of racist acts and other acts of intolerance that have occurred
on the University of Connecticut campus. There have, of course, been
many of these deplorable and despicable actions at the University and
at colleges and universities throughout the nation. Why? That is what
I would like to address in the few minutes allotted me here. Black folk
routinely experience what Professor Joe Fagin of the University of
Texas at Austin calls "micro-aggressions," daily insults and put-downs
as a result of their color.

As a black person in this society, and as a historian of the
African-American experience, and having lived and taught in the
midwest, west coast, and east coast, I find nothing new about the issues we are addressing here today. This for me is personally very
sad. This could be the commission hearing in 1949 or 1963. We talk
about "multi-culturalism" and "Afro-centrism" but more than forty
years ago we were talking about the same thing, although the termi-
nology was different. I had a personal flash or deja vu when I
looked at the names of student participants and saw one named
Howard Lindsey on the program for this afternoon; fascinating.
One of my very best friends is Professor Howard O. Lindsey who is
a historian at DePaul University in Chicago. That Howard Lindsey
was a student activist at the University of Michigan in the 1960s
and helped start the Black Student Movement on that campus; and

is a founding member of the National Council For Black Studies. Lindsey was engaged in student activism at Michigan at the same time I was engaged in similar activity at the University of Illinois at Urbana-Champaign. So please excuse my flash of deja vu. I trust that the Howard Lindsey who is on the panel of students this afternoon does not have Otis as his middle name? If he does, I may begin to suspect that all of us here may be trapped in an old re-run of the "Twilight Zone." What it does say, seriously, is how history so often continues to repeat itself and that so many issues of the past are still the same issues before us.

Let me return to my original question of "why?" Why are the racist acts and other acts of intolerance occurring on our college and university campuses today? The answer to that is the same answer to the question of why the sales clerk is not helpful; why the kid working at the local McDonald's doesn't say thank you; why the student at your office door comes in without knocking; why some employers think that Blacks, Latinos and other people of color will not work hard; or where some men think that there are some professions and occupations that women can't excel at; or why some people hold stereotypical views of Asians or blame the Japanese for America's economic woes. It is the same answer to "why" that, I would suggest, is a sub-theme that united Gerald Gills study *Meanness Mania: The Changing Mood*, to Paul Rothenberg's *Racism and Sexism: An Integrated Study*, to Ronald Takaki's *Iron Cages: Race and Culture in Nineteenth Century America*, to William Chafe's *Civilities and Civil Rights*. It seems to me that it is that same answer to "why" that is found, albeit peripheral at times, in the various commission reports of the 1960s: *The Walker Report, The Skolnick Report, The Graham and Gurr Report*, and, of course, *The Kerner Commission Report*. What is the one underlying cause that runs through all of these reports, books, and studies that examine police brutality, race riots, gang violence, racism, sexism, harassment, xenophobia, campus unrest? I am not a reductionist, but the one common factor is *ignorance*—a basic lack of understanding of one another and hence a basic lack of respect for one another as human beings.

The problem of intolerance that we have on our college campuses is symptomatic of the problem that is pervasive throughout the larger society. We are a society that with the passage of each day is becoming fundamentally less educated. Someone said many years ago: "Civilization is only one generation deep." I fear that assessment is correct. So when we fail as we have been doing to provide quality education at the primary and secondary levels, fail to give proper nurturing in the home and positive role models specifically, there should be no surprise when we as a society reap the bitter fruit produced by a lack of proper cultivation. We are in the midst of an epidemic. Ask yourself how bad is the situation if these manifestations are occurring on college campuses, the citadels of learning and knowledge, the ivory towers of tolerance?

What must we do? First, we must identify the enemy and that enemy is foremost, I believe, *ignorance*. Second, as Kwame Nkrumah once said: "Thought without action is meaningless." Having identified our foe we must declare WAR ON IGNORANCE, like the WAR ON POVERTY in the 1960s, and commit ourselves to educating our population at every level, inculcating them with an appreciation of and respect for human diversity. Our universities and colleges must take the lead in this initiative. We are, after all, at the top of the educational food chain and, as such, the responsibility to spearhead this WAR ON IGNORANCE falls upon us.

Second, we must, in my opinion, develop a micro and a macro plan of action at every college and university in the United States. The Institute for African-American Studies at the University of Connecticut is a micro effort, but we are trying to do our part. The IAAS is involved in educating the campus community about the African-American experience; recruiting more minority faculty and more minority graduate students; we host a "critical issues" lecture series that brings to campus distinguished scholars of the African-American experience who share with us their research and insights; we are developing an undergraduate major in African-American studies; and we are committed to public service through our outreach program, hosting public seminars and teacher workshops in Hartford and elsewhere; and bringing inner-city youngsters to visit Storrs, thus helping to demystify the university for them and encouraging them to go on to college. At the macro level, the University's leadership must, as a general does with an army, inventory his/her holdings and effectively integrate each division, unit, department, and individual foot soldier into a master plan, a strategic and coordinated campaign against the enemy, which in this case is *ignorance*. And at the national level, the supreme commander and chief must do the same.

Thank you for the opportunity to share these observations with you.*

---

* Remarks published in Campus Tensions in Connecticut: Searching for Solutions in the Nineties, Report of the Connecticut Advisory Committee to the U.S. Commission on Civil Rights (Washington, DC: Government Printing Office, September 1994).

ENDNOTES

PROLOGUE

1. Roy P. Basler, ed., *The Collected Works of Abraham Lincoln* (Brunswick, NJ: Rutgers University Press, 1953–1955), V, 537; see, for example, Martin Luther King, Jr.'s speech, "Police Brutality Will Backfire," given at Brown's Chapel on March 21, 1965 prior to resuming the Selma March.

I. RACE FIRST: AN INTRODUCTION TO BLACK HISTORY
a). The New Critical Race Theory

1. Courtroom Television Network, *What the Jury Saw in Cal. V. Powell*, videocassette (Oak Forest, IL: MPI Home Videos, 1992); NAACP, *Beyond the Rodney King Story: NAACP Report on Police Conduct and Community Reactions, 1993*; an engaging discussion of the wider implications of the Simpson trial is given in Toni Morrison and Claudia Brodsky Lacour, ed., *Birth of a Nation: Gaze, Script, and Spectacle in the O.J. Simpson Case* (New York, NY: Random House, 1996).

2. Lena Williams, "When Blacks Shop, Bias often Accompanies a Sale," *New York Times*, 30 April 1991, A1, A9; Joe R. Feagin and Melvin P. Sikes, *Living with Racism: The Black Middle-Class Experience* (Boston, MA: Beacon Press, 1994), 37, 45, 53; Ira Winderman, "Just Because We're Black Doesn't Mean We're Thugs," *Sun-Sentinel* (Fort Lauderdale and Miami), 4 November 1994, 1H, 4–5H; Powell remarks made in interview on Larry King Show, 18 September 1995 and in several other venues during his promotional tour for his book, *My American Journey*.

3. See Derrick Bell, *And We Are Not Saved: The Elusive Quest for Racial Justice* (New York, NY: Basic Books, 1987), *Faces at the Bottom of the Well: The Permanence of Racism* (New York, NY: Basic Books, 1992), and *Confronting Authority: Reflections of an Ardent Protester* (Boston, MA: Beacon Press, 1994); Patricia J. Williams, *The Alchemy of Race and Rights* (Cambridge, MA: Harvard University Press, 1991); Stephen L. Carter, *Reflections of an*

Affirmative Action Baby (New York, NY: Basic Books, 1991); Lani Guinier, *The Tyranny of the Majority* (New York, NY: Free Press, 1994), 1; Cornel West, *Race Matters* (Boston, MA: Beacon Press, 1993), x; Constance Baker Motley, *Equal Justice Under Law* (New York, NY: Farrar, Straus & Giroux, 1998); Randall Robinson, *Defending the Spirit: A Black Life in America* (New York, NY: Dutton, 1998); Houston Baker, *Black Studies, Rap, and the Academy* (Chicago, IL: University of Chicago Press, 1993); Charles Johnson, *Being and Race: Black Writings since 1970* (Bloomington, IN: Indiana University Press, 1990); on the emerging field of Critical Race Theory see Charles J. Ogletree, Jr., "The Conference on Critical Race Theory: When the Rainbow is Not Enough," *New England Law Review* 31:3 (Spring 1997), 705–708; K.C. Nebeker, "Critical Race Theory: A White Graduate Student's Struggle with the Growing Area of Scholarship," *International Journal of Qualitative Studies in Education* (Special Issue on Critical Race Theory) 11:1 (1998), 25–42; Richard Delgado, ed., *Critical Race Theory: The Cutting Edge* (Philadelphia, PA: Temple University Press, 1995).

4. Quoted in Alfred A. Moss, Jr., *The American Negro Academy: Voices of the Talented Tenth* (Baton Rouge, LA: Louisiana State University Press, 1981), 1, 25; John Hope Franklin, *The Color Line: Legacy for the Twenty-First Century* (Columbia, MO: University of Missouri Press, 1993), xi; Donald Spivey, "African-American History and the New Critical Race Theory," address given at the University of South Florida, Institute on Black Life, 26 October 1995.

b). The Politics of the Scholarship of African-American History

5. L.D. Reddick, "A New Interpretation of Negro History," *Journal of Negro History* (January 1937).

6. Carter G. Woodson, "Negro Historians of Our Time," *Negro History Bulletin*, 8 (October 1946), 155–156, 158–159. James Baldwin, lecture given at University of Illinois, Urbana-Champaign, circa 1969. I was in attendance at Baldwin's lecture. Unfortunately the actual date of his talk escapes me but the words he delivered do not. Woodson quote is taken from Sister Anthony Scally's "Woodson and the Genesis of ASALH," *Negro History Bulletin* (January/February 1977), 653–655. For discussion of the early years in black history writing and the movement see Earl E. Thorpe, *Black Historians: A Critique* (New York, NY: William Morrow, 1971), 3–13; John Hope Franklin, *George Washington Williams: A Biography* (Chicago, IL: University of Chicago Press, 1985), 100–116, 164–179; Lorenzo J. Greene, (Arvarh E. Strickland, ed.),

Working with Carter G. Woodson, the Father of Black History (Baton Rouge, LA: Louisiana State University Press, 1989); Vincent Harding, *There Is A River: the Black Struggle for Freedom in America* (New York, NY: Vintage, 1983), xi; and the excellent treatment on the nineteenth century component in particular see Wilson J. Moses's recent work, *Afrotopia: The Roots of African American Popular History* (New York, NY: Cambridge University Press, 1998), especially 3–95, 96–112. A content analysis of the JNH articles and their multi-disciplinary approaches was conducted by the Institute for African-American Studies at the University of Connecticut in 1989 under the supervision of then IAAS director Donald Spivey.

7. Third College incident cited in Nick Aaron Ford, *Black Studies: Threat or Challenge* (Port Washington, NY: Kennikat Press, 1973), 74, also see 42–54; Raymond Wolters, *The New Negro on Campus: Black College Rebellions of the 1920s* (Princeton, NJ: Princeton University Press, 1975), 29–70, 82–86. The position for "objective" history void of politics is given in Oscar Handlin, *Truth in History* (Cambridge, MA: Harvard University Press, 1979), 23, 54, 101–108, 133, 372; for solid treatments of the history discipline and schools of thought see Fritz Stern, ed., *The Varieties of History: From Voltaire to the Present* (New York, NY: Vintage, 1973), 1, 40, 46, 54–70, 129, especially C. Van Woodward's controversial essay, "Clio and Crisis," 474–490, including his statement regarding black history as "too important to be left entirely in the hands of Negro historians," 486; Peter Burke, *The French Historical Revolution: The Annales School, 1929–89* (Stanford, CA: Stanford University Press, 1990), 1–11, 94–111; Francois Bedarida, *The Social Responsibility of the Historian* (Providence, RI: Berghahn Books, 1994), 2–5, 47, 51–61. For an engaging discussion of the politics of African-American history writing see Ernest Kaiser, "In Defense of the People's Black and White History and Culture," *Freedomways* 2 (1970), 17–37. For a feel for Woodson's inclusive scholarly approach see Carter G. Woodson, *African Myths Together with Proverbs: A Supplementary Reader Composed of Folk Tales from Various Parts of Africa* (Washington, DC: Associated Publishers, 1928).

8. Carter G. Woodson, "Personal: Thomas Jesse Jones," *Journal of Negro History*, 35 (1950), 107–109, "Negro Life and History in Our Schools," *Journal of Negro History*, 4 (1919), 273–280, and "An Accounting for Twenty-Five Years," *Journal of Negro History* 25 (1940), 422–431; Carter G. Woodson, "Democracy," *Negro History Bulletin* 6 (October 1942), 3–4, 14. One of the best discussions in many years of the black history movement and the many obsta-

cles it faced is Jacqueline Goggin, *Carter G. Woodson: A Life in Black History* (Baton Rouge, LA: Louisiana State University Press, 1993), see especially 50, 60–63, 92–93,135–137,172–174. Thomas Jesse Jones and several of the major funding agencies exported their conservative funding approach to Africa as well, see Donald Spivey, "The African Crusade For Black Industrial Schooling," *Journal of Negro History* 63 (January 1978), 1–17. See also Sister Anthony Scally, *Carter G. Woodson: A Bio-Bibliography* (Westport, CT: Greenwood Press, 1985); August Meier and Elliott Rudwick, *Black History and the Historical Profession, 1915–1980* (Urbana, IL: University of Illinois Press, 1986), 3, 25, 67–71, 88, 109; Harold Cruse, *The Crisis of the Negro Intellectual* (New York, NY: William Morrow, 1967), 145, 164–169, 337, 377; Kenneth O. Reilly, *Racial Matters: The FBI's Secret File on Black America, 1960–1972* (New York, NY: The Free Press, 1986), 14, 128–129, 141, FBI-COINTEL File confirmed that agency had informants within the OAH as cited in O'Reilly, 290; on the Apetheker incident at Yale, a joint committee of the American Historical Association and the Organization of American Historians investigated the matter and sided with the Yale history department's refusal to sponsor the one-semester visiting appointment and concluded that academic freedom and 1st Amendment rights were not violated, see *New York Times,* 15 January 1978, 44, 22 August 1976, 23, 30 April 1976, Sec. 2, 1, 26 March 1976, 40, 11 April 1976, 26, 28 April 1976, 30.

c). Race or Gender

9. Gloria T. Hull, Barbara Smith, Pat Bell Scott, eds., *But Some of Us Are Brave* (Old Westbury, NY: Feminist Press, 1987), Ellen Pence, "Racism—A White Issue, 46, Barbara Smith, "Racism and Women's Studies," 51; Beverly Guy-Sheftall, *Phylon* 1 (1992), 33–41; Bell Hooks, *Ain't I A Woman: Black Women and Feminism* (Boston, MA: South End Press, 1990) and *Killing Rage: Ending Racism* (New York, NY: Henry Holt, 1995), 1–22, 174–212; Evelyn Brooks Higginbotham, "African-American Women's History and the Metalanguage of Race," *Signs: Journal of Women in Culture and Society* 17:2 (1992), 95; Elizabeth Spelman, *Inessential Woman: Problems of Exclusion in Feminist Thought* (Boston, MA: Beacon Press, 1988); Deborah White, Aren't I a Woman: *Female Slaves in the Plantation South* (New York, NY: Norton, 1985), 1–37, 184–198; A. Leon Higginbotham, Jr., "Race, Sex, Education and Missouri Jurisprudence: Shelley v. Kraemer in a Historical Perspective," *Washington University Law Quarterly*

LXVII (1989), 684–685, as cited in Evelyn Brooks Higginbotham, "African-American Women's History and the Metalanguage of Race," 97–98. For further discussion along these lines see Louise Michele Newman, *White Women's Rights: The Racial Origins of Feminism in the United States* (New York, NY: Oxford University Press, 1998).

d). The New Anti-Critical Race Theorists

10. The new anti-critical race theorists have spewed forth numerous publications both academic and non-academic. The following books fairly represent their points of view on major issues: Diane Ravitch, *The Troubled Crusade: American Education, 1945–1980* (New York, NY: Basic Books, 1983); Allan Bloom, *The Closing of the American Mind* (New York, NY: Simon and Schuster, 1987); Walter E. Williams, *The State Against Blacks* (New York, NY: McGraw Hill, 1982); Thomas Sowell, *Race, Culture and Equality* (Stanford, CA: Hoover Institute, 1998); Shelby Steele, *The Content of Our Character: A New Vision of Race in America* (New York, NY: Harper Collins, 1990); Nat Hentoff, *Free Speech for Me But Not for Thee: How the American Left and Right Relentlessly Censor Each Other* (New York, NY: Harper Collins, 1992); Mary Lefkowitz, *Not Out of Africa: How Afrocentrism Became an Excuse to Teach Myth as History* (New York, NY: Harper Collins, 1996); William Bennett, *The Death of Outrage: Bill Clinton and the Assault on American Ideals* (New York, NY: Free Press, 1998); Dinesh D'Souza, *Illiberal Education: The Politics of Race and Sex on Campus* (New York, NY: Vintage, 1992); Arthur Schlesinger, Jr., *The Disuniting of America: Reflections on a Multicultural Society* (New York, NY: Norton, 1992; revised and enlarged 1998); John McWorter, *Losing the Race: Self-Sabotage in Black America* (New York, NY: Free Press, 2000).

11. Schlesinger, *Disuniting of America*, 9–10.

12. *Ibid.*, 76–78, 81.

13. The "ice and sun people" hypothesis was first made in 1978 by the white author Michael Bradley, *The Iceman Inheritance: Prehistoric Sources of Western Man's Racism, Sexism and Aggression* (New York, NY: Kayode Publishing, Inc., 1991 rept. of 1978 edn.); Schlesinger, 77, 81, 83–84, 86–88. As additional correctives to Schlesinger's thesis consult W. E. B. Du Bois, *The World and Africa: An Inquiry into the part which Africa has Played in World History* (New York, NY: International Publishers, 1947), especially chapter V, "Egypt," 98–114; Leopold Sedar Senghor, "Negritude and the Civilization of the Universal," in Carlos Moore, et. al., eds., *African*

Presence in the Americas (Trenton, NJ: Africa World Press, 1995); also see Janet G. Vaillant, *Black, French, and African: A Life of Leopold Sedar Senghor* (Cambridge, MA: Harvard University Press, 1990), 243–271; Cheikh Anta Diop, *The Cultural Unity of Black Africa* (Chicago, IL: Third World Press, 1978); Ivan van Sertima, ed., *Blacks in Science: Ancient and Modern* (New Brunswick, NJ: Transaction Books, 1983).

14. For a reasoned and extensive treatment of the question of academic canons see Henry Louis Gates, Jr., *Loose Canons: Notes on the Culture Wars* (New York, NY: Oxford University Press, 1992); D'Souza, *Illiberal Education*, xviii, 1.

15. D'Souza, 16, 18–22, 101, 124–125.

16. *Ibid.*, 197–206, 64, 211–212. For detailed and enlightened discourse that further serves as correctives to D'Souza's misunderstanding of academe consult Lawrence W. Levine, *The Opening of the American Mind: Canons, Culture, and History* (Boston, MA: Beacon Press, 1996), 35–102, 121–131; Robin D.G. Kelley, *Yo' Mama's Disfunktional: Fighting the Culture Wars in Urban America* (Boston, MA: Beacon Press, 1997); and William G. Bowen and Derek Bok, *The Shape of the River: Long-Term Consequences of Considering Race in College and University Admissions* (Princeton, NJ: Princeton University Press, 1998).

17. George M. Fredrickson, *New York Review of Books* 42:16 (1995), 10–11; Derrick Bell, guest lecture, "Confronting Authority," Coral Gables, Florida, 29 February 1996; Eric Foner, "Race and the Conservatives," *Dissent* 43:1 (1996), 105, 109; Sean Wilentz, "Color-Blinded," *The New Yorker* (October 1995), 91, 94;

e). Afrocentrism and the Challenge to Eurocentrism

18. Molefi Kete Asante, *Afrocentricity* (Trenton, NJ: Africa World Press, 1991), vii, 1, 107; Frank L. Matthews, "Academic Agitator: Dr. John Henrik Clarke," *Black Issues in Higher Education* (5 November 1992), 30–34. Also see Samir Amin, *Eurocentrism* ((New York, NY: Monthly Review Press, 1989), 89–117; Herb Boyd, "In Class with the Controversial Dr. Leonard Jeffries," *Emerge* 3 (February 1992), no.4, 34–37; Ed Wiley, III, "Afrocentrism: Many Things to Many People," *Black Issues in Higher Education* 8:17 (October 1991), 1, 20–21; *The Afrocentric Scholar: The Journal of the National Council for Black Studies* 1:1 (May 1992),1; K.K. Dompere, *Afrocentricity and African Nationalism: Philosophy and Ideology for Africa's Complete Emancipation* (Langley, MD: I.A.A.S. Publishers, Inc., 1992), 87–113.

19. Vine Deloria, *We Talk, You Listen: New Tribes, New Turf* (New York, NY: Dell, 1972), 39; "A vast, complex system of Eurocentrism permeates the entire academic curriculum" and we are engaged in an "intellectual war," is the conclusion of Professor Cain Hope Fedler of Howard University as cited in *Chronicle of Higher Education* (16 June 1993), A7; a feel for politics on campus is given in "Telling the Truth: A Report on the State of the Humanities in Higher Education," *Humanities*, 13:5 (September/October 1992), 1–11; William M. Chace, "The Real Challenge of Multi-Culturalism is Yet to Come," *Academe* (November/December 1990), 20–23; Mary Lefkowitz, "Afrocentrism Poses a Threat to the Rationalist Tradition," *Chronicle of Higher Education* (6 May 1992), A52.

20. Malcolm quote from George Breitman, ed., *Malcolm X on Afro-American History* (New York, NY: Pathfinder Press, 1974), 6. Buchanan quote from his column of 22 November 1984 and cited in Lars-Erik Nelson's editorial in *The New York Daily News*, 31 July 1986, 21A, under title, "Pretoria's White House Voice."

21. Charles Darwin, *the Origin of Species by Means of Natural Selection* (New York, NY: Random House rept. of 1859 edition) and *The Descent of Man and Selection in Relation to Sex* (New York, NY: Random House rept. of 1871 edition), Chp. VII, "On the Races of Man;" Richard Leakey, *The Origin of Humankind* (New York, NY: Basic Books, 1994), 1–20, 79–100; Louis S.B. Leakey, *Adam's Ancestors: the Evolution of Man and Culture* (New York, NY: Harper Torchbooks, 1960), *Olduvai Gorge, 1951–1961* (London, England: Cambridge University Press, 1965), *The Progress and Evolution of Man in Africa* (New York, NY: Oxford University Press, 1962); Basil Davidson, *African Civilization Revisited* (Trenton, NJ: Africa World Press, 1993), 1–46; Donald Johanson and Maitland A. Edey, *Lucy: The Beginnings of Humankind* (New York, NY: William Morrow, 1981), *Blueprints: Solving the Mystery of Evolution* (New York, NY: William Morrow, 1989); Donald Johanson and James Shreeve, *Lucy's Child: The Discovery of a Human Ancestor* (New York, NY: William Morrow, 1989), 45–101; PBS original broadcast 27 January 1987, "Children of Eve," (Boston, MA: WGBH Nova Transcripts, 1987), 1–29.

22. St. Clair Drake, *Black Folk Here and There* (Los Angeles, CA: CAAS, 1987), I., 115–239; Stanley Burstein, ed., *Ancient African Civilizations: Kush and Axum* (Princeton, NJ: Markus Wiener Publishers, 1998), 1–52, 53–55, 97–100; Martin Bernal, *Black Athena* (New Brunswick, NJ: Rutgers University Press, 1987), 1–38, 202–212, 294–296, 435–438; Jacob H. Carruthers, "Outside Academia: Bernal's Critique of Black Champions of Ancient Egypt,

Journal of Black Studies 22 (June 1992), no. 4, 459–476; Joseph E. Harris, *Africans and Their History* (New York, NY: New American Library, 1972), 11–58; Basil Davidson, *African Civilization Revisited* (Trenton, NJ: Africa World Press, 1993), 11, 25, 63, 81; Basil Davidson, "Africa: Different But Equal (Part I)" and "Africa: Mastering A Continent (Part 2)" *BBC Educational Videos* (1984); W.E.B. Du Bois, *The World and Africa: An Inquiry Into the Part which Africa has Played in World History* (New York, NY: International Publishers, 1969), 98–147; E. Jefferson Murphy, *History of African Civilization* (New York, NY: Thomas Y. Crowell, 1972), 18–63; I.E.S. Edwards, *The Pyramids of Egypt* (New York, NY: Penguin Books, 1979), 53,61,222, 292; George G.M. James, *Stolen Legacy* (San Franciso, CA: Julian Richardson Associates, Publishers, 1988 rept. of 1945 edn.); John G. Jackson, *Introduction to African Civilizations* (Secaucus, NJ: The Citadel Press, 1974), "Introduction by John Henrik Clarke," 3–35, 37–92; Cheikh Anta Diop, *The African Origin of Civilization: Myth or Reality* (Westport, CT: Lawrence Hill & Co., 1974), 1–9, 100–133, 237, 276–277; Victor Oguejiofor Okafor, "Diop and the African Origin of Civilization: An Afrocentric Analysis," *Journal of Black Studies* 22 (December 1991), no. 22, 252–268; Chancellor Williams, *the Destruction of Black Civilization: Great Issues of a Race from 4500 B.C. to 2000 A.D.* (Chicago, IL: Third World Press, 1974), 62–124; *The Mummy*, Universal Studios Picture, 1932; Yosef ben-Jochannan, *Black Man of the Nile* (New York, NY: Alkebu-lan Books Associates, 1970), 114–250, and *Africa: Mother of Western Civilization* (Alkebu-lan Books Associates, 1973), 75–167, 304–347; John Noble Wilford, "Rescued Nubian Treasures Reflect Black Influence on Egypt," *New York Times* (11 February 1992), C1, C10.

23. Leo Wiener, *Africa and the Discovery of America* ((Philadelphia, PA: Innes and Sons, 1922), I, II, and III; R.A. Jairazbhoy, *Ramses III: Father of Ancient America* (London, England: Karnak House, 1992); Ivan van Sertima, *They Came Before Columbus: The African Presence in Ancient America* (New York, NY: Random House, 1976), and ed., *African Presence in Early America* (New Brunswick, NJ: Transaction Books, 1992); Joseph E. Harris, *The African Presence in Asia* (Evanston, IL: Northwestern University Press, 1971); Floyd W. Hayes, III, "The African Presence in America," *Black World* (July 1973), 5–23; Smithsonian Institution, *Disease and Demography in the Americas* (Washington, DC: Smithsonian Institution Press, 1992), i–x, 1–147; Association of American Geographers, *The Americas Before and After 1492* (Washington, DC: Association of American Geographers, 1992); John Henrik Clarke, "The Africans,

Christopher Columbus and the Myth of the New World Discovery,"
Pan-African Scholars Quarterly, 2:4 (1991), 2–8.

II. THE DESTRUCTION OF A PEOPLE

a). The Beginning of the African-American Journey from Respectability to Degradation

1. Basil Davidson, *The Lost Cities of Africa* (Boston, MA: Little, Brown & Co., 1959); Joseph E. Harris, *Africans and Their History* (New York, NY: New American Library, 1972), 34–70; J.C. deGraft-Johnson, *African Glory: The Story of Vanished Negro Civilizations* (Baltimore, MD: Black Classic Press, 1978), 53–126; Ivan Van Sertima, ed., *Golden Age of the Moor* (New Brunswick, NJ: Transaction Publishers, 1993), 1–8, 27–84; T.A. Osae, S.N. Nwabara and A.T.O. Odunsi, *A Short History of West Africa* (New York, NY: Hill and Wang, 1973), 13–86; Cheikh Anta Diop, *Precolonial Black Africa* (Chicago, IL: Lawrence Hill Books, 1987), 21–45, 89–129; Said Hamdun and Noel King, *Ibn Battuta in Black Africa* (Princeton, NJ: Markus Wiener Publishers, 1994); Basil Davidson, *The African Genius* (Boston, MA: Little, Brown and Co., 1969), 45–79, 160–167; Richard Hull, *African Cities and Towns Before the European Conquest* (New York, NY: Norton, 1976), ix–xx. Reliable overviews are given in Robert I. Rotberg, *A Political History of Tropical Africa* (New York, NY: Harcourt, Brace and World, 1965), 5–50; Philip S. Foner, *History of Black Americans: From Africa to the Emergence of the Cotton Kingdoms* (Westport, CT: Greenwood Press, 1975), 34–57; and E. Jefferson Murphy, *History of African Civilization* (New York, NY: Thomas Y. Crowell Co., 1972), 82–129.

2. Jordan's book remains the finest treatment of the subject. Winthrop D. Jordan *White Over Black: American Attitudes Toward the Negro, 1550–1812* (New York, NY: Pelican Books, 1969), 3–43. Also see Anthony Barthelemy, *Black Face, Maligned Race: The Representation of Blacks in English Drama from Shakespeare to Southerne* (Baton Rouge, LA: Louisiana State University Press, 1987).

3. Edgar Rice Burroughs, *Tarzan of the Apes* (Shelton, CT: First Edition Printing, 1998 rept. of 1914 edn.); John H. Griffin, *Black Like Me* (New York, NY: Penguin, 1996 rept. of 1961 edn.).

b). They Came, We Were Brought

4. A good collection of the leading arguments regarding the slave trade is David Northrup, ed., *The Atlantic Slave Trade* (Lexington, MA: D.C. Heath, 1994). Basil Davidson, *The African Slave Trade:*

Precolonial History, 1450–1850 (Boston, MA: Little, Brown and Co., 1961), xiii, 31–39; Eric Williams, *Capitalism and Slavery* (New York, NY: Capricorn Books, 1966 rept. of 1943 edn.), 30–107; Walter Rodney, *How Europe Underdeveloped Africa* (Dar-es Salaam, Tanzania: Tanzania Publishing House, 1972), 40–123; J.E. Inikori, "Measuring the Atlantic Slave Trade: An Assessment of Curtin and Anstey," *Journal of African History* 17 (1976), no. 2, 197–223; Philip D. Curtin, *The Atlantic Slave Trade* (Madison, WI: University of Wisconsin Press, 1969), 265–273; Roger Anstey, "The Volume and Profitability of the British Slave Trade, 1761–1807," in Stanley Engerman and Eugene Genovese, ed., *Race and Slavery in the Western Hemisphere* (Princeton, NJ: Princeton University Press, 1975), 3–31; Daniel P. Mannix and Malcolm Cowley, *A History of the Atlantic Slave Trade* (New York, NY: The Viking Press, 1962), 27–130; Alexander Falconbridge, *An Account of the Slave Trade on the Coast of Africa*, (London, England: J. Phillips Pub., 1788); W.E.B. Du Bois, *The Suppression of the African Slave Trade* (New York, NY: Schocken Books, 1969 rept. of 1896 edn.), 1–37, 40–45; Immanuel Wallerstein, *The Modern World-System I: Capitalist Agriculture and the Origins of the European World-Economy in the Sixteenth Century* (New York, NY: Academic Press, 1974), 43–44, 83–90.

5. Vincent Bakpetu Thompson, *The Making of the African Diaspora in the Americas, 1441–1900* (New York, NY: Longman Inc., 1987), 1–107; J.M. Blaut, ed., *1492: The Debate on Colonialism, Eurocentrism and History* (Trenton, NJ: Africa World Press, 1992), passim; David Brian Davis, *Slavery and Human Progress* (New York, NY: Oxford University Press, 1984), 23–31, 51–81; Herbert S. Klein, *African Slavery in Latin America and the Caribbean* (New York, NY: Oxford University Press, 1986), 1–45, 67–138; Stanley Stein, *Vassouras: A Brazilian Coffee Country, 1850–1900* (New York, NY: Atheneum, 1976); Carl M. Degler, *Neither Black Nor White: Slavery and Race Relations in Brazil and the United States* (New York, NY: Macmillan, 1971), 23–54; Richard S. Dunn, Sugar and Slaves: The Rise of the Planter Class in the English West Indies, 1624–1713 (New York, NY: Norton, 1972), 46–116, 188–262; Franklin W. Knight and Colin A. Palmer, ed., *The Modern Caribbean* (Chapel Hill, NC: University of North Carolina Press, 1989), 1–20; Karia M. de Querios Mattoso, *To Be a Slave in Brazil, 1550–1888* (New Brunswick, NJ: Rutgers University Press, 1986), 1–84; Allan Kulikoff, *Tobacco and Slaves: The Development of Southern Cultures in the Chesapeake, 1680–1800* (Chapel Hill, NC: University of North Carolina Press, 1986), 23–77; Frank Tannen-

baum, *Slave and Citizen: The Negro in the Americas* (New York, NY: Vintage Books, 1946); Stanley M. Elkins, *Slavery: A Problem in American Institutional and Intellectual Life* (Chicago, IL: University of Chicago Press, 1959), 1–97; Arthur Ramos, *The Negro in Brazil* (Washington, DC: Associated Publishers, 1939), 34–35; Gilberto Freyre, *The Masters and the Slaves* (New York, NY: Knopf, 1946), 351, 392; see especially Marvin Harris, "The Myth of the Friendly Master" in Laura Foner and Eugene D. Genovese, ed., *Slavery in the New World: A Reader in Comparative History* (Englewood Cliffs, NJ: Prentice-Hall, 1969), 38–47; Moses D.E. Nwulia, *Britain and Slavery in East Africa* (Washington, DC: Three Continents Press, 1975), 1–29, 96–110; Roger Norman Buckley, *Slaves in Red Coats: The British West India Regiments, 1795–1815* (New Haven, CT: Yale University Press, 1979), 63–81; Evelyn Brooks Higginbotham, "African-American Women's History and the Metalanguage of Race," *Signs: Journal of Women in Culture and Society* 17:2 (1992), 95; 93–98.

III. DEMOCRACY CONTRADICTED

a). Black in "the Land of the Free"

1. Richard Hakluyt, *A Discourse on Western Planting* (Cambridge, England: Press of J. Wilson and Son, 1877 rept., microfilm copy by University Microfilms, Ann Arbor, Michigan, 1956); Thomas Paine, *Common Sense* (Boston, MA: John H. Dunham, 1803); Lorenzo J. Greene, *The Negro in Colonial New England* (New York, NY: Atheneum, 1969), 15–47, 50–69; William D. Piersen, *Black Yankees: The Development of an Afro-American Subculture in Eighteenth-Century New England* (Amherst, MA: University of Massachusetts Press, 1988), 1–28; David Brion Davis, *The Problem of Slavery in the Age of Revolution, 1770–1823* (Ithaca, NY: Cornell University Press, 1975), 255–267, 274–279, 285–286; Benjamin Quarles, *The Negro in the American Revolution* (Chapel Hill, NC: University of North Carolina Press, 1961), 33–50; Bernard Bailyn, *The Ideological Origins of the American Revolution* (Cambridge, MA: Harvard University Press, 1967), passim; Susan M. Kingsbury, *Records of the Virginia Company of London* (Washington, DC: Government Printing Office, 1906–1935), III, 241–48; Wesley Frank Craven, *White Red and Black: The Seventeenth-Century Virginian* (Charlottesville, VA: University Press of Virginia, 1971), 73–77, 102–103; A. Leon Higginbotham, Jr., *In the Matter of Color: Race and The American Legal Process: The Colo-*

nial Period (New York, NY: Oxford University Press, 1978), 5–7, 371–390; Paul Finkelman, *Slavery and the Founders: Race and Liberty in the Age of Jefferson* (Armonk, NY: M.E. Sharpe, 1996), 80–104; Donald G. Nieman, *Promises to Keep: African-Americans and the Constitutional Order, 1776 to the Present* (New York, NY: Oxford University Press, 1991), 3–29; Richard Hofstadter, *The American Political Tradition* (New York, NY: Vintage, 1974), 22–55; Gary B. Nash, *Red, White, and Black: The Peoples of Early America* (Englewood Cliffs, NJ: Prentice-Hall, 1974), 13–26; J. Hector St. John de Crevecoeur, *Letters from an American Farmer* (New York, NY: E.P. Dutton, 1957 rept.), 17–19, 155–168; Lerone Bennett, Jr., *Before the Mayflower: A History of Black America* (New York, NY: Penguin Books, 1982), 55–85; Nathan I. Huggins, *Black Odyssey: The Afro-American Ordeal in Slavery* (New York, NY: Vintage, 1977), 3–24.

2. W.E.B. Du Bois, *The Souls of Black Folk* (New York, NY: Fawcett, 1961 rept. of 1903 edn.), v; Donald Spivey, "Point of Contention: An Historical Perspective on the African-American Presence in Hartford," *The State of Black Hartford* (Hartford, CT: The Urban League of Greater Hartford, Inc., 1994), 45–61.

3. Marion and Ellsworth Grant, *The City of Hartford, 1784–1984* (Hartford, CT: Connecticut Historical Society, 1986), 1–6; Will I. Twitchell, ed., *Hartford in History: A Series of Papers By Resident Authors* (Hartford, CT: Press of the Plimpton Mfg. Co., 1907), 97, 122–124; Charles W. Burpee, *History of Hartford County Connecticut, 1633–1928* (Hartford, CT: S.J. Clarke Publishing, 1928), I., 74, 166; Barbara W. Brown and James M. Rose, *Black Roots in Southeastern Connecticut, 1650–1900* (Detriot, MI: Gale Research Co., 1980), 10, 67, 144, 296, 337, 362; Elizabeth Donnan, *Documents Illustrative of the History of the Slave Trade to America* (New York, NY: Octagon Books, 1969), III., 2, 32, 70; Piersen, 1, 14, 18–49, 100, 104; Greene, 28–75; William C. Nell, *Colored Patriots of the American Revolution* (Salem, NH: Boston, MA: Robert F. Wallcut, 1855), 132–144; David O. White, *Connecticut's Black Soldiers, 1775–1783* (Chester, CT: Pequot Press, 1973); John E. Rogers, *Inner City Bicentennial Booklet, 1776–1976* (Westport, CT: University of Hartford, 1975); Richard D. Brown, "Not Only Extreme Poverty, But the Worst Kind of Orphanage: Lemuel Haynes and the Boundaries of Racial Tolerance on the Yankee Frontier, 1770–1820," *The New England Quarterly* 61:4 (December 1988), 502–518; Ordell Shepard, *Connecticut Past and Present* (New York, NY: Knopf, 1939), 23, 31, 106–120; Albert E. Van Dusen, *Connecticut* (New York, NY: Random House, 1961), III., 1–46; see Christopher Collier and Bonnie Collier, "Slaver

and the Black Experience," in *The Literature of Connecticut History* (Middle Town, CT: Connecticut Humanities Council, 1983); Shepard, 111.

4. James D. Essig, "Connecticut Ministers and Slavery, 1790–1795," *Journal of American Studies* I (1981, no. 15, 27–44; Leonard Richards, *Gentlemen of Property and Standing: Anti-Abolition Mobs in Jacksonian America* (New York, NY: Oxford University Press, 1970), 37–41; James W.C. Pennington, *The Fugitive Blacksmith, or Events in the History of James W. C. Pennington, Pastor of a Presbyterian church, New York, Formerly a Slave in the State of Maryland, United States* (London, England: Charles Gilpin, 1850); Connecticut Historical Commission and the Center for Connecticut Studies, Eastern Connecticut State University, "James W.C. Pennington," in *Connecticut History and Culture: An Historical Overview and Resource Guide for Teachers* (Hartford, CT: Connecticut Historical Commission, 1986), 132; David O. White, "Fugitive Blacksmith of Hartford: James W.C. Pennington," *Connecticut Historical Society Bulletin,* 49:1 (Winter 1984), 5–30 and "Augustus Washington, Black Daguerreotypist of Hartford," 39:1 (Winter 1974), 14–19; Arthur White, "Prince Saunders: An Instance of Social Mobility Among Antebellum New England Blacks," *Journal of Negro History* 60:4 (October 1975), 526–536; Frank A. Stone, *African American Connecticut: African Origins, New England Roots* (Storrs, CT: Issac Thut World Education Center, 1991), 110; *Rebecca Primus Papers,* Connecticut Historical Society, passim.

5. The best overview of the black condition in the antebellum North is Leon F. Litwack's long-standing, *North of Slavery: The Negro in the Free States, 1790–1860* (Chicago, IL: University of Chicago Press, 1961), 3–29 and passim. Lorenzo Greene's work remains the finest treatment to date of the black experience in the colonial period: *The Negro in Colonial New England* (New York, NY: Atheneum, 1969), 257–315; William D. Piersen, *Black Yankees: The Development of an Afro-American Subculture in Eighteenth-Century New England* (Amherst, MA: University of Massachusetts Press, 1988), 87–96, 117–128; Gary B. Nash, *Forging Freedom: The Formation of Philadelphia's Black Community, 1720–1840* (Cambridge, MA: Harvard University Press, 1988), 172–281; Roi Ottley and William J. Weatherby, ed., *The Negro in New York: An Informal Social History, 1626–1940* (New York, NY: Praeger, 1967), 1–128; Spivey, "A Point of Contention: An Historical Perspective on the African-American Presence in Hartford," 46–55.

6. James Mellon, ed., *Bullwhip Days: The Slaves Remember: An Oral History* (New York, NY: Weidenfeld and Nicolson, 1988), 3–24, 55–82; John Blassingame, *Slave Testimony: Two Centuries of*

Letters, Speeches, Interviews, and Autobiographies (Baton Rouge, LA: Louisiana State University Press, 1977), 121–366; Thomas Jefferson, *Notes on the State of Virginia* (New York, NY: Norton, 1974 rept.), 138–143; on Jefferson's relationship with his slave Sally Hemings see Annette Gordon-Reed, *Thomas Jefferson and Sally Hemings: An American Controversy* (Charlottesville, VA: University Press of Virginia, 1997), and Michael Durey, *With the Hammer of Truth: America's Early National Heroes* (Charlottesville, VA: University Press of Virginia, 1990). Matthew T. Mellon, *Early American Views on Negro Slavery* (New York, NY: Mentor Books, 1969); Kenneth M. Stampp, *The Peculiar Institution* (New York, NY: Vintage, 1956), especially 3–140, 237–382; C.L.R. James, *The Black Jacobins: Toussaint L'Overture and the San Domingo Revolution* (New York, Vintage, 1963), 145–198; Ulrich B. Phillips, *American Negro Slavery* (Baton Rouge, LA: Louisiana State University Press, 1966 rept. of 1918 edn.), 228–343, 359–453; Eugene D. Genovese, *The Political Economy of Slavery* (New York, NY: Vintage, 1965), *The World the Slaveholders Made* (New York, NY: Vintage, 1971), especially vi–ix, 96–113, and *Roll Jordan Roll: The World the Slave Made* (New York, NY: Vintage, 1976); Robert W. Fogel and Stanley L. Engerman, *Time on the Cross: The Economics of American Negro Slavery* (New York, NY: Little, Brown and Co., 1974), especially 3–12, 40–58, 127–157; Herbert G. Gutman, *Slavery and the Numbers Game: A Critique of Time on the Cross* (Urbana, IL: University of Illinois Press, 1975), and *The Black Family in Slavery and Freedom, 1750–1925* (New York, NY: Vintage, 1976), 20–44, 185–230, 432–460; George M. Fredrickson, *The Black Image in the White Mind: The Debate on Afro-American Character and Destiny, 1817–1914* (New York, NY: Harper and Row, 1971), 43–75; H. Shelton Smith, *In His Image But: Racism in Southern Religion, 1780–1910* (Durham, NC: Duke University Press, 1974), 129–165; Richard C. Wade, *Slavery in the Cities: The South, 1820–1860* (New York, NY: Oxford University Press, 1977), 4–23, 30–54, 65–71, 136–173; John W. Blassingame, *The Slave Community: Plantation Life in the Antebellum South* (New York, NY: Oxford University Press, 1979), 149–222; Leslie H. Owens, *This Species of Property: Slave Life and Culture in the Old South* (New York, NY: Oxford University Press, 1976), 19–120; Robert S. Starobin, *Industrial Slavery in the Old South* (New York, NY: Oxford University Press, 1970), 35–74; T.H. Breen and Stephen Innes, *Myne Owne Ground: Race and Freedom on Virginia's Eastern Shore, 1640–1676* (New York, NY: Oxford University Press, 1980), 36–67; Barbara Jeanne Fields, *Slavery and Freedom on the Middle*

Ground (New Haven, CT: Yale University Press, 1985), 23–62, 194–206; Jacqueline Jones, *Labor of Love, Labor of Sorrow: Black Women, Work and the Family, from Slavery to the Present* (New York, NY: Vintage, 1986), 11–43; see Alex Haley, *Roots: The Saga of an American Family* (New York, NY: Doubleday, 1976); *The Negro Family: The Case for National Action* [commonly known as the Moynihan Report after Committee Chair, Daniel Patrick Moynihan] (Washington, DC: Government Printing Office, 1965), 1–78; Joyce A. Ladner, *Tomorrow's Tomorrow: The Black Woman* (New York, NY: Doubleday, 1971); William Julius Wilson, *The Truly Disadvantaged: The Inner City, the Underclass, and Public Policy* (Chicago, IL: University of Chicago Press, 1987), 96–97, 110–111, 144–153, 184–186.

b). The Culture of Survival

7. Vincent Bakpetu Thompson, *The Making of the African Diaspora in the Americas, 1441–1900* (New York, NY: Longman, 1987), 9–21, 131–159, 255–300; Joseph H. Harris, *The Global Dimension of the African Diaspora* (Washington, DC: Howard University Press, 1982), 1–92; Lawrence W. Levine, *Black Culture and Black Consciousness: Afro-American Folk Thought from Slavery to Freedom* (New York, NY: Oxford University Press, 1977), 5–80, 136–189; Sterling Stuckey, *Slave Culture: Nationalist Theory and the Foundations of Black America* (New York, NY: Oxford University Press, 1987), 1–97; see Joseph E. Holloway, ed., *Africanisms in American Culture* (Bloomington, IN: Indiana University Press, 1991); Sylvia Ardyn Boone, *Radiance From the Waters: Ideals of Feminine Beauty in Mende Art* (New Haven, CT: Yale University Press, 1986), 1–12, 45–54, 81–95; John S. Mbiti, *African Religions and Philosophy* (New York, NY: Anchor Books, 1970), 29–36, 130–142, 266–273, 355–363; Diane Marie Spivey, *The Peppers, Cracklings and Knots of Wool Cookbook: The Global Migration of African Cuisine* (Albany, NY: State University of New York Press, 1999) explores the culinary link between Africa and the entire diaspora. Gwendolyn Midlo Hall, *Africans in Colonial Louisiana: The Developments of Afro-Creole Culture in the Eighteenth Century* (Baton Rouge, LA: Louisiana State University Press, 1992), 186–200, 275–315; also see Michael A. Gomez, *Exchanging Our Country Marks: The Transformation of African Identities in the Colonial and Antebellum South* (Chapel Hill, NC: University of North Carolina Press, 1998), 244–290; Margaret T. Drewal, *Yoruba Ritual: Performers, Play, Agency* (Bloomington, IN: Indiana

University Press, 1992); Pedro Perez Sarduy and Jean Stubbs, ed., *AfroCuba: An Anthology of Cuban Writing on Race, Politics and Culture* (New York, NY: Center for Cuban Studies, 1993) 3–27; Margaret Washington Creel, *A Peculiar People: Slave Religion and Community-Culture Among the Gullahs* (New York, NY: New York University Press, 1988), 45–66, 113–147, 259–307; Albert J. Raboteau, *Slave Religion: The Invisible Institution in the Antebellum South* (New York, NY: Oxford University Press, 1978), 211–318; Whittington B. Johnson, *Black Savannah, 1788–1864* (Fayetteville, AS: University of Arkansas Press, 1996), 85–132; John B. Boles, ed., *Masters and Slaves in the House of the Lord: Race and Religion in the American South, 1740–1870* (Lexington, KY: University Press of Kentucky, 1988), passim; Lesleie H. Owens, *This Species of Property: Slave Life and Culture in the Old South* (New York, NY: Oxford University Press, 1976), 50–69; Mellon, *Bullwhip Days*, 33–54; Thomas L. Webber, *Deep Like the Rivers: Education in the Slave Quarters Community, 1831–1865* (New York, NY: Norton, 1976), 27–59, 91–102; Robert C. Toll, *Blacking Up: The Minstrel Shows in Nineteenth-Century America* (New York, NY: Oxford University Press, 1974), 65–133; Melville J. Herskovits, *The Myth of the Negro Past* (Boston, MA: Beacon Press, 1990), 54–85; John W. Blassingame, *The Slave Community: Plantation Life in the Antebellum South* (New York, NY: Oxford University Press, 1979), 105–148; Roger D. Abrahams, ed., *Afro-American Folktales: Stories from Black Traditions in the New World* (New York, NY: Pantheon, 1985); Deborah G. White, "Female Slaves: Sex Roles and Status in the Antebellum Plantation South," in J. William Harris, ed., *Society and Culture in the Slave South* (New York, NY: Routledge, 1992), 225–243; Georgia Writers' Project, *Drums and Shadows: Survival Studies Among the Georgia Coastal Negroes* (Athens, GA: University of Georgia Press, 1986 rept.), illustrations; Harriet A. Jacobs, *Incidents in the Life of a Slave Girl* (Cambridge, MA: Harvard University Press, 1987 rept.), 68–79; Nancy Prince, *The Narrative of Nancy Prince: Black Woman's Odyssey Through Russia and Jamaica* (New York, NY: Markus Wiener Pubs., 1990 rept. of 1850 edn.); M.M. Manring, *Slave in a Box: The Strange Career of Aunt Jemima* (Charlottesville, VA: University Press of Virginia, 1998), 1–78; Elizabeth Fox-Genovese, *Within the Plantation Household: Black and White Women of the Old South* (Chapel Hill, NC: University of North Carolina Press, 1988), 146–191; William Loren Katz, *Black Indians: A Hidden Heritage* (New York, NY: Atheneum, 1986), 35–73; Daniel F. Littlefield, Jr., *Africans and Seminoles: From Removal to Emancipation*

(Westport, CT: Greenwood Press, 1977), 15–35, 162–179; Wade, *Slavery in the Cities*, 55–79; Ira Berlin, *Slaves Without Masters: The Free Negro in the Antebellum South* (New York, NY: Oxford University Press, 1974), 284–315; Ortiz M. Walton, *Music: Black, White and Blue* (New York, NY: William Morrow and Co., 1972),1–37, 73–92; Francis Berry, *African Music: A People's Art* (Westport, CT: Lawrence Hill & Co., 1975, 17–39; Paul Oliver, *Savannah Syncopators: African Retentions in the Blues* (New York, NY: Stein and Day, 1970), 84–101; Geneva H. Southall, *Blind Tom: The Post-Civil War Enslavement of a Black Musical Genius* (Minneapolis, MN: Challenge Production, Inc., 1979); LeRoi Jones, *Blues People: The Negro Experience in White America and the Music that Developed From it* (New York, NY: William Morrow, 1963), 17–32, 60–80, 166–175; Dena J. Epstein, *Sinful Tunes and Spirituals: Black Folk Music to the Civil War* (Urbana, IL: University of Illinois Press, 1977), 47–76; Timothy White, *Catch a Fire: the Life of Bob Marley* (New York, NY: Henry Holt, 1991), 23, 103, 128, 135; for discussion of the emergence of the modern music scene and the African-American contribution see Nelson George, *The Death of Rhythm and Blues* (New York, NY: Pantheon Books, 1988), also thoughtful is Frank Kofsky, *Black Nationalism and the Revolution in Music* (New York, NY: Pathfinder, 1970).

8. Bertram Wyatt-Brown, "Male Slave Psychology in the Old South," in J. William Harris, ed., *Society and Culture in the Slave South* (New York, NY: Routledge, 1992), 100–127; Elizabeth Fox-Genovese, "Women Who Opposed Slavery," in *Within the Plantation Household*, 290–333; Blassingame, *The Slave Community*, 284–322; Stanley M. Elkins, *Slavery: A Problem in American Institutional and Intellectual Life* (Chicago, IL: University of Chicago Press, 1959), 81–139; Gordon W. Allport, *Personality: A Psychological Interpretation* (New York, NY: Henry Holt and Co., 1948) and *The Nature of Prejudice* (Boston, MA: Beacon Press, 1954); George Spindler, *Education and Cultural Process* (Prospect Heights, IL: Waveland Press, 1987); Frantz Fanon, *Black Skin, White Masks* (New York, NY: Grove Press, 1967), Chp. VI., "The Negro and Psychopathology," 141–209.

c). Trying Just to be Free, Not an American

9. African resistance to enslavement began on the shores of Africa, see Ali Mazrui and Robert Rothberg, *Protest and Power in Black Africa* (New York, NY: Oxford University Press, 1970), I. Peter Wood, *Black Majority: Negroes in Colonial South Carolina from 1670 through the Stono Rebellion* (New York, NY:

Norton, 1974), 285–330; Alfred N. Hunt, *Haiti's Influence on Antebellum America* (Baton Rouge, LA: Louisiana State University Press, 1988), 84–106; Herbert Aptheker, *American Negro Slave Revolts* (New York, NY: International Publishers, 1993 6th edn.); Gerald W. Mullin, *Flight and Rebellion: Slave Resistance in Eighteenth-Century Virginia* (New York, NY: Oxford University Press, 1972), 140–164; Nat Turner, *The Confessions of Nat Turner* (Richmond, VA: T.R. Gray, 1832); James T. Baker, *Nat Turner: Cry Freedom in America* (New York, NY: Harcourt Brace, 1998); John Hope Franklin, *Runaway Slaves: Rebels on the Plantation* (New York, NY: Oxford University Press, 1999); Wade, *Slavery in the Cities*, 204–242; Howard Jones, *Mutiny on the Amistad: The Saga of a Slave Revolt and its Impact on American Abolition, Law, and Diplomacy* (New York, NY: Oxford University Press, 1987); Donald Spivey, "Implications of the Amistad Revolt of 1839," lecture delivered at New Haven Colony Historical Society Workshop for Teachers Grades K-12, 1 February 1992; Elizabeth Donnan, ed., *Documents Illustrative of the History of the Slave Trade to America* (New York, NY: Octagon Books, 1969), II., 266.

10. Robert P. Smith, "William Cooper Nell: Crusading Black Abolitionist," *Journal of Negro History* LV:3 (1970), 182–199; Stanley W. Campbell, *The Slave Catchers: Enforcement of the Fugitive Slave Law, 1850–1860* (New York, NY: Norton, 1970); Earl Conrad, *Harriet Tubman* (Washington, DC: Associated Pubs., 1943); Harriet A. Jacobs, *Incidents in the Life of a Slave Girl*, 17–27, 53–57; Benjamin Quarles, *Black Abolitionists* (New York, NY: Oxford University Press, 1969), 33, 143–167; *Prigg v. Pennsylvania* (1842); John L. Thomas, ed., *Slavery Attacked: The Abolitionist Crusade* (Englewood Cliffs, NJ: Prentice-Hall, 1965), 76–79, 99–104; Leonard L. Richards, *Gentlemen of Property and Standing: Anti-Abolition Mobs in Jacksonian America* (New York, NY: Oxford University Press, 1970), 4–5, 36–54, 85–96; Joel Schor, *Henry Highland Garnet: A Voice of Black Radicalism in the Nineteenth Century* (Westport, CT: Greenwood Press, 53–64; Paul Jefferson, ed., *The Travels of William Wells Brown* (New York, NY: Markus Wiener Pubs., 1991), 21–71; William Cheek and Aimee Lee Cheek, *John Mercer Langston and the Fight for Black Freedom, 1829–65* (Urbana, IL: University of Illinois Press, 1989), 349–382; David Walker, *David Walker's Appeal to the Coloured Citizens of the World, but in Particular, and Very Expressly, to Those of The United States of America* (New York, NY: Hill and Wang, 1985 rept. of 1829 edn.).

IV. OUTRIGHT VIOLENCE

a). Parallels to the Modern Civil Rights Movement

1. Donald Spivey, "The Contemporary Civil Rights Movement and Parallels to John Brown," paper prepared for Commemoration Symposium on "Images of John Brown," Torrington, Connecticut, 9 May 1992; Benjamin Quarles, *Blacks on John Brown* (Urbana, IL: University of Illinois Press, 1972), *Black Abolitionists* (New York, NY: Oxford University Press, 1969), 235–245, and *Lincoln and the Negro* (New York, NY: Da Capo, 1962), 56–144; James A. Rawley, *Race and Politics: Bleeding Kansas and the Coming of the Civil War* (Philadelphia, PA: J.B. Lippincott, 1969), 133–134; Richard O. Curry, ed., *Radicalism, Racism, and Party Realignment: The Border States During Reconstruction* (Baltimore, MD: Johns Hopkins Press, 1969, xiii–xxvi; LaWanda Cox, *Lincoln and Black Freedom* (Urbana, IL: University of Illinois Press, 1985), 119–125, 142–184; Lerone Bennett, *Forced to Glory: Abraham Lincoln's White Dream* (Chicago, IL: Johnson Publishing, 2000); Kwame Nkrumah, *Ghana: The Autobiography of Kwame Nkrumah* (New York, NY: International Publishers, 1971 rept. of 1957 edn.), 147–156; Schor, *Henry Highland Garnet*, 60–61, 136, 163–164; W.E.B. Du Bois, *John Brown* (Philadelphia, PA: George W. Jacobs & Co., 1909), 342; Douglass quote cited in Stuckey, *Slave Culture*, 166.

2. W.E.B. Du Bois, *The autobiography of W.E.B. Du Bois* (New York, NY: International Publishers, 1968), 251; Oswald Garrison Villard, *John Brown* (New York, NY: Houghton Mifflin, 1910); Victor Ullman, *Martin R. Delany: The Beginnings of Black Nationalism* (Boston, MA: Beacon Press, 1971), 191–200, 249, 283, 460; Mildred J. Thompson, *Ida B. Wells-Barnett: An Exploratory Study of an American Black Woman, 1893–1930* (Brooklyn, NY: Carlson Publishing, Inc., 1990), 183; Kelly Miller quote cited in Tony Martin, *Race First: The Ideological and Organizational Struggles of Marcus Garvey and the Universal Negro Improvement Association* (Westport, CT: Greenwood Press, 1976), 195; George Brietman, ed., *Malcolm X on Afro-American History* (New York, NY: Pathfinder Press, 1974), 66; Du Bois, *John Brown*, 140; *Sports Illustrated* (26 February 1968), 25–26; David Garrow, *Bearing the Cross: Martin Luther King, Jr., and the Southern Christian Leadership Conference* (New York, NY: William Morrow, 1986), 393.

3. See Gene Marine, *The Black Panthers* (New York, NY: Signet Books, 1969) and Bobby Seale, *Seize the Time: The Story of the Black Panther Party and Huey P. Newton* (New York, NY: Vintage Books, 1970), passim; Herbert Aptheker, *Slave Guerrilla Warfare and Mili-*

tant Abolitionism (New York, NY: International Publishers, 1968), 58, 68–69; Du Bois, *John Brown*, 396; "White Expert Tells How Racism is Taught and Learned," *Jet Magazine* (13 July 1992), 14; Spivey, "The Contemporary Civil Rights Movement and Parallels to John Brown," 4–5.

b). Civil War Lessons

4. James McPherson, *Battle Cry of Freedom: The Civil War Era* (New York, NY: Oxford University Press, 1988), 78–144, 202–233, 689–717, and passim; Eric Foner, *Free Soil, Free Labor, Free Men* (New York, NY: Oxford University Press, 1970), 11–39, 103–185, 301–318; Lincoln quote is cited in LaWanda Cox, *Lincoln and Black Freedom*, 21; James L. Roark, *Masters Without Slaves: Southern Planters in the Civil War and Reconstruction* (New York, NY: Norton, 1977), 35–67; William J. Cooper, Jr., *Liberty and Slavery: Southern Politics to 1860* (New York, NY: Knopf, 1983), 120–147, 213–247; Don E. Fehrenbacher, *Slavery, Law, and Politics: The Dred Scott Case in Historical Perspective* (New York, NY: Oxford University Press, 1981), 102–120; Paul Finkelman, *Dred Scott v. Sandford: A Brief History with Documents* 1997); R. Kent Newmyer, *The Supreme Court under Marshall and Taney* (New York, NY: Harlan Davidson, 1968), 122–146; Kenneth M. Stampp, *The Imperiled Union: Essays on the Background of the Civil War* (New York, NY: Oxford University Press, 1980), 105–162; Richard Moe, *The Last Full Measure: The Life and Death of the First Minnesota Volunteers* (New York, NY: Henry Holt, 1993), 13; Mark Rimsley, "In Not So Dubious Battle: The Motivations of American Civil War Soldiers," *Journal of Military History* 62:1 (January 1998), 175–195; George M. Fredrickson, *The Inner Civil War: Northern Intellectuals and the Crisis of the Union* (New York, NY: Harper Torchbooks, 1965), 65–97, and *The Arrogance of Race: Historical Perspectives on Slavery, Racism, and Social Inequality* (Middletown, CT: Wesleyan University Press, 1988), 28–52; see *Record of the Service of the Fifty-fifth Regiment of Massachusetts Volunteer Infantry* (Salem, NH: Aver Co. Publishers, 1991 rept. of 1868 edn.); David W. Blight, *Frederick Douglass' Civil War: Keeping Faith in Jubilee* (Baton Rouge, LA: Louisiana State University Press, 1989), 101–174; James M. McPherson, *The Negro's Civil War* (New York, NY: Vintage, 1965), 38–68, 183–188; Samuel May, *The Fugitive Slave Law and Its Victims* (Freeport, NY: Black Heritage Library Collection, 1970 rept. of 1861 edn.); Stanley W. Campbell, *The Slave Catchers: Enforcement of the Fugitive Slave*

Law, 1850–1860 (New York, NY: Norton, 1970), 26–49, 80–95; Herbert Aptheker, *Slave Guerrilla Warfare,* 75–145; Thomas Wentworth Higginson, *Army Life in a Black Regiment* (New York, NY: Norton, 1984 rept. of 1869 edn.), 231–247; Joseph T. Glattahaar, *Forged in Battle: The Civil War Alliance of Black Soldiers and White Officers* (New York, NY: Meridian Books, 1991), 143–168; Susie King Taylor, *A Black Woman's Civil War Memoirs* (New York, NY: Markus Wiener Publishing, 1988 rept. of 1848 edn.), 55–67; John Hope Franklin, *The Militant South* (Boston, MA: Beacon Press, 1964), 63–79, 227–250; Harriet Beecher Stowe, *Uncle Tom's Cabin* (New York, NY; Signet, 1965 rept. of 1852 edn.).

c). Reconstruction

5. Eric Foner, *Reconstruction: America's Unfinished Revolution, 1863–1877* (New York, NY: Harper & Row, 1988), 35–59, 78–101, 307–315; Kenneth M. Stampp and Leon F. Litwack, *Reconstruction: An Anthology of Revisionist Writings* (Baton Rouge, LA: Louisiana State University Press, 1969), 221; for a stellar grasp of the politics surrounding the emancipation act see John Hope Franklin, *The Emancipation Proclamation* (New York, NY: Doubleday, 1965); David Warren Bowen, *Andrew Johnson and the Negro* (Knoxville, TN: University of Tennessee Press, 1989), 133–156; W.E.B. Du Bois, "Reconstruction and Its Benefits," *American Historical Review* 15 (July 1910), 781–799, and *Black Reconstruction* (New York, NY: Meridian Books, 1968 rept. of 1935 edn.), 670–710; Shirley Graham Du Bois, *His Day Is Marching On: A Memoir of W.E.B. Du Bois* (Philadelphia, PA: J.B. Lippincott Co., 1971), passim; Kenneth M. Stampp, *The Era of Reconstruction, 1865–1877* (New York, NY: Vintage Books, 1965), 186–216. For a feel of the old Dunningnite school see William A. Dunning, *Reconstruction, Political and Economic, 1865–1877* (New York, NY: Harper & Brothers, 1907 rept. 1962), Claude G. Bowers, *The Tragic Era: The Revolution after Lincoln* (Cambridge, MA: Harvard University Press, 1929), E. Merton Coulter, *The South During Reconstruction* (Baton Rouge, LA: Louisiana State University Press, 1947). For a feel for the revisionist see Vernon L. Wharton, *The Negro in Mississippi, 1865–1890* (New York, NY: Harper Torchbooks, 1947), and Stampp, *Reconstruction: An Anthology,* 3–12; Curry, *Radicalism, Racism, and Party Realignment,* 100–104; Joel Williamson, *New People: Miscegenation and Mulattoes in the United States* (New York, NY: New York University Press, 1980), 87–91; Pinchback quote cited in John Hope Franklin, *Reconstruc-*

tion *After the Civil War* (Chicago, IL: University of Chicago Press, 1961), 91, also see Chp. VI, "The South's New Leaders," 85–103, ed., *The Autobiography of John Roy Lynch* (Chicago, IL: University of Chicago Press, 1970 rept.), ix–xxxix, 45–58; Arnold Taylor, *Travail and Triumph: Black Life and Culture in the South since the Civil War* (Westport, CT: Greenwood Press, 1976), 1–22. A critical assessment of South Carolina Republicanism during Reconstruction is offered in Thomas Holt, *Black Over White* (Urbana, IL: University of Illinois Press, 1977). For a superb overview of the Reconstruction era and its significance to African Americans see John Hope Franklin's classic text, (with Alfred A. Moss, Jr.), *From Slavery to Freedom: A History of African Americans* (New York, NY: McGraw-Hill, 1994, 7th edn.), 220–263; racist poem in *Louisiana Times*, 9 November 1867 as cited in Coulter, *The South During Reconstruction*, 59.

d). Seeking the Dream

6. Willie Lee Rose, *Rehearsal for Reconstruction* (New York, NY: Vintage, 1964), 14–21, 32–62, 308–340; Margaret Washington Creel, *A Peculiar People: Slave Religion and Community-Culture Among the Gullahs* (New York, NY: New York University Press, 1988), 259–276, 323–326; Whittington B. Johnson, *Black Savannah, 1788–1864* (Fayetteville, AR: University of Arkansas Press, 1996), 85–106, 155–176; Ira Berlin, *Slaves Without Masters: The Free Negro in the Antebellum South* (New York, NY: Oxford University Press, 1974), 284–315; John B. Boles, *Slack Southerners, 1619–1869* (Lexington, KY: University Press of Kentucky, 1984), 140–181; Robert F. Engs, *Freedom's First Generation: Black Hampton, Virginia, 1861–1890* (Philadelphia, PA: University of Pennsylvania Press, 1979), 3–24, 99–120.

7. The roots of my present take on this subject evolved from my previously published study, *Schooling for the New Slavery: Black Industrial Education, 1868–1915* (Westport, CT: Greenwood Press, 1978), Chp. I, "The Making of Free Slaves," 3–15. James H. Brewer, *The Confederate Negro: Virginia's Craftsmen and Military Laborers, 1861–1865* (Durham, NC: Duke University Press, 1969), 3–16; James Purcell Guild, *Black Laws of Virginia: A Summary of the Legislative Acts of Virginia Concerning Negroes from Earliest Times to the Present* (New York, NY: Negro University Press, 1936), 395. Black labor was also exploited by the Union Army before Reconstruction. See John Oliver to American Missionary Association, 5 August 1862, *American Missionary Association Collec-*

tion, Fisk University (now at Dillard University); John Lockwood to American Missionary Association, 7 April 1862, AMA Collection; Edward L. Pierce, *Enfranchisement and Citizenship: Addresses and Papers*, ed., A.N. Stevens (Boston, MA: Roberts Brothers, 1896), 36–50; Thirty-seventh Congress, 2nd Session, House of Representatives Executive Document No. 85, "Africans in Fort Monroe Military District: A Letter from the Secretary of War" (Washington, DC: Government Printing, 1863), 2; C.B. Wilder to General Orlando Brown, 18 October 1865 and 18 January 1866, *Records of the Bureau of Refugees, Freedmen, and Abandoned Lands (BRFAL)*, National Archives; Armstrong quotes from Samuel Chapman Armstrong to General Orlando Brown, "Quarterly Report," 30 June 1866 and 30 June 1868, *BRFAL*; Samuel Chapman Armstrong to Mrs. Clarissa Armstrong, 15 March 1867, *Armstrong Family Papers*, Williams College; William McFeely, *Yankee Stepfather: General O.O. Howard and the Freedmen* (New York, NY: Norton, 1968), 45–83, 84–91, 267. McFeely's still remains the best overall critical assessment of the Freedman's Bureau. Edward K Graham's manuscript, "A Tender Violence: The Biography of a College," yet unpublished but provides a thorough treatment of the black community of Hampton (Hampton Institute, Hampton, VA). Robert F. Engs reaches similar conclusions in his important book, *Freedom's First Generation*, 199–204.

V. THE NEW SLAVERY

a). If You are Black, Stay Back

1. A most comprehensive treatment that the reader can consult with great benefit is Leon Litwack's *Trouble in Mind: Black Southerners in the Age of Jim Crow* (New York, NY: Knopf, 1998) and, especially for the period immediately after the Civil War, *Been In the Storm So Long: The Aftermath of Slavery* (New York, NY: Vintage, 1979). The tumultuous race relationship in the emerging New South is masterfully captured in Joel Williamson, *The Crucible of Race: Black-White Relations in the American South Since Emancipation* (New York, NY: Oxford University Press, 1984) and a faithfully condensed version *A Rage for Order: Black-White Relations in the American South Since Emancipation* (New York, NY: Oxford University Press, 1986). Nell Irvin Painter, *Standing at Armageddon: The United States, 1877–1919* (New York, NY: Norton, 1987), 216–230. Rayford Logan's treatment of the subject of the federal government's abandonment of blacks after Reconstruction is

a classic and still valuable to consult: *The Betrayal of the Negro: From Rutherford B. Hayes to Woodrow Wilson* (New York, NY: Collier Books, 1972 rept. of 1954 edn.). Hayes quote cited in Logan, 26.

2. Larry Greene, "Black Populism and the Quest for Racial Unity," *Telos*, 103 (1995), 127–129. One of the best discussions of fusion politics is that of Paul Kleppner, *The Cross of Culture: A Social Analysis of Midwestern Politics, 1850–1900* (New York, NY: Free Press, 1970). Also see Helen G. Edmonds, *Fusion Politics in North Carolina* (Chapel Hill, NC: University of North Carolina Press, 1951); William H. Chafe, "The Negro and Populism: A Kansas Case Study," *Journal of Southern History*, 34:3 (1968), 402–419; Norman Pollack, *The Populist Response to Industrial America* (New York, NY: Norton, 1966); C. Vann Woodward, *Origins of the New South* (Baton Rouge, LA: Louisiana State University Press, 1951), 205–234; Philip S. Foner, *The Great Labor Uprising of 1877* (New York, NY: Monad Books, 1977), 122–126; Charles A. Lofgren, *The Plessy Case: A Legal-Historical Interpretation* (New York, NY: Oxford University Press, 1987), 16–27, 28–43, 174–195.

3. Litwack *Trouble in Mind* gives extensive coverage. Still worth consulting is C. Vann Woodward's short book, *The Strange Career of Jim Crow* (New York, NY: Oxford University Press, 1957). Splendid discourses on Social Darwinism are provided by: Albert Somit, *Darwinism, Dominance, and Democracy: the Biological Bases of Authoritarianism* (Westport, CT: Praeger, 1997); Carl M. Degler, *In Search of Human Nature: The Decline and Revival of Darwinism in American Social Thought* (New York, NY: Oxford University Press, 1991); John C. Greene, *Science, Ideology and World View: Essays in the History of Evolutionary Ideas* (Berkeley, CA: University of California Press, 1981); and Richard Hofstadter's timeless piece, *Social Darwinism in American Thought* (Philadelphia, PA: University of Pennsylvania Press, 1944) which has been reprinted in many editions since then. William Stanton, *The Leopard's Spots: Scientific Attitudes Toward Race in America, 1915–1859* (Chicago, IL: University of Chicago Press, 1960), passim; Richard O. Curry, ed., *Freedom at Risk: Secrecy, Censorship, and Repression in the 1980s* (Philadelphia, PA: Temple University Press, 1988), 3–44; Jack Temple Kirby, *Darkness at the Dawning: Race and Reform in the Progressive South* (New York, NY: J.B. Lippincott & Co., 1972), 7–25; also see Thomas G. Dyer, *Theodore Roosevelt and the Idea of Race* (Baton Rouge, LA: Louisiana State University Press,

1980), 89–122; Donald Davidson, *Still Rebels, Still Yankees* (Baton Rouge, LA: Louisiana State University Press, 1972), 231–253; Robert Cruden, *The War that Never Ended: The American Civil War* (Englewood Cliffs, NJ: Prentice-Hall, 1973), 133–152, 191–192; see J.C. Lester and D.L. Wilson, *Ku Klux Klan: Its Origin, Growth, and Disbandment* (New York, NY: Da Capo Press, 1973 rept. of 1905 edn.), a sympathetic account of the KKK; David M. Chambers, *Hooded Americanism: The History of the Ku Klux Klan* (New York, NY: New Viewpoints, 1981), 8–27; also see Kenneth Jackson, *The Ku Klux Klan in the City, 1915–1930* (New York, NY: Oxford University Press, 1967); for a sense of the crimes perpetrated against black women consult Gerda Lerner, ed., *Black Women in White America: A Documentary History* (New York, NY: Vintage, 1972), 173–193; see report on Hose lynching in *Birmingham Age-Herald*, 26 April 1899; William Ivy Hair, *Carnival of Fury: Robert Charles and the New Orleans Race Riot of 1900* (Baton Rouge, LA: Louisiana State University Press, 1976); Williamson, *The Crucible of Race*, 180–223; Dominic J. Capeci and Jack C. Knight, "Reckoning with Violence: W.E.B. Du Bois and the 1906 Atlanta Race Riot," *Journal of Southern History* 62:4 (1996), 727–766; Maxine D. Jones and Kevin M. McCarthy, *African Americans in Florida* (Sarasota, FL: Pineapple Press, Inc., 1993), "The Rosewood Massacre," 83–84; for a sense of the efforts to demonize blacks see Thomas Dixon, Jr., *The Leopard's Spots* (New York, NY: Doubleday, 1902), Robert W. Shufeldlt, *The Negro a Menace to American Civilization* (Boston, MA: R. G. Badger, 1907), Claude H. Nolen, *The Negro's Image in the South: The Anatomy of White Supremacy* (Lexington, KY: University of Kentucky Press, 1968), especially 3–17, and Forrest G. Wood, *Black Scare: The Racist Response to Emancipation and Reconstruction* (Berkeley, CA: University of California Press, 1970), 1–16, 156–172. The lasting linkages of those images to the contemporary setting can be discerned from Peter Noble, *The Negro in Films* (London, England: Knapp, Drewett & Sons, 1954), and James R. Nesteby, *Black Images in American Films, 1896–1954* (Lanham, MD: University Press of America, 1982). Tillman quotes taken from Francis Butler Simkins, *Pitchfork Ben Tillman: South Carolinian* (Baton Rouge, LA: Louisiana State University Press, 1967), 393–395; Thomas Dixon, *The Clansman: An Historical Romance of the Ku Klux Klan* (New York, NY: Doubleday, 1916 rept. of 1905 edn.); see "Birth of A Nation" (New York Film Annex rept., 1998 (2) videos of 1915 film); Du Bois, *The Souls of Black*

Folk, Chp. V, "Of the Wings of Atalanta," 65–73; W.E.B. Du Bois, *The Autobiography of W.E.B. Du Bois* (New York, NY: 1969 edn.), 229.

b). At the Back Door

4. Paulo Freire, *Pedagogy of the Oppressed* (New York, NY: Herder and Herder, 1972), 55; my earlier views of Booker T. Washington have not substantially changed over the past twenty years except a stronger conviction that others held substantial control over him and that he underestimated the depths of American racism, see Donald Spivey, *Schooling for the New Slavery,* especially Chp. 2, "Shine, Booker, Shine: The Black Overseer of Tuskegee," 45–70. Washington's statement regarding accepting denial of accommodation in a restaurants is from Booker T. Washington, "Some Results of the Armstrong Idea," Address Delivered at Hampton Institute in Celebration of Founder's day (31 January 1909), 11, *Armstrong Family Papers*, Williams College; Washington quote on penchant of whites for money and social position is taken from Booker T. Washington, "The South as an Opening for a Business Career," Address Delivered at Lincoln University (26 April 1888), *Booker T. Washington Papers*, Library of Congress; his statement urging blacks on as peaceful elements of labor that will be protected is from Booker T. Washington, "Address Delivered at Raleigh, North Carolina" (30 October 1903), *BTWP*; Washington advocacy of his philosophy as the correct one for blacks to attain leverage and power is given succinctly in Booker T. Washington, "The Progress of the Negro," Address Delivered at a Meeting of the New York Congregational Club (16 January 1893), *BTWP*. Sidney Willhelm, *Who Needs the Negro?* (New York, NY: Doubleday, 1971), 64–66, 288; the theme of black uselessness to the labor market is given more recent exclamation from a reading of William Julius Wilson, *When Work Disappears: The World of the New Urban Poor* (New York, NY: Knopf, 1996) and Jeremy Rifkin, *The End of Work: The Decline of the Global Labor Force and the Dawn of the Post-Market Era* (New York, NY: Tarcher/Putnam Books, 1996); see, for example, Du Bois's classic, "Of Mr. Booker T. Washington and Others," Chp. III, in *The Souls of Black Folk*, 42–54; Ida B. Wells, "Booker T. Washington and His Critics," *World Today*, April 1904, 518–521, rept. in Thompson, *Ida B. Wells-Barnett: An Exploratory Study of an American Black Woman*, 255–260; Ida B. Wells-Barnett, *On Lynchings: Southern Horrors, A Red Record* (Salem, New Hamp-

shire: Ayers, 1991 rept. of 1892 & 1894 edns.); Booker T. Washington, *My Larger Education* (New York, NY: Doubleday, 1911), 3; Kelly Miller, *Radicals and Conservative and Other Essays on the Negro in America* (New York, NY: Schocken Books, 1968 rept. of 1908 edn.), especially 42–70; T. Thomas Fortune, *Black and White: Land, Labor and Politics in the South* (New York, NY: Arno Press, 1969 rept.), 27–36; Pete Daniel, *Peonage In the South, 1901–1969* (New York, NY: Oxford University Press, 1973), 19–42; Daniel A. Novak, *The Wheel of Servitude: Black Forced Labor after Slavery* (Lexington, KY: University Press of Kentucky, 1978), 1–9, 44–62.

c). Seeking the Land of the Free and Trying to Make Your Own Home of the Brave

5. Albert N. Hunt, *Haiti's Influence on Antebellum America: Slumbering Volcano in the Caribbean* (Baton Rouge, LA: Louisiana State University Press, 1988), 147–188; Charles Morrow Wilson, *Liberia: Black Africa in Microcosm* (New York: Harper & Row, 1971); Gus Liebenow, *Liberia: The Evolution of Privilege* (Ithaca, NY: Cornell University Press, 1969); M.R. Delany and Robert Campbell, *Search for a Place* (Ann Arbor, MI: University of Michigan Press, 1969 rept.); M.B. Akpah, "Black Imperialism: Americo-Liberian Rule Over the African Peoples of Liberia, 1841–1964," *Canadian Journal of African Studies* 7 (1973), 217–236; also see Donald Spivey, *The Politics of Miseducation: The Booker Washington Institute of Liberia, 1929–1984* (Lexington, KY: University Press of Kentucky, 1986), 15–33; I.K. Sundiata, *Black Scandal: America and the Liberian Labor Crisis, 1929–1936* (Philadelphia, PA: Institute for the Study of Human Issues, 1980); Amos J. Beyan, *The American Colonization Society and the Creation of the Liberian State, 1822–1900* (Lanham, MD: University Press of America, 1991); Wilson Moses, *The Golden Age of Black Nationalism, 1850–1925* (New York, NY: Oxford University Press, 1978), 32–58, and *Alexander Crummell: A Study of Civilization and Discontent* (New York, NY: Oxford University Press, 1989), 119–145, 196–221; Theodore Draper, *The Rediscovery of Black Nationalism* (New York, NY: Viking Press, 1970), 48–56; Alphonso Pinkney, *Red, Black, and Green: Black Nationalism in the United States* (New York, NY: Cambridge University Press, 1976), 1–36; Rodney Carlisle, *The Roots of Black Nationalism* (Port Washington, NY: Kennikat Press, 1975), 24–45; Lamont D. Thomas, *Rise To Be A People: A*

Biography of Paul Cuffe (Urbana, IL: University of Illinois Press, 1986), 13–21, 72–81, 101–106; Sheldon H. Harris, *Paul Cuffe: Black America and the African Return* (New York, NY: Simon and Schuster, 1972), 80–86, 139–144; Victor Ullman, *Martin R. Delany: The Beginnings of Black Nationalism* (Boston, MA: Beacon Press, 1971), 195–246, 507–519; Hollis R. Lynch, *Edward Wilmot Blyden: Pan-Negro Patriot, 1832–1912* (New York, NY: Oxford University Press, 1970), 10–31, 84–104; see also Stephen W. Angell, *Henry McNeal Turner and African-American Religion in the South* (Knoxville, TN: University of Tennessee Press, 1992). Turner quotes from Henry M. Turner, "The Negro Has Not Sense Enough" and "God is a Negro," *Voice of Missions*, 1 July 1900 and 1 February 1898 as cited in John H. Bracey, August Meier, and Elliott Rudwick, eds., *Black Nationalism in America* (Indianapolis, IN: Bobbs-Merrill Co., 1970), 173, 154; and quote on self-government and empowerment, from Henry McNeal Tuner in the *Christian Recorder*, 22 February and 21 June 1883 as cited in Edwin S. Redkey, *Black Exodus: Black Nationalism and Back-to-Africa Movements, 1890–1910* (New Haven, CT: Yale University Press, 1969), 34.

d). A Dream Deferred

6. See, Stuart Creighton Miller, *The Unwelcome Immigrant: The American Image of the Chinese, 1785–1862* (Berkeley, CA: University of California Press, 1969), 83–92, 113–123, 145–166; Ronald Takaki, *Iron Cages: Race and Culture in 19th-Century America* (New York, NY: Oxford University Press, 1990), 215–229; John Higham, *Strangers in the Land: Patterns of American Nativism, 1860–1925* (New York, NY: Atheneum, 1973), 18, 25, 170; William R. Brock, *Conflict and Transformation: The United States, 1844–1877* (New York, NY: Penguin Books, 1973), 436–438.

7. Colin Powell, *My American Journey* (New York, NY: Random House, 1995), 276–280, 554–557; see, for example, William Loren Katz, *Black Indians: A Hidden Heritage* (New York, NY: Atheneum, 1986), 148–188; and Sucheng Chan, Douglas Henry Daniels, Mario T. Garcia, Terry P. Wilson, eds., *Peoples of Color in the American West* (Lexington, MA: D.C. Heath, 1994).

8. Nell Irvin Painter, *Exodusters: Black Migration to Kansas after Reconstruction* (New York, NY: Knopf, 1977), 108–117, 184–201; Arthur L. Tolson, *The Black Oklahomans: A History, 1541–1972* (New Orleans, LA: Edwards Printing Co., 1974), 73–77; Mozell C. Hill, "The All-Negro Communities of Okla-

homa," *Journal of Negro History,* 31:3 (July 1946), 254–268; Jere W. Robinson, "Edward P. McCabe and the Langston Experiment," *The Chronicles of Oklahoma* LI:3 (Fall 1973), 343–355; Kaye M. Teall, ed., *Black History in Oklahoma* (Norman, OK: Oklahoma Public Schools, 1971), 167–171.

9. My thanks to the Oklahoma Historical Society for allowing me to draw material from my article "Crisis on a Black Campus: Langston University and its Struggle for Survival," *The Chronicles of Oklahoma* LIX:4 (Winter 1981–1982), 430–447. McCabe quotes are from the *Langston Herald,* 22 October 1891, 1, and 17 November 1892, 1; *San Francisco Examiner,* 3 March 1890, 3. For background on John Mercer Langston see his authored autobiography, *From the Virginia Plantation to the National Capitol or the First and Only Negro Representative in Congress from the Old Dominion* (Hartford, CT: American Publishing Co., 1894), and *Freedom and Citizenship* (Washington, DC: Rufus H. Dardy Publishers, 1883); and the only scholarly biography on Langston, William Cheek and Aimee Lee Cheek, *John Mercer Langston and the Fight for Black Freedom, 1829–1865* (Urbana, IL: University of Illinois Press, 1989).

10. Cited in Teall, *Black History in Oklahoma,* 187; Spivey, "Crisis on a Black Campus: Langston University and its Struggle for Survival," 433–436. The Langstonite's statement supporting Booker T. Washington's analogy of separate as the fingers on the hand is cited in Mozell C. Hill, "The All-Negro Society in Oklahoma" (unpublished Ph.D. Dissertation, University of Chicago, 1946), 125. Hill concludes that by the 1920s the Langston community was closer to the ideology of Garveyism than that of Booker T. Washington or W.E.B. Du Bois. "Highest on the priority of organizations that Langstonites favored," Hill says, "was the Universal Negro Improvement Association." (p. 120). Hill's observation accurately reflects the temperament of the community. It is clear, however, that after the 1920s, the political ideology of the town began to move toward integrationism. Increasing numbers of Langstonites joined the NAACP. The makeup of the community, nevertheless, remained one hundred percent African American. Moon quote is cited in Teall, 190. Dunjee quote from the *Black Dispatch,* 4 January 1923, 1. Quote equating Langston to an educational Athens is from the *Oklahoma Guide,* Guthrie, Oklahoma, 11 April 1901, 6. McCabe quote of "black man's land" is from undated bulletin found in the *E. P. McCabe Negro History Collection,* Oklahoma Historical Society; and similar notices and comments found in the "Inman E. Page Files" of the *Melvin B. Tolson Black Heritage Collection,* Langston University.

11. Young remarks reported in the *Black Dispatch*, 4 January 1923, 2, 5. The General Education Board was self-serving. The GEB was the brainchild of northern industrialists who had large economic interests in the south. The economic interests were inextricably tied to black labor. Industrial schooling stood for the heightened exploitation of that labor. The GEB industrialists considered blacks basically in terms of what they could produce in day-to-day labor. To make the blacks even more valuable as workers, as the industrialists saw it, they had to be "properly" educated—in short, given industrial schooling, a limited brand of education geared to produce a more tractable labor force. The GEB gave its financial support to education programs that supported this order of things. For further discussion see Spivey, *Schooling for the New Slavery*, 90–101. Zack Hubert to General Education Board, 31 August 1930; Jackson Davis to Hubert, 17 September 1930; GEB to Hubert, 1 December 1930; Hubert to General Education Board, 9 January 1931; GEB to Langston University, 2 February 1931; Leo M. Favrot to J.W. Sanford, 30 March 1936, all from *General Education Board Collection*, File no. OK 2: "Langston University," Series 1, Box 120, Rockefeller Archives, Tarreytown, New York; "Colored Agricultural and Normal University, Langston," May 23, 1936, General Education Board, File no. OK 2. Also see William H. Martin, "Current Trends and Events of National Importance in Negro Education/Section A: Recent Development in the Education of Negro Teachers in Oklahoma," *Journal of Negro Education*, XVIII:1 (Winter 1949), 77–80. The Martin study of Langston was much more favorable. Martin's, however, was an in-house survey. At the time, he was Director of Education at Langston University. Copy of the report was filed with the General Education Board. See file no. OK 2. "Sanford vs. Howard," no. 8513, Office of the Court Clerk, Guthrie, Oklahoma; *Black Dispatch*, 30 September 1939, 1–7; John W. Sanford, *Melvin B. Tolson Black Heritage Collection*; unidentified newspaper clipping, General Education Board, File no. OX 2; *Black Dispatch*, 7 October 1939, 1; "Negro President Quits Job After One-Day Tenure," *Oklahoma City Times*, 9 October 1939, 1; Albert L. Turner to Fred A. Holman, 7 October 1939, Langston University Archives; *Colored Agricultural and Normal University, Langston, Bulletin* (September 1939), 1–2, *Melvin B. Tolson Black Heritage Collection*; "Politics Drive Turner From Langston Post," *Black Dispatch*, 14 October 1939, 1.

12. Dunjee cited in *Black Dispatch*, 20 January 1940, 1; Foresman remarks cited in *Tulsa Tribune*, 3 June 1960, 2; Harris state-

ment from *Langston University Bulletin* (June 1960), 1–2, G. Lamar Harris File, *Melvin B. Tolson Black Heritage Collection*; Tatel quote, HEW spokesperson's statement, and NOBUCS comments, from "U.S. Accepts 3 States' Plans for Desegregation, Rejects 3: HEW's civil rights office passes proposals of Arkansas, Oklahoma, and Florida, but turns down Georgian's, Virginia's, and a portion of North Carolina's programs," *Chronicle of Higher Education*, 13 February 1978, 3–4. For further discussion of the dilemma facing black colleges see Charles V. Willie and Ronald Edmonds, ed., *Black Colleges in America: Challenge, Development, Survival* (New York, NY: Columbia University Teachers College Press, 1978).

VI. URBAN BLACKS: NEW CONSCIOUSNESS AND NEW VOICE TO THE AMERICAN DILEMMA

a). Northern Hope

1. Florette Henri, *Black Migration Movement North, 1900–1920* (New York, NY: Doubleday, 1976), vi–vii, 40–80, 237–268, and passim; Kenneth W. Goings, et.al., *The New African-American Urban History* (Thousand Oaks, CA: Sage, 1996), 1–64; Beverly A. Bunch-Lyon, *And they Come: The Migration of African-American Women from the South to Cincinnati, Ohio 1900–1950* (unpublished Ph.D. Dissertation, Miami University, Depart. Of Psychology, 1995), 1–12, 89–111; Sam Joseph Dennis, *African-American Exodus and White Migration, 1900–1950: A Comprehensive Analysis of Population Movements and their Relations to Labor and Race Relations* (New York, NY: Garland Pub., 1989), 217–245; Louis M. Kyriakoudes, "Southern Black Rural-Urban Migrations in the Era of the Great Migration: Nashville and Middle Tennessee, 1890–1930," *Agricultural History* 72:2 (1998), 341–351; Stewart E. Tolnay, "The Great Migration and Changes in the Northern Black Family," *Social Forces* 75:4 (1997), 1213–1238; June Sochen, *The Unbridgeable Gap: Blacks and Their Quest for The American Dream, 1900–1930* (Chicago, IL: Rand McNally, 1972), 27–48; Howard N. Rabinowitz, *Race Relations in the Urban South, 1865–1890* (Urbana, IL: University of Illinois Press, 1980), 18–30; Nicholas Lemann, *The Promised Land: The Great Black Migration and How it Changed America* (New York, NY: Vintage, 1992), 223–340; also see Gilbert Osofsky, *Harlem: The Making of a Negro Ghetto* (New York, NY: Harper Torchbooks, 1968), 71–90; Allan H. Spear, *Black Chicago: The Making of a Negro Ghetto, 1890–1920* (Chicago, IL: University of Chicago Press,

1967),129–146; Arnold R. Hirsch, *Making the Second Ghetto: Race & Housing in Chicago, 1940–1960* (New York, NY: Cambridge University Press, 1985), 1–8; David M. Katzman, *Before the Ghetto: Black Detroit in the Nineteenth Century* (Urbana, IL: University of Illinois Press, 1975), 207–212; David Gordon Nielson, *Black Ethos: Northern Urban Negro Life and Thought, 1890–1930* (Westport, CT: Greenwood Press, 1977), 121–156; David Allan Levine, *Internal Combustion: The Races in Detroit* (Westport, CT: Greenwood Press, 1976), 153–198), 14; Joe William Trotter, Jr., *Black Milwaukee: The Making of an Industrial Proletariat, 1915–45* (Urbana, IL: University of Illinois Press, 1988), 39–79; Kenneth L. Kusmer, *A Ghetto Takes Shape: Black Cleveland, 1870–1930* (Urbana, Illinois: University of Illinois Press, 1978), 157–173. A classic and still highly valuable treatment of the black urban experience is Ray Stannard Baker, *Following the Color Line: American Negro Citizenship in the Progressive Era* (New York, NY: Harper Torchbooks, 1964 rept. of 1908 edn.). Editorial quotes from the *Chicago Defender*, 1912–1919, for example, "Farewell, Dixie Land," 12 October 1919, "Getting the South Told," 25 November 1916, "Attitude," 10 February 1917, "The Soul of a Lyncher," 10 July 1920. For listings of black inventors and other African-American accomplishments from the period consult Alton Hornsby, *The Black Almanac* (Woodbury, NY: Barron's Educational Series, Inc., 1977); Portia P. James, *The Real McCoy: African-American Invention and Innovation, 1619–1930* (Washington, DC: Smithsonian Institution Press, 1989); and McKinley Burt, Jr., *Black Inventors of America* (Portland, OR: National Book Co., 1989); Ivan Van Sertima, ed., *Blacks in Science: Ancient and Modern* (New Brunswick, NJ: Transaction Books, 1983), 215–292.

b). Black Voices

2. James Weldon Johnson, *Black Manhattan* (New York, NY: Atheneum, 1930), 3, 146–147; Jervis Anderson, *This Was Harlem, 1900–1950* (New York, NY: Farrar Straus Giroux, 1983), 185–203; A. Peter Bailey, *The Harlem Hospital Story: 100 Years of Struggle Against Illness, Racism and Genocide* (Richmond, VA: Native Sons Publishers, 1991), 27–55; Langston Hughes, *The Best of Simple* (New York, NY: Hill and Wang, 1969), 20; on H.L. Mencken see his *Notes on Democracy* (New York, NY: Knopf, 1926), and *In Defense of Women* (New York, NY: Knopf, 1922); W.E.B. Du Bois, "Close Ranks," *The Crisis* (July 1918), editorial; Alain LeRoy Locke, *The New Negro: An Interpretation* (New York, NY: Simon

and Schuster, 1997 rept. of 1925 edn), 5, 6–7; see Claude McKay, *Home to Harlem* (New York, NY: Pocket Books, 1969 rept.); McKay's poem and Hughes's poem from Langston Hughes and Arna Bontemps, eds., *The Poetry of the Negro, 1746–1949* (Garden City, NY: Doubleday, 1949), 333, 105–106 respectively; Abraham Chapman, *Black Voices: An Anthology of Afro-American Literature* (New York, NY: New American Library, 1968). For an interesting take on the connection between the music and the literature of the Harlem Renaissance see Steven C. Tracy, *Langston Hughes and the Blues* (Urbana, IL: University of Illinois Press, 1988), especially 59–140.

   3. For a variety of perspectives to gain the full magnitude of the black Renaissance the following are most useful: George Hutchinson, *The Harlem Renaissance in Black and White* (Cambridge, MA: Harvard University Press, 1997); Cary D. Wintz, *Black Culture and the Harlem Renaissance* (College Station, TX: Texas A&M Press, 1996); Cheryl A. Wall, *Women of the Harlem Renaissance* (Bloomington, IN: Indiana University Press, 1995); David L. Lewis, *When Harlem was in Vogue* (New York, NY: Penguin Books, 1997); Steven Watson, *The Harlem Renaissance: Hub of African-American Culture, 1920–1930* (New York, NY: Pantheon Books, 1995); Jervis Anderson, *This Was Harlem, 1900–1950* (New York, NY: Farrar Straus Giroux, 1983); Nathan Irvin Huggins, *Harlem Renaissance* (New York, NY: Oxford University Press, 1971); John Henrik Clarke, *Harlem: A Community in Transition* (New York, NY: Citadel, 1969); Sterling Brown, *Negro Poetry and Drama and the Negro in American Fiction* (New York, NY: Atheneum, 1969 rept.); Tony Martin, ed., *African Fundamentalism: A Literary and Cultural Anthology of Garvey's Harlem Renaissance* (Dover, MA: The Majority Press, 1991). For a feel for the development of the African-American music scene from blues to big band see, for example, Jeff Todd Titon, *Early Downhome Blues: A Musical and Cultural Analysis* (Urbana, IL: University of Illinois Press, 1977); Daphne D. Harrison, *Black Pearls: Blues Queens of the 1920s* (New Brunswick, NJ: Rutgers University Press, 1988); Robert Dixon and John Godrich, *Recording the Blues* (New York, NY: Stein and Day, 1970); Charles Keil, *Urban Blues* (Chicago, IL: University of Chicago Press, 1970), 50–68; Allen Woll, *Black Musical Theatre: From Coontown to Dreamgirls* (New York, NY: Da Capo, 1989); Derek Jewell, *Duke: A Portrait of Duke Ellington* (New York, NY: Norton, 1977); and Samuel A. Floyd, Jr., ed., *Black Music in the Harlem Renaissance* (Westport, CT: Greenwood Press, 1990). The art scene in Harlem is given serious attention in Romare Bearden

and Harry Henderson, *A History of African-American Art, 1972 to the Present* (New York, NY: Pantheon, 1993); Amy Helene Kirschke, *Aaron Douglas: Art, Race, and the Harlem Renaissance* (Jackson, MS: University of Mississippi Press, 1995); Hayward Gallery Exhibition, *Rhapsodies in Black: Art of the Harlem Renaissance* (London, England: Hayward Gallery, 1997).

c). Passing on the Word: Urban Black Activism

4. Trotter quote on Booker T. Washington as cited in Stephen R. Fox, *The Guardian of Boston: William Monroe Trotter* (New York, NY: Atheneum, 1970), 29. The reader can reliably consult the Fox book which is the only published scholarly account of Trotter's life story.

d). The Messenger's Message

5. Randolph's and Owens's "aim" for the Messenger as taken from *Messenger*, November 1917, 1. Randolph's editorials in the *Messenger* magazine from 1917 to 1928 were extensively consulted for the development of the author's perspective on the labor leader and specific comments cited herein. On Randolph and Socialism see Sterling D. Spero and Abram L. Harris, *The Black Worker* (New York, NY: Atheneum, 1959), 390, 404; Roi Ottley and William J. Weatherby, ed., *The Negro in New York: An Informal Social History, 1626–1940* (New York, NY: Praeger, 1967), 226.

6. "Crisis of the Crisis," *Messenger,* July 1918; "A Supreme Negro Jamaican Jackass," *Messenger,* January 1923, 561; Jervis Anderson, *A Philip Randolph: A Biographical Portrait* (New York, NY: Harcourt Brace Jovanovich, Inc., 1973), 83–96, 115–119, 139, 146–147; "The Most Dangerous Negro in America," *Negro Digest,* September 1961; Randolph's views criticized by the black press, see Ottley and Weatherby, ed., *The Negro in New York: An Informal Social History, 1626–1940,* 225–227.

7. Interesting takes on Randolph, his conflicts with other African-American leaders, and the labor struggles of the BSCP are provided in Paula F. Pfeffer, *A. Philip Randolph: Pioneer of the Civil Rights Movement* (Baton Rouge, LA: Louisiana State University Press, 1996); William H. Harrison, *Keeping the Faith: A. Philip Randolph, Milton P. Webster, and the Brotherhood of Sleeping Car Porters, 1925–1937* (Urbana, IL: University of Illinois Press, 1977); Brailsford R. Brazeal, *The Brotherhood of Sleeping Car Porters* (New York, NY: Harper & Row, 1946); Jarvis Anderson, *A. Philip Randolph*; Spero

and Harris, *The Black Worker*; Ray Marshall, *The Negro Worker* (New York, NY: Random House, 1967).

e). Working from Without

8. Garvey quote from Amy Jacques-Garvey, ed., *The Philosophy and Opinions of Marcus Garvey* (New York, NY: Arno Press, 1969), 93. Primary sources on Garvey and the UNIA are now readily available in Robert A. Hill, ed., *The Marcus Garvey and Universal Negro Improvement Association Papers* (Berkeley, CA: University of California Press, 1983–1990), 7 Vols. An extensively researched treatment of Garvey and the UNIA is Tony Martin, *Race First: The Ideological and Organization Struggles of Marcus Garvey and the Universal Negro Improvement Association* (Westport, CT: Greenwood Press, 1976). Also see Theodore Vincent, *Black Power and the Garvey Movement* (San Francisco, CA: Ramparts, 1972); Rupert Lewis, *Marcus Garvey: Anti-Colonial Champion* (Trenton, NJ: Africa World Press, 1988); and John Henrik Clarke, ed., *Marcus Garvey and the Vision of Africa* (New York, NY: Vintage, 1974). Judith Stein offers a largely class perspective on Garvey in her book, *The World of Marcus Garvey: Race and Class in Modern Society* (Baton Rouge, LA: Louisiana State University Press, 1986). Stilted and outdated but a part of the development historiographically on Garveyism is E. David Cronon, *Black Moses: The Story of Marcus Garvey and the Universal Negro Improvement Association* (Madison, WI: University of Wisconsin, 1955).

9. For extensive document sources of Hoover and Justice Department efforts to infiltrate and destroy the Garvey movement consult "Marcus Garvey FBI Investigation File," microfilm, *Scholarly Resources*, 1978; Robert Hill, ed., *The Marcus Garvey and Universal Negro Improvement Association Papers*, Vols. I–III, indexed listings under "Bureau of Investigation." Tony Martin offers a chilling and detailed accounting of the government's tactics against Garvey. See Martin, *Race First: The Ideological and Organization Struggles of Marcus Garvey and the Universal Negro Improvement Association*, Chp. 9, "U.S.A. versus UNIA," 174–220. Garvey and Hoover quotes as cited in Martin, 174, 176, Kelly Miller quote, 195. Classic treatments of the Red Scare and Alien and Sedition Acts are provided in: James Morton Smith, *Freedom Fetters: The Alien and Sedition Laws and American Civil Liberties* (Ithaca, NY: Cornell University Press, 1966); William Preston, Jr., *Aliens and Dissenters: Federal Suppression of Radicals, 1903–1933* (New York, NY: Harper Torchbooks, 1963), especially chapter on IWW, 35–62; and John Higham, *Strangers in the Land: Patterns of American Na-*

tivism, 1860–1925 (New York, NY: Atheneum, 1973), 210–233. The problems between the IWW and the U.S. government are captured in Melvyn Dubofsky, *We Shall Be All: A History of the IWW"* (Chicago, IL: Quadrangle Books, 1969); and Philip S. Foner, *The Black Worker During the Era of the Knights of Labor* (Philadelphia, PA: Temple University Press, 1978). Marguerite Green, *The National Civic Federation and the American Labor Movement, 1900–1925* (Washington, DC: Catholic University Press, 1956), 402–409.

VII. SEEKING SALVATION DURING MORE HARD TIMES

1. National Association for the Advancement of Colored People, *Thirty Years of Lynching in the United States, 1889–1918* (New York, NY: NAACP, 1919), and *Supplement: A Generation of Lynching in the United States, 1921–1946* (New York, NY: NAACP, 1946); see too, James R. McGovern, *Anatomy of a Lynching: The Killing of Claude Neal* (Baton Rouge, LA: Louisiana State University Press, 1982), 115–139; Richard B. Sherman, *The Republican Party and Black America: From McKinley to Hoover, 1896–1933* (Charlottesville, VA: University Press of Virginia, 1973), 1–23, 174–175, 198–200, 252–259; NAACP statement urging blacks to be independent voters and to side with friends from *Annual Report of the NAACP* (1926), 32. Hoover and his depression policies are given careful attention in Harris Gaylor Warren, *Herbert Hoover and the Great Depression* (New York, NY: Norton, 1967), 188–206.

2. Roi Ottley and William J. Weatherby, ed., *The Negro in New York: An Informal Social History, 1626–1940* (New York, NY: Praeger, 1967), 265; public utility companies executive responses from *Messenger*, January 1927, and cited in Ottley and Weatherby, 268–269; Ella Baker and Marvel Cooke, "The Bronx Slave Market," *Crisis*, November 1935, 330–331, 340. For insider and personal perspectives on the ravages of the Great Depression see Studs Terkel, *Hard Times* (New York, NY: Avon Books, 1970).

a). New Deal or Old Deal

3. Warren, *Herbert Hoover and the Great Depression*, 36–38; Richard B. Sherman, *The Republican Party and Black America*, 231–233; Leslie Fishel, "The Negro in the New Deal Era," *Magazine of Wisconsin History* (1964–65), 111–117, 120–123; Frank Freidel, *Franklin D. Roosevelt: A Rendezvous with Destiny* (New York, NY: Little, Brown, 1990), 123–124, 244–246, 508–509,

520–521; William E. Leuchtenburg, *Franklin D. Roosevelt and the New Deal, 1932–1940* (New York, NY: Harper Torchbooks, 1963), 126, 138–141, 185–192; Ellis W. Hawley, *The New Deal and the Problem of Monopoly* (Princeton, NJ: Princeton University Press, 1966), 277, 301–318; Robert C. Weaver, *Negro Labor: A National Problem* (New York, NY: Harcourt, Brace and Co., 1946), 3–40; Herbert R. Northrup, "Organized Labor and Negro Workers," in Bernard Sternsher, ed., *The Negro in Depression and War* (Chicago, IL: Quadrangle Books, 1969), 127–149; Wilkins quote from Roy Wilkins to Dorthea F. Nichols, 9 March 1938, NAACP Files as cited in Raymond Wolters, *Negroes and the Great Depression: The Problem of Economic Recovery* (Westport, CT: Greenwood Press, 1970), 106.

b). Working From Within

4. The section on Bethune relied heavily on the several Bethune biographies that are permanent properties of the Floridian Collection of the Archives and Special Collections of the Richter Library of the University of Miami: Rackham Holt, *Mary McLeod Bethune: A Biography* (Garden City, NY: Doubleday, 1964); Emma Gelders Sterne, *Mary McLeod Bethune* (New York, NY: Knopf, 1957); and Catherine Owens, *Mary McLeod Bethune* (New York, NY: Vanguard Press, 1951). Also see Elaine M. Smith, "Mary McLeod Bethune's Last Will and Testament: A Legacy for Race Vindication," *Journal of Negro History* 81:1–4 (1996), 105–122. A forthcoming study that promises to yield new light on Bethune's work and historical legacy as a role model especially for young African-American women is Joyce Hanson's *The Ties that Bind: Mary McLeod Bethune and the Political Mobilization of African-American Women* (Columbia, Missouri: University of Missouri Press, forthcoming). Bethune quotes are from her Diary and Last Will and Testament, Bethune-Cookman College, Daytona Beach, Florida.

c). God Incorporated

5. Clifford Burke in Studs Terkel, *Hard Times* (New York, NY: Avon Books, 1970), 104–105. John Henrik Clarke in Sara Harris, *Father Divine* (New York, NY: Macmillian, 1971), ix. The studies on Father Divine and his Peace Missions organization run the gamut from accusing him of being a charlatan to complimenting him for his community service. My take on Father Divine falls into the highly skeptical and critical camp although I have drawn heavily

both from those critical and those complimentary of Divine and his work. The most extensive coverages of Divine and his organizational efforts are: Jill Watts, *God, Harlem U.S.A.: The Father Divine Story* (Berkeley, CA: University of California Press, 1992); Sara Harris, *Father Divine*; Robert Weisbrot, *Father Divine and the Struggle for Racial Equality* (Urbana, IL: University of Illinois Press, 1983); Kenneth E. Burnham, *God Comes to America: Father Divine and the Peace Mission Movement* (Boston, MA: Lambeth Press, 1979); Robert Allerton Parker, *The Incredible Messiah: The Deification of Father Divine* (Boston, MA: Little, Brown and Co., 1937). I have also found the following of value and helped to inform this essay: Father Divine, *The Condescension of God* (Divine Peace Mission, 1957), *Father Divine: His Words of Spirit and Hope* (Divine Peace Mission, 1961), *Here's the Answer* (Divine Peace Mission, 1900); "The New Day," microfilm, (New York, NY: New Day Pub. Co., 1936), Vol 1.; Bruce Hum, *Father Divine: God or Man* (Lenoir City, TN: Lenoir Pub. Co., 1949); John Hoshor, *God in a Rolls Royce: The Rise of Father Divine: Madman, Menace, or Messiah* (Freeport, NY: Books for Libraries Press, 1936); Velmer J. Gardner, *I Spent Saturday Night in the Devil's House: An Exposure of Father Divine* (Springfield, MO: Velmer Gardner Evangelistic Association, Inc., 1952); Gains S. Reid, *Who is Father Divine?* (New York, NY: Reid Pub., 1947); E.J. Daniels, *Father Divine: The World's Chief False Christ* (Winter Gardens, FL: Biblical Echo Press, 1937).

6. Divine quotes from *Father Divine: His Words of Spirit and Hope*, and *Here's the Answer*.

7. Harris, *Father Divine*, 49–56, 248–251; Claude McKay, *Harlem: Negro Metropolis* (New York, NY: Harcourt Brace Jovanovich, Inc., 1968 rept. of 1940 Dutton edn.), 73–85; Weisbrot, 80–81, 100–104; Father Divine, *Father Divine: His Words of Spirit and Hope*; Gayraud S. Wilmore, *Black Religion and Black Radicalism* (New York, NY: Doubleday, 1972), 214–216.

VIII. BATTLING ON EVERY FRONT

a). The Military Front

1. The participation of blacks in America's wars is a subject area awaiting scholarly development. There are several first-person accounts available on the Civil War period and a few other accounts on some of the later wars and African-American involvement. The U.S. Park Service has a pamphlet it distributes that outlines the contributions and sacrifices made by blacks. The

very few serious analytical treatments available formed the basis of the discussion presented in this chapter: Robert W. Mullen, *Blacks in America's Wars: The Shift in Attitudes from the Revolutionary War to Vietnam* (New York, NY: Anchor Foundation, 1991), especially 38–51, and *Black Americans/African Americans: Vietnam through the Gulf War* (Needham Heights, MA: Ginn Press, 1991); Danny Duncan Collum, ed., *African Americans in the Spanish Civil War: "This Ain't Ethiopia, But It'll Do"* (New York, NY: G.K. Hall & Co., 1992); *The Medal of Honor and African Americans in the United States Army during World War II* (Raleigh, NC: Shaw University, 1995); "Returning Soldiers," *Crisis*, May 1919; Rudolf J. Friederich, "54 Black Heroes: Medal of Honor Winners," *Crisis*, June–July 1969; Benjamin O. Davis, *Benjamin O. Davis, Jr. — American: An Autobiography* (New York, NY: Plume, 1992), passim; James E. Westheider, *Fighting on Two Fronts: African Americans and the Vietnam War* (New York, NY: New York University Press, 1997); and Terry Wallace, *Bloods: An Oral History of the Vietnam War by Black Veterans* (New York, NY: Ballantine Books, 1984).

2. Scholarly assessments of the Brownsville and Houston episodes are provided in: Ann J. Lane, *The Brownsville Affair: National Crisis and Black Reaction* (Port Washington, NY: Kennikat Press, 1971); Robert V. Haynes, "The Houston Mutiny and Riot of 1917," *Southwestern Historical Quarterly*, 76:4 (April 1973), 418–438.

b). The African Front

3. Bonnie K. Holcomb and Sisai Ibssa, *The Invention of Ethiopia: The Making of a Dependent Colonial State in Northeast Africa* (Trenton, NJ: The Red Sea Press, 1990), 193–213; Danny Duncan Collum, ed., *African Americans in the Spanish Civil War: "This Ain't Ethiopia, But It'll Do,"* 6, 16–19, 123–124, 146–147; David Nicolle, *The Italian Invasion of Abyssinia* (London, England: Osprey, 1997); Stephen U. Chukumba, *The Big Powers Against Ethiopia: Anglo-Franco American Diplomatic Maneuvers During the Italo-Ethiopian Dispute, 1934–1938* (Washington, DC: University Press of America, Inc., 1979), 1–3, 40, 59, 191–193, 357–358; Du Bois quote from W.E.B. Du Bois, "Inter-Racial Implications of the Ethiopian Crisis," *Foreign Affairs*, 14:1 (October 1935), 86–89. An excellent history of the CAA is given in a relatively small but important book by Hollis Lynch, *Black American Radicals and the Libera-*

tion of Africa: The Council on African Affairs, 1937–1955 (Ithaca, NY: Africana Studies and Research Center Monograph Series, 1978).

4. Lynch, *Black American Radicals and the Liberation of Africa: The Council on African Affairs, 1937–1955,* 18–19, 21–22, 26–29, 32, 39. Martin B. Duberman, *Paul Robeson: A Biography* (New York, NY: Ballantine Books, 1989), 254–285, 296–299, 340–341, 437; a good take on Ralph Bunche and his more feisty earlier years is provided in Charles P. Henry, *Ralph Bunche: Model Negro or American Other?* (New York, NY: New York University Press, 1998). "Council on African Affairs," in *General Office File, NAACP, 1940–1955,* microfilm, (Frederick, MD: University Publications of America, 1992); I. B. Tabata, *8 Million Demand Freedom* (New York, NY: Council on African Affairs, 1946), microfilm; "Seeing is Believing," (New York, NY: Council on African Affairs, 1947), Schomburg Research Center, New York Public Library.

c). The Communist Front: Better Red than American?

5. The works upon which this analysis draws extensively are the following: *The Daily Worker,* from 1930 to 1950; Mark Naison, *Communists in Harlem During the Depression* (Urbana, IL: University of Illinois Press, 1983), 203–217; Harold Cruse, *Plural But Equal: Blacks and Minorities in America's Plural Society* (New York, NY: William Morrow, 1987), 76, 96–98, 176, 214–218, and *Crisis of the Negro Intellectual* (New York, NY: William Morrow, 1967), 16–18, 161–162, 467–470; Wilson Record, *The Negro and the Communist Party* (New York, NY: Atheneum, 1971 rept. of 1951 edn.), 21–36, 162–164, 209, 287; Julius Jacobson, ed., *The Negro and the American Labor Movement* (New York, NY: Doubleday & Co., 1968), 193–198; on the charges of genocide see William L. Patterson, ed., *We Charge Genocide: the Crime of Government Against the Negro People* (New York, NY: International Pubs., 1951).

d). The Labor Front

6. Herbert Hill, "The Importance of Race in American Labor History," *International Journal of Politics, Culture, and Society* 9:2 (Winter 1995), 317–333; Jerry A. Jacobs, Mary Blair-Loy, "Gender, Race, Local Labor Markets and Occupational Devaluation," *Sociological Focus* 29:3 (1996), 209–230; Eric Tscheschlok, "So Goes the Negro: Race and Labor in Miami, 1940–1963," *Florida Historical*

Quarterly 75:1 (Summer 1996), 42–67; Michael Goldfield, "Race and Labor Organization in the United States," *Monthly Review* 49:3 (1997), 80–97; Franklin D. Wilson, Marta Tienda, Lawrence Wu, "Race and Unemployment: Labor Market Experiences of Black and White Men, 1968–1988," *Work and Occupations* 22:3 (1995), 245–270; Gary Fink, et. al., *Race, Class and Community in Southern Labor History* (Tuscaloosa, AL: University of Alabama Press, 1994), 94–98, 278–281; Art Preis, *Labor's Giant Step: Twenty Years of the CIO* (New York, NY: Pathfinder Press, 1972), 9–15, 375–376, 455–456, 514–516; Saul D. Alinsky, *John L. Lewis: An Unauthorized Biography* (New York, NY: Vintage, 1970), passim; Harvey Schwartz, *The March Inland: Origins of the ILWU Warehouse Division, 1934–1938* (Los Angeles, CA: Institute of Industrial Relations, University of California, 1978), 106–141; Irving Bernstein, *Turbulent Years: A History of the American Worker, 1933–1941* (Boston, MA: Houghton Mifflin, 1971), 87–89, 189–190, 454; David Brody, *Workers in Industrial America: Essays on the 20th Century Struggle* (New York, NY: Oxford University Press, 1980), 158–166; Ronald L. Lewis, *Black Coal Miners in America: Race, Class, and Community Conflict, 1780–1980* (Lexington, KY: University Press of Kentucky, 1987), 79–120; Robert C. Weaver, *Negro Labor: A National Problem* (New York, NY: Harcourt, Brace and Co., 1946), 97–108, 236–246; Ray Marshall, *The Negro Worker* (New York, NY: Random House, 1967), 30–42; Sterling D. Spero and Abram L. Harris, *The Black Worker* (New York, NY: Atheneum, 1959), 337–351, 461–469; Hill's findings about JLC and ILGWU presented in Ray Marshall, *The Negro Worker* (New York, NY: Random House, 1967), 36–38; King statement to UAW quoted in *Labor Today*, 22 (Spring 1962), 12 as cited in Marshall, 40.

7. The following list of sources will also give the reader a feel for the evolution of my thinking and thesis on the inter-relationship of the world economy, labor and the condition of people of color worldwide: Philip S. Foner, *Organized Labor and the Black Worker, 1619–1973* (New York, NY: Praeger, 1974), 312–331, 397–424, 431–435; Celso Furtado, *Obstacles to Development in Latin America* (New York, NY: Doubleday & Co., 1970), 17–25, 58–64, 137–140, 180–184; James Petras and Maurice Zeitlin, ed., *Latin America: Reform or Revolution* (Greenwich, CT: Fawcett Pubs., 1968), especially Luis Vitale, "Latin America: Feudal or Capitalist?," 32–43, and Maurice Halperin, "Growth and Crisis in the Latin American Economy," 44–75; Osvaldo Sunkel, "Change and Frustration in Chile," in Claudio Veliz, ed., *Obstacles to Change in*

Latin America (New York, NY: Oxford University Press, 1969), 116–144; Rudolfo Stavenhagen, "Challenging the Nation-State in Latin America," in Michael B. Whiteford and Scott Whiteford, ed., *Crossing Currents: Continuity and Change in Latin America* (Upper Saddle River, NJ: Prentice-Hall, Inc., 1998), 13–23; William J. Pomeroy, *American Neo-Colonialism: Its Emergence in the Philippines and Asia* (New York, NY: International Pubs., 1970), 195–228; Imamu Amiri Baraka, *African Congress: A Documentary of the First Modern Pan-African Congress* (New York, NY: William Morrow, 1972), 154–156; Selwyn R. Cudjoe, *Movement of the People: Essays on Independence* (Ithaca, NY: Calaloux Pubs., 1983), 121-153; a good start to gain historical perspective on the situation in Haiti is Bernard Diederich and Al Burt, *Papa Doc* (New York, NY: Avon, 1969), 156–175; Walter Rodney, *How Europe Underdeveloped Africa* (Dar-es Salaam, Tanzania: Tanzania Publishing House, 1972), 224–260; Kwame Nkrumah, *Neo-Colonialism: The Last Stage of Imperialism* (New York, NY: International Pubs., 1965), 145–164, 178–182, 187–191, 224, 230; Amii Omara-Otunnu, *Politics and the Military in Uganda* (New York, NY: St. Martin's Press, 1987), 180–181; Eric Wolf, *Sons of the Shaking Earth* (Chicago, IL: University of Chicago Press, 1959), 252–256; Julius Jacobson, ed., *The Negro and the American Labor Movement*, 226–231; Henry Pelling, *Amerian Labor* (Chicago, IL: University of Chicago Press, 1960), 195–198; Selig Perlman, *The Theory of the Labor Movement* (New York, NY: Augustus M. Kelley Pubs., 1970), 207–253; Donald Spivey, *The Politics of Miseducation: The Booker Washington Institute of Liberia, 1929–1984* (Lexington, KY: University Press of Kentucky, 1986), 33–48; Sidney M. Wilhelm, *Who Needs the Negro?* (New York, NY: Doubleday & Co., 1971), in particular 271–324; Jeremy Rifkin, *The End of Work: The Decline of the Global Labor Force and the Dawn of the Post-Market Era* (New York, NY: Tarcher/Putnam Book, 1996), especially 208–220, 249–274.

e). The Sports Front

8. I am grateful to the editors of *Phylon* for permission to draw from my previously published article, "Sport, Protest, and Consciousness: The Black Athlete in Big-Time Intercollegiate Sports, 1941–1968," *Phylon* XLIV:2 (June 1983), 116–125; Donald Spivey, "Taking Charge: Historicizing of the Social and Political Challenges to the Black Student Athlete in Big-Time Intercollegiate Sport," paper presented at symposium on *Sport Matters: Black Intellectuals*

Respond to and Transcend Darwin's Athletes, New York University, 4 April 1998; Jesse Owens, *Jesse: The Man Who Outran Hitler* (New York, NY: Fawcett, 1978), 56–59, 133–142, and *Blackthink: My Life as Black Man and White Man* (New York, NY: William Morrow, 1970), 195–209; Joe Louis, *My Life* (Hopewell, NJ: Ecco Press, 1997 rept. of 1978 edn.), 135–172; Richard Bax, *Joe Louis* (New York, NY: Da Capo, 1998); Anthony Edmonds, "The Second Louis-Schmeling Fight: Sport, Symbol, and Culture," *Journal of Popular Culture* 37:1 (Summer 1973), 42–50; Jeffrey T. Sammons, *Beyond the Ring: The Role of Boxing in American Society* (Urbana, IL: University of Illinois Press, 1988), 96–129; William Montague Cobb, "The Negro as a Biological Element in the American Population," *Journal of Negro Education* 8 (1939), 336–346, and "Race and Runners," *Journal of Health and Physical Education* (January 1936), 1–7; Kenneth Manning, "Montague Cobb and the Science of Human Sameness," paper delivered at symposium on *Sport Matters: Black Intellectuals Respond to and Transcend Darwin's Athletes,* New York University, 4 April 1998; James H. Jones, *Bad blood: The Scandalous Story of the Tuskegee Experiment— When Government Doctors Played God and Science Went Mad* (New York, NY: The Free Press, 1981), 7–11, 156–170, 204, 206–219; Martin Luther King, Jr., *Where Do We Go From Here: Chaos or Community* (New York, NY: Bantam Books, 1968), 80.

9. Spivey, "Sport, Protest, and Consciousness: The Black Athlete in Big-Time Intercollegiate Sports, 1941–1968," 118–121; Robert Petersen, *Only the Ball was White: A History of Legendary Black Players and All-Black Professional Teams* (New York, NY: Oxford University Press, 1992 rept. of 1970 edn.), 129–144; on the integration of baseball and signing of Jackie Robinson see Jules Tygiel, *Baseball's Great Experiment: Jackie Robinson and his Legacy* (New York, NY: Oxford University Press, 1997 & 1983), Arnold Rampersad, *Jackie Robinson: A Biography* (New York, NY: Knopf, 1997); on the first woman to cross the color line in tennis: Althea Gibson, *I Always Wanted to Be Somebody* (New York, NY: Harper, 1958); Allen Guttman, *Sports Spectators* (New York, NY: Columbia University Press, 1986); Edwin B. Henderson, *The Negro in Sports* (Washington, DC: Associated Publishers, 1949); "Bates Must Play Group Adopts Four Resolutions," *Education Sun,* 23 October 1940, 1; *Heights Daily News,* 23 October 1940, 1, New York University Archives. For a detailed examination of the NYU protest see Donald Spivey, "End Jim Crow in Sports: The Protest at New York University, 1940–1941," *Journal of Sport History* 15:3 (Winter 1988), 282–303.

10. *Daily Worker*, 9 December 1952, 9; *Chicago Bee*, an African-American newspaper, applauded the *Daily Worker* for its fight against discrimination in sports: *Chicago Bee*, 7 June 1942, 2; See list of All-America players in Christy Walsh, *College Football and All America Review* (Hollywood, CA: House-Warven, 1951); *Sporting News*, 14 October 1947, 1; *Daily Worker*, 22 January 1950, 8; stated regarding motives of Branch Rickey from *Daily Worker*, 12 November 1847, 15; John Underwood, "The True Crisis," *Sports Illustrated*, 20 May 1963, 17; *United Press International*, 20 February 1951; Donald Spivey and Thomas A. Jones, "Intercollegiate Athletic Servitude: A Case Study of the black Illini Student-Athletes, 1931–1967," *Social Science Quarterly 55* (March 1975), 939–947; J. Robert Evans, *Blowing the Whistle on Intercollegiate Sports* (Chicago, IL: 1974), 39–82; Joseph Durso, *The Sports Factory: An Investigation into College Sports* (New York, NY: Quadrangle, 1975), 18–30; Randy Roberts and James Olson, *Winning is the Only Thing: Sports in America Since 1945* (Baltimore, MD: Johns Hopkins University Press, 1989), 73–94; Kenneth L. Shropshire, *In Black and White: Race and Sports* (New York, NY: New York University Press, 1996), 20–35.

11. Donald Spivey, "Black Consciousness and Olympic Protest Movement, 1964 1980" in *Sport in America: New Historical Perspectives* (Westport, CT: Greenwood Press, 1985), 239–262; Clippings, Avery Brundage Collection, Box 287, University of Illinois Archives, Urbana-Champaign; *Chicago Defender*, 6 July–12 July 1968, 4, 27, July–2, August 1968, 6; Harry Edwards, *The Revolt of the Black Athlete* (New York, NY: The Free Press, 1969), 91–93, 175–182; Frederic Cople Jaher, "White America Views Jack Johnson, Joe Louis, and Muhammad Ali," in Spivey, ed., *Sport in America: New Historical Perspectives*, 145–192; "The Giant They Love to Hate: Muhammad Ali," *Sports Illustrated*, 6 December 1965, 40–45, 106–109; Ali A. Mazrui, "Boxer Muhammad Ali and Soldier Idi Amin As International Political Symbols: The Bioeconomics of Sport and War," *Comparative Studies in Society and History*, 19 (April 1977), 189–215; Muhammad Ali, *The Greatest* (New York, NY: Ballantine Books, 1975); also see Gerald Early, *The Muhammad Ali Reader* (Hopewell, NJ: Ecco Press, 1998); and on Curt Flood see Curt Flood, *The Way It Is* (New York, NY: Pocket Books, 1972), and "Curt Flood Act of 1997," *Report of the Senate Committee on the Judiciary*, *105th United States Congress* (Washington, DC: Government Printing Office, 1997), 105–118; *New York Times*, 6 May 1979; Interview of Harry Edwards on CBS program "60 minutes," 19 October 1980; "Blues for Curt Flood," *Chicago Defender*, 19 July 1972, 32; *New York Times*, 19 July 1972; "Boy-

cott of the 1968 Games," Avery Brundage Collection, Box 287; John Morin, "The Bloody Olympiad," *Daily World*, 5 October 1968, 12, and 4 October 1968, 12; International Athletes' Club to Avery Brundage, 18 April 1966, Brundage Collection, Box 176; *Chicago Daily News*, 2 February 1968, 24–26; Bob Ottum, "Grim Countdown to the Games," *Sports Illustrated*, 14 October 1968, 36–43; Pete Axthelm, "Boycott Now—Boycott Later?," *Sports Illustrated*, 26 February 1968, 24–26; *Chicago Defender*, 1–7 June 1968, 15, and 19–25 October 1968, 18; *Daily World*, 12 October 1968, 12; *Chicago Defender,* 24 February–1 March 1968, 12, and 4–10 May 1968, 18, and 9–15 March 1968, 15; "After 32 years, Owens is Still Example for Youth," *Chicago Defender*, 11–17 May 1968, 31; Edwards quotes that the boycott is still on: *Daily World*, 9 August 1968, 12, and 3 September 1968, 12, and 19 October 1968, 12; *World Sports, January 1969*, 11; *Los Angeles Times*, 8 April 1970, 9; *New York Times*, 6 October 1968; Detroit Free Press, 14 October 1972; Tommie Smith remarks about the "tameness" of the boycott is from Mike Jay, "Tommie Smith: After Four Years," *Daily World*, 14 October 1972, m-11.

f). The Civil Rights Front and Beyond

12. King quote on duality as cited in his book, *Where Do We Go From Here: Chaos or Community* (New York, NY: Bantam Books, 1968), 80. King quote from speech to National Jewish Committee, New York City, 20 May 1965. A valuable in-depth examination of the linkages between the Civil Rights Movement and the teachings of Gandhi is provided in Sudarshan Kapur, *Raising Up A Prophet: The African-American Encounter with Gandhi* (Boston, MA: Beacon Press, 1992). Major sources author drew from in formulating interpretation of civil rights organizations and activist political strategies: David Garrow, *Bearing the Cross: Martin Luther King, Jr., and the Southern Christian Leadership Conference* (New York, NY: William Morrow, 1986); Robert Weisbrot, *Freedom Bound: A History of America's Civil Rights Movement* (New York, NY: Plume, 1991); Clayborne Carson, *In Struggle: SNCC and the Black Awakening of the 1960s* (Cambridge, MA: Harvard University Press, 1982); Howard Zinn, SNCC: The New Abolitionists (Boston, MA: Beacon Press, 1965); Theodore Cross, *The Black Power Imperative: Racial Inequality and the Politics of Nonviolence* (New York, NY: Faulkner Books, 1987); Vincent Harding, *The Other American Revolution* (Los Angeles, CA: Center for Afro-American Studies, 1980); James McEvoy and Abraham Miller, ed., *Black*

Power and Student Rebellion (Belmont, CA: Wadsworth Pubs., 1969); Louis E. Lomax, *The Negro Revolt* (New York, NY: Signet, 1963); August Meier and Elliott Rudwick, *Core: A Study in the Civil Rights Movement* (Urbana, IL: University of Illinois Press, 1975), and *Black Protest in the Sixties* (Chicago, IL: Quadrangle, 1970); Nancy J. Weiss, *The National Urban League, 1910–1940* (New York, NY: Oxford University Press, 1974); Wunyabari O. Maloba, *Mau Mau and Kenya: An Analysis of a Peasant Revolt* (Bloomington, IN: Indiana University Press, 1993); Joseph R. Washington, Jr., *Black Religion: The Negro and Christianity in the United States* (Boston, MA: Beacon Press, 1964); Gene Marine, *The Black Panthers* (New York, NY: Signet, 1969); Angela Y. Davis, *Women, Race and Class* (New York, NY: Vintage, 1983); Elaine Brown, *A Taste of Power: A Black Woman's Story* (New York, NY: Pantheon, 1992); James H. Cone, *Black Theology and Black Power* (New York, NY: The Seabury Press, 1969); Stokely Carmichael and Charles V. Hamilton, *Black Power: The Politics of Liberation in America* (New York, NY: Vintage, 1967); Michael B. Preston, Lenneal J. Henderson, Jr., and Paul Puryear, ed., *The New Black Politics: The Search for Political Power* (West Plains, NY: Longman, Inc., 1982).

13. King often acknowledges his intellectual ties to Walter Rauschenbusch, *Christianity and the Social Crisis* (New York, NY: Macmillian, 1916), and Reinhold Niebuhr, *Moral Man and Immoral Society: A Study in Ethics and Politics* (New York, NY: Scribner's & Sons, 1941). King's epiphany of the coffee cup remarks were made at a speech that I heard in Chicago in September 1966 and in other talks before and after that date; also cited in Garrow, *Bearing the Cross*, 89. "Content of their character" from King's "I Have a Dream" speech before the March on Washington for Jobs and Freedom, Washington, D.C., 28 August 1963. King's sentiments regarding Black Power are given in detail in his own words in his book, *Where Do We Go From Here: Chaos or Community*, 27–77. Sources underlying my interpretation and providing personal reflections on the movement: Martin Luther King, Jr. and other African-American leaders and activist organizations of the period: Martin Luther King, Jr., *Where Do We Go From Here: Chaos or Community* (New York, NY: Bantam, 1968), *Stride Toward Freedom: The Montgomery Story* (New York, NY: Harper & Row, 1958), *Why We Can't Wait* (New York, NY: Signet, 1963); Taylor Branch, *Parting the Waters: America in the King Years 1954–1963* (New York, NY: Simon and Schuster, 1988); Stephen B. Oates, *Let the Trumpet Sound: The Life of Martin Luther King,*

Jr. (New York, NY: Plune, 1982); Hanes Walton, Jr., *The Political Philosophy of Martin Luther King, Jr.* (Westport, CT: Greenwood Press, 1976), and *Invisible Politics: Black Political Behavior* (Albany, NY: State University of New York Press, 1985); Peter J. Albert and Ronald Hoffman, ed., *We Shall Overcome: Martin Luther King, Jr. and the Black Freedom Struggle* (New York, NY: Da Capo, 1993); Clayborne Carson, ed., *The Papers of Martin Luther King, Jr.: Called to Serve* I (Berkeley CA: University of California Press, 1992); Steve Clark, *Malcolm X: The Final Speeches* (New York, NY: Pathfinder, 1992); Malcolm X with Alex Haley, *The Autobiography of Malcolm X* (New York, NY: Grove Press, 1964); George Breitman, ed., *Malcolm X: By Any Means Necessary* (New York, NY: Pathfinder, 1987 rept. of 1970 edn.); Juan Williams, *Thurgood Marshall: American Revolutionary* (New York, NY: Times Books, 1998); Willie Morris, *The Ghosts of Medgar Evers: A Tale of Race, Murder, Mississippi, and Hollywood* (New York, NY: Random House, 1998); Roy Wilkins, *Standing Fast: The Autobiography of Roy Wilkins* (New York, NY: Viking Press, 1982); James Meredith, *James Meredith vs. Ole Miss* (Jackson, MS: Meredith Pub., 1995), and *Three Years in Mississippi* (Bloomington, IN: Indiana University Press, 1966); Stokely Carmichael, *Stokely Speaks: Black Power Back to Pan-Africanism* (New York, NY: Vintage, 1971); Bobby Seale, *Seize the Time: The Story of the Black Panther Party and Huey P. Newton* (New York, NY: Vintage, 1970); Eldridge Cleaver, *Soul on Ice* (New York, NY: McGraw-Hill, 1968); Angela Davis, *Angela Davis: An Autobiography* (New York, NY: International Pubs., 1988); James Farmer, *Lay Bare the Heart: An Autobiography of the Civil Rights Movement* (New York, NY: Plume, 1985); Andrew Young, *An Easy Burden: The Civil Rights Movement and the Transformation of America* (New York, NY: HarperCollins, 1996); Charles V. Hamilton, *Adam Clayton Powell, Jr.: The Political Biography of an American Dilemma* (New York, NY: Atheneum, 1991); Gayraud S. Wilmore, *Black Religion and Black Radicalism* (New York, NY: Doubleday, 1972); Frady Marshall, *Jesse: The Life and Pilgrimage of Jesse Jackson* (New York, NY: Random House, 1996); Joanne Grant, *Ella Baker: Freedom Bound* (New York, NY: Wiley, 1998); John Lewis, *Walking with the Wind: A Memoir of the Movement* (New York, NY: Simon & Schuster, 1998); Chana Kai Lee, *For Freedom's Sake: The Life of Fannie Lou Hamer* (Urbana, IL: University of Illinois Press, 1999).

14. Hugh Davis Graham and Ted Robert Gurr, *Violence in America: The Complete Official Report to the National Commis-*

sion on the Causes and Prevention of Violence (New York, NY: Signet, 1969); *Report of the National Advisory Commission on Civil Disorder* [a.k.a. The Kerner Commission Report] (New York, NY: Bantam, 1968). Lyndon Johnson quote from a speech at a civil rights conference at Johnson Library as cited in Paul K. Conkin, *Big Daddy from the Pedernales: Lyndon Baines Johnson* (Boston, MA: Twyane, 1986), 295. Sources underlying my interpretation of economic and social condition of African-Americans: Alphonso Pinkney, *The Myth of Black Progress* (New York, NY: Cambridge University Press, 1986), and *Black Americans* (Englewood Cliffs, NJ: Prentice-Hall, 1987); *The Negro Family: The Case for National Action* [commonly known as the Moynihan Report after Committee Chair, Daniel Patrick Moynihan] (Washington, DC: Government Printing Office, 1965); Marian Wright Edelman, *The Measure of Our Success: A Letter to My Children and Yours* (Boston, MA: Beacon Press, 1994); Theodore R. Kennedy, *You Gotta Deal With It: Black Family Relations in a Southern Community* (New York, NY: Oxford University Press, 1980); David L. Kirp, *Just Schools: The Idea of Racial Equality in American Education* (Berkeley, CA: University of California Press, 1982); Jonathan Kozol, *Death at an Early Age* (New York, NY: Bantam 1967), and *Savage Inequalities: Children in America's Schools* (New York, NY: Crown, 1991); Anne Moody, *Coming of Age in Mississippi* (New York, NY: Dell, 1968); William H. Grier and Price M. Cobbs, *Black Rage* (New York, NY: Bantam, 1969); Manning Marable, *The Crisis of Color and Democracy: Essays on Race, Class and Power* (Monroe, ME: Common Courage Press, 1992); David R. Goldfield, *Black, White, and Southern: Race Relations and Southern Culture 1940 to the Present* (Baton Rouge, LA: Louisiana State University Press, 1991); J. Anthony Lukas, *Common Ground: A Turbulent Decade in the Lives of Three American Families* (New York, NY: Vintage, 1986); Shelley Green and Paul Pryde, *Black Entrepreneurship in America* (New Brunswick, NJ: Transaction Pubs., 1990); Waldo E. Martin, Jr., *Brown v. Board of Education: A Brief History* (Boston, MA: Bedford/St. Martin's, 1998); Kofi Lomotey, ed., *Going to School: The African-American Experience* (Albany, NY: State University of New York Press, 1990); Lawrence J. Hanks, *The Struggle for Black Political Empowerment in Three Georgia Counties* (Knoxville, TN: University of Tennessee Press, 1987); William Julius Wilson, *The Truly Disadvantaged: The Inner City, the Underclass, and Public Policy* (Chicago, IL: University of Chicago Press, 1990); David Glasgow, *The Black Underclass:*

Poverty, Unemployment and Entrapment of Ghetto Youth (New York, NY: Vintage, 1981); Fober M. Fogelson, *Violence as Protest: A Study of Riots and Ghettos* (New York, NY: Doubleday, 1971); James P. Comer, *School Power: Implication of an Intervention Project* (New York, NY: The Free Press, 1980); J. Harvie Wilkinson III, *From Brown to Bakke: The Supreme Court and School Integration: 1954–1978* (New York, NY: Oxford University Press, 1979); Roy L. Brooks, *Rethinking the American Race Problem* (Berkeley, CA: University of California Press, 1990); Paul Jacobs, *Prelude to Riot: A View of Urban America from the Bottom* (New York, NY: Vintage, 1968); Andrew Hacker, *Two Nations: Black and White, Separate, Hostile, Unequal* (New York, NY: Scribners, 1992); Gerald R. Gill, *Meanness Mania: The Changed Mood* (Washington, DC: Howard University Press, 1980); William H. Chafe, *Civilities and Civil Rights: Greensboro, North Carolina, and the Black Struggle for Freedom* (New York, NY: Oxford University Press, 1981); Gerald David Jaynes and Robin M. Williams, Jr., *A Common Destiny: Blacks and American Society; Report of the Committee on the Status of Black Americans, National Research Council* (Washington, DC: National Academy Press, 1989). Sources underlying my interpretation of government's reactions to the Civil Rights Movement and beyond: Kenneth O'Reilly, *Racial Matters: The FBI's Secret File on Black America, 1960–1972* (New York, NY: The Free Press, 1989); David Burner, *John F. Kennedy and a New Generation* (New York, NY: HarperCollins, 1989); Anthony Summers, *Official and Confidential: The Secret Life of J. Edgar Hoover* (New York, NY: Putnam, 1993); Natalie Robins, *Alien Ink: The FBI's War on Freedom of Expression* (New Brunswick, NJ: Rutgers University Press, 1993); David J. Garrow, *The FBI and Martin Luther King, Jr.* (New York, NY: Penguin, 1981); Robert F. Burk, *The Eisenhower Administration and Black Civil Rights* (Knoxville, TN: University of Tennessee Press, 1985); Samuel F. Yette, *The Choice: The Issue of Black Survival in America* (New York, NY: Berkley Medallion, 1975); Michael B. Katz, *The Undeserving Poor: From the War on Poverty to the War on Welfare* (New York, NY: Pantheon, 1989); Jerome H. Skolnick, *The Politics of Protest: The Skolnick Report to the National Commission on the Causes and Prevention of Violence* (New York, NY: Ballantine, 1969. Vietnam War: George Donelson Moss, *Vietnam: An American Ordeal* (Englewood Cliffs, NJ: Prentice-Hall, 1990); Marvin E. Gettleman, *Vietnam: History, Documents, and Opinions on a Major World Crisis* (New York, NY: Fawcett, 1966);

Richard O. Curry, ed., *Freedom at Risk: Secrecy, Censorship, and Repression in the 1980s* (Philadelphia, PA: Temple University Press, 1988), and *An Uncertain Future: Thought Control and Repression During the Reagan-Bush Era* (Los Angeles, CA: First Amendment Foundation, 1992).

RACE TO THE FUTURE

Toward a Conclusion

1. Donald Spivey, "Mandela the Boxer," remarks made at program in celebration of the release of Nelson Mandela, Afro-American Cultural Center, University of Connecticut, 12 February 1990. For further discussion of the issues raised I recommend: Randall Robinson, *Defending the Spirit: A Black Life in America* (New York, NY: Dutton, 1998); Fatima Meer, *Higher Than Hope: The Authorized Biography of Nelson Mandela* (New York, NY: Harper & Row, 1988); Bernard Magubane, *The Ties That Bind: African-American Consciousness of Africa* (Trenton, NJ: Africa World Press, 1989), and *South Africa: From Soweto to Uitenhage: The Political Economy of the South African Revolution* (Trenton, NJ: Africa World Press, 1989); Elie Kedourie, ed., *Nationalism in Asia and Africa* (New York, NY: Meridian Books, 1970); George M. Fredrickson, *White Supremacy: A Comparative Study in American and South African History* (New York, NY: Oxford University Press, 1981); Toni Morrison, ed., *Race-ing Justice, En-Gendering Power: Essays on Anita Hill, Clarence Thomas, and the Construction of Social Reality* (New York, NY: Pantheon, 1992).

2. Malcolm X's admonitions are captured in *By Any Means Necessary* (New York, NY: Pathfinder, 1987), and *Malcolm X Speaks* (New York, NY: Grove Press, 1965). Account of Gates dinner party cited in *Boston Globe*, 7 March 1996, 67. *Report of the Advisory Committee on One America in the 21st Century—The President's Initiative on Race*, Washington, D.C., 18 September 1998; also see Mary Owen and Darci McConnell, "Race Report Meets with Skepticism, Proposal for Help," *Detroit Free Press*, 19 September 1998, 1A; Sonya Ross, "Colorblind Society Won't Erase Stereotypes, Race Advisers Say," and "Report Urges Clinton to Confront Prejudice, Privilege in U.S. Whites Benefit While Others Are Disfranchised," *Associated Press*, 8 July 1998, A03 and 18 September 1998, A18, respectively. For further discussion of the contemporary racial divide from a variety of useful perspectives see: Bob Blauner, *Black Lives, White Lives: Three Decades of Race Relations in America* (Berkeley, CA: University of California Press, 1990); Studs Terkel, *Race: How*

Blacks and Whites Think and Feel About the American Obsession (New York, NY: Anchor Books, 1992); Herbert Aptheker, ed., *Against Racism: Unpublished Essays, Papers, Addresses, 1887–1961 By W.E.B. Du Bois* (Amherst, MA: University of Massachusetts Press, 1985); John Hope Franklin, *Race and History: Selected Essays, 1938–1988* (Baton Rouge, LA: Louisiana State University Press, 1989); Henry Louis Gates, Jr. and Cornel West, *The Future of the Race* (New York, NY: Vintage, 1997); Stanley Crouch, *The All-American Skin Game, or the Decoy of Race* (New York, NY: Vintage, 1997); and Richard Delgado, *The Coming Race War? And Other Apocalyptic Tales of America After Affirmative Action and Welfare* (New York, NY: New York University Press, 1996).

AFRICAN-AMERICAN HISTORY: A SUGGESTED READING LIST

(The following list is meant to be suggestive not exhaustive of the rich field of African-American history)

General Overviews and Texts

Aptheker, Herbert, (ed) *A Documentary History of the Negro People in the United States vols. I–II* (New York, NY: Citadel, 1968)

Bain, Mildred and Lewis, Ervin, (ed) *From Freedom to Freedom: African Roots in American Soil* (New York, NY: Random House, 1977)

Bennett, Lerone, *Before the Mayflower: A History of Black America* (New York, NY: Penguin, 1984; rev. 1961)

Chambers, Bradford, (ed) *Chronicles of Black Protest* (New York, NY: Mentor, 1968)

Du Bois, W.E.B., *Black Folk Then and Now* (New York, NY: Holt, 1939)

Finkenline, Roy, *Sources of the African-American Past* (New York, NY: Longman, 1997)

Foner, Philip S., *History of Black Americans*, vols. I–III (Westport, CT: Greenwood Press, 1975–1981)

Franklin, John Hope, *From Slavery to Freedom: A History of Negro Americans* Sixth Edition (New York, NY: Knopf, 1987)

Franklin, John Hope, *Race and History: Selected Essays, 1938–1988* (Baton Rouge, LA: LSU Press, 1989)

Frazier, Thomas R., *Afro-American History: Primary Sources* (Chicago, IL: Dorsey, 1988)

Frazier, Thomas R., *Afro-American History: Primary Sources* (New York, NY: Dorsey Press, 1988)

Genovese, Eugene D., *In Red and Black: Marxian Explorations in Southern and Afro-American History* (New York, NY: Pantheon, 1969)

Goggin, Jacqueline, *Carter G. Woodson: A Life in Black History* (Baton Rouge, LA: LSU Press, 1997)

Harding, Vincent, *The Other American Revolution* (Los Angeles, CA: Center for Afro-American Studies, 1980)

Hine, Darlene Clark, et. al., *African-American Odyssey* (New York, NY: Prentice Hall, 1999)

Holt, Thomas C., and Brown, Elsa Barkley, *Major Problems in African-American History* Vols. I&2 (New York, NY: Houghton Mifflin, 2000)

Huggins, Nathan I. and Kilson, Martin, and Fox, Daniel M., *Key Issues in the Afro-American Experience* vols. I–II (New York, NY: Harcourt Brace, 1971)

Jacobs, Paul and Landau, Saul, eds., *To Serve the Devil: A Documentary Analysis of America's Racial History and Why it has Been Kept Hidden* vols. I–II (New York, NY: Vintage, 1971)

Kelley, Robin D.G., and Lewis, Earl, eds., *To Make Our World Anew: A History of African Americans* (New York, NY: Oxford University Press, 2000)

Logan, Rayford W., *The Negro in the United States* (Princeton, NJ: Nostrand Co., 1957)

Meltzer, Milton, (ed) *In Their Own Words: A History of the American Negro* vols. I–II (New York, NY: Mentor, 1965)

Miller, Kelly, *Radicals and Conservatives: Essays on the Negro in America* (New York, NY: Schocken, 1968; rpt. 1908)

Myrdal, Gunnar, *An American Dilemma: The Negro Problem and Modern Democracy* Vols. I&II (New York, NY: Harper, 1969; rpt. 1944)

Nieman, Donald G., *Promises to Keep: African-Americans and the Constitutional Order, 1776 to the Present* (New York, NY: Oxford University Press, 1991)

Quarles, Benjamin, *The Negro in the Making of America* (New York, NY: Collier Books, 1964)

Scheiner, Seth and Edelstein, Tilden, (ed) *The Black Americans: Interpretive Readings* (New York, NY: Holt, Reinhart 1971)

Toppin, Edgar A., *A Biographical History of Blacks in America Since 1528* (New York, NY: McKay, 1971)

Williams, George W., *History of the Negro Race in America* vols. I&II, (Salem, NH: Ayer, 1989; Rept. 1883)

African Legacy and Diaspora

Abrahams, Peter, *Wild Conquest: A Novel of Boer Aggression and African Resistance in South Africa* (New York, NY: Doubleday, 1971)

Africa Information Service, (ed) *Return to the Source: Selected Speeches of Amilcar Cabral* (New York, NY: Modern Reader, 1973)

Asante, Molefi Kete, *Afrocentricity* (Trenton, NJ: Africa World Press, 1991)

Awoonor, Kofi, *The Bread of the Earth: A Survey of the History, Culture and Literature of Africa South of the Sahara* (New York, NY: Anchor Press, 1976)

Balandier, Georges, *Ambiguous Africa* (New York, NY: Pantheon, 1966)

Ben-Jochannan, Yosef, *Africa: Mother of Western Civilization* (New York, NY: Alkebu-Lan Books, 1971)

Bennett, Norman Robert, *Mirambo of Tanzania* (London, ED: Oxford University Press, 1971)

Bernal, Martin, *Black Athena* (New Brunswick, NJ: Rutgers University Press, 1987)

Beyan, Amos J., *The American Colonization Society and the Creation of the Liberian State* (Lanham, MA: University Press of America, 1991)

Buckley, Roger Norman, *Congo Jack: A Novel* (Mt. Kisco, NY: Pinto Press, 1997)

Burstein, Stanley, *Ancient African Civilizations: Kush and Axum* (Princeton, NJ: Marcus Wiener, 1998)

Cartey, Wilfred and Kilson, Martin, (ed), *The Africa Reader* (New York, NY: Vintage, 1970)

Chaliand, Gerard, *Armed Struggle in Africa* (New York, NY: Modern Reader, 1969)

Chukumba, Stephen U., *The Big Powers Against Ethiopia* (Lanham, MD: University Press of America, 1979)

Cole, Hubert, *Christophe: King of Haiti* (New York, NY: Viking, 1967)

Davidson, Basil, *A History of East and Central Africa* (New York, NY: Doubleday, 1969)

Davidson, Basil, *African Civilization Revisited* (Trenton, NJ: Africa World Press, 1993)

Davidson, Basil, *The Lost Cities of Africa* (Boston, MA: Little, Brown & Co., 1959)

DeGraft-Johnson, J.C., *African Glory: The Story of Vanished Negro Civilizations* (Baltimore, MD: Black Classic Press, 1986; Rept. 1954)

Denoon, Donald, *Southern Africa Since 1800* (New York, NY: Praeger, 1973)

Diederich, Bernard and Burt, Al, *Papa Doc: The Truth About Haiti Today* (New York, NY: Avon, 1969)

Diop, Cheikh Anta, *Civilization or Barbarism* (Brooklyn, NY: Lawrence Hill Books, 1991; Rept. 1981)

Diop, Cheikh Anta, *The African Origin of Civilization: Myth or Reality* (Westport, CT: Lawrence Hill, 1974)

Dobler, Lavinia and Brown, William A., *Great Rulers of the African Past* (New York, NY: Doubleday, 1965)

Drake, St. Clair, *Black Folk Here and There* (Los Angeles, CA: Center for Afro-American Studies, 1987)

Du Bois, W.E.B., *The World and Africa* (New York, NY: International Pubs., 1965; rpt. 1947)

Edwards, I.E.S., *The Pyramids of Egypt* (New York, NY: Penguin, 1971; rpt)

Fage, F.D., *A History of West Africa* (Cambridge, ED: Cambridge University Press, 1969)

Falola, Toyin, ed., *Africa* Vols. 1–5 (Durham, NC: Carolina Academic Press, 2000–2003)

Fanon, Frantz, *The Wretched of the Earth* (New York, NY: Grove Press, 1963)

Fanon, Frantz, *Toward the African Revolution* (New York, NY: Grove, 1967)

Frank, Andre Gunder, *Crisis: In the Third World* (New York, NY: Holmes and Meier, 1981)

Furtado, Celso, *Obstacles to Development in Latin America* (New York, NY: Anchor, 1970)

Gibson, Thelma, *Forbearance: The Life Story of a Coconut Grove Native* (Homestead, FL: Helena Enterprises, 2000)

Guevara, Che, *The Diary of Che Guevara* (New York, NY: Bantam Books, 1968)

Harris, Joseph E., *Africans and Their History* (New York, NY: New American Library, 1972)

Hodder, B.W., *Africa Today* (New York, NY: Africana, 1978)

Hull, Richard, *African Cities and Towns Before the European Conquest* (New York, NY: Norton, 1976)

Jackson, John, *Introduction to African Civilization* (Secaucus, NJ: Citadel, 1974)

James, George G.M., *Stolen Legacy* (San Franciso, CA: Julian Richardson Associates, Publishers, 1988 rept. 1945)

Jansoon, Kurt, et. al., *The Ethiopian Famine* (London, ED: Zed Books, 1987)

Johanson, Donald and Shreeve, James, *Lucy's Child: The Discovery of a Human Ancestor* (New York, NY: William Morrow, 1989)

Johnson, Michael, and Roark, James L., *Black Masters: A Free Family of Color in the Old South* (New York, NY: W.W. Norton, 1984)

Johnson, Whittington B., *Race Relations in the Bahamas, 1784–1834* (Fayetteville, AR: 2000)

Kedourie, Elie, (ed) *Nationalism in Asia and Africa* (New York, NY: Meridian Books, 1970)

Keesing's Research Report, *Africa Independent: A Study of Political Developments* (New York, NY: Scribner's, 1972)

Kenyatta, Jomo, *Facing Mt. Kenya* (New York, NY: Vintage, 1965)

Knight, Franklin W., and Palmer, Colin A., ed., *The Modern Caribbean* (Chapel Hill, NC: University of North Carolina Press, 1989)

Kotecha, Ken C. and Adams, Robert W., *African Politics* (Washington, DC: University Press of America, 1981)

La Guma, Ales, (ed) *Apartheid* (New York, NY: International Pubs., 1971)

Lavan, George, (ed) *Che Guevara Speaks* (New York, NY: Grove, 1967)

Lelyveld, Joseph, *Move Your Shadow: South Africa, Black and White* (New York, NY: Penguin Books, 1985)

Lierde, Jean Van, (ed) *Lumumba Speaks: The Speeches and Writings of Patrice Lumumba* (Boston, MA: Little, Brown, 1972)

Lynch, Hollis R., *Black American Radicals and the Liberation of Africa: The Council on African Affairs, 1937–1955* (Ithaca, NY: Africana Studies Press, Cornell Univ., 1978)

Lynch, Hollis R., *Edward Wilmot Blyden: Pan-Negro Patriot* (London, ED: Oxford University Press, 1967)

Magubane, Bernard, *The Ties That Bind: African-American Consciousness of Africa* (Trenton, NJ: Africa World Press, 1989)

Marcus, Harold G., *Haile Sellassie I: The Formative Years, 1892–1936* (Lawrenceville, NJ: Red Sea Press, 1995)

Mathabane, Mark, *Kafir Boy: The True Story of a Black Youth's Coming of Age in Apartheid South Africa* (New York, NY: Plume, 1986)

Mattoso, Katia M. de Queriros, *To Be a Slave in Brazil, 1550–1888* (New Brunswick, NJ: Rutgers University Press, 1986)

Mbiti, John S., *African Religions and Philosophy* (New York, NY: Anchor, 1969)

Meer, Fatima, *Higher Than Hope: The Authorized Biography of Nelson Mandela* (New York, NY: Harper, 1988)

More, Carlos, *Castro, the Blacks, and Africa* (Los Angeles, CA: UCLA Center for Afro-American Studies, 1988)

Morel, E.D., *The Black Man's Burden* (New York, NY: Modern Reader, 1969)

Murphy, E. Jefferson, *History of African Civilization* (New York, NY: Crowell, 1972)

Naipaul, V.S., *Among the Believers: An Islamic Journey* (New York, NY: Knopf, 1981)

Nascimento, Abdias Do, and Nascimento, Elisa Larkin, *Africans in Brazil* (Trenton, NJ: Africa World Press, 1992)

Nkrumah, Kwame, *Challenge of the Congo* (New York, NY: International Publishers, 1967)

Nkrumah, Kwame, *Class Struggle in Africa* (New York, NY: International Publishers, 1970)

Nkrumah, Kwame, *Ghana: The Autobiography of Kwame Nkrumah* ((New York, NY: International Pubs., 1971; rpt.)

Nyerere, Julius K., *Man and Development* (New York, NY: Oxford University Press, 1974)

Ogot, B.A., (ed) *Zamani: A Survey of East African History* (London: Longman, 1968)

Ogot, Bethwell A., (ed) *War and Society in Africa* (London, ED: Frank Cass, 1972)

Omara-Otunnu, Amii, *Politics and the Military in Uganda, 1890–1985* (New York, NY: St. Martin's Press, 1987)

Osae, T.A., et. al., *A Short History of West Africa* (New York, NY: Hill and Wang, 1968)

Padmore, George, *The Life and Struggles of Negro Toilers* (Hollywood, CA: Sun Dance Press, 1971)

Petras, James and Zeitlin, Maurice, (ed) *Latin America: Reform or Revolution?* (New York, NY: Fawcett, 1968)

Plummer, Brenda Gayle, *Haiti and the Great Powers, 1902–1915* (Baton Rouge, LA: LSU Press, 1988)

Rodney, Walter, *How Europe Underdeveloped Africa* (Washington, DC: Howard University Press, 1974)

Rotberg, Robert I., *A Political History of Tropical Africa* (New York, NY: Harcourt, Brace, 1965)

Segal, Ronald, *The Race War: The World-Wide Clash of White and Non-White* (New York, NY: Bantam, 1967)

Sertima, Ivan Van, ed., *African Presence in Early America* (New Brunswick, NJ: Transaction Press, 1992)

Sertima, Ivan Van, ed., *Blacks in Science: Ancient and Modern* (New Brunswick, NJ: Transaction Books, 1983)

Sertima, Ivan Van, ed., *Golden Age of the Moor* (New Brunswick, NJ: Transaction Books, 1993)

Sertima, Ivan Van, ed., *Great African Thinkers: Cheikh Anta Diop* (New Brunswick, NJ: Transaction Books, 1992)

Sertima, Ivan Van, *They Came Before Columbus: The African Presence in Ancient America* (New York, NY: Random House, 1976)

Seth, Ronald, *Milestones in African History* (Philadelphia, PA: Chilton Book Co., 1969)

Shinnie, Margaret, *Ancient African Kingdoms* (New York, NY: Mentor, 1965)

Spivey, Diane M., *The Peppers, Cracklings, and Knots of Wool Cookbook: The Global Migration of African Cuisine* (Albany, NY: State University of New York Press, 1999)

Spivey, Donald, *The Politics of Miseducation: The Booker Washington Institute of Liberia, 1929–1984* (Lexington, KY: University Press of Kentucky, 1986)

Sundiata, I.K., *Black Scandal: America and the Liberian Labor Crisis, 1929–1936* (Philadelphia, PA: Institute for the Study of Human Issues, 1980)

Taylor, John H., *Egypt and Nubia* (Cambridge, MA: Harvard University Press, 1991)

Thompson, Vincent, *The Making of the African Diaspora in the Americas 1441–1900* (New York, NY: Longman, 1987)

Tutuola, Amos, *The Palm-Wine Drunkard: A Novel from Africa* (New York, NY: Grove 1953)

Veliz, Claudio, (ed) *Obstacles to Change in Latin America* (London: Oxford University Press, 1965)

Wallerstein, Immanuel, *Africa: The Politics of Independence* (New York, NY: Vintage, 1961)

Ward, W.E.F. and White, L.W., *East Africa: A Century of Change, 1870–1970* (New York, NY: Africana, 1971)

Weissman, Stephen R., *American Foreign Policy in the Congo, 1960–1964* (Ithaca, NY: Cornell University Press, 1974)

West, Richard, *Congo: An Account of a Century of European Exploration and Exploitation in the Heart of Africa* (New York, NY: Holt, Rinehart, Winston, 1972)

Wiener, Leo, *Africa and the Discovery of America* Vols. I–III (Philadelphia, PA: Innes & Sons, 1922 (Vol. I pub. in 1920))

Williams, Chancellor, *The Destruction of Black Civilization* (Chicago, IL: Third World Press. 1974)

Woodson, Carter G., *African Myths* (Washington, DC: Associated Publishers, 1928)

Slavery, Race, Early America

Alford, Terry, *Prince Among Slaves* (New York, NY: Oxford University Press, 1977)

Aptheker, Herbert, *Nat Turner's Slave Rebellion* (New York, NY: Grove, 1966)

Archer, Leonie, *Slavery and Other Forms of Unfree Labour* (New York, NY: Routledge, 1988)

Berlin, Ira, *Slaves Without Masters: The Free Negro in the Antebellum South* (New York, NY: Vintage, 1974)

Blassingame, John W., *Black New Orleans, 1860–1880* (Chicago, IL: University of Chicago Press, 1973)

Blassingame, John W., *The Slave Community* (New York, NY: Oxford University Press, 1972)

Blauner, Bob, *Black Lives, White Lives: Three Decades of Race Relations in America* (Berkeley, CA: University of California Press, 1989)

Boles, John B., *Black Southerners, 1619–1869* (Lexington, KY: 1984)

Boles, John B., *Master and Slaves in the House of the Lord: Race and Religion in the American South, 1740–1870* (Lexington, KY: 1988)

Bontemps, Arna, ed., *Five Black Lives* (Middletown, CT: Wesleyan University Press, 1971)

Bracey, John, et. al., (ed) *American Slavery: The Question of Resistance* (Belmont, CA: Wadsworth, 1971)

Breen, T.H., *Myne Owne Ground: Race and Freedom on Virginia's Eastern Shore, 1640–1676* (New York, NY: Oxford University Press, 1980)

Brown, Richard D. and Rabe, Stephen G., (ed) *Slavery in American Society* (Lexington, MA: D.C. Heath, 1969)

Campbell, Stanley W., *The Slave Catchers: Enforcement of the Fugitive Slave Law, 1850–1860* (New York, NY: W.W. Norton, 1968)

Clarke, John Henrik, et. al., *William Styron's Nat Turner: Ten Black Writers Respond* (Boston, MA: Beacon Press, 1968)

Curtin, Philip D., *The Atlantic Slave Trade* (Madison, WN: University of Wisconsin, 1969)

Davidson, Basil, *The African Slave Trade* (Boston, MA: Little, Brown, 1961)

Davis, David Brion, *Slavery and Human Progress* (New York, NY: Oxford University Press, 1984)

Davis, David Brion, *The Problem of Slavery in the Age of Revolution, 1770–1823* (Ithaca, NY: Cornell University Press, 1975)

Davis, David Brion, *The Problem of Slavery in Western Culture* (Ithaca, NY: Cornell University Press, 1966)

Degler, Carl N., *Neither Black Nor White: Slavery and Race Relations in Brazil and the United States* (New York, NY: Macmillan, 1971)

Donnan, Elizabeth, (ed) *Documents Illustrative of the History of the Slave Trade to America* Vols. I–IV (New York, NY: Octagon Books, 1969; rpt. 1930)

Douglass, Frederick, *Narrative of the Life of Frederick Douglass* (New York, NY: Dolphin Book, 1963; rpt. 1845)

Du Bois, W.E.B., *The Suppression of the African Slave-Trade* (New York, NY: Schocken, 1969; rpt. 1896)

Edwards, G. Franklin, (ed) *E. Franklin Frazier on Race Relations* (Chicago, IL: University of Chicago Press, 1968)

Elkins, Stanley M., *Slavery* (Chicago, IL: University of Chicago, 1959)

Equiano, Olaudah, *The Interesting Narrative of the Life of Olaudah Equiano* (Boston, MA: Bedford/St. Martin's, 1995)

Fanon, Frantz, *Black Skin White Masks: The Experiences of a Black Man in a White World* (New York, NY: Grove, 1967)

Fast, Howard, *Freedom Road* (New York, NY: Bantam, 1972, rpt. 1944)

Fehrenbacher, Don. E., *The Dred Scott Case: Its Significance in American Law and Politics* (New York, NY: Oxford University Press, 1979)

Finkelman, Paul, *Slavery and the Founders: Race and Liberty in the Age of Jefferson* (New York, NY: M.E. Sharpe, 1996)

Fogel, Robert William and Engerman, Stanley L., *Time on the Cross: The Economics of American Negro Slavery* (New York, NY: Little, Brown, 1974)

Foner, Laura and Genovese, Eugene, (ed) *Slavery in the New World: A Reader in Comparative History* (Englewood Cliffs, NJ: Prentice-Hall, 1969)

Foner, Philip S., *Blacks in the American Revolution* (Westport, CT: Greenwood Press, 1975)

Franklin, John Hope, *Runaway Slaves: Rebels on the Plantation* (New York, NY: Oxford University Press, 1999)

Fredrickson, George M., *The Arrogance of Race: Historical Perspectives on Slavery, Racism, and Social Inequality* (Middletown, CT: Wesleyan, 1988)

Fredrickson, George M., *The Black Image in the White Mind: The Debate on Afro-American Character and Destiny, 1817–1914* (New York, NY: Harper and Row, 1971)

Fredrickson, George M., *White Supremacy: A Comparative Study in American and South African History* (New York, NY: Oxford University Press, 1981)

Fuller, Louis, *Slavery in the United States of America* (New York, NY: Norstrand, 1972)

Genovese, Eugene D., *The Political Economy of Slavery* (New York, NY: Vintage, 1965)

Genovese, Eugene D., *The World the Slaveholders Made* (New York, NY: Vintage 1971)

Georgia Writers' Project, *Drums and Shadows: Survival Studies Among the Georgia Coastal Negroes* (Athens, GA: University of Georgia Press, 1986; rept 1940)

Greene, Lorenzo Johnston, *The Negro in Colonial New England* (New York, NY: Atheneum, 1969; rpt. 1942)

Grenberg, Kenneth, ed., *The Confessions of Nat Turner and Related Documents* (Boston, MA: Bedford/St. Martin's 1996)

Gutman, Herbert G., *The Black Family in Slavery and Freedom, 1750–1925* (New York, NY: Vintage, 1976)

Harding, Vincent, *There Is A River: The Black Struggle for Freedom in America* (New York, NY: Vintage, 1983)

Herskovits, Melville J., *The Myth of the Negro Past* (Boston, MA: Beacon Press, 1958; rpt. 1941)

Higginbotham, A. Leon, *In The Matter of Color: Race and the American Legal Process* (New York, NY: Oxford University Press, 1978)

Huggins, Nathan Irvin, *Black Odyssey: The Afro-American Ordeal in Slavery* (New York, NY: Vintage, 1977)

Jacobs, Harriet A., *Life of a Slave Girl* (Cambridge, MA: Harvard, 1987; rpt.)

James, C.L.R., *The Black Jacobins: Toussaint L'Ouverture and the San Domingo Revolution* (New York, NY: Vintage, 1973)

Jefferson, Paul, ed., *The Travels of William Wells Brown* (New York, NY: Marcus Wiener, 1991; Repts. 1848 & 1855)

Jefferson, Thomas, *Notes on the State of Virginia* (New York, NY: Norton, 1972; rpt.)

Johnson, Michael P. and Roark, James L., *Black Masters: A Free Family of Color in the Old South* (New York, NY: Norton, 1984)

Johnson, Whittington B., *Black Savannah, 1788–1864* (Fayetteville, AR: University of Arkansas Press, 1996)

Jones, Howard, *Mutiny on the Amistad* (New York, NY: Oxford University Press, 1987)

Jordan, Winthrop D., *White Over Black: American Attitudes Toward the Negro, 1550–1812* (Chapel Hill, NC: University of North

Carolina Press, 1968)

Klein, Herbert S., *African Slavery in Latin America and the Caribbean* (New York, NY: Oxford University Press, 1986)

Kolchin, Peter, *Unfree Labor: American Slavery and Russian Serfdom* (Cambridge, MA: Harvard University Press, 1987)

Kulikoff, Allan, *Tobacco and Slaves* (Chapel Hill, NC: University of North Carolina Press, 1986)

Levine, Lawrence W., *Black Culture and Black Consciousness: Afro-American Folk Thought from Slavery to Freedom* (New York, NY: Oxford University Press, 1977)

Littlefield, Daniel C., *Rice and Slaves: Ethnicity and the Slave Trade in Colonial South Carolina* (Urbana, IL: University of Illinois Press, 1991)

Litwack, Leon F., *North of Slavery: The Negro in the Free States, 1790–1860* (Chicago, IL: University of Chicago Press, 1961)

Lynd, Staughton, *Class Conflict, Slavery, and the United States Constitution* (Indianapolis, NY: Bobbs-Merrill, 1967)

Mannix, Daniel P., *Black Cargoes: A History of the Atlantic Slave Trade* (New York, NY: Viking, 1965)

Manring, M.M., *Slave in a Box: The Strange Career of Anunt Jemima* (Charlottesville, VA: University Press of Virginia, 1998)

Mattoso, Katia M. Queriros, *To Be a Slave in Brazil, 1550–1888* (New Brunswick, NJ: 1986)

May, Samuel, *Fugitive Slave Law and Its Victims* (1861, Rept. Freeport, NY: Black Heritage Library Collection, 1970)

McKitrick, Eric L., (ed) *Slavery Defended* (Englewood Cliffs, NJ: Prentice-Hall, 1963)

Mellon, James, ed., *Bullwhip Days: The Slaves Remember* (New York, NY: Weidenfeld, 1988)

Mellon, James, ed., *Bullwhip Days: The Slaves Remember: An Oral History* (New York, NY: Weidenfeld, 1988)

Mintz, Steven, ed., *African American Voices: The Life Cycle of Slavery* (St. James, NY: Brandywine Press, 1993)

Morner, Magnus, *Race Mixture in the History of Latin America* (Boston, MA: Little, Brown, 1967)

Mullin, Gerald W., *Flight and Rebellion: Slave Resistance in Eighteenth-Century Virginia* (New York, NY: Oxford University Press, 1972)

Nash, Gary B., *Forging Freedom: The Formation of Philadelphia's Black Community, 1720–1840* (Cambridge, MA: Harvard, 1988)

Nash, Gary B., *Red, White, and Black* (Englewood Cliffs, NJ: Prentice Hall, 1974)

Nell, William C., *The Colored Patriots of the American Revolution* (Salem, NH: Ayer, 1986; Rept. 1855)

Northup, Solomon, *Twelve Years A Slave: The Narrative of Solomon Northup* (New York, NY: Miller, Orton, 1856)

Nwulia, Moses D.E., *Britain and Slavery in East Africa* (Washington, DC: Three Continents Press, 1975)

Osofsky, Gilbert, *The Burden of Race: A Documentary History of Negro-White Relations in America* (New York, NY: Harper, 1967)

Owens, Leslie Howard, *This Species of Property: Slave Life and Culture in the Old South* (New York, NY: Oxford University Press, 1976)

Phillips, Ulrich B., *American Negro Slavery* (Baton Rouge, LA: LSU Press, 1966; rpt. 1918)

Piersen, William D., *Black Yankees: The Development of an Afro-American Subculture in Eighteenth-Century New England* (Amherst, MA: University of Massachusetts Press, 1988)

Quarles, Benjamin, *Frederick Douglass* (New York, NY: Atheneum, 1968)

Quarles, Benjamin, *The Negro in the American Revolution* (Chapel Hill, NC: University of North Carolina Press, 1961)

Raboteau, Albert J., *Slave Religion* (New York, NY: Oxford University Press, 1978)

Ringer, Benjamin, *'We The People' and Others: Duality and America's Treatment of Its Racial Minorities* (London, ED: Tavistock Publications, 1983)

Roark, James L., *Masters Without Slaves* (New York, NY: Norton, 1977)

Rogers, J.A., *From Superman to Man* (New York, NY: Helga Rogers, 1971; rpt. 1957)

Rose, Willie Lee, (ed) *A Documentary History of Slavery in North America* (New York, NY: Oxford University Press, 1976)

Rose, Willie Lee, *Slavery and Freedom* (New York, NY: Oxford University Press, 1982)

Stanton, William, *The Leopard's Spots: Scientific Attitudes Toward Race in America, 1815–59* (Chicago, IL: University of Chicago Press, 1960)

Stowe, Harriet Beecher, *Uncle Tom's Cabin* (New York, NY: Signet, 1965; rpt. 1852)

Stuckey, Sterling, *Slave Culture: Nationalist Theory and the Foundations of Black America* (New York, NY: Oxford University Press, 1987)

Styron, William, *The Confessions of Nat Turner* (New York, NY:

Signet, 1966)

Takaki, Ronald, *Iron Cages: Race and Culture in 19th-Century America* (New York, NY: Oxford University Press, 1990)

Tannenbaum, Frank, *Slave and Citizen* (New York, NY: Knopf, 1946)

Thomas, John L., (ed) *Slavery Attacked* (Englewood Cliffs, NJ: Prentice Hall, 1965)

Van Deburg, William L., *The Slave Drivers: Black Agricultural Labor Supervisors in the Antebellum South* (New York, NY: Oxford University Press, 1979)

Wade, Richard C., *Slavery in the Cities: The South 1820–1860* (New York, NY: Oxford University Press, 1964)

Walker, David, *David Walker's Appeal* (New York, NY: Hill and Wang, 1985; rpt.)

Weinsten, Allen and Gatell, Frank Otto, (ed) *American Negro Slavery: A Modern Reader* (New York, NY: Oxford University Press, 1968)

White, David O., *Connecticut's Black Soldiers, 1775–1783* (Chester, CT: Pequot Press, 1973)

White, Shane, *Somewhat More Independent: The End of Slavery in New York City, 1770–1810* (Athens, GA: University of Georgia Press, 1991)

Williams, Eric, *Capitalism and Slavery* (Chapel Hill, NC: University of North Carolina Press, 1944)

Wood, Peter H., *Black Majority: Negroes in Colonial South Carolina from 1670 through the Stono Rebellion* (New York, NY: W.W. Norton, 1974)

Civil War and Reconstruction, Abolitionism

Aptheker, Herbert, *To Be Free* (New York, NY: International Pubs., 1968; rpt)

Bennett, Lerone *Forced into Glory: Abraham Lincoln's White Dream* (Chicago, IL: Johnson Pub. Co. 2000)

Buck, Paul H., *The Road to Reunion* (Boston, MA: Little, Brown, 1937)

Butchart, Ronald E., *Northern Schools, Southern Blacks, and Reconstruction* (Westport, CT: Greenwood Press, 1980)

Cheek, William and Cheek, Aimee Lee, *John Mercer Langston and the Fight for Black Freedom, 1829–65* (Urbana, IL: University of Illinois Press, 1989)

Conrad, Earl, *Harriet Tubman: Negro Soldier and Abolitionist* (New York, NY: International Pubs., 1942)

Cox, LaWanda and Cox, John H., *Politics, Principle, and Prejudice, 1865–1866* (New York, NY: Atheneum, 1969)

Cox, LaWanda, *Lincoln and Black Freedom* (Urbana, IL: University of Illinois Press, 1985)

Cruden, Robert, *The War that Never Ended: The American Civil War* (Englewood Cliffs, NJ: Prentice Hall, 1971)

Curry, Richard O., (ed) *Radicalism, Racism, and Party Realignment: The Border States During Reconstruction* (Baltimore, MD: Johns Hopkins University Press, 1969)

Du Bois, W.E.B., *Black Reconstruction in America, 1860–1880* (New York, NY: Atheneum, 1977; rpt. 1935)

Du Bois, W.E.B., *John Brown* (Philadelphia, PA: Jacobs Pubs., 1909)

Engs, Robert Francis, *Freedom's First Generation: Black Hampton, Virginia, 1861–1890* (Philadelphia, PA: University of Pennsylvania Press, 1979)

Foner, Eric, *Reconstruction: America's Unfinished Revolution, 1863–1877* (New York, NY: Harper & Row, 1988)

Franklin, John Hope, (ed) *Reminiscences of an Active Life: The Autobiography of John Roy Lynch* (Chicago, IL: University of Chicago Press, 1970)

Franklin, John Hope, *Reconstruction After the Civil War* (Chicago, IL: University of Chicago Press, 1961)

Franklin, John Hope, *The Emancipation Proclamation* (New York, NY: Doubleday, 1965)

Franklin, John Hope, *The Militant South* (Boston, MA: Beacon, 1964)

Friedheim, William, *Freedom's Unfinished Revolution: An Inquiry Into the Civil War and Reconstruction* (New York, NY: The New Press, 1996)

Glatthaar, Joseph T., *Forged in Battle: The Civil War Alliance of Black Soldiers* (New York, NY: Meridian, 1991)

Higginson, Thomas Wentworth, *Army Life in a Black Regiment* (New York, NY: Collier, 1962; rpt.)

Holt, Thomas, *Black Over White: Negro Political Leadership in South Carolina During Reconstruction* (Urbana, IL: University of Illinois Press, 1977)

Kraditor, Aileen S., *American Abolitionism* (New York, NY: Vintage, 1967)

Lerner, Gerda, *The Grimke Sisters* (New York, NY: Shocken, 1971)

Litwack, Leon F., *Been in the Storm so Long: The Aftermath of Slavery* (New York, NY: Vintage, 1979)

Mcfeely, William S., *Yankee Stepfather: General O.O. Howard and the Freedmen* (New York, NY: Norton, 1968)

Mcpherson, James M., *Battle Cry of Freedom: The Civil War Era* (New York, NY: Oxford University Press, 1988)

Mcpherson, James M., *The Abolitionist Legacy* (Princeton, NJ: Princeton University Press, 1975)

Mcpherson, James M., *The Negro's Civil War* (New York, NY: Vintage, 1965)

Oates, Stephen B., *The Fires of Jubilee: Nat Turner's Fierce Rebellion* (New York, NY: Mentor, 1975)

Painter, Nell, *Sojourner Truth* (New York, NY: W. W. Norton, 1996)

Quarles, Benjamin, *Black Abolitionists* (New York, NY: Oxford University Press, 1969)

Rawley, James A., *Race and Politics: Bleeding Kansas and the Coming of the Civil War* (Philadelphia, PA: Lippincott, 1969)

Record of the Service of the Fifty-Fifth Regiment of Massachusetts Volunteer Infantry (Salem, NH: Ayer, 1991; Rept. 1868)

Richards, Leonard L., *Gentlemen of Property and Standing: Anti-Abolition Mobs in Jacksonian America* (New York, NY: Oxford University Press, 1970)

Rose, Willie Lee, *Rehearsal for Reconstruction: The Port Royal Experiment* (New York, NY: Vintage, 1964)

Sewell, Richard H., *Ballots for Freedom: Antislavery Politics in the United States, 1837–1860* (New Yor, NY: W. W. Norton, 1976)

Singletary, Otis A., *Negro Militia and Reconstruction* (New York, NY: McGraw-Hill, 1963)

Stampp, Kenneth M. and Litwack, Leon F., (ed) *Reconstruction: An Anthology of Revisionist Writings* (Baton Rouge, LA: LSU Press, 1969)

Starobin, Robert S., *Industrial Slavery in the Old South* (New York, NY: Oxford University Press, 1970)

Sterling, Dorothy, (ed) *We Are Your Sisters: Black Women in the Nineteenth Century* (New York, NY: W.W. Norton, 1984)

Still, William, *The Underground Railroad* (Salem, NH: Ayer Co., 1992; Rept. 1872)

Swift, David E., *Black Prophets of Justice: Activist Clergy Before the Civil War* (Baton Rouge, LA: LSU Press, 1989)

Vaughn, William Preston, *Schools For All: The Blacks and Public Education in the South, 1865–1877* (Lexington, KY: University Press of Kentucky, 1974)

Wood, Forrest G., *Black Scare: The Racist Response to Emancipation and Reconstruction* (Berkeley, CA: University of California

Press, 1970)

Wyatt-Brown, Bertram, *Honor and Violence in the Old South* (New York, NY: Oxford University Press, 1986)

Nadir, 1877–1920, New South

Baker, Ray Stannard, *Following the Color Line: American Negro Citizenship in the Progressive Era* (New York, NY: Harper Row, 1964; rpt. 1908)

Bond, Horace Mann, *Negro Education in Alabama: A Study in Cotton and Steel* (New York, NY: Atheneum, 1969)

Chalmers, David M., *Hooded Americanism: The History of the Ku Klux Klan* (Chicago, IL: Quadrangle, 1968)

Collum, Danny Duncan, ed., *African Americans in the Spanish Civil War* (New York, NY: G. K. Hall, 1992)

Daniel, Pete, *The Shadow of Slavery: Peonage in the South, 1901–1969* (Urbana, IL: University of Illinois Press, 1972)

Davis, Allison, et. al., *Deep South* (Los Angeles, CA: UCLA Center for Afro-American Studies, 1988; rept 1941)

Du Bois, W.E.B., *Darkwater: Voices from Within the Veil* (New York, NY: Shocken Books, 1969; rpt. 1920)

Du Bois, W.E.B., *Dusk of Dawn* (New York, NY: Shocken, 1968; rpt)

Du Bois, W.E.B., *The Souls of Black Folk* (Greenwich, CT: Fawcett, 1961; rpt. 1903)

Fortune, Timothy Thomas, *Black and White: Land, Labor and Politics in the South* (New York, NY: Arno, 1968; rpt.)

Fry, Gladys-Marie, *Night Riders* (Knoxville, TN: University of Tennessee Press, 1975)

Gilmore, Al-Tony, *Bad Nigger: The National Impact of Jack Johnson* (Port Washington, NY: Kennikat, 1975)

Goldfield, David R., *Black, White, and Southern: Race Relations and Southern Culture 1940 to the Present* (Baton Rouge, LA: LSU Press, 1990)

Greene, Lorenzo J., et. al., *Missouri's Black Heritage* (Columbia, MO: University of Missouri Press, 1980)

Harris, Sheldon H., *Paul Cuffe: Black America and the African Return* (New York, NY: Clarion, 1972)

Jones, James H., *Bad Blood: The Scandalous Story of the Tuskegee Experiment* (New York, NY: Free Press, 1981)

Kirby, Jack, *Darkness at the Dawning: Race and Reform in the Progressive South* (New York, NY: Lippincott, 1972)

Kremer, Gary R., *James Milton Turner and the Promise of America* (Columbia, MO: University of Missouri Press, 1991)

Lester, J.C. and Wilson, D.L., *The Ku Klux Klan* (New York, NY: Da Capo, 1973)

Litwack, Leon, *Trouble in Mind: Black Southerners in the Age of Jim Crow* (New York, NY: Knopf, 1998)

Lofgren, Charles A., *The Plessy Case* (New York, NY: Oxford University Press, 1987)

Logan, Rayford W., *The Betrayal of the Negro: From Rutherford B. Hayes to Woodrow Wilson* (New York, NY: Collier Books, 1972 rpt.)

Lynk, Miles V., *The Black Troopers in the Spanish-American War* (New York, NY: AMS, 1971; rpt 1899)

Meier, August, *Negro Thought in America, 1880–1915* (Ann Arbor, MI: University of Michigan Press, 1963)

Moore, John Hammond, *Before and After: The Relations of the Races in the South* (Baton Rouge, LA: LSU Press, 1967)

Moses, Wilson J., *The Golden Age of Black Nationalism, 1850–1925* (New York, NY: Oxford University Press, 1978)

Nolen, Claude H., *The Negro's Image in the South: The Anatomy of White Supremacy* (Lexington, KY: University Press of Kentucky, 1968)

Novak, Daniel A., *The Wheel of Servitude: Black Forced Labor After Slavery* (Lexington, KY: University Press of Kentucky, 1978)

Painter, Nell Irvin, *Standing at Armageddon: The United States, 1877–1919* (New York, NY: W.W. Norton, 1987)

Rabinowitz, Howard N., *Race Relations in the Urban South, 1865–1890* (Urbana, IL: University of Illinois Press, 1980)

Sherer, Robert G., *Subordination or Liberation: The Development and Conflicting Theories of Black Education in Nineteenth Century Alabama* (Birmingham, AL: University of Alabama Press, 1977)

Sherman, Richard, *The Republican Party and Black America From McKinley to Hoover* (Charlottesville, VA: University Press of Virginia, 1973)

Spivey, Donald, *Schooling for the New Slavery: Black Industrial Education, 1868–1915* (Westport, CT: Greenwood Press, 1978)

Tindall, George Brown, *South Carolina Negroes, 1877–1900* (Baton Rouge, LA: LSU Press, 1966)

Tuttle, William M., *Race Riot: Chicago in the Red Summer of 1919* (New York, NY: Atheneum, 1975)

Washington, Booker T., *My Larger Education* (New York, NY: Doubleday, 1911)

Williamson, Joel, *A Rage for Order: Black-White Relations in the American South Since Emancipation* (New York, NY: Osford, 1986)

Wolters, Raymond, *The New Negro on Campus: Black College Rebellions of the 1920s* (Princeton, NJ: Princeton University Press, 1975)

Woodward, C. Vann, *Origins of the New South, 1877–1913* (Baton Rouge, LA: LSU Press, 1951)

Woodward, C. Vann, *The Strange Career of Jim Crow* (New York, NY: Oxford University Press, 1957)

Wynes, Charles E., *Charles Richard Drew: The Man and the Myth* (Urbana, IL: University of Illinois Press, 1988)

Black Exodus, Urban North

Bloch, Herman D., *The Circle of Discrimination: An Economic and Social Study of the Black Man in New York* (New York, NY: New York University Press, 1969)

Clarke, John Henrik, (ed) *Harlem: A Community in Transition* (New York, NY: Citadel, 1964)

Connolly, Harold, *A Ghetto Grows in Brooklyn* (New York, NY: New York University Press, 1977)

Drake, St. Clair and Cayton, Horace R., *Black Metropolis: A Study of Negro Life in a Northern City* Vols I & II (New York, NY: Harper, Row, 1945)

Du Bois, W.E.B., *The Philadelphia Negro* (New York, NY: Schocken, 1899)

Henri, Florette, *Black Migration Movement North, 1900–1920* (New York, NY: Anchor, 1976)

Hirsch, Arnold R., *Making the Second Ghetto: Race and Housing in Chicago, 1940–1960* (New York, NY: Cambridge, 1983)

Homel, Michael W., *Down From Equality: Black Chicagoans and the Public Schools, 1920–41* (Urbana, IL: University of Illinois Press, 1984)

Katzman, David M., *Before the Ghetto: Black Detroit in the Nineteenth Century* (Urbana, IL: University of Illinois Press, 1975)

Keil, Charles, *Urban Blues* (Chicago, IL: University of Chicago Press, 1966)

Kusmer, Kenneth, *A Ghetto Takes Shape: Black Cleveland, 1870–1930* (Urbana, IL: University of Illinois, 1978)

Lemann, Nicholas, *The Promised Land: The Great Black Migration and How it Changed America* (New York, NY: Vintage, 1992)

Levine, David Allan, *Internal Combustion: The Races in Detroit, 1915–1926* (Westport, CT: Greenwood Press, 1976)

McGovern, James R., *Anatomy of a Lynching: The Killing of Claude Neal* (Baton Rouge, LA: LSU Press, 1982)

Meister, Richard J., (ed) *The Black Ghetto: Promised Land or Colony?* (Lexington, MA: Heath, 1975)

Nielson, David Gordon, *Black Ethos: Northern Urban Negro Life and Thought, 1890–1930* (Westport, CT: Greenwood Press, 1977)

Osofsky, Gilbert, *Harlem: The Making of a Negro Ghetto* (New York, NY: Harper Row, 1963)

Ottley, Roi and Weatherby, William J., (ed) *The Negro in New York* (New York, NY: Praeger, 1967)

Painter, Nell Irvin, *Exodusters: Black Migration to Kansas after Reconstruction* (New York, NY: Knopf, 1977)

Philpott, Thomas Lee, *The Slum and the Ghetto: Neighborhood Deterioration and Middle-Class Reform, Chicago, 1880–1930* (New York, NY: Oxford University Press, 1978)

Sherman, Richard B., (ed) *The Negro and the City* (Englewood Cliffs, NJ: Prentice-Hall, 1970)

Spear, Allan H., *Black Chicago: The Making of a Negro Ghetto, 1890–1920* (Chicago, IL: University of Chicago, 1967)

Spero, Sterling D. and Harris, Abram L., *The Black Worker* (New York, NY: Atheneum, 1968; rpt. 1931)

Tolson, Arthur L., *The Black Oklahomans, A History: 1541–1972* (New Orleans, LA: Edwards Printing, 1974)

Trotter, Joe William, Jr., *River Jordan: African American Urban Life in the Ohio Valley* (Lexington, KY: University Press of Kentucky, 1998)

Weiss, Nancy J., *The National Urban League, 1910–1940* (New York, NY: Oxford University Press, 1974)

Wolters, Raymond, *Negroes and the Great Depression* (Westport, CT: Greenwood Press, 1970)

Wright, Richard, *Black Boy* (New York, NY: Harper Row, 1967; rpt. 1937)

Harlem Renaissance, Black Literature

Abrahams, Peter, *Mine Boy* (New York, NY: Collier, 1970)

Abrahams, Roger D., (ed) *Afro-American Folktales* (New York, NY: Pantheon, 1985)

Achebe, Chinua, *Anthills of the Savannah* (New York, NY: Anchor Books, 1987)

Anderson, Jervis, *This Was Harlem, 1900–1950* (New York, NY: Farrar Straus, 1981)

Angelou, Maya, *I Know Why the Caged Bird Sings* (New York, NY: Random House, 1970)

Baldwin, James, *Another Country* (New York, NY: Dell, 1960)

Baldwin, James, *Giovanni's Room* (New York, NY: Dell, 1956)

Baldwin, James, *Go Tell It On The Mountain* (New York, NY: Dell, 1965)

Baldwin, James, *Going to Meet the Man* (New York, NY: Dell, 1965)

Baldwin, James, *Just Above My Head* (New York, NY: Dial, 1979)

Baldwin, James, *Nobody Knows My Name* (New York, NY: Dell, 1961)

Baldwin, James, *Notes Of A Native Son* (Boston, MA: Beacon, 1955)

Baldwin, James, *The Devil Finds Work* (New York, NY: Dial, 1967)

Baldwin, James, *The Fire Next Time* (New York, NY: Dell, 1962)

Barksdale, Richard and Kinnamon, Kenneth, (ed) *Black Writers of America: A Comprehensive Anthology* (New York, NY: Macmillan, 1972)

Berry, Faith, (ed) *Langston Hughes: Good Morning Revolution* (New York, NY: Lawrence Hill, 1973)

Brooks, Gwendolyn, *Maud Martha* (New York, NY: Popular Library, 1953)

Brown, Claude, *Manchild in the Promised Land* (New York, NY: Signet, 1965)

Brown, Sterling, *Negro Poetry and Drama and the Negro in American Fiction* (New York, NY: Atheneum, 1969; rpt. 1937)

Chapman, Abraham, *Black Voices: An Anthology of Afro-American Literature* (New York, NY: New American Library, 1968)

Chesnutt, Charles W., *The Wife of His Youth* (Boston, MA: Cresset, 1899)

Clarke, John Henrik, (ed) *American Negro Short Stories* (New York, NY: Hill and Wang, 1969)

Cooker, Mercer, and Henderson, Stephen E., *The Militant Black Writer in Africa and the United States* (Madison, Wis: University of Wisconsin Press, 1969)

Couch, William, (ed) *New Black Play Wrights: An Anthology* (Baton Rouge, LSU Press, 1968)

Dickinson, Donald C., (ed) *A Bio-bibliography of Langston Hughes, 1902–1967* (New York, NY: Archon Books, 1967)

Doctorow, E.L., *Ragtime* (New York, NY: Fawcett, 1974)

Ellison, Ralph, *Invisible Man* (New York, NY: Random House, 1952)

Ellison, Ralph, *Shadow and Act* (New York, NY: Vintage, 1972; rpt)

Fairweather, Stephen, *The Baymen of Belize* (Miami, FL: Society

Pubs., 1992)

Floyd, Samuel Floyd, ed., *Music of the Harlem Renaissance* (Knoxville, TN: University of Tennessee Press, 1993)

Gates, Henry Louis, Jr., *The Signifying Monkey: A Theory of African-American Literary Criticism* (New York, NY: Oxford University Press, 1988)

Gayle, Addison, (ed) *The Black Aesthetic* (New York, NY: Doubleday, 1971)

Genet, Jean, *The Blacks: A Clown Show* (New York, NY: Grove, 1960)

Harper, Michael S. and Stepto, Robert B., (ed) *Chant of Saints: A Gathering of Afro-American Literature, Art, and Scholarship* (Urbana, IL: University of Illinois Press, 1979)

Hughes, Langston and Bontemps, Arna, (ed) *The Poetry of the Negro, 1746–1949* (New York, NY: Doubleday, 1949)

Hughes, Langston, *The Best of Simple* (New York, NY: Hill and Wang, 1961)

Hughes, Langston, *The Big Sea* (New York, NY: Hill and Wang, 1968; rpt. 1940)

Hurston, Zora Neale, *Dust Tracks on a Road: An Autobiography* (1942; Rept. Urbana, IL: University of Illinois Press, 1984)

Jahn, Janheinz, *Neo-African Literature: A History of Black Writing* (New York, NY: Grove, 1966)

Johnson, Charles, *Being and Race: Black Writings since 1970* (Bloomington, IN: Indiana University Press, 1990)

Johnson, Charles, *Middle Passage* (New York, NY: Plume, 1990)

Johnson, James Weldon, *Black Manhattan* (New York, NY: Atheneum, 1968; rpt. 1930)

Johnson, James Weldon, *God's Trombones* (New York, NY: Viking, 1966; rpt. 1927)

Jones, LeRoi, (ed) *Black Fire: An Anthology of Afro-American Writing* (New York, NY: William Morrow, 1968)

Jones, LeRoi, *Dutchman and the Slave* (New York, NY: Apollo, 1964)

Jones, LeRoi, *Tales By LeRoi Jones* (New York, NY: Grove, 1967)

Jones, LeRoi, *The Dead Lecturer* (New York, NY: Grove, 1964)

Kirschke, Amy, *Aaron Douglas: Art, Race, and the Harlem Renaissance* (Jackson, MS: University of Mississippi Press, 1995)

Locke, Alain, *The New Negro* (New York, NY: Atheneum, 1969; rpt)

Mathabane, Mark, *Kaffir Boy* (New York, NY: New American Library, 1986)

McKay, Claude, *Harlem: Negro Metropolis* (New York, NY:

Harvest, 1968; rpt. 1940)

McKay, Claude, *Home to Harlem* (New York, NY: Pocket Books, 1969; rpt)

Morrison, Toni, *Beloved* (New York, NY: Knopf, 1987)

Morrison, Toni, *Playing in the Dark: Whiteness and the Literary Imagination* (Cambridge, MA: Harvard University Press, 1992)

Perry, Nelson, *Black Fire: The Making of An American Revolutionary* (New York, NY: The New Press, 1994)

Rampersad, Arnold, *The Life of Langston Hughes* (New York, NY: Oxford University Press, 1986)

Rampersad, Arnold, *The Life of Langston Hughes Vol I: 1902–1941* (New York, NY: Oxford University Press, 1986)

Shockley, Ann Allen, *Afro-American Women Writers, 1746–1933* (New York, NY: Meridian, 1989)

Soyinka, Wole, *The Interpreters* (London, ED: Heineman, 1965)

Teague, Bob, *Letters to a Black Boy* (New York, NY: Walker, 1968)

Thomas, Piri, *Down These Mean Streets* (New York, NY: Vintage, 1967)

Thompson, Robert Farris, *Flash of Spirit: African and Afro-American Art and Philosophy* (New York, NY: Vintage, 1984)

Toomer, Jean, *Cane* (New York, NY: Harper Row, 1969; rpt. 1923)

Tracy, Steven C., *Langston Hughes and the Blues* (Urbana, IL: University of Illinois Press, 1988)

Vincent, Theodore G., (ed) *Voice of a Black Nation: Political Journalism in the Harlem Renaissance* (San Francisco, CA: Ramparts, 1973)

Wagner, Jean, *Black Poets of the United States* (Urbana, IL: University of Illinois Press, 1973

Walker, Margaret, *Jubilee* (New York, NY: Bantam, 1966)

Waters, Ethel, *His Eye is on the Sparrow: An Autobiography* (New York, NY: Da Capo, 1992; Rept. 1950)

Wideman, John Edgar, *Brothers and Keepers* (New York, NY: Penguin, 1984)

Williams, John A., *The Man Who Cried I am* (New York, NY: Signet, 1967)

Wright, Ellen and Fabre, Michael, (ed) *Richard Wright: A Reader* (New York, NY: Harper and Row, 1978)

Wright, Richard, *Eight Men* (New York, NY: Avon, 1961)

Wright, Richard, *Native Son* (New York, NY: Harper, Row, 1970)

Wright, Richard, *Savage Holiday* (New York, NY: Award Books,

1969)

Wright, Richard, *The Outsider* (New York, NY: Harper and Row, 1953)

Wright, Richard, *Uncle Tom's Children* (New York, NY: Harper, Row, 1936)

Wright, Richard, *White Man Listen* (New York, Anchor, 1964)

Black Music

Abdul, Raoul, *Blacks in Classical Music* (New York, NY: Dodd, Mead, 1977)

Bebey, Francis, *African Music* (Westport, CT: Lawrence Hill, 1975)

Berendt, Joachim, *The Jazz Book* (Westport, CT: Lawrence Hill, 1975)

Buerkle, Jack V. and Barker, Danny, *Bourbon Street Black: The New Orleans Black Jazzman* (New York, NY: Oxford University Press, 1973)

Charles, Ray and Ritz, David, *Brother Ray* (New York, NY: Dial, 1978)

Charters, Samuel, *The Blues Makers* (New York, NY: Da Capo, 1967)

Collier, James L., *Louis Armstrong: An American Success Story* (New York, NY: Atheneum, 1994)

Curtis, Susan, *Dancing to a Black Man's Tune: A Life of Scott Joplin* (Columbia, MO: University of Missouri Press, 1994)

Davis, Stephen, and Simon, Peter, *Reggae Bloodlines in Search of the Music and Culture of Jamaica* (New York, NY: Da Capo, 1992)

Dixon, Robert and Godrich, John, *Recording the Blues* (New York, NY: Stein and Day, 1970)

Dixon, Willie, and Snowden, Don, *I am the Blues: The Willie Dixon Story* (New York, NY: Da Capo, 1989)

Feather, Leonard, *From Satchmo to Miles* (New York, NY: Stein and Day, 1974)

George, Nelson, *The Death of Rhythm and Blues* (New York, NY: Pantheon, 1988)

Harrison, Daphne D., *Black Pearls: Blues Queens of the 1920s* (New Brunswick, NJ: Rutgers, 1988)

Hentoff, Nat, et. al., (ed) *Jazz* (New York, NY: Holt, Rinehart, 1959)

Jewell, Derek, *Duke: A Portrait of Duke Ellington* (New York, NY: Norton, 1977)

Jones, Bessie, et. al., *Step It Down: Games, Plays, Songs and Stories from the Afro-American Heritage* (Athens, GA: University of

Georgia Press, 1987)

Kofsky, Frank, *Black Nationalism and the Revolution in Music* (New York, NY: Pathfinder, 1970)

Litweiler, John, *The Freedom Principle: Jazz After 1958* (New York, NY: Da Capo, 1984)

Lomax, Alan, *Mister Jelly Roll* (Berkeley, CA: University of California Press, 1950)

Marquis, Donald M., *In Search of Buddy Bolden: First Man of Jazz* (Baton Rouge, LA: LSU Press, 1978)

Mingus, Charles, *Charles Mingus: Beneath the Underdog* (New York, NY: Penguin, 1971)

Montgomery, Elizabeth Rider, *William C. Handy: A Father of the Blues* (New York, NY: Dell, 1968)

Morrison, Toni, *Jazz* (New York, NY: Knopf, 1992)

Murray, Albert, *Stomping the Blues* (New York, NY: McGraw Hill, 1976)

Nketia, J.H. Kwabena, *The Music of Africa* (New York, NY: Norton, 1974)

Oliver, Paul, *Bessie Smith* (New York, NY: A.S. Barnes, 1971)

Palmer, Robert, *Deep Blues: A Musical and Cultural History of the Mississippi Delta* (New York, NY: Penguin, 1982)

Riis, Thomas L., *Just Before Jazz: Black Musical Theater in New York, 1890–1915* (Washington, DC: Smithsonian, 1989)

Sackheim, Eric, (ed) *The Blues Line: A Collection of Blues Lyrics* (New York, NY: Schirmer Books, 1969)

Sargeant, Winthrop, *Jazz, Hot and Hybrid* (New York, NY: Da Capo, 1975)

Simpkins, C.O., *Coltrane: A Biography* (Brooklyn, NY: Herndon House, 1975)

Southall, Geneva H., *Blind Tom: The Post-Civil War Enslavement of a Black Musical Genius* (Minneapolis, MN: Challenge, 1979)

Southern, Eileen, *The Music of Black Americans* (New York, NY: Norton, 1971)

Stewart-Baxter, Derrick, *Ma Rainey and the Classic Blues Singers* (New York, NY: Stein and Day, 1970)

Thomas, J.C., *Coltrane: Chasin' the Trane* (New York, NY: Da Capo, 1975)

Tirro, Frank, *Jazz: A History* (New York, NY: Norton, 1977)

Titon, Jeff Todd, *Early Downhome Blues* (Urbana, IL: University of Illinois Press, 1977)

Walton, Ortiz M. *Music: Black White and Blue* (New York, NY: Morrow, 1972)

White, Timothy, *Catch A Fire: The Life of Bob Marley* (New York, NY: Henry Holt, 1991)

Woll, Allen, *Black Musical Theatre: From Coontown to Dreamgirls* (New York, NY: Da Capo, 1989)

Black Leaders, Nationalism

Anderson, Jervis A. *Philip Randolph* (New York, NY: Harcourt Brace, 1972)

Baraka, Imamu Amiri, (ed) *African Congress: A Documentary of the First Modern Pan-African Congress* (New York, NY: William Morrow, 1972)

Bracey, John H., Meier, August, and Rudwick, Elliott, (ed) *Black Nationalism in America* (Indianapolis, IN: Bobbs-Merrill, 1970)

Broderick, Francis L., *W.E.B. Du Bois: Negro Leader in a Time of Crisis* (Stanford, CA: Stanford University Press, 1959)

Carlisle, Rodney, *The Roots of Black Nationalism* (Port Washington, NY: Kennikat, 1975)

Clarke, John Henrik, ed., *Marcus Garvey and the Vision of Africa* (New York, NY: Vintage, 1974)

Cruse, Harold, *Plural But Equal* (New York, NY: Morrow, 1987)

Cruse, Harold, *Rebellion or Revolution* (New York, NY: William Morrow, 1968)

Cruse, Harold, *The Crisis of the Negro Intellectual* (New York, NY: Morrow, 1967)

Davis, Angela, *Autobiography of Angela Davis* (New York, NY: International Publishers, 1988)

Davis, Benjamin O., Jr., *Benjamin O. Davis, Jr., American: An Autobiography* (New York, NY: Plume, 1992)

Deal, Phillip Hayes, *Paul Robeson* (Garden City, NY: Nelson Doubleday, 1978)

Delany, Martin R. and Campbell, Robert, *Search for a Place: Black Separatism and Africa, 1860* (Ann Arbor, MI: University of Michigan Press, 1969; rpt. 1860)

Delany, Martin R., *Blake or The Huts of America* (Rept. Boston, MA: Beacon Press, 1970)

Dick, Robert C., *Black Protest: Issues and Tactics* (Westport, CT: Greenwood Press, 1974)

Dompere, K.K., *Afrocentricity and African Nationialism* (Langley Park, MD: IAAS Press, 1992)

Draper, Theodore, *The Rediscovery of Black Nationalism* (New York, NY: Viking 1969)

Du Bois, Shirley Graham, *His Day is Marching On: A Memoir of W.E.B. Du Bois* (Philadelphia, PA: Lippincott, 1971)

Du Bois, W.E.B., *An ABC of Color* (New York, NY: International Pubs., 1969; rpt)

Du Bois, W.E.B., *The Autobiography of W.E.B. Du Bois* (New York, NY: International Publishers, 1968)

Duberman, Martin B., *Paul Robeson* (New York, NY: Ballantine, 1989)

Epps, Archie, (ed) *The Speeches of Malcolm X at Harvard* (New York, NY: Apollo, 1968)

Evanzz, Karl, *The Messenger: The Rise and Fall of Elijah Muhammad* (New York, NY: Pantheon, 1999)

Fox, Stephen R., *The Guardian of Boston: William Monroe Trotter* (New York, NY: Atheneum, 1971)

Franklin, John Hope, et. al., *Black Leaders of the Twentieth Century* (Urbana, IL: University of Illinois Press, 1982)

Franklin, John Hope, *George Washington Williams* (Chicago, IL: University of Chicago, 1985)

Garrow, David J., *Bearing The Cross: Martin Luther King, Jr. and the Southern Christian Leadership Conference* (New York, NY: Morrow, 1986)

Geismar, Peter, *Fanon: The Revolutionary as Prophet* (New York, NY: Grove, 1969)

Goldman, Peter, *The Death and Life of Malcolm X* (Urbana, IL: University of Illinois Press, 1979)

Greene, Lorenzo J., *Working With Carter G. Woodson, the Father of Black History a Diary 1928–1930* (Baton Rouge, LA: LSU Press 1989)

Hamilton, Charles V., *Adam Clayton Powell, Jr. The Political Biography of an American Dilemma* (New York, NY: Atheneum, 1991)

Harlan, Louis R., *Booker T. Washington: The Making of a Black Leader, 1856–1901* (New York, NY: Oxford University Press, 1972)

Harris, Sara, *Father Divine* (New York, NY: Collier, 1953)

Harris, Sheldon H., *Paul Cuffe: Black America and the African Return* (New York, NY: Simon and Schuster, 1979)

Hill, Robert A., ed., *The Marcus Garvey and Universal Negro Improvement Association Papers* (Berkeley, CA: University of California Press, 1983–1990), 7 Vols.

Hudson, Hosea, *Black Worker in the Deep South* (New York, NY: International Pubs., 1971)

Jacques-Garvey, Amy, (ed) *Philosophy and Opinions of Marcus*

Garvey (New York, NY: Arno Press, 1969)

Johnson, James Weldon, *Along This Way: The Autobiography of James Weldon Johnson* (New York, NY: Viking, 1968; rpt)

Jones, J. Raymond, *The Harlem Fox* (Albany, NY: SUNY Press, 1989)

King, Kenneth James, *Pan-Africanism and Education: A Study of Race Philanthropy and Education in the Southern States of America and East Africa* (London, ED: Oxford University Press, 1971)

Lewis, David Levering, *W.E.B. Du Bois: Biography of a Race, 1868–1919* (New York, NY: Henry Holt, 1993)

Lewis, David Levering, *W.E.B. Du Bois: The Fight for Equality and The American Century, 1919–1963* (New York, NY: Henry Holt, 2000)

Lewis, Rupert, *Marcus Garvey: Anti-Colonial Champion* (Trenton, NJ: Africa World Press, 1988)

Litwack, Leon, et. al., *Black Leaders of the Nineteenth Century* (Urbana, IL: University of Illinois Press, 1988)

Love, Spencie, *One Blood: The Death and Resurrection of Charles R. Drew* (Chapel Hill, NC: University of North Carolina Press, 1996)

Malcolm X, *The Autobiography of Malcolm X* (New York, NY: Grove, 1964)

Manning, Kenneth R., *Black Apollo of Science: The Life of Ernest E. Just* (New York, NY: Oxford University Press, 1983)

Marable, Manning, *W.E.B. Du Bois: Black Radical Democrat* (Boston, MA: G.K. Hall, 1986)

Martin, Tony, *Marcus Garvey, Hero* (Dover, MA: The Majority Press, 1983)

Martin, Tony, *Race First: The Ideological and Organization Struggles of Marcus Garvey and the Universal Negro Improvement Association* (Westport, CT: Greenwood, 1976)

Mathurin, Owen Charles, *Henry Sylvester Williams and the Origins of the Pan-African Movement, 1869–1911* (Westport, CT: Greenwood, 1976)

McMurry, Linda O., *Recorder of the Black Experience: A Biography of Monroe Nathan Work* (Baton Rouge, LA: LSU Press, 1985)

Moses, Wilson J., *Afrotopia: The Roots of African American Popular History* (New York, NY: Cambridge University Press, 1998)

Moses, Wilson, *Alexander Crummell: A Study of Civilization and Discontent* (New York, NY: Oxford University Press, 1989)

Moss, Alfred A. Jr., *The American Negro Academy* (Baton Rouge, LA: LSU Press, 1981)

Moss, Alfred A., Jr., *The American Negro Academy: Voices of the Talented Tenth* (Baton Rouge, LA: LSU Press, 1981)

Painter, Nell Irvin, *The Narrative of Hosea Hudson: His Life as a Negro Communist in the South* (Cambridge, MA: Harvard, 1979)

Perry, Bruce, *Malcolm: The Life of a Man Who Changed Black America* (Barrytown, NY: Station Hill, 1991)

Pinkney, Alphonso, *Red, Black, and Green: Black Nationalism in the United States* (New York, NY: Cambridge University Press, 1976)

Redkey, Edwin S., *Black Exodus: Black Nationalist and Back-to-Africa Movements, 1890–1910* (New Haven, CT: Yale University Press, 1969)

Reynolds, Babrara A., *Jesse Jackson: America's David* (Washington, DC: JFA Associates, 1985)

Robeson, Paul, *Here I Stand* (Boston, MA: Beacon, 1958)

Rudwick, Elliott M., *W.E.B. Du Bois: Propagandist of the Negro Protest* (New York, NY: Atheneum, 1969)

Scally, Sister Anthony, *Carter G. Woodson: A Bio-Bibliography* (Westport, CT: Greenwood, 1985)

Schor, Joel, *Henry Highland Garnet: A Voice of Black Radicalism in the Nineteenth Century* (Westport, CT: Greenwood, 1977)

Stein, Judith, *The World of Marcus Garvey: Race and Class in Modern Society* (Baton Rouge, LA: LSU Press, 1986)

Sundquiest, Eric J., ed., *The Oxford W.E.B. Du Bois Reader* (New York, NY: Oxford University Press, 1996)

Thomas, Lamont D., *Rise To Be A People: A Biography of Paul Cuffe* (Urbana, IL: University of Illinois, 1986)

Thornbrough, Emma Lou, (ed) *Booker T. Washington* (Englewood Cliffs, NJ: Prentice-Hall, 1969)

Ullman, Victor, *Martin R. Delany: The Beginnings of Black Nationalism* (Boston, MA: Beacon, 1971)

Vincent, Theodore G., *Black Power and the Garvey Movement* (San Francisco, CA: Ramparts, 1972)

Washington, Booker T., *Up From Slavery* (New York, NY: Doubleday, 1901)

Weisbrot, Robert, *Father Divine and the Struggle for Racial Equality* (Urbana, IL: University of Illinois Press, 1983)

White, John, *Black Leadership in America, 1895–1968* (London, ENG: Longman, 1985)

Wilkins, Roy, *Standing Fast: The Autobiography of Roy Wilkins* (New York, NY: Penguin, 1984)

Wintz, Gary, ed., *African American Political Thought, 1890–1930: Washington, Du Bois, Garvey, and Randolph* (Ar-

monk, NY: ME. Sharpe, 1996)
Wynes, Charles, *Charles Richard Drew* (Urbana, IL: University of Illinois Press, 1988)

Post-WW II Era

Berman, William C., *The Politics of Civil Rights in the Truman Administration* (Columbus, OH: Ohio State University Press, 1970)

deCoy, Robert H., *The Nigger Bible* (Los Angeles, CA: Holloway House, 1967)

Du Bois, W.E.B., *Color and Democracy: Colonies and Peace* (New York, NY: Harcourt Brace, 1945)

Dunn, Marvin, *Black Miami in the Twentieth Century* (Gainesville, FL: University Press of Florida, 1997)

Fogelson, Robert M., *Violence as Protest* (New York, NY: Doubleday, 1971)

Franklin, John Hope and Starr, Isidore, (ed) *The Negro in 20th Century America* (New York, NY: Vintage, 1967)

Harrington, Michael, *The Other America: Poverty in the United States* (Baltimore, MD: Penguin Books, 1963)

Kain, John F., (ed) *Race and Poverty: The Economics of Discrimination* (Englewood Cliffs, NJ: Prentice-Hall, 1969)

Killian, Lewis and Grigg, Charles, *Racial Crisis in America* (Englewood Cliffs, NJ: Prentice-Hall, 1964)

Kluger, Richard, *Simple Justice: The History of Brown v. Board of Education* (New York, NY: Vintage, 1975)

Lincoln, C. Eric, *Race, Religion and the Continuing American Dilemma* (New York, NY: Hill and Wang, 1984)

Noer, Thomas J., *Cold War and Black Liberation* (Columbia, MO: University of Missouri Press, 1985)

Patterson, William L., (ed) *We Charge Genocide* (New York, NY: International Pubs., 1971; rpt. 1951)

Polenberg, Richard, *One Nation Divisible: Class, Race, and Ethnicity in the United States since 1938* (New York, NY: Penguin, 1980)

Preston, Michael, et. al., (ed) *The New Black Politics* (London, ED: Longman, 1982)

Silberman, Charles E., *Crisis in Black and White* (New York, NY: Vintage, 1964)

Wallace, Terry, *Bloods: An Oral History of the Vietnam War by Black Veterans* (New York, NY: Ballantine Books, 1984)

Weaver, Robert C., *Negro Labor: A National Problem* (New

York, NY: Harcourt Brace, 1946)

Westheider, James E., *Fighting on Two Fronts: African Americans and the Vietnam War* (New York, NY: New York University Press, 1997)

Willhelm, Sidney, *Who Needs the Negro?* (New York, NY: Anchor, 1971)

Civil Rights Movement, Contemporary Black America

Albert, Peter, and Hoffman, Ronald, ed., *We Shall Overcome: Martin Luther King, Jr. and the Black Freedom Struggle* (New York, NY: Da Capo, 1993)

Baker, Houston, *Black Studies, Rap, and the Academy* (Chicago, IL: University of Chicago Press, 1993)

Baldwin, James, *No Name in the Street* (New York, NY: Dial, 1972)

Baldwin, Lewis, and Woodson, Aprille, *Freedom is Never Free: A Biographical Portrait of Edgar Daniel Nixon, Sr.,* (Nashville, TN: Office of Minority Affairs, 1992)

Bardolph, Richard, *The Civil Rights Record: Black Americans and the Law, 1849–1970* (New York, NY: Crowell, 1970)

Barndt, Joseph R., *Why Black Power?* (New York, NY: Friendship Press, 1968)

Bell, Derrick, *And We Are Not Saved: The Elusive Quest for Racial Justice* (New York, NY: Basic Books, 1987)

Bell, Derrick, *Confronting Authority: Reflections of an Ardent Protester* (Boston, MA: Beacon Press, 1994)

Bell, Derrick, *Faces at the Bottom of the Well: The Permanence of Racism* (New York, NY: Basic Books, 1992)

Bennett, Lerone Jr., *Confrontation: Black and White* (Baltimore, MD: Penguin, 1972)

Blaustein, Albert and Ferguson, Clarence C., *Desegregation and the Law: The Meaning and Effect of the School Desegregation Cases* (New York, NY: Vintage, 1962)

Branch, Taylor, *Parting the Waters: America in the King Years, 1954–63* (New York, NY: Simon and Schuster, 1988)

Breitman, George, (ed) *Malcolm X on Afro-American History* (New York, NY: Pathfinder, 1970)

Breitman, George, (ed) *Malcolm X Speaks* (New York, NY: Grove, 1965)

Breitman, George, (ed) *The Assassination of Malcolm X* (New York, NY: Pathfinder, 1976)

Burns, W. Haywood, *The Voices of Negro Protest* (New York, NY: Oxford University Press, 1966)

Carmichael, Stokely and Hamilton, Charles V., *Black Power: The Politics of Liberation in America* (New York, NY: Vintage, 1967)

Carmichael, Stokely, *Stokely Speaks: Black Power to Pan-Africanism* (New York, NY: Vintage, 1965)

Carson, Clayborne, ed., *The Papers of Martin Luther King, Jr.: Vol. I: Called to Serve* (Berkeley, CA: University of California Press, 1992)

Carson, Clayborne, et. al., *The Eyes on the Prize Civil Rights Reader* (New York, NY: Penguin, 1987)

Carson, Clayborne, *In Struggle: A History of SNCC* (Cambridge, MA: Harvard University Press, 1983)

Chafe, William H., *Civilities and Civil Rights: Greensboro, North Carolina, and the Black Struggle for Freedom* (New York, NY: Oxford University Press, 1980)

Clark, Kenneth B., *Dark Ghetto* (New York, NY: Harper, Row, 1965)

Clarke, John Henrik, (ed) *Malcolm X: The Man and His Times* (New York, NY: Collier Books, 1969)

Cleaver, Eldridge, *Soul on Ice* (New York, NY: McGraw-Hill, 1968)

Cross, Theodore, *The Black Power Imperative* (New York, NY: Faulkner Books, 1987)

Cudjoe, Selwyn R., *A Just and Moral Society* (Ithaca, NY: 1984)

Delgado, Richard, ed., *Critical Race Theory: The Cutting Edge* (Philadelphia, PA: Temple University Press, 1995)

Duberman, Martin, *The Uncompleted Past* (New York, NY: E.P. Dutton, 1971)

Dyson, Michael Eric, *Navigating the Race Rules* (New York, NY: Vintage, 1996)

Farmer, James, *Lay Bare the Heart: An Autobiography of the Civil Rights Movement* (New York, NY: Plume, 1986)

Fogelson, Robert M., *Violence as Protest: A Study of Riots and Ghettos* (New York, NY: Anchor, 1971)

Franklin, John Hope, *The Color Line: Legacy for the Twenty-First Century* (Columbia, MO: University of Missouri Press, 1993)

Garrow, David J., *The FBI and Martin Luther King, Jr.* (New York, NY: Penguin, 1981)

Gates, Henry Louis, Jr., and West, Cornel, *The Future of the Race* (New York, NY: Vintage Press, 1996)

Gill, Gerald R., *Meanness Mania: The Changed Mood* (Washington, DC: Howard University Press, 1980)

Glasgow, Douglas G., *The Black Underclass* (New York, NY: Oxford University Press, 1980)

Graham, Hugh Davis, and Gurr, Ted Robert, *Violence in America* (New York, NY: Signet, 1969)

Grant, Joanne, *Ella Baker: Freedom Bound* (New York, NY: Wiley, 1989)

Green, Shelley and Pryde, Paul, *Black Entrepreneurship in America* (New Brunswick, NJ: Transaction, 1990)

Gregory, Dick, *The Shadow That Scares Me* (New York, NY: Pocket Books, 1968)

Grier, William H. and Cobbs, Price M., *Black Rage* (New York, NY: Bantam, 1968)

Guinier, Lani, *The Tyranny of the Majority* (New York, NY: Free Press, 1994)

Gwaltney, John Langston, *Drylongso: A Self-Portrait of Black America* (New York, NY: Vintage, 1980)

Hacker, Andrew, *Two Nations: Black and White, Separate, Hostile, Unequal* (New York, NY: Scribners, 1992)

Haley, Alex, *The Autobiography of Malcolm X* (New York, NY: Grove, 1964)

Harding, Vincent, *The Other American Revolution* (Los Angeles, CA: UCLA Center for Afro-American Studies, 1980)

Hare, Nathan, *The Black Anglo-Saxons* (New York, NY: Marzani, 1965)

Hersey, John, *The Algiers Motel Incident* (New York, NY: Bantam, 1968)

Jacobs, Paul, *Prelude to Riot: A View of Urban America from the Bottom* (New York, NY: Vintage, 1967)

Jaynes, Gerald D., et. al., *A Common Destiny: Blacks and American Society* (Washington, DC: National Academy Press, 1989)

Kapur, Sudarshan, *Raising Up A Prophet: The African-American Encounter with Gandhi* (Boston, MA: Beacon Press, 1992)

Katz, Michael B., *The Underserving Poor: From the War on Poverty to the War on Welfare* (New York, NY: Pantheon, 1989)

Kelley, Robin D. G., *Yo' Mama's Disfunktional! Fighting the Culture Wars in Urban America* (Boston, MA: Beacon Press, 1997)

Khanga, Yelena, *Soul to Soul: The Story of a Black Russian American Family, 1865–1992* (New York, NY: W.W. Norton, 1992)

Killian, Lewis M., *The Impossible Revolution: Black Power and the American Dream* (New York, NY: Random House, 1968)

King, Martin Luther, Jr., *Stride Toward Freedom: The Montgomery Story* (New York, NY: Harper and Row, 1958)

King, Martin Luther, *Where Do We Go From Here* (New York, NY: Harper Row, 1967)

King, Martin Luther, *Why We Can't Wait* (New York, NY: New American Library, 1963)

Kirp, David L., *Just Schools: The Idea of Racial Equality in American Education* (Berkeley, CA: University of California Press, 1982)

Lawson, Steven F., *Running for Freedom: Civil Rights and Black Politics in America Since 1941* (Philadelphia, PA: Temple University Press, 1991)

Lee, Chana Kai, *For Freedom's Sake: The Life of Fannie Lou Hamer* (Urbana, IL: University of Illinois Press, 1999)

Leiden, Carl, and Schmitt, Karl M., *The Politics of Violence: Revolution in the Modern World* (Englewood Cliffs, NJ: Prentice-Hall, 1968)

Lester, Julius, *Look Out Whitey! Black Power's Gon' Get Your Mama!* (New York, NY: Grove, 1968)

Levine, Lawrence, *The Opening of the American Mind: Canons, Culture, and History* (Boston, MA: Beacon Press, 1996)

Lincoln, C. Eric, *The Black Muslims in America* (Boston, MA: Beacon Press, 1961)

Lomax, Louis E., *The Negro Revolt* (New York, NY: Signet, 1962)

Lukas, J. Anthony, *Common Ground: A Turbulent Decade in the Lives of Three American Families* (New York, NY: Vintage, 1986)

Manis, Andrew M., *A Fire You Can't Put Out: The Civil Rights Life of Birmingham's Revered Fred Shuttlesworth* (Tuscaloosa, AL: University Press of Alabama, 1999)

Mann, Eric, *Comrade George: An Investigation Into the Life, Political Thought, and Assassination of George Jackson* (New York, NY: Harper Row, 1972)

Marable, Manning, *The Crisis of Color and Democracy: Essays on Race, Class and Power* (Monroe, ME: Common Courage Press, 1992)

Marine, Gene, *The Black Panthers* (New York, NY: Signet, 1969)

Martin, Waldo E., Jr., *Brown v. Board of Education* (Boston, MA: Bedford/St. Martin's, 1989)

McEvoy, James and Miller, Abraham, (ed) *Black Power and Student Rebellion* (Belmont, CA: Wadsworth Publishing, 1969)

Meier, August and Rudwick, Elliott, *CORE: A Study in the Civil Rights Movement, 1942–1968* (Urbana, IL: University of Illinois Press, 1975)

Meier, August and Rudwick, Elliott, (ed) *Black Protest in the Six-*

ties (Chicago, IL: Quadrangle Books, 1970)

Meredith, James, *Three Years in Mississippi* (Bloomington, IN: Indiana University Press, 1966)

Moody, Anne, *Coming of Age in Mississippi* (New York, NY: Dell, 1968)

Morris, Aldon D., *The Origins of the Civil Rights Movement* (New York, NY: Free Press, 1984)

Motley, Constance, *Equal Justice Under Law* (New York, NY: Farrar, Straus & Giroux, 1998)

Muse, Benjamin, *The American Negro Revolution: From Nonviolence to Black Power, 1963–1967* (Bloomington, IN: Indiana University Press, 1968)

Naison, Mark, *White Boy: A Memoir* (Philadelphia, PA: Temple University Press, 2002)

Norrell, Robert J., *Reaping the Whirl-Wind: The Civil Rights Movement in Tuskegee* (New York, NY: Vintage, 1985)

Oates, Stephen B., *Let the Trumpet Sound: The Life of Martin Luther King, Jr.* (New York, NY: New American Library, 1982)

Olson, Lynne, *Freedom's Daughters: The Unsung Heroines of the Civil Rights Movement From 1830 to 1970* (New York, NY: Scribner, 2001)

O'Reilly, Kenneth, *Racial Matters: The FBI's Secret File on Black America, 1960–1972* (New York, NY: Free Press, 1989)

Pinkney, Alphonso, *The Myth of Black Progress* (New York, NY: Cambridge, 1984)

Preston, Michel B., et. al., *The New Black Politics* (New York, NY: Longman, 1982)

Purcell, Theodore V. and Cavanagh, Gerald F., *Blacks in the Industrial World* (New York, NY: Free Press, 1972)

Reed, Merl E., *Seedtime for the Modern Civil Rights Movement: The President's Committee on Fair Employment Practice, 1941–1946* (Baton Rouge, LA: LSU Press, 1991)

Report to the National Commission on the Causes and Prevention of Violence, *Shoot-Out in Cleveland* (New York, NY: Bantam, 1969)

Robinson, Randall, *Defending the Spirit: A Black Life in America* (New York, NY: Dutton, 1998)

Robinson, Randall, *The Debt: What America Owes to Blacks* (New York, NY: Dutton, 2000)

Scheer, Robert, (ed) *Eldridge Cleaver: Post-Prison Writings and Speeches* (New York, NY: Random House, 1967)

Schultz, John, *The Chicago Conspiracy Trial* (New York, NY: Da Capo, 1993)

Seale, Bobby, *Seize the Time: The Story of the Black Panther*

Party and Huey P. Newton (New York, NY: Vintage, 1970)

Silver, James W., *Mississippi: The Closed Society* (New York, NY: Harcourt Brace, 1963)

Sitkoff, Harvard, *A New Deal for Blacks: The Emergence of Civil Rights as a National Issue* (New York, NY: Oxford University Press, 1978)

Skolnick, Jerome, *The Politics of Protest* (New York, NY: Ballantine Books, 1969)

Terkel, Studs, *Race: How Blacks and Whites Think and Feel About the American Obsession* (New York, NY: Anchor, 1992)

Terry, Wallace, *Bloods: An Oral History of the Vietnam War by Black Veterans* (New York, NY: Ballantine, 1984)

Toplin, Robert Brent, *Unchallenged Violence: An American Ordeal* (Westport, CT: Greenwood Press, 1975)

Tyson, Timothy, *Radio Free Dixie: Robert F. Williams and the Roots of Black Power* (Chapel Hill, NC: University of North Carolina Press, 1999)

Urban League, *The State of Black America 1992* (annual) (New York, NY: National Urban League, 1992; published annually)

Wagstaff, Thomas, *Black Power: The Radical Response to White America* (Beverly Hills, CA: Glencoe Press, 1969)

Walton, Hanes, *The Political Philosophy of Martin Luther King, Jr.* (Westport, CT: Greenwood, 1971)

Weinberg, Kenneth G., *Black Victory: Carl Stokes and the Winning of Cleveland* (Chicago, IL: Quadrangle Books, 1968)

Weisbord, Robert G., and Kazarian, Richard, Jr., *Israel in the Black American Perspective* (Westport, CT: Greenwood Press, 1985)

Weisbrot, Robert, *Freedom Bound: A History of America's Civil Rights Movement* (New York, NY: Plume, 1990)

West, Cornel, *Race Matters* (Boston, MA: Beacon Press, 1993)

Williams, Juan, *Thurgood Marshall: American Revolutionary* (New York, NY: Times Books, 2000)

Williams, Patricia J., *The Alchemy of Race and Rights* (Cambridge, MA: Harvard University Press, 1991)

Williams, Walter E., *The State Against Blacks* (New York, NY: McGraw-Hill, 1982)

Wilson, William Julius, *The Truly Disadvantaged: The Inner City, the Underclass, and Public Policy* (Chicago, IL: University of Chicago Press, 1987)

Wright, Jr., Nathan, *Black Power and Urban Unrest* (New York, NY: Hawthorn Books, 1967)

Yette, Samuel F., *The Choice: The Issue of Black Survival in*

America (New York, NY: Berkley, 1971)

Young, Andrew, *An Easy Burden: The Civil Rights Movement and the Transformation of America* (New York, NY: Harper Collins, 1996)

Zinn, Howard, *SNCC: The New Abolitionists* (Boston, MA: Beacon, 1964)

The Black Struggle, Topical: Education, Family, Labor, Religion, Women

Allen, George, Carol, *Segregated Sabbaths: Richard Allen and the Rise of Independent Black Churches, 1760–1840* (New York, NY: Oxford University Press, 1973)

Aptheker, Herbert, (ed) *The Education of Black People: Ten Critiques, 1906–1960 by W.E.B. Du Bois* (New York, NY: Monthly Review Press, 1975)

Bailey, A. Peter, *The Harlem Hospital Story: 100 Years of Struggle Against Illness, Racism and Genocide* (Richmond, VA: Native Sun Pubs., 1991)

Baker, Houston A., Jr., *Black Studies: Rap and the Academy* (Chicago, IL: University of Chicago Press, 1993)

Billingsley, Andrew, *Black Families in White America* (Englewood Cliffs, NJ: Prentice-Hall, 1968)

Boskin, Joseph, *Sambo: The Rise and Demise of an American Jester* (New York, NY: Oxford University Press, 1986)

Brown, Elaine, *A Taste of Power: A Black Woman's Story* (New York, NY: Pantheon, 1992)

Bullock, Henry Allen, *A History of Negro Education in the South* (New York, NY: Praeger, 1970)

Burt, McKinley, Jr., *Black Inventors of America* (Portland, OR: National Book Co., 1989)

Cade, Toni, (ed) *The Black Woman: An Anthology* (New York, NY: New American Library, 1970)

Carnoy, Martin, *Education as Cultural Imperialism* (New York, NY: McKay, 1974)

Clarke, John Henrik, *Notes for an African World Revolution* (Trenton, NJ: Africa World Press, 1991)

Cone, James H., *Black Theology and Black Power* (New York, NY: Seabury, 1969)

Cox, George O., *Education for the Black Race* (New York, NY: African Heritage Publishers, 1974)

Davis, Angela Y., *Women, Race and Class* (New York, NY: Vintage, 1983)

Du Bois, W.E.B., (ed), *The Negro American Family* (Atlanta, GA: Atlanta University Press, 1909)

Evans, Sara M. *Born for Liberty: A History of Women in America* (New York, NY: Free Press, 1989)

Foner, Philip S. and Lewis, Ronald L., *The Black Worker During the Era of the Knights of Labor* vols. I–III (Philadelphia, PA: Temple University Press, 1978)

Foner, Philip S., *Organized Labor and the Black Worker, 1619–1973* (New York, NY: Praeger, 1974)

Franklin, E. Franklin, *The Negro Church in America* (New York, NY: Schocken, 1964)

Frazier, E. Franklin, *Black Bourgeoisie: The Rise of a New Middle Class* (New York, NY: Free Press, 1957)

Frazier, E. Franklin, *Negro Youth at the Crossways* (New York, NY: Schocken, 1967)

Frazier, E. Franklin, *The Negro Family in the United States* (Chicago, IL: University of Chicago Press, 1939)

Gallagher, Buell G., *American Caste and the Negro College* (New York, NY: Gordian Press, 1966)

Gates, Henry Louis, Jr., *Loose Canons: Notes on the Culture Wars* (New York, NY: Oxford University Press, 1992)

Green, Shelley and Pryde, Paul, *Black Entrepreneurship in America* (New Brunswick, NJ: Transaction Books, 1990)

Harlan, Louis R., *Separate and Unequal* (New York, NY: Atheneum, 1968)

Harris, William H., *The Harder We Run: Black Workers Since the Civil War* (New York, NY: Oxford University Press, 1982)

Hernton, Calvin C., *Sex and Racism* (New York, NY: Doubleday, 1965)

Higginbotham, Evelyn Brooks, *Righteous Discontent: The Women's Movement in the Black Baptist Church, 1880–1920* (Cambridge, MA: Harvard University Press, 1993)

Hine, Darlene Clark, ed., *Black Women in America: An Historical Encyclopedia* (Bloomington, IN: Indiana University Press, 1994)

Hooks, Bell, *Ain't I A Woman: Black Women and Feminism* (Boston, MA: South End Press, 1990)

Jacobson, Julius, (ed) *The Negro and the American Labor Movement* (New York, NY: Anchor, 1968)

Jaynes, Gerald D., *Branches Without Roots: Genesis of the Black Working Class in the American South, 1862–1882* (New York, NY: Oxford University Press, 1986)

Jones, Jacqueline, *Labor of Love, Labor of Sorrow: Black*

Women, Work and the Family, From Slavery to the Present (New York, NY: Vintage, 1986)

Kennedy, Theodore R., *You Gotta Deal With It: Black Family Relations in a Southern Community* (New York, NY: Oxford University Press, 1980)

Kozol, Jonathan, *Death at an Early Age* (New York, NY: Bantam, 1967)

Kozol, Jonathan, *Savage Inequalities: Children in America's Schools* (New York, NY: Crown, 1991)

Ladner, Joyce A., *Tomorrow's Tomorrow: The Black Woman* (New York, NY: Doubleday, 1971)

Lerner, Gerda (ed), *Black Women in White America: A Documentary History* (New York, NY: Vintage, 1973)

Lewis, Ronald L., *Black Coal Miners in America* (Lexington, KY: University Press of Kentucky, 1987)

Logan, Rayford W., *Howard University: The First Hundred Years, 1867–1967* (New York, NY: New York University Press, 1969)

Lomotey, Kofi, ed., *Going to School: The African-American Experience* (Albany, NY: State University of New York Press, 1990)

Majors, M.A., *Noted Negro Women: Their Triumphs and Activities* (Salem, NH: Ayer, 1986; Rept.)

Malson, Micheline R., et. al., *Black Women in America* (Chicago, IL: University of Chicago Press, 1988)

Marshall, Ray, *The Negro Worker* (New York, NY: Random House, 1965)

Mays, Benjamin E., *The Negro's God As Reflected in His Literature* (New York, NY: Antheneum, 1969)

McCaul, Robert, *The Black Struggle for Public Schooling in Nineteenth-Century Illinois* (Carbondale, IL: Southern Illinois University Press, 1987)

Meier, August, and Rudwick, Elliott, *Black Detroit and the Rise of the UAW* (New York, NY: Oxford University Press, 1979)

Meier, August, et. al., (ed) *Black Workers and Organized Labor* (Belmont, CA: Wadsworth, 1971)

Mullen, Robert W. *Blacks in America's Wars* (New York, NY: Pathfinder, 1973)

Murray, Albert, *The Omni Americans: Black Experience and American Culture* (New York, NY: Da Capo, 1970)

Newman, Michele, *White Women's Rights: The Racial Origins of Feminism in the United States* (New York, NY: Oxford University Press, 1999)

Patterson, Haywood and Conrad, Earl, *Scottsboro Boys* (New

York, NY: Collier, 1950)

Pettigrew, Thomas F., *A Profile of the Negro American* (New York, NY: Norstrand, 1964)

Record, Wilson, *The Negro and the Communist Party* (Chapel Hill, NC: University of North Carolina Press, 1951)

Rothenberg, Paula S., *Race, Class, and Gender in the United States* (New York, NY: St. Martins, 1993)

Santino, Jack, *Miles of Smiles, Years of Struggle: Stories of Black Pullman Porters* (Urbana, IL: University of Illinois Press, 1989)

Sertima, Ivan Van, (ed) *Blacks in Science: Ancient and Modern* (New Brunswick, NJ: Rutgers University Press, 1983)

Smith, H. Shelton, *In His Image, But: Racism in Southern Religion, 1780–1910* (Durham, NC: Duke University Press, 1972)

Sollors, Werner, ed., *The Invention of Ethnicity* (New York, NY: Oxford University Press, 1989)

Sowell, Thomas, *Black Education: Myths and Tragedies* (New York, NY: McKay, 1972)

Thompson, Mildred I., *Ida B. Wells-Barnett: An Exploration Study of an American Black Woman, 1893–1930* (Brooklyn, NY: Carlson, 1990)

Washington, Joseph R., *Black Religion: The Negro and Christianity in the United States* (Boston, MA: Beacon Press, 1964)

White, Deborah, *Aren't I a Woman: Female Slaves in the Plantation South* (New York, NY: Norton, 1985)

Wilkinson, J. Harvie, *From Brown to Bakke* (New York, NY: Oxford University Press, 1979)

Willie, Charles V. and Edmonds, Ronald R., (ed) *Black Colleges in America: Challenge, Development, Survival* (New York, NY: Teachers College Press, Columbia Univ., 1978)

Wilmore, Gayraud S., *Black Religion and Black Radicalism* (New York, NY: Doubleday, 1972)

Wilson, William Julius, *When Work Disappears: The World of the New Urban Poor* (New York, NY: Knopf, 1996)

Woodson, Carter G., *The Miseducation of the Negro* (New York, NY: Associated Pubs., 1933)

Blacks in Sports, Arts and Entertainment, etc.

Ashe, Arthur and Rampersad, Arnold, *Days of Grace: A Memoir* (New York, NY: Ballantine Books, 1994)

Ashe, Arthur, *A Hard Road to Glory: A History of the African-American Athlete* 3 vols. (New York, NY: Amistad, 1988, 1993)

Bak, Richard, *Turkey Sternes and the Detroit Stars: the Negro Leagues in Detroit, 1919–1933* (Detroit, MI: Wayne State University Press, 1994)

Behee, John, *Hail to the Victors: Black Athletes at the University of Michigan* (Ann Arbor, MI: Ulrich's Books, 1974)

Boskin, Joseph, *Sambo: The Rise and Demise of An American Jester* (New York, NY: Oxford University Press, 1986)

Brashler, William: *Josh Gibson: A Life in the Negro Leagues* (New York, NY: Harper Row, 1978)

Bruce, Janet, *The Kansas City Monarchs: Champions of Black Baseball* (Lawrence, KS: University Press of Kansas, 1985)

Cahn, Susan K., *Coming On Strong: Gender and Sexuality in Twentieth-Century Women's Sport* (Cambridge, MA: Harvard University Press, 1994)

Carroll, John M., *Fritz Pollard: Pioneer in Racial Advancement* (Urbana, IL: University of Illinois Press, 1992)

Chalk, Ocania, *Black College Sport* (New York, NY: Dodd, Mead & Co., 1976)

Dates, Jannette L. and Barlow, William, ed., *Split Image: African Americans in the Mass Media* (Washington, DC: Howard University Press, 1990)

Dawkins, Marvin P., and Kinloch, Graham C., *African American Golfers During the Jim Crow Era* (Westport, CT: Praeger, 2000)

Early, Gerald, ed., *The Muhammad Ali Reader* (New York, NY: Weisbach Books, 1999)

Early, Gerald, *Tuxedo Junction: Essays on American Culture* (New York, NY: Ecco, 1989)

Edwards, Harry, *Revolt of the Black Athlete* (New York, NY: Free Press, 1969)

Ely, Melvin Patrick, *The Adventures of Amos 'N' Andy: A Social History of an American Phenomenon* (New York, NY: Free Press, 1991)

Farr, Finis, *Black Champion: The Life and Times of Jack Johnson* (New York, NY: Scribner's, 1964)

Gibson, Bob, *From Ghetto to Glory: The Story of Bob Gibson* (Englewood Cliffs, NJ: Prentice-Hall, 1968)

Henderson, Edwin Bancroft, *The Negro in Sports* (Washington, DC: Associated Pubs., 1949)

Hoberman, John, *Darwin's Athletes: How Sport Has Damaged Black America and Preserved the Myth of Race* (New York, NY: Houghton Mifflin, 1997)

James, C.L.R., *Beyond A Boundary* (Durham, NC: Duke University Press, 1993)

Johnson, Abby A., and Johnson, Ronald M., *Propaganda and Aesthetics: The Literary Politics of African-American Magazines in the Twentieth Century* (Amherst, MA: University of Massachusetts Press, 1979)

Johnson, Jack, *Jack Johnson: In the Ring and Out* (London, ED: Protesus, 1977; rpt.)

LaFeber, Walter, *Michael Jordan and the New Global Capitalism* (New York, NY: W.W. Norton, 2000)

Lapsick, Richard E., *The Politics of Race and International Sport* (Westport, CT: Greenwood Press, 1975)

LeFlore, Ron, *One In A Million: The Ron LeFlore Story* (New York, NY: Warner Books, 1978)

Louis, Joe, *Joe Louis: My Life* (New York, NY: Harcourt Brace, 1978)

Mead, Chris, *Champion: Joe Louis, Black Hero in White America* (New York, NY: Penguin, 1985)

Musick, Phil, *Hank Aaron: The Man Who Beat the Babe* (New York, NY: Popular Library, 1974)

Newcombe, Jack, *Floyd Patterson: Heavyweight King* (New York, NY: Bartholomew House, 1961)

Noble, Peter, *The Negro in Films* (London, ED: Knapp, Drewett, 1948)

Orr, Jack, *The Black Athlete* (New York, NY: Pyramid Books, 1970)

Overmyer, James, *Queen of the Negro Leagues: Effa Manley and the Newark Eagles* (Lanham MD: Scarecrow Press, 1998)

Owens, Jesse, *Blackthink: My Life and Black Man and White Man* (New York, NY: William Morrow, 1970)

Payton, Walter, *Sweetness* (Chicago, IL: Contemporary Books, 1978)

Peterson, Robert, *Only the Ball Was White* (Englewood Cliffs, NJ: Prentice-Hall, 1970)

Peterson, Robert, *Only The Ball Was White: A History of Legendary Black Players and All-Black Professional Teams* (New York, NY: Oxford University Press, 1992)

Pratt, Alan, ed., *Black Humor* (New York, NY: Garland, 1998)

Roberts, Randy, *Papa Jack: Jack Johnson and the Era of White Hopes* (New York, NY: Free Press, 1983)

Robinson, Jackie, *Baseball Has Done It* (Philadelphia, PA: Lippincott, 1964)

Robinson, Sugar Ray, *Sugar Ray* (New York, NY: Da Capo, 1994)

Ruck, Rob, *Sandlot Seasons: Sport in Black Pittsburgh* (Urbana, IL: University of Illinois Press, 1987)

Russell, Bill, *Second Wind* (New York, NY: Ballantine, 1979)

Sammons, Jeffrey T., *Beyond the Ring: The Role of Boxing in American Society* (Urbana, IL: University of Illinois Press, 1988)

Spivey, Donald, (ed) *Sport in America: New Historical Perspectives* (Westport, CT: Greenwood Press, 1985)

Toll, Robert C., *Blacking Up: The Minstrel Show in Nineteenth-Century America* (New York, NY: Oxford University Press, 1974)

Tygiel, Jules, *Baseball's Great Experiment: Jackie Robinson and His Legacy* (New York, NY: Oxford University Press, 1983)

Watkins, Mel, *On the Real Side: A History of African American Comedy* (Chicago, IL: Lawrence Hill, 1994)

Wiggins, David K., *Glory Bound: Black Athletes in a White America* (Syracuse, NY: Syracuse University Press, 1997)

Wolf, David, *Foul: The Connie Hawkins Story* (New York, NY: Holt, Rinehart, 1972)

Young, Doc, *Sonny Liston: The Champ Nobody Wanted* (Chicago, IL: Johnson Publishing Co., 1963)

INDEX